Gone with the Wind

# Gone with the Wind

Sidney Howard

*Based on the novel by*
*Margaret Mitchell*

*Edited and with an introduction by*
*Richard Harwell*

*faber and faber*
LONDON · BOSTON

First published in 1981
by Lorrimer Publishing Limited
Reissued in 1990
by Faber and Faber Limited
3 Queen Square London WCIN 3AU

Printed in Great Britain by
Richard Clay Ltd Bungay Suffolk

A CIP record for this book is
available from the British Library

ISBN 0-571-12579-4

# CONTENTS

# INTRODUCTION

Margaret Mitchell was a movie fan. One of her most memorable assignments as a young reporter on the Atlanta *Journal* was an interview with Rudolph Valentino. She was of an age with the film industry. Born in 1900, she grew up with *The Perils of Pauline* and reached for maturity with *The Birth of a Nation*. As a student at Smith College she enjoyed watching a youthful William Powell in a local stock company and later followed his career in Hollywood. She could lose herself watching a romantic film, but her greatest enthusiasm was reserved for such comedy stars as W.C. Fields and Mae West. The Marx Brothers occupied a special pinnacle at the peak of fame. Her reaction to their antics was uninhibited if not downright raucous. Her friends insisted that she could be located in a theater's audience by her rollicking, contagious laughter.

No one looked forward to the film of *Gone with the Wind* more avidly than its author. She feared what Hollywood would do to her story and she dreaded the hoopla that was bound to surround the film's premiere in Atlanta, but in the end she was genuinely pleased with the movie. Some years later the distinguished diplomat Joseph C. Grew told how he saw it in her company while he was visiting Atlanta in 1945: "The two of us sat watching it for four and a half hours—she for the eleventh and a half time—laughing and crying, taking as fresh delight in it as if it were her first time and she had nothing to do with it but enjoy it!"

From the time motion picture rights to the novel were purchased by Selznick International Pictures in July 1936, all aspects of its filming were matters of public concern. As Miss Mitchell wrote to Katharine Brown on February 14, 1937: "As you probably know wherever two or more of ye are gathered together these days, the two or more talk about the movie."

Miss Mitchell was writing to suggest a friend for a post the Selznickers (as she called them) had wanted her to undertake herself:

My suggestion is—why not take Susan Myrick [of the Macon *Telegraph*] out to the Coast in some capacity while the picture is being made? . . . You said that you'd like to have me there to pass on the authenticity and rightness of this and that, the accents of the white actors, the dialect of the colored ones, the minor matters of dress and deportment, the small touches of local color, etc. Well, I can't go and you know why. But I thought if you

7

really wanted a Georgian for the job there wouldn't be anyone better than Sue. In fact, she would be a better person for the job than I would because she knows more about such matters than I do.

Miss Myrick got the job as a Technical Adviser and became one of the principal conduits through which Miss Mitchell kept in far closer touch with the filming of GWTW than she was willing to admit. Another constant and reliable source of information was Wilbur G. Kurtz, Atlanta artist and architect, who was appointed Historian for the film. He and his wife Annie Laurie and Miss Myrick wrote Miss Mitchell letters from Hollywood that comprise a running account of what was going on at the Selznick International Studios in Culver City.

Katharine Brown, however, was Miss Mitchell's strongest link to the film. It was Kay Brown who, according to David O. Selznick, was "the very first to recognize the film possibilities of the novel." How she called the book to the attention of Selznick prior to its publication and persuaded him to buy it despite strong misgivings is a thrice-told story and does not need repeating here. Miss Brown was "Story Editor" for Selznick and ran his New York office in 1936. When Margaret Mitchell went to New York to sign the film contract on July 30, one month after the publication date of *Gone with the Wind*, she was, as her husband John R. Marsh put it, suffering from too much fame too fast. She was fatigued from the whirlwind of bestsellerdom that had caught her in its vortex. She was dismayed by the potential complications embedded in the contract as written by the Selznick organization. Meeting a charming and capable businesswoman even younger than herself as Selznick's eastern representative was a relief and a delight.

After returning home she wrote:

You and Miss Modisett must have thought me several kinds of a varmint for not writing you sooner to thank you for what you did in the matter of the sale of "Gone With the Wind" and also for your many courtesies to me. . . . My eyes were so bad when I was in New York that I could barely see. That was the reason for my unmannerly desire to get the contract closed up immediately. I had overstrained my eyes on the proof reading of the book and had about finished them on the heavy correspondence that followed . . . Thank you so much for your enthusiasm about the book, your cordiality to me—and the cocktails! Being a "Provincial Lady" and coming from a state that has been bone dry for about fifty years, that cocktail was about the first legal cocktail I ever drank!

*Susan Myrick, technical adviser on Southern customs and speech, checks a portion of the GWTW script with actress Evelyn Keyes, her fellow Georgian.*

*...sistant Director Eric Stacey ...d "the camera gang." Left ...right: Arthur Arling, opera-...e cameraman; Ernest ...ller, chief cameraman; ...rry Wolf, camera assis-...nt; and Stacey.*

MGM, © 1939, 1967. Collection of Richard Harwell.

MGM, © 1939, 1967. Atlanta Historical Society, Wilbur G. Kurtz Collection.

That meeting of Kay Brown and Margaret Mitchell was the beginning of a long and rewarding personal and business relationship. Miss Brown quickly became the author's contact with Selznick International Pictures and with David Selznick himself. Relations between Miss Mitchell and the filmmakers occasionally were strained—especially when PR man Russell Birdwell became involved—but Selznick used Miss Brown as his Special Ambassador in Charge of the Author and tensions were always eventually brought under control.

As early as October 6, 1936, Miss Mitchell wrote Miss Brown: "Life has been awful since I sold the movie rights! I am deluged with letters demanding that I do not put Clark Gable in as Rhett. Strangers telephone me or grab me on the street, insisting that Katharine Hepburn will never do. It does me no good to point out sarcastically that it is Mr. Selznick and not I who is producing this picture." Similar statements run like a refrain through more than two years of correspondence.

Miss Mitchell was bedeviled with opinions about the possible casting more than on any other point, but she was also constantly besieged by requests from correspondents who wanted her to get them into the movies, "and also their tap-dancing daughters, their grandmothers and their colored cooks and chauffeurs." She was approached by friends of Georgian Lamar Trotti who wanted him hired to write the screenplay. Later, such well known authors as DuBose Heyward and Stark Young let her know that they would not be averse to having their names dropped in the right Hollywood circles. She told all comers variations of what she wrote one ambitious actor friend on October 13, 1936: "Regardless of what you may read in the papers, regardless of what anyone may tell you, I have *nothing* to do with the moving picture production of 'Gone With the Wind.' Nothing to do with the script or the casting, costuming, backgrounds. I sold the movie rights out right with no strings tied and I have nothing whatsoever to do with it any more." The pressures on her constantly increased. She told her old friend Willie Snow Ethridge on January 16, 1937: "I never go any where I want to go, see anyone I want to see[,] do anything I want to do. If it goes on much longer I shall be in a worse state than 'Aunt Pittypat' was ever in."

She learned to live with a situation she could not prevent and which even her closest friends could scarcely believe, but she never learned to like it. She wrote Bishop Gerald O'Hara, who by coincidence had been made Bishop of Savannah just weeks too late for the fictional Gerald's name to be altered, advising him against requesting

*Katharine Brown, Selznick's East Coast representative, and John Hay ("Jock") Whitney, Selznick's principal backer, in London in 1936 when the purchase of GWTW by Selznick International Pictures was announced.*

a name change in the film. If nothing else, she reasoned, too many people would raise the question "Why?"

I base this opinion on some of my own experiences with "Gone With the Wind." The book is my own creation but it has long since gotten out of my hands. It belongs apparently, not to me, but to its readers, and the number of them is greater than I have even been able to comprehend. . . .

Personal experience has shown me that the public interest centered around "Gone With the Wind" is a force of such magnitude that it is not to be trifled with. I do not trifle with it myself and I would not advise anyone else to trifle with it.

Margaret Mitchell knew only too well that the point at which *Gone with the Wind* was most likely "to be trifled with" was when a screenplay was adapted from it. The first positive announcement about the making of the film was that George Cukor would be its director. Early in October Miss Brown wrote the author that Cukor would soon be paying a visit to Atlanta and mentioned that someone would come with him to discuss "changes in continuity."

In keeping with her hands-off policy Miss Mitchell replied:

Of course, I would love to help out in any way I can but I have no ideas at all about any changes and could be of no help whatsoever in such a matter. Besides, if the news got out that I was in even the slightest way responsible for any deviations from the book, then my life wouldn't be worth living. You see, this section has taken the book to its heart and that is something which makes me prouder than anything else. But each and every reader feels that he has part ownership in it and they are determined that nothing shall be changed. I am dogged by people who say they'll never speak to me again if "I let the movie people change one line." So I would not be of any assistance in the continuity.

"The movie people," of course, were going to have to change a great many lines. On October 13 Miss Brown wrote that Sidney Howard would do the job for them. Her letter was quickly followed by one from Selznick praising Howard's reputation as a playwright. Howard himself got around to writing her in mid-November:

You know that you have given me more story than I can properly compress into the two hours a picture is, at the outside, permitted. Some things will have to go because nothing is less adequate than a picture which tries to cover too much ground and so covers none of it properly. I shall ask you to look at our first lay-out of the material when it is in shape and, if you are willing, to tell me what you think of the script as it comes along. I have, on occasion, made Red Lewis do this for me and it has helped me with the script and eased the shock of outcome for him.

I may also tell you that if I find myself obliged to write any additional dialogue for the colored folks you will have to lend me a hand. Those are the best written darkies, I do believe, in all literature. They are the only ones I have ever read which seem to come through without white patronizing. I once asked Hugh Walpole why he did not make a picture of "Martin Chuzzlewit" and he asked me how I would enjoy the job of writing added lines for Sarah Gamp. I feel that way about your negroes.

Miss Mitchell shot back a letter explaining that she was having nothing to do with script writing—politely, but very definitely. Howard replied that the Selznick office had dealt through his agent and had told him nothing about her policy. "My notion in writing you as I did," he explained, "was chiefly to assure you—in so far as it is in my power to assure you—that you would have all possible measure of approval or criticism of your picture before it reaches the irrevocable stage of celluloid. . . . I take you at your word and shall not trouble you." This time Miss Mitchell responded: "Now that the misunderstandings have been cleared away . . . I am even more confident than before that the book is in good hands." She never met Howard, but, by mail, they grew to be firm friends.

Had Howard been less modest he might have reassured Miss Mitchell further by referring her to the published version of his dramatization of *Dodsworth*. For it both Howard and Lewis wrote introductory material. Lewis concluded: "The one thing a dramatization should not be is a mere dramatization. It is quite as much an act of creation as any play based entirely upon the dramatist's own design, and an acute study of the tale to be dramatized is less important than the process of imaginative reflection which recasts the original elements for the stage."

Howard told how, as a writer for the stage, he had looked enviously toward dramatizing a novel for the screen. "How fine," he wrote, "to revel in the freedom of motion pictures, to flash from place to place, to order mobs about over real deserts and to sail real ships upon a genuine ocean!" He had discussed *Dodsworth* with Lionel Barrymore, who wanted to play it on the stage. Of this he said:

"The result," I said, "cannot be anything but a libel on the novel. We should have to leave out too much on the stage. On the screen," I said, "it might be effective. There might be something in setting a novel up and photographing a continuous illustration to the text." Novel and screen seemed to be crying for each other—and for me to bring them properly together. . . . I found myself trying my theories on "Arrowsmith." . . . Our first script managed to cover perhaps one half of the book's extent and could have been made into a nice picture for a couple of million more than Mr. Goldwyn had on hand at the moment, a picture which would have run about four hours. Thus I learned that the ratio of initial cost to maximum possible return applies as ruthlessly to the screen as to the stage. Moreover it is an ancient and sound rule that no picture may run longer than ninety minutes. . . . My motion picture version of "Arrowsmith" taught me that the filmed novel bears no more relationship to the real thing than any other variety of illustration. To my dismay the Lewis characters seemed farther from me and from reality on the screen than they would have seemed in the most average stage version. And this, I decided, was because the screen (and let no master of "directors' touches" tell me otherwise) is virtually incapable of comment or implication and both comment and implication are important aspects of good novel writing. . . . Though conscience quailed, we dropped the middle of the Lewis story, shortened the end and beginning and barely sketched in the remainder. "Arrowsmith" is indeed a remarkable work. It survived even the murderous treatment to which we subjected it. . . . Most remarkable of all, Sinclair Lewis had a good time when he saw it.

Howard did an admirable job on *Arrowsmith* and a superb job on *Dodsworth*. He regarded the latter as "good" but, he said, "it remains far less than the novel and therein lies my dissatisfaction with it and my reason for saying that I shall hardly attempt another dramatization. Works of art are best left in the form their creators selected for them."

Here, before its time, was the story of the screenplay of *Gone with the Wind*. How lucky Margaret Mitchell was that Selznick could tempt Howard into doing another dramatization.

Howard was thoroughly professional. Once started, he worked rapidly, and on January 8, 1937, wrote Miss Mitchell that he expected "to have the script mailed in about ten days." Apparently he finished a draft even more quickly than he predicted, for Miss Mitchell wrote him on January 12: "I talked by long distance with the Selznick New York office yesterday and they were so enthusiastic about your script that I had goose bumps up and down my back. How glad I am that you wrote it!"

The dramatist planned a trip to Atlanta in March but Selznick called him to California to work with him on the finished draft. Instead

Cukor and his staff went to Atlanta in early April. Miss Mitchell described their visit in a letter to her friend Herschel Brickell:

> Mr. Cukor, who is to direct "Gone With the Wind," has been here with his technical staff, and I took them all over the red rutted roads of Clayton County. The dogwood was just coming out and the flowering crabs blooming like mad. The movie people wanted to see old houses that had been built before Sherman got here and I obligingly showed them. While they were polite, I am sure they were dreadfully disappointed, for they had been expecting architecture such as appeared in the screen version of "So Red the Rose." . . . I besought them to please leave Tara ugly, sprawling, columnless, and they agreed. I imagine, however, that when it comes to Twelve Oaks they will put columns all around the house and make it as large as our new city auditorium.

She next heard from Howard in a letter of June 5, having hesitantly agreed, at Selznick's request, to see him "in an unofficial way."

> I had planned—during the period when I was fool enough to believe that my work on your book would have been finished when my contract said—to drop in on you with all that behind both of us. . . . As you know, none of those connected with the picture has yet got down to brass tacks and I sat in Hollywood for five weeks drawing a pleasant salary and doing my own work the while. They wanted me to see you only to give themselves the illusion of action. I am scheduled to go back in July for four weeks to complete the script for even more salary but I am a bit of an agnostic on the subject of their ever getting down to work in my few years this side of the grave.

Miss Mitchell asked, if the screenplay were not finished, what was the stack of manuscript pages that had been on Cukor's desk when he was in Atlanta? Howard answered: "Picture scripts are written and later re-written in collaboration with the director, who has, after all, to make the picture. The script of 'Gone With the Wind' is written but not yet re-written." Kay Brown wrote on August 27: "Sidney Howard has just completed the adaptation and I understand there is only about two more weeks of revision to be done. I haven't seen a copy of this last script, but when Sidney gets home, I shall snag one from him."

In October Howard was once again working on GWTW. "Some spirit of madness" he wrote from New York, "moved Selznick to load the whole kit and kaboodle on a private car and bring them East to work with me here, which is just fine, because I am rehearsing a play

MGM, © 1939, 1967. Collection of Richard Harwell.

at the same time. But Selznick likes things to be as complicated as possible and believes that our script will be ready to shoot some day, I am beginning to wonder."

The "completed" version of Howard's screenplay is dated November 27, 1937, but only the day before he had written Miss Mitchell: "Selznick left New York with the script still uncompleted and is now urging me to come back to Hollywood for another two weeks in January, which I hope to be able to do, not only because I should hate like the devil to turn the job over to some other writer but also because I am interested to see how much money a picture producer is willing to spend to pay men for not being allowed to earn their pay." The portion of the screenplay that follows Scarlett and Rhett's honeymoon was written during that January stint.

Wilbur G. Kurtz's diary recorded Feburary 2, 1938:

While over the boards [the drawing boards at the Selznick studio] Sidney Howard walked in. He said this was his last day. His manner of being preoccupied never deserts him. But on his way out he wheeled, threw back his large shoulders and, with incisive speech somewhat on the sardonic side, orated, "Yes, I'm through. It's not a movie script. It's a transcription from the book. But what else could I do. I just used Miss Mitchell's words and scenes." All with an air of talking down his trying efforts and the results he got. No one seemed to agree with him. "See you later." And he was gone.

In his October letter Howard had asked questions about Atlanta in 1863. In his letter of November 26 he told Miss Mitchell how her full and cooperative answers had been put to use in the screenplay:

I think that we can take one small historical liberty and see an iron fence wrecked in the summer of '63 because, for picture reasons, it seems convenient to give the camera a long walk through Atlanta and let the audience see how things are going in the city just before the battle of Gettysburg and because it is extremely difficult to do this earlier in the picture. I took care of the refugees in the course of this walk by showing a farm wagon of them unloading along the street into the welcoming arms of Atlanta ladies. Your suggestion of seeing them in a park is good, too, but the action of climbing out of a wagon may be more pictorial.

The script written and rewritten, there was a long hiatus before activity on that front resumed. Work in other areas continued, but without great pressure. Selznick knew he would deal for Clark Gable to play Rhett and that Gable's commitments would prevent the start of filming for nearly another year.

Kay Brown had written Miss Mitchell back in October 1936: "My own personal theory is not to put a well-known actress in as Scarlett as everyone will be bound to say she is Katharine Hepburn, or Margaret Sullavan, or Joan Crawford playing Joan Crawford, and not Scarlett O'Hara. My feeling is that if we have a completely new person audiences will be more generally satisfied that she is their conception." Selznick had a precedent for a talent search in his hunt that had turned up Tommy Kelly for the title role in *The Adventures of Tom Sawyer*. Trying to find a Scarlett kept publicity about GWTW rolling and was lampooned in Clare Boothe's successful play *Kiss the Boys Good-Bye*. It was not, however, the charade that many suspected but for real—in hopes if not in results.

A research office was set up at Selznick's Culver City studio and Ruth Leone, Librarian, and Eric Stacey, Assistant Director, began systematically to collect the background information Cukor wanted. Wilbur Kurtz went to the Coast for a while, compiled masses of historical information, and lent a modicum of respectability to the concept of the grand houses the movie people dreamed up as Tara and Twelve Oaks.

Many chapters were added to the interminable arguments about Southern accents. Miss Mitchell wrote a correspondent in Columbia, South Carolina, in April 1937: "About the Southern accent in the film version of 'Gone With the Wind'—Mr. Cukor . . . was very interested in Southern accents and in correct Negro dialect, and he laughingly said that every Southerner he had met had told him that the late Confederate States of America would again secede from the Union if he permitted a Southern character to say 'you all' when addressing one person." Actually she was convinced that the film would be better if the actors talked in good stage voices than if they tried to fake Southern speech.

The signing of Gable to play Rhett became official in August 1938. That meant a start of filming not later than February 1939. Selznick was still hoping for an unknown actress to play Scarlett, but in the fall Paulette Goddard looked like the front-runner for the part.

Yes, the screenplay had been written and rewritten. It had not been broken down into the detailed scenes necessary for a shooting script. And Selznick was still not satisfied with it. Miss Mitchell dictated a note of her October 12 telephone conversation with Miss Brown:

Katharine phoned from New York to invite me to go to Sweden with her and Mr. and Mrs. S., or to go to Bermuda. At my refusal to accompany them to either place, she said Mr. S. would compromise and meet me somewhere near Charleston or any place I would designate. I refused, telling her of social engagements during the coming two months as well as my worry about Father's health.

The reason for the call and the invitation was that Mr. S. is preparing to cut the script and the making of "bridgeovers" or transitions. He wanted Mr. Howard to take a boat trip with him so that they could do this job, but Mr. Howard refused to leave New York as he was expecting a baby and had bought a dairy farm. Mr. S. is unable to work in California or New York and thought the job could be done on a sea voyage. Failing Mr. Howard, he and Katharine thought I would be just the person to assist in the job, "either with or without credit." I replied that I knew nothing about the technique necessary for such a job, and, for reasons above, could neither leave town nor promise to do any work.

Miss Mitchell stayed in Atlanta. Miss Brown sailed for Sweden to see through Selznick International's purchase of *Intermezzo*. Mr. and Mrs. Selznick went to Bermuda, taking his scenario assistant Barbara Keon and her young son with them. There they worked with Jo Swerling on the construction of the screenplay. From Bermuda Selznick requested Dan O'Shea of SIP to find him a new script writer and an additional dialogue writer. For the first he suggested Oliver H. P. Garrett. For the dialogue he asked for Robert Sherwood, Stark Young, James Boyd, Rachel Field, Evelyn Scott, or MacKinlay Kantor. None of these was available, but Garrett was. He and Wilbur Kurtz, back on duty as Historian, met Selznick in New York November 25.

Mr. Kurtz described the meeting in the Selznick offices in a letter home:

Mr. Selznick paced the rug and outlined what problems had to be faced regarding script-cutting. The revision seems to be along the lines of condensation. I was handed a recently cooked-up one line revised continuity, which is a brief, indicating what scenes are to be shown. The Tarleton twins turn up *missing*, and only a few glimpses of Belle Watling are vouchsafed.

Selznick, Garrett, Keon, and Kurtz continued their "conferences" on the train ride to Los Angeles. Not much was accomplished during the trip, but it was made memorable by Selznick's assertion: "Miss Mitchell has such a childlike faith that I am going to make a good picture!" Little could have been farther from the truth. In replying to some of Susan Myrick's reports of script difficulties early in 1939 Miss Mitchell wrote:

I hate to say "I told you so" but there is no one but you to whom I can say it. When movie agents were hounding me in 1936 to let them unload GWTW on the movies, I refused, saying it wasn't possible to make a movie of it. This remark drove them to hysteria. Finally, I let The Macmillan Company sell it. Before I signed the contract I told Katharine Brown and the other Selznickers assembled in the room they were making a great mistake, for a picture could not be made from that book. They all laughed pityingly and patted me, saying "there, there." They said it was a natural and just look at all that dialogue! Why they would not have to write another line. I said yes indeed and thank you, but I knew how that book was written. It had taken me ten years to weave it as tight as a silk pocket handkerchief. If one thread were broken or pulled an ugly ravel would show clear through to the other side of the material. Yet they would have to cut for a script, and when they began cutting they would discover they had technical problems they never dreamed about. . . . Now they have run into exactly the problem I foresaw. And may God have mercy on their souls.

Selznick and Garrett continued work on the script. Selznick asked Franclien Macconnell, who had done a fine condensation of GWTW for him long before, to comb the book for suggestions as to what could best be eliminated. He asked her also to note dialogue not in the script that might be lifted for use instead of some other writer's new dialogue. Shortly after F. Scott Fitzgerald was released from his stint on GWTW he wrote Maxwell Perkins, his editor at Scribner's: "It is wonderful to be writing again instead of patching—do you know in that 'Gone With the Wind' job I was absolutely forbidden to use any words except those of Margaret Mitchell, that is, when new phrases had to be invented one had to thumb through it and check out phrases of hers which would cover the situation!" Having said in November that he did not want Howard back after his refusal of further work the month before, Selznick now tried to recall him at $3,000 a week.

The accelerated activity on GWTW stepped up requests from the studio to Miss Mitchell. On November 29, 1938, she wrote Ruth Leone of the Research Department concerning a long list of questions from Eric Stacey. She answered Mrs. Leone's letter in part and reminded her of Mr. Kurtz's imminent arrival in Hollywood. On December 16 she wrote him in response to a query she had received from one of the wardrobe staff:

I'm returning the sketches of the head rag, and you will note that I have not ok-ed them. . . . I am not connected with the film and I do not think it my place to pass upon anything of this nature. During the past year or more I have received several letters from the Selznick offices asking for information of one kind or another. I have answered some of the questions and have been glad to do it if the information was readily available. I was also glad to assist the Selznick people in getting a list of books and people they might consult in their research work. However, I am not a technical adviser on this job. I have given some pretty broad hints of my attitude in several of my previous letters, but now I think I had better state my position more directly. . . . I don't mind being obliging and I am hopeful that the picture will be accurate as to background, costumes, etc., but I can't and won't take on the responsibilities of serving as an adviser and we might as well understand each other on that point before we go any farther. . . . When Sue Myrick and Annie Laurie get there you ought to be able to handle the situation without needing any help from me and much better than I could.

For the next few weeks—until Vivien Leigh was signed to play Scarlett and the casting of her, Olivia de Havilland, and Leslie Howard was announced on January 13, 1939—there was a spirited series of telephone calls between Miss Brown and Miss Mitchell. How would the announcements be made? Should screen tests of Scarlett be sent to Atlanta for a private viewing? Etc., etc. Miss Mitchell declined the offer of the screen tests; it would be impossible to see them without giving away the secret. Finally the announcements of the principals to play along with Clark Gable were telegraphed to her in great detail at roughly the same time they were released to the press.

The selection of the stars was chief among a myriad of details that beset producer and staff getting ready to begin filming. Further work in Hollywood and urgent calls to New York filled out the cast. Walter Plunkett, costume designer; Joseph Platt, interior designer; and Florence Yock, landscape architect were frantically busy. Selznick was still worrying about the screenplay, searching for scenes to shorten or to drop, calling in Fitzgerald to work with Garrett, and pausing in the midst of it all to shoot off to Miss Mitchell a question about the appearance of Tara's grounds.

Filming began January 26, but the screenplay was far from final. It would not be final for another nine months, but the immediate problem was a large and especially vexing one: the continuity of the script between the bazaar scene and the scene in which Rhett gives Scarlett a Paris bonnet. Miss Brown wired Miss Mitchell that she would call her about this and forwarded by mail a detailed account of the problem as Selznick saw it.

That interim version of the screenplay moves from the bazaar to a scene of lawyers Randolph and Merriwether engaged in talk of Gen. Robert E. Lee's invasion of Pennsylvania. It then describes Rhett and Belle riding together in her carriage. As they reach Aunt Pittypat's house it becomes obvious that Rhett has with him a fancy, unopened hatbox. From there the script proceeds to the end of the bonnet scene pretty well as it was finally realized.

Miss Brown's questions are not part of the record, but they can be surmised from notes Miss Mitchell made of their telephone conversation:

I never [in the novel] went into Belle's house.

Rhett would not drive publicly with her because it would be *ungentlemanly*. His horse could stand in front of her house but he could not drive with her. No one could or would receive him after this.

To alight from her carriage in front of Aunt Pitty's would show he had no respect for Melly or Pitty. After such conduct even Melly would not receive him. She would be forced to believe all the bad things she heard were true.

Rhett would not have been rude to Belle.

Suggestion—Belle without hat following him from her front door to his horse. Bonnet slung over saddle pommel.

Belle must not be familiar with coachman. Scarlett could be familiar but Belle not because she was not nice. Coachman could show disdain for her but not impertinence. (His position one that would have embarrassed him if he were well brought up.) Poor whites more on their dignity with Negroes than nice people as they hated Negroes. Negroes did not respect or like them.

"Producers and what they do with scripts," Miss Mitchell's friend Susan Myrick wrote her on January 11, 1939, "is like a chef making soup. The chef gets an idea from a soup he ate. He spends days making a stock that is just right. He tastes, adds seasonings, tastes again, adds again. Perfect. Then he does more things to it until he has the finest soup in the universe. Whereupon, he calls in the other chefs and they all stand around and pee in it! And this, the treasonable ones of us seem to agree is what has happened about GWTW."

Garrett, she reported, progressed slowly on the script but gossip blamed his lack of progress on Selznick's constant changes. As Miss Mitchell's eyes and ears in Hollywood, she remarked on Scott Fitzgerald's brief period of collaboration with Garrett and his early departure from the set. She reported periodically on the script—how little she thought of the ending of the Garrett revision, for example. "I

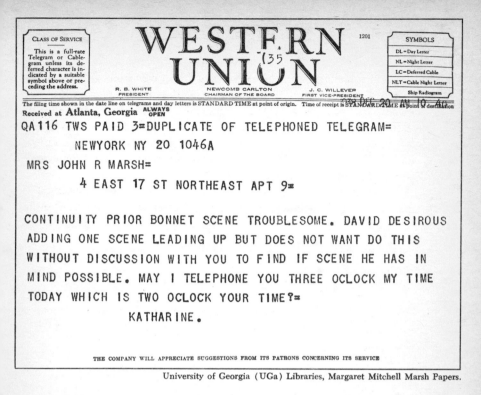

# WESTERN UNION

1201

R. B. WHITE
PRESIDENT

NEWCOMB CARLTON
CHAIRMAN OF THE BOARD

J. C. WILLEVER
FIRST VICE-PRESIDENT

The filing time shown in the date line on telegrams and day letters is STANDARD TIME at point of origin. Time of receipt is STANDARD TIME at point of destination

Received at Atlanta, Georgia   ALWAYS OPEN

QA116 TWS PAID 3=DUPLICATE OF TELEPHONED TELEGRAM=

NEWYORK NY 20 1046A

MRS JOHN R MARSH=

4 EAST 17 ST NORTHEAST APT 9=

CONTINUITY PRIOR BONNET SCENE TROUBLESOME. DAVID DESIROUS
ADDING ONE SCENE LEADING UP BUT DOES NOT WANT DO THIS
WITHOUT DISCUSSION WITH YOU TO FIND IF SCENE HE HAS IN
MIND POSSIBLE. MAY I TELEPHONE YOU THREE OCLOCK MY TIME
TODAY WHICH IS TWO OCLOCK YOUR TIME?=

KATHARINE.

University of Georgia (UGa) Libraries, Margaret Mitchell Marsh Papers.

*Kay Brown's telegram to Margaret Mitchell concerning a particularly
difficult sequence in the screenplay.*

MGM, © 1939, 1967. Collection of Yvette Curran, Rego Park, New York.

knew," she wrote on January 20, "they'd manage some way to make it seem like a happy ending. Lord knows they need to after they have telescoped the story to make everybody die within half an hour. Honestly! What Garrett has done is leave the first half of the script just as long as ever (though he has re-written it—and not to its improvement, if I do say so as shouldn't) and shortened the last part to make it look as if someone dies every few minutes."

Once again Selznick called on Miss Mitchell for help. This time he wanted aid in transmitting to film audiences something that would indicate Melanie's character when she was first introduced in the film. As before, Miss Mitchell politely declined.

On January 25 Selznick sent Jock Whitney, his partner and financial backer of SIP, copies of Howard's screenplay, the Howard-Garrett version, and what then existed as a shooting script. He cautioned Whitney not to be alarmed at the meager proportion of shooting script. He said that large portions of the Howard and Howard-Garrett versions would be incorporated into the shooting script and that he had the whole film already firmly fixed in his mind. He admitted to discouragements along the way but declared that now, on the eve of starting to film, he was sure that he would achieve a picture that would fulfill all expectations.

Shooting began as scheduled. Miss Myrick quickly became a partisan of George Cukor, as Miss Mitchell had been ever since she first met him in 1937. In response to a rumor in July 1938 she had written Miss Brown: "Do, please, tell me if it is true that George Cukor is out of the picture. I have very little interest in who will act in the picture, but I am sorry if George will not direct. I thought him a grand person and a brilliant one." In mid-February 1939 differences between Cukor and Selznick reached a climax and they parted ways, somewhat less than amicably, after less than three weeks of filming.

The exact reasons for the break are uncertain, and hints, surmises, and rumors have been thoroughly aired in the ever-growing literature about GWTW. Susan Myrick's contemporaneous account is as good as any, probably more trustworthy than most, and has never before been published. She wrote Miss Mitchell on February 14:

When the morning *Hollywood Reporter* said Cukor would quit I refused to believe it. But on the set I knew there must be truth in the report for all faces were wreathed in gloom and crew gathered in knots of threes or twos to talk in muted tones. George came in a moment later, cheery as usual with a Good Morning for everybody and no hint of anything unusual on his face.

Morning wore on and everybody asked everybody else about it. Finally, I got up nerve enough to ask Eric Stacey and he gloomily said he thought there was no hope of patching it all up and his only reaction was that George had been damned patient not to have resigned before.

It is really and actually true; George finally told me all about it. When there was a lull and I had a chance I said to him I was upset over what I'd heard and he said come and talk to him. So; we sat down and he talked— not for publication he said, but because he liked me, felt responsible for getting me into a mess and wanted me to know the truth. He hated it very much he said but he could not do otherwise. In effect he said he is an honest craftsman and he cannot do a job unless he knows it is a good job and he feels the present job is not right. For days, he told me, he has looked at the rushes and felt he was failing. He knew he was a good director and knew the actors were good ones, yet the thing did not click as it should.

Gradually he became more and more convinced that the script was the trouble. . . . David, himself, thinks HE is writing the script and he tells poor Bobby Keon and Stinko Garrett what to write. And they do the best they can with it, in their limited way. Garrett is just a professional scenario writer while Howard knows dramatic values and—oh hell, you know what Howard is.

And George has continuously taken script from day to day, compared the Garrett-Selznick version with the Howard, groaned and tried to change some parts back to the Howard script. But he seldom could do much with the scene. . . .

So George just told David he would not work any longer if the script was not better and he wanted the Howard script back. David told George he was a director, not an author, and he (David) was the producer and the judge of what is a good script (or words to that effect) and George said he was a director and a damn good one and he would not let his name go out over a lousy picture and if they didn't go back to the Howard script (he was willing to have them cut it down shorter) he, George, was through.

And bull-headed David said "OK, get out!"

There followed a lapse in filming; a new director, Victor Fleming; and a new script writer, Ben Hecht. Historians of *Gone with the Wind* have given too much credence to Hecht's account in his *A Child of the Century* of how he wrote the first nine reels of GWTW in seven days. Hecht's account is so full of demonstrable untruths and exaggerations (as is the rest of that autobiography) that it should be heavily discounted. He told of the difficulty of finding a copy of the Howard script "discarded three years before," of toasting the "dead craftsman"

*Lydia Schiller, script assistant, and Wilbur G. Kurtz, historian. Taken on location at Big Bear Lake June 14, 1939, by Katherine Causey.*

*Vivien Leigh studying the day's script on the set for Tara at the Selznick studio lot "Forty Acres," Culver City. Snapshot by Wilbur G. Kurtz, June 9, 1939.*

*Director Victor Fleming (center) and Assistant Director Eric Stacey (back to camera). Snapshot at Forty Acres while preparing for the scene of the wounded at the carshed. Snapshot by Wilbur G. Kurtz.*

*George Cukor, Clark Gable, and William McClain in the bazaar scene.*

Atlanta Historical Society, Kurtz Collection.

MGM, © 1939, 1967. Collection of Yvette Curran.

(seven months before Howard's untimely death in August 1939), etc., etc. Selznick, he said, promised him $15,000 for a week's work and he refused to work longer. He failed to say that he had John van Druten working with him or that he worked two weeks instead of one. He declared that on the fourth day a blood vessel in Fleming's right eye broke and that on the fifth Selznick "toppled into a torpor while chewing on a banana." He neglected to tell that he did the last of his work in a hospital.

Hecht's principal contribution was a series of titles connecting the chief sequences of the film. He has been credited with the idea of projecting these over montages of the progress of the war. This idea was already written into the Howard-Garrett screenplay. Wilbur Kurtz was directed toward the end of February to prepare historical data on which Hecht would base his titles. Kurtz, Val Lewton, and Winston Miller spent endless hours from then until June working out elaborate montages. They were much too detailed and too heavily burdened with history to help move the story along and, except for a few brief vignettes, were eventually discarded. In late September Selznick wired Hecht in New York asking him to write the seven titles actually used in the film. He commented that some of the titles could be based on the ones written while Hecht was in Hollywood.

The titles are an effective device and serve the film well—all except the very first, which Miss Mitchell felt set a falsely romantic tone to the whole story. Virginius Dabney, of Richmond, in a 1942 book commented that the lines badly distort the spirit of the novel. Writing to him she said:

I am glad you made the statement about the prologue of the motion picture and its reference to cavaliers in the South. Some people gave me the credit for writing it and thought it was "just beautiful"; others, who knew the section about which I wrote, belabored me for dislocating one of the central ideas of the book. It was useless for me to protest that I had nothing to do with the matter. I certainly had no intention of writing about cavaliers.

Hecht's lines appear over the rolling title of *Gone with the Wind* as

> There was a land of Cavaliers and
> Cotton Fields called the Old South . . .
>
> Here in this pretty world
> Gallantry took its last bow . . .

Here was the last ever to be seen
of Knights and their Ladies Fair,
of Master and of Slave . . .

Look for it only in books, for it
is no more than a dream remembered,
a Civilization gone with the wind . . .

Vivien Leigh was even more a partisan of Cukor than was Miss Myrick. She did not care for Fleming and found acting under his direction difficult. She and Miss Myrick were also together in their devotion to Howard's script. In her letter to Miss Mitchell on February 14, Miss Myrick wrote:

I just re-read your sentence "I have an idea they are using the Sidney Howard script for the first part of the movie . . . I imagine they are following the book up to the end of the war with few changes." Well dearie, you got another thought. The Howard script is beautiful. If I wasn't scared of my life I'd mail you one. It is just the book in spirit, every inch. The Garrett opus does follow the book in a fashion but it does such queer things. For instance there are numerous scenes that are pure exposition and not disguised at all and no actress on earth can say them so they don't sound like they are exposition.

Miss Leigh echoed this criticism of the screenplay in writing to her husband on April 2: "As far as the film goes, it creeps along—very long hours and very little work done—principally I think because every scene is so hard to play because of the appalling dialogue. However, David Selznick promises me that Sidney Howard is coming back on the script."

"Have they got a script yet?" Miss Mitchell wrote to Mr. and Mrs. Kurtz March 11. "I read in some theatrical paper that the last people who were hired to do the script refused to do a day-to-day job and said they had to be at least ten days ahead. That sounded as if the script were not completed yet." She added that a Hollywood producer visiting in Atlanta had told her Robert Benchley had been approached with an offer to work on it. "I regret to state," she reported, "that I was overtaken by unseemly merriment and laughed until I cried. I could not tell the man why I laughed, but I was thinking that Groucho Marx, William Faulkner and Erskine Caldwell would probably be on the script before this business was over. As you can gather, I do get a great deal of fun out of this affair, and my greatest enjoyment comes from a sense of thanksgiving that I have nothing to do with it and am not in Hollywood."

On March 12 Miss Myrick wrote that Hecht was gone and van Druten and John Balderston were working on the script. "We have 60 pages marked 'completed script,'" she said, "but every few days we get some pink pages marked 'substitute script' and we tear out some yellow pages and set in the new pink ones. We expect blue or orange pages any day now."

Soon the staff and cast were receiving blue pages as substitutes for the substitute pink pages. Thus the shooting script eventually also became known among aficionados of *Gone with the Wind* as the "rainbow script."

Victor Fleming won over Miss Myrick (though she still missed Cukor) and flattered her by asking her to write some ad lib lines. He told her—in her words—"that God knows they'd had fifteen writers, I'd just as well try my hand at it and probably couldn't be any worse than the others!" Miss Myrick particularly disliked the over-grand Twelve Oaks designed for the film and loved it when Fleming said: "Maybe the po' white trash will like it because they can say it is just like Grandpa's that Sherman burned down."

On April 9 Miss Myrick wrote news good enough to suit the Easter it was: "SIDNEY HOWARD IS BACK ON THE SCRIPT! Came back last week." She added: "I haven't the faintest idea how many folks that makes in all who have done script. I lost count after the first ten and all I know is Howard is somewhere around the sixteenth, though he may be the twentieth." She counted better than she thought she did. The full list of writers and tinkerers on the script is John Balderston, F. Scott Fitzgerald, Michael Foster, Oliver H. P. Garrett, Ben Hecht, Barbara Keon, Wilbur G. Kurtz, Val Lewton, Charles MacArthur, John Lee Mahin, Edwin Justus Mayer, Winston Miller, David O. Selznick, Donald Ogden Stewart, Jo Swerling, and John van Druten—to say nothing of Margaret Mitchell or Sidney Howard.

Miss Mitchell wrote back: "I suppose Mr. Howard discovered that there was practically nothing left of his original script. I would not be surprised to learn that the script of the other sixteen had been junked and Mr. Howard's original script put into production." Howard was not again mentioned by Miss Myrick in the brief period he was back on the scene. On May 28 she wrote:

Sidney Howard is long gone and I miss him. He was so delightful and so understanding of the true situation. When he left he came to say good

*Vivien Leigh prepares for a scene with William Bakewell as the Confederate dispatch rider, June 13, 1939.*

bye to me and I asked if the script were finished. He said yes but no doubt David would re-write it and it would not surprise Howard if D O S called him back from N Y in a month or so to re-write it once more. You know, I think that the script is now about fifty pages more than when Howard first wrote it.

Everyone on the set—Selznick most of all—had trepidations when filming began. Enthusiasm reached a low point when Cukor left. Luckily Selznick retained Whitney's faith and financial support, and shared the financier's confidence in the production. Now that things had gone full circle with the script, attitudes brightened. In her Easter letter Miss Myrick wrote:

One day I think this pix is going to be a grand mess. Next day I am thrilled over it and think it is going to be marvelous. The street scenes are so fine I think the thing is a Birth of a Nation. And the new script we have for the scene with Scarlett and Dr. Meade in the hospital for the wounded men is thrilling as can be.

In late May all the film so far put together was shown to the staff. Mrs. Annie Laurie Kurtz wrote an Atlanta friend: "This was the crucial moment. . . . We watched with bated breath—and found that it was more than we had hoped for. It is truly beautiful!"

The man who counted wrote to Howard Dietz, Director of Advertising and Publicity for MGM, that the picture would surpass everything predicted for it and would have to be publicized and promoted accordingly. In an uncharacteristic understatement he estimated that the film might gross as much as twelve or thirteen million dollars.

Filming was officially completed on June 27, with a number of retakes and with a company party after the finish of the day's work. There remained further retakes, montages, bridgeovers, and various special film effects to carry work well into the fall. The filming of added bits and retakes was still going on as late as October 24. That day's work included a retake of the final scene. This was Selznick's triumph in the fullest sense. Here he clinched success for his film, bringing to it something of the equivocation—the "comment and implication," to quote Howard—with which Margaret Mitchell had closed her novel. If Miss Mitchell had ever lacked faith that Selznick was going to make a good picture, David O. Selznick had never really doubted. Now he had done it.

Max Steiner's score was not ready until late November. Last minute cut-ins (including a brief scene shot on November 11) and the scoring pushed completion perilously close to the announced date of the film's first showing. But on December 11 Selznick wired Kay Brown, already in Atlanta for the premiere on December 15, that *Gone with the Wind* was completed.

*Gone with the Wind* was David Selznick's film. No matter how entertaining and exciting Miss Mitchell's novel, no matter how felicitous Sidney Howard's screenplay, no matter what directors and actors contributed—the film was Selznick's through and through.

In a letter early in 1940 to Frank Capra, Selznick bragged that he had made *Gone with the Wind* his way and against the advice of all of his associates. "Everything," he said, "in 'Gone With the Wind,' without exception, is as I wanted it to be. I took the gamble on my own conceptions, and on my own methods."

In the souvenir program for GWTW's first run Dietz quotes Selznick in more gracious comments: "The production of 'Gone With the Wind' represents the complete devotion to their respective jobs, and the coordinated efforts, of a hundred artists, technicians and department heads. I should like to take this opportunity to express publicly my deep appreciation to those credited on the screen and in the program, including especially Victor Fleming, William Cameron Menzies, Jack Cosgrove, and Hal Kern; and also to others too numerous to mention, in particular Katharine Brown." The producer added a special tribute to Sidney Howard as the author of the screenplay: "Having had the pleasure and privilege of being associated in close daily collaboration for over a year with that great craftsman, the late Sidney Howard, on the screenplay, it is my deepest regret . . . that he did not live to see the realization of his work."

Most of the material in the film that is not taken directly from Margaret Mitchell was created by Selznick himself. He credited a few scenes each to Howard and Hecht, a very few to van Druten, and only scattered words to Garrett. He claimed responsibility—and credit—for 80 per cent of the film's construction, dividing the rest among Swerling, Howard, and Hecht.

Almost none of Fitzgerald's relatively small amount of original work on GWTW survives in the film. The screenplay, however, was considerably affected by his competent editing, work the Garrett revision of Howard's script sorely needed. He worked most with the difficult continuity from the bazaar through Ashley's Christmas leave. He achieved remarkable improvement of Garrett's lines by following Selznick's edict that the dialogue should use Margaret Mitchell's words as much as possible. He cut redundancies in the Garrett-Howard script and restored lines originally in the book or in Howard's version.

Garrett (or Selznick or Keon) had acted on Miss Mitchell's suggestion to have Belle bring the bonnet out to Rhett already mounted on his horse. On that version Fitzgerald commented: "Somehow sordid—as it *isn't* in the book. Belle shouldn't be a harridan. Have rewritten on next page." (It is Fitzgerald's rewritten version of this scene that is incorporated into this book.) When the working screenplay seemed to refer slightingly to the Confederate "cause" one too many times, he noted: "We're running 'the Cause' into the ground. Mitchell satirizes but does not burlesque."

Andrew Turnbull recorded in 1962 that Fitzgerald found *Gone with the Wind* "'good' but 'not very original . . . . There are no new characters, new techniques, new observations—none of the elements that make literature—especially no new examination into human emotions. But on the other hand it is interesting, surprisingly honest, consistent and workmanlike throughout.'" Most of Fitzgerald's marginal comments on Garrett's version of the screenplay relate to its dramatic weaknesses. Some clearly show his respect for Miss Mitchell's work. Again and again occur such notes as: "Book restored. Why must this good dialogue be made trite and stagey?" and "Book restored. It is infinitely more moving." His most frequent notation was, in fact, "Book restored."

It is difficult to measure Jo Swerling's contribution, if any. Scarlett's fall which caused her miscarriage is not in Howard's version but appears in the Howard-Garrett script, whether put there by Garrett, Selznick, or Swerling is not possible to say.

Garrett's reworking is, as Susan Myrick stated and Vivien Leigh hinted, marred by too much exposition disguised as dialogue and by clumsy introductions of history into the script. Perhaps Garrett was too good a student of Wilbur Kurtz when the historian gave him a crash course in Civil War history on their transcontinental ride in 1938. Selznick, however, was much taken with the device of using montages to explicate the course of the war. But one of the wisest moves he made during the cutting and editing of the film was to cut the montages almost completely. Some footage was made for these scenes. According to E. D. C. Campbell, Jr., Director of the Museum of the Confederacy, portions of it turn up as stock film used in *Raintree County* and in *Shenandoah*. Likewise, some Mississippi River shots made by James Fitzpatrick (of travelogue fame) for use in GWTW found their way into the 1950's remake of *Showboat*.

The version of *Gone with the Wind* presented here does not follow from start to finish any of the various single versions prepared during the course of filming. These are the Howard screenplay, the Howard-Garrett version, the shooting script, and the Moviola version. The Moviola version is one made by taking the words of the action directly from the film as by dictation. Even that version, however, is not an exact transcript. Ben Hecht's flowery words in the rolling titles, for example, differ slightly in the film from the way they are printed in the Moviola transcript.

Selznick was undoubtedly right in giving Howard sole credit for the screenplay. He felt that the work of no other writer merited attention. The version of *Gone with the Wind* that is presented here is fully 85 per cent Howard's. It includes a few scenes Howard wrote that are not in the final screenplay—Scarlett's arrival at the Atlanta depot in 1863, the delightful scene between Rhett and Belle Watling as they watch Atlanta society entering the armory for the great bazaar, the scene showing Peachtree Street as it had been affected by war just before Gettysburg, and the not-too-successful scene that shows postwar conditions in Jonesboro.

The only scene of great importance added to Howard's version is Scarlett's fall down the stairs. Scenes of lesser value which appear in later versions and not in Howard's are those of lawyers Randolph and Merriwether discussing Lee's campaign, Rhett leaving Belle's place with the bonnet for Scarlett, Uncle Peter chasing the ancient rooster for Ashley's Christmas dinner, the night scene in the makeshift hospital, Scarlett and Rhett's post-honeymoon visit to Tara, the scene between Frank Kennedy and Big Sam just after the Shantytown incident, and Rhett's visit to London with Bonnie. Howard wrote the lines assigned to the London nurse as Scarlett's. The later transfer of them was a good move.

Other scenes underwent changes as work on the film progressed. There were scores of revised pages of script, but often the revisions covered no more than a slight change in stage directions. For the most part, the scenes that Howard wrote retained most of his lines all the way through filming. Howard never got to the stage of working with the director in making the shot-by-shot version of the script. One can guess that he was joking—and expecting a rewrite—when he had Ashley and his friends in their feigned drunkenness sing "Marching Through Georgia," and it was a jocular leg-pull of his friend George Cukor when he wrote as a direction after a childish sentence of Wade Hampton's: "Mr. Cukor will coach the child actor in this pronunciation."

The sequence of the Paris bonnet scene gave the most trouble. The

# SELZNICK INTERNATIONAL PICTURES, INC.

# CALL SHEET

DATE **FRIDAY, JUNE 9, 1939**

PICTURE **"GONE WITH THE WIND"** PROD. NO. **108** DIRECTOR **VICTOR FLEMING**

SET **EXT. TARA** **NOVEMBER 1865**

LOCATION **40 ACRES** SET NO. **1** SCENES **469 to 484F**

| NAME | TIME CALLED | | CHARACTER, DESC., WARDROBE |
|---|---|---|---|
| | ON SET | MAKE-UP | |
| Vivien Leigh | 8:00 AM | 7:00 AM | Scarlett #14 |
| Thomas Mitchell | 8:00 AM | 6:30 AM | Gerald #6 |
| Victor Jory | 9:00 AM | 8:00 AM | Jonas Wilkerson #3 |
| Isabel Jewell | 9:00 AM | 8:00 AM | Emmy Slattery #1 |
| Oscar Polk | Will call | | Pork #3 |
| Stand-ins | 7:30 AM | 7:00 AM | -- |
| | | | PROPERTY DEPT. |
| | | | Wilkerson's buggy and horse as used - - - - 8:00 AM |

**I N   C A S E   O F   B A D   W E A T H E R**

INT. LOWER HALL-RHETT'S HOUSE - STAGE #14 - SET #54 - SCS. 681-2 -AUTUMN 1872

| | | | |
|---|---|---|---|
| Vivien Leigh | 9:00 AM | 8:00 AM | Scarlett #32 |
| Clark Gable | 9:00 AM | 8:30 AM | Rhett #31 |
| Stand-ins | 8:15 AM | 8:00 AM | |

| | | SPECIAL EFFECTS: |
|---|---|---|
| CAMERAS - - - - - - - - | 7:00 AM | Fog - - - - - Will notify |
| SOUND (Ready) - - - - - | 8:15 AM | |
| P.A.SYSTEM (Ready) - - | 7:30 AM | |
| COSGROVE - - - - - - - | Will notify | NOTE TO ALL DEPTS. |
| LUNCHES (Ready to serve) | 12:00 M | |
| TRANSPORTATION - - - - | As ordered | If company shoots on 40 acres, the Call Times may be changed, depending on time company completes shooting, Thursday, June 8th. If there is any change, Depts. will be notified on completion of day's shooting. |

ADVANCE SHOOTING SCHEDULE ON
REVERSE SIDE OF CALL SHEET

*The cast and staff's call sheet for June 9, 1939. The number following a character's name is the character's costume number for that scene.*

Saturday, June 10  -  Int. Hall-Rhett's House     Stage #14
               AT NIGHT
               Menzies Unit to lineup and shoot
               Fog Sequence on Stage #3 as soon
               as Miss Leigh is available.

Monday, June 12  -  Int. Scarlett's Room     Stage #11
               (Now scene after miscarriage with
                    Scarlett and Mammy)
               Retake Closeup of Scarlett in Library
               Retake Closeup of Scarlett in 12 Oaks Room
               Closeup Aunt Pitty in PROVOST MARSHAL SEQ.
               IN P.M.
               Ext. Streets (PROCESS) Fire-Escape Seq.
                    With Rhett & Scarlett
                    NOTE: This sequence will be used
                           as cover from day to day.
               AT NIGHT
               Ext. Road Near Edge of Town     Ext.Stage #14
                    Rhett-Scarlett-Wagon-Extras

Tuesday, June 13  -  Ext. Peachtree Street     40 Acres
               Scarlett's Curse
               Note; Have Mr. Selznick standby
                       during shooting of this sc.
               Dispatch Rider Scene
               IN P.M.
               Ext. Streets (PROCESS) - Fire-Escape Seq.

Wednesday, June 14 - Ext. Tara - Gerald & Scarlett's Walk    Malibu Lake

Thursday, June 15  -  Ext. Tara - End of Honeymoon Dissolve    40 Acres
               (With Gerald & Scarlett)
               IN.P.M.
               Scarlett's Oath - PROCESS

Friday, June 16  -  Ext. Peachtree St.     40 Acres
               Baby Buggy Sc. with Rhett-Scarlett
               IN P.M.
               Process - Pickups, etc.

Saturday, June 17  -  Ext. Tara - Gerald & Scarlett
               IN P.M.
               Trek (if necessary) or Honeymoon

Monday, June 19  -  Honeymoon or Trek
Tuesday, June 20  -  Attack Seq. (sooner if possible)
Wednesday, June 21 - Scarlett as a Business Woman
Thursday, June 22  -  Honeymoon or Trek
Friday, June 23  -  Honeymoon or Trek
Saturday, June 24  -  Ext. Rhett's Garden - Bonnie's Riding Lesson

version used in the film does not completely jibe with Howard's version, but his way of telling it is so much the superior one that it—plus less than a page of Fitzgerald's work—is used here. The reader will have to make small adjustments in logic and sequence for himself. Similarly, Howard included a few characters who did not survive script changes or editing. These include Jeems, the Tarleton twins' servant; Cade Calvert, Honey Wilkes, Dilcey, a Captain Randall and a Miss Blessington (neither of whom was in the novel), and various bit characters and extras. Their speeches are used here as written. There are other minor inconsistencies which remain in this amalgamated text, such as Charles Hamilton being a corporal in one scene and a captain in the next; but these are of no importance. The text has been carefully selected to eliminate major inconsistencies. The Tarleton twins, for example, are killed in three different ways and in one intermediate version a Grandmother Tarleton, whom Margaret Mitchell never knew, is invented to receive the news. In this version they die only once.

The text has been chosen to emphasize the pleasure of reading *Gone with the Wind* as a screenplay and to give the reader as full as possible a dramatic version of the story. Each reader will enjoy for himself discovering alterations from the novel and from the final form of the film. It is estimated that this version, filmed in its entirety, would make a picture five hours and eight minutes long.

The beginning and end of the screenplay were trouble spots, as they are in the composition of almost any narrative. Howard dived right in to Scarlett's scene with the Tarleton boys. The Howard-Garrett version begins with a "Foreword title dealing with the period and the locale, with a comment on the Southern aristocracy." It then fades in on the jacket of the novel and follows with the first few lines of the text. The shooting script drops the clumsy and already hackneyed device of using photographs of the book, substituting a long shot of Fort Sumter with the Confederate flag being raised. The final version, with its pictorial rolling title and Hecht's grandiose lines, is a refinement of the introduction to the Howard-Garrett script.

When Miss Myrick and the Kurtzes wrote Miss Mitchell of Selznick's idea of an opening shot of Fort Sumter, she said in her answering letter to Mr. and Mrs. Kurtz:

I must confess that at this news John and I yelled with laughter. I have yet to see a war picture that did not open with Fort Sumter, and it is too much to hope that "Gone With the Wind" would be different. Movie pro-

*Vivien Leigh poses for a scene not used in the film.*

ducers are just like vaudeville actors. I once asked a vaudeville actor why he and others of his profession persisted in cracking jokes that came from Joe Miller's joke book. I felt that an occasional new joke would be relished by the public. He said, seriously, that I was all wrong. Far from relishing a new joke, the public resented one bitterly. They were confused by the newness and did not know whether to laugh or not. They knew what to expect when an actor said, "Who was that lady I seen you with last night?" and they laughed dutifully. Probably Mr. Selznick feels that audiences are accustomed to Fort Sumter and will know when they see it that a picture about the War will inevitably follow.

Selznick planned from the time the fire sequences were made December 10, 1938, to use them on a "grandeur" screen made up of three ordinary screens. This plan failed because there was not enough usable footage. There were plenty of shots of the burning sets of old films, but Yakima Canutt, the great stunt man who as a stunt double played Rhett in them, did not match Clark Gable closely enough in dress and bearing for many of them to be used.

In Howard's script the last scene is:

EXTERIOR–THE STREET IN FRONT OF THE NEW HOUSE–DAY
*From* SCARLETT'S *angle (over her shoulder if possible)* RHETT *can be seen as he gets into the carriage and drives off. A final cry from her.*
SCARLETT: Rhett!
MAMMY *appears beside her. She falls back against her for support. The* CAMERA GOES CLOSE *as she turns to* MAMMY.
SCARLETT: I'll go crazy if I think about this now! I'll think about it tomorrow! We'll go home to Tara tomorrow, Mammy! I'll get strength from Tara! And think of some other way to get him back! After all, tomorrow is . . . another day.

*FADE OUT*

That scene certainly did not catch the spirit of the novel as effectively as Howard usually did. It became worse, much worse, in Garrett's revision:

EXTERIOR–OUTSIDE FRONT DOOR–*SEMI-LONG SHOT*
SCARLETT *remains helplessly gazing after* RHETT. *Now* MAMMY *appears at the open doorway behind* SCARLETT.
MAMMY [*gently*]: Honey, chile—
SCARLETT *turns and flings herself into* MAMMY'S *arms. CAMERA SWIFTLY MOVES IN CLOSER.* SCARLETT *sobs like a little girl.*

SCARLETT: O, Mammy, he's gone. He's gone again! How'll I ever get him back?

MAMMY: He'll come back. D'in Ah say de last time? He'll do it agin. Ah always knows.

FADE OUT

In early June Selznick devised an idea in which Scarlett would realize her love for Rhett in her walk through the mist from Melanie's deathbed. In a highly melodramatic scene she hurries in search of Rhett:

As she nears the top of the hill the realization comes to her that she is in love with Rhett. And to her unthinking panic in her chase of him, there is added first a clarifying of her emotions which we read on her face, which slowly changes to joy at the realization of her emotions. And where before she had called to him and searched for him without knowing why, now her pace accelerates still further and she runs with an eagerness and ecstasy to the man she knows she loves.

This "Scarlett's walk" was to be accompanied by a series of dissolves, half obscured by the mist, of remembered moments with Rhett.

At the same time, June 5, Selznick sent alternate script which was also filmed. This was simply a strengthening of the Howard ending by the omission of Mammy and fading out on an extremely large close-up of Scarlett's face or fading to a sunset shot of the spot at Tara where Gerald had spoken to her of love of the land. In a close-up "The sunset rim-lights her face. She is ecstatic that she still has what is most deeply rooted in her affections." In an alternate to this Scarlett is saying: "Rhett! . . . Rhett! . . . You'll come back . . . I *know* you will!" Either way there was a return to the sunset shot when "*CAMERA DRAWS BACK* as we once did on Scarlett and Gerald until the tiny silhouetted figure of Scarlett is outlined against Gerald's Tara."

On June 8 the producer sent to the set the script for the ending as millions upon millions who have seen the film know it. Selznick was pleased with the ending as he finally filmed it. He told Miss Brown that it would probably not seem good on paper to her or to Miss Mitchell but guaranteed that it worked. He was excited with the reception it got at a geniune "sneak preview" in Riverside September 12. No preview cards bore comments against it. Selznick felt it gave the end of the film both a lift and just the proper amount of uncertainty to portray the equivocation of the end of the novel.

There remained one point, small but of special significance. Joseph

UGa Libraries, Medora Field Perkerson Collection.

UGa Libraries, Perkerson Collection.

UGa Libraries, Perkerson Collection.

I. Breen of the Hays office had forbidden the use of the word "damn." In Howard's script when Scarlett asks "What's to become of me?" Rhett replies: "I wish I cared, but I don't." In the Howard-Garrett version his line became: "My dear, I don't give a damn." It was filmed using "damn" but also, as insurance, saying "I don't care." Only in Selznick's June 9 rewrite did the telling adverb appear, the little addition that made so much difference; and only after six months of pleas to Will S. Hays, President of the Motion Picture Producers and Distributors of America, and payment of a token fine, was Rhett permitted to say *Gone with the Wind*'s most memorable line: "Frankly, my dear, I don't give a damn."

DAVID O. SELZNICK'S

PRODUCTION OF *Margaret Mitchell's*

# "*GONE WITH THE WIND*"

STARRING

## Clark Gable
## Vivien Leigh
## Leslie Howard   Olivia de Havilland

A Selznick International Picture–Produced by David O. Selznick

| DIRECTED BY | SCREEN PLAY BY | MUSIC BY |
|---|---|---|
| Victor Fleming | Sidney Howard | Max Steiner |

Released by METRO-GOLDWYN-MAYER INC.

**CENTR M 105**

# ORCHESTRA
Loew's Grand Theatre
Friday Evening, Dec. 15, 1939

# THE PLAYERS

*In the order of their appearance:*

| | |
|---|---|
| BRENT TARLETON | Fred Crane |
| STUART TARLETON | George Reeves |
| SCARLETT O'HARA | Vivien Leigh |
| MAMMY | Hattie McDaniel |
| BIG SAM | Everett Brown |
| ELIJAH | Zack Williams |
| GERALD O'HARA | Thomas Mitchell |
| PORK | Oscar Polk |
| ELLEN O'HARA | Barbara O'Neil |
| JONAS WILKERSON | Victor Jory |
| SUELLEN O'HARA | Evelyn Keyes |
| CARREEN O'HARA | Ann Rutherford |
| PRISSY | Butterfly McQueen |
| JOHN WILKES | Howard Hickman |
| INDIA WILKES | Alicia Rhett |
| ASHLEY WILKES | Leslie Howard |
| MELANIE HAMILTON | Olivia de Havilland |
| CHARLES HAMILTON | Rand Brooks |
| FRANK KENNEDY | Carroll Nye |
| CATHLEEN CALVERT | Marcella Martin |
| RHETT BUTLER | Clark Gable |
| AUNT "PITTYPAT" HAMILTON | Laura Hope Crews |
| DOCTOR MEADE | Harry Davenport |
| MRS. MEADE | Leona Roberts |
| MRS. MERRIWETHER | Jane Darwell |
| RENÉ PICARD | Albert Morin |
| MAYBELLE MERRIWETHER | Mary Anderson |
| FANNY ELSING | Terry Shero |
| OLD LEVI | William McClain |

47

| | |
|---|---|
| UNCLE PETER | Eddie Anderson |
| PHIL MEADE | Jackie Moran |
| REMINISCENT SOLDIER | Cliff Edwards |
| BELLE WATLING | Ona Munson |
| THE SERGEANT | Ed Chandler |
| A WOUNDED SOLDIER | George Hackathorne |
| A CONVALESCENT SOLDIER | Roscoe Ates |
| A DYING SOLDIER | John Arledge |
| AN AMPUTATION CASE | Eric Linden |
| A COMMANDING OFFICER | Tom Tyler |
| A MOUNTED OFFICER | William Bakewell |
| THE BARTENDER | Lee Phelps |
| THE YANKEE DESERTER | Paul Hurst |
| THE CARPETBAGGER'S FRIEND | Ernest Whitman |
| A RETURNING VETERAN | William Stelling |
| A HUNGRY SOLDIER | Louis Jean Heydt |
| EMMY SLATTERY | Isabel Jewell |
| THE YANKEE MAJOR | Robert Elliott |
| HIS POKER-PLAYING CAPTAINS | George Meeker, Wallis Clark |
| THE CORPORAL | Irving Bacon |
| A CARPETBAGGER ORATOR | Adrian Morris |
| JOHNNY GALLEGHER | J.M. Kerrigan |
| A CARPETBAGGER BUSINESSMAN | Olin Howland |
| A RENEGADE | Yakima Canutt |
| HIS COMPANION | Blue Washington |
| TOM, A YANKEE CAPTAIN | Ward Bond |
| BONNIE BLUE BUTLER | Cammie King |
| BEAU WILKES | Mickey Kuhn |
| BONNIE'S NURSE | Lillian Kemble Cooper |

# STAFF

| | |
|---|---|
| *The Production designed by* | William Cameron Menzies |
| *Art direction by* | Lyle Wheeler |
| *Photographed by* | Ernest Haller, A.S.C. |
| *Technicolor Associates* | Ray Rennahan, A.S.C. |
| | Wilfrid M. Cline, A.S.C. |
| *Musical Score by* | Max Steiner |
| *Associate* | Lou Forbes |
| *Special Photographic effects by* | Jack Cosgrove |
| *Associate: Fire effects* | Lee Zavitz |
| *Costumes designed by* | Walter Plunkett |
| *Scarlett's hats by* | John Frederics |
| *Interiors by* | Joseph B. Platt |
| *Interior decoration by* | Edward G. Boyle |
| *Supervising Film Editor* | Hal C. Kern |
| *Associate Film Editor* | James E. Newcom |
| *Scenario Assistant* | Barbara Keon |
| *Recorder* | Frank Maher |
| *Makeup and hairstyling* | Monty Westmore |
| *Associates* | Hazel Rogers, Ben Nye |
| *Dance Directors* | Frank Floyd, Eddie Prinz |
| *Historian* | Wilbur G. Kurtz |
| *Technical Advisers* | Susan Myrick, Will Price |
| *Research* | Lillian K. Deighton |
| *Production Manager* | Raymond A. Klune |
| *Technicolor Co. Supervision* | Natalie Kalmus |
| *Associate* | Henri Jaffa |
| *Assistant Director* | Eric G. Stacey |
| *Second Assistant Director* | Ridgeway Callow |
| *Production continuity* | Lydia Schiller, Connie Earle |
| *Mechanical Engineer* | R.D. Musgrave |
| *Construction Superintendent* | Harold Fenton |

| | |
|---:|:---|
| *Chief Grip* | Fred Williams |
| *In Charge of Wardrobe* | Edward P. Lambert |
| *Associates* | Marian Dabney, Elmer Ellsworth |
| *Casting Managers* | Charles Richards, Fred Schuessler |
| *Location Manager* | Mason Litson |
| *Scenic Department Superintendent* | Henry J. Stahl |
| *Electrical Superintendent* | Wally Oettel |
| *Chief Electrician* | James Potevin |
| *Properties:* | |
| *Manager* | Harold Coles |
| *On the set* | Arden Cripe |
| *Greens* | Roy A. McLaughlin |
| *Drapes* | James Forney |
| *Special properties made by* | Ross B. Jackman |
| *Tara landscaped by* | Florence Yock |
| *Still photographer* | Fred Parrish |
| *Camera operators* | Arthur Arling, Vincent Farrar |
| *Assistant Film Editors* | Richard van Enger, Ernest Leadley |

FADE IN:

There was a land of Cavaliers and
Cotton Fields called the Old South. . . .

Here in this patrician world the
Age of Chivalry took its last bow. . . .

Here was the last ever to be seen
of Knights and their Ladies Fair,
of Master and of Slave. . . .

Look for it only in books, for it
is no more than a dream remembered,
a Civilization gone with the wind. . . .

FADE OUT

# First
# Sequence

# EXTERIOR–TARA–THE GARDEN–DAY

*Begin where two superb hunters and a lesser mount are tied to the hitching post in front of the house. Three or four dogs lie on the gravel safely behind the horses' heels. The CAMERA turns slowly to take in a considerable extent of lawn, box-bordered, where the drive curves away toward the stables. A wall of trees edges the lawn in the distance and isolated trees are spotted here and there. The life of the plantation is shuffling along paths and across the drive and, as the CAMERA turns, the ear is offended by the gobble of a turkey as a Little Colored Boy pursues it out of the flower beds, across the lawn, and out of sight. This sound blends, the CAMERA still turning, with the laughter of young people's voices—*SCARLETT'S, STUART TARLETON'S, BRENT TARLE-TON'S—*and the CAMERA pulls up at last beneath the columned verandah of the house, where* JEEMS, *the Tarleton groom, grins amidst the security of a cape jessamine bush. The laughter subsiding,* BRENT TARLETON *is speaking off-screen.*

BRENT'S VOICE: Don't know why we should care about being expelled from college! We'd have had to come home before term was out anyway.

SCARLETT'S VOICE: Why would you?

STUART'S VOICE: The war, goose! The war's going to . . .

THE VERANDAH–DAY

SCARLETT: If you boys say "war" just once again, I'll walk into the house and slam the door! Pa talks war morning, noon, and night and all the gentlemen who come here talk war and Fort Sumter and secession and Abe Lincoln till I could scream! And this war talk's just ruining every party I go to. There isn't going to be any war!

BRENT: Not going to be any war!

STUART: Why, Scarlett, honey, of course there's going to be a war!

SCARLETT *rises to make good her threat.*

BRENT: All right, Scarlett! All right! We'll talk about something else!

SCARLETT *sits again.*

STUART: We'll talk about the barbecue and ball at Twelve Oaks tomorrow. We came over to make sure we get all your waltzes tomorrow night. [SCARLETT, *pleased, settles back in her chair.*] First Brent, then me, then Brent again and so on . . .

MGM, © 1939, 1967. Collection of Yvette Curran.

SCARLETT: Now wouldn't that be just lovely, if only . . . [*Both boys sit forward as* SCARLETT *holds her fire for just long enough.*] . . . if only I didn't have every one of 'em taken!
CATASTROPHE.
BRENT AND STUART [*together*]: Why, honey!
SCARLETT: Well, I couldn't risk being a wallflower, waiting on you two to come home from Atlanta, could I, now?
*The boys exchange a look as though to say that conditions are now very bad indeed; then:*
STUART: How about if we tell you a secret, Scarlett?
SCARLETT *sits forward eagerly.*
SCARLETT: Oh, what?
STUART: You know the Wilkeses cousin who lives in Atlanta—Miss Melanie Hamilton?
SCARLETT: That goody-goody! Who cares about her?
BRENT: Ashley Wilkes does. And the Wilkeses have invited her to stay at Twelve Oaks over the barbecue because Ashley Wilkes is going to marry her.
*Neither boy perceives the sudden death of all* SCARLETT's *animation.*
SCARLETT: It isn't so.
STUART: Yes, it is so. You know the Wilkeses always marry their cousins.
BRENT: They're announcing the engagement tomorrow night.
STUART: Well, that's the secret. Now do we get the waltzes?
SCARLETT [*automatic*]: If you want 'em. Yes.
BRENT: And do we eat barbecue with you, too?
SCARLETT [*as before*]: Of course. Why not? Good night.
*The boys are astounded.*
BRENT [*to* STUART]: Yee-aay-ee! I'll bet the other boys will be hoppin' mad.
STUART: Let 'em be mad. We two can handle 'em. Yee-aay-ee!
*In their enthusiasm they haven't noticed that* SCARLETT *has risen to her feet and has started away. Suddenly they are aware of this and leap to their feet.*
BRENT: Scarlett!
STUART: Where're you going?
LONG SHOT—FRONT VIEW *of TARA—CAMERA SHOOTING TOWARD VERANDAH*
*Walking swiftly, determinedly away from the verandah toward* CAMERA *comes* SCARLETT, *her face a study in pain and shock. Beyond*

ABOVE: *Vivien Leigh prepares for a retake of GWTW's opening scene at Tara.* BELOW: *The camera set-up for the scene. Miss Leigh is shown at the lower right of this picture with her back to the camera. Snapshots by Wilbur G. Kurtz, taken June 26, 1939.*

MGM, © 1939, 1967. Collection of Yvette Curran.

*her the twins may be seen at the top of the verandah steps, gazing after
her in consternation.*

BRENT [*calling*]: Scarlett, honey, come back here.

STUART: Please, Scarlett—

*But she pays no attention. Her expression strained, taut, she cuts
across the drive and over the lawn, PASSING CAMERA.*

INTERIOR–THE DRAWING ROOM–DAY

MAMMY—*aged and mountainous, but filled with the dignity of her
race at its finest—stands with* PORK *at the window which overlooks
the verandah. From their angle the three young people can be seen as
the two boys rise, astounded. Suddenly* STUART TARLETON *turns angrily
on his heel and walks down the verandah steps, shouting:*

STUART: Jeems! Jeems, we're going home!

BRENT *follows him and* JEEMS *is seen to join them and they go, all
three, toward the horses at the hitching post.* PORK *turns to* MAMMY.

PORK: Mammy, whut's de meanin' of dat?

MAMMY: Looks ter me lak she sent dem home. [*She goes through
the French window onto the verandah, the CAMERA following.*]
Huccome you din' ask dem ter stay for supper, Miss Scarlett? Ah done
tell Poke ter lay two extry plates fer dem. You got no mo' manners
dan a fe'el han'! Settin' out hyah widout yo' shawl, too, an' de night
air fixin' ter set in!

*In the background, the two* TARLETONS *and their groom mount and
ride away.*

SCARLETT: I'm going right on setting out here, Mammy, till Pa comes
home, so you run fetch my shawl.

MAMMY: Me run!

*She goes indignantly. The CAMERA moves close to* SCARLETT.

SCARLETT: Oh, Ashley! Ashley!

*Her young face contracts with misery. Then she rises suddenly and
runs down the verandah steps.*

EXTERIOR–BELL TOWER–TARA–SUNSET

*Two little pickaninnies are on the huge wheel above the ground,
forcing it to revolve by throwing their weight from one side to the
other. This causes the quitting bell to ring—which is the message to
the field hands that the day's work is finished.*

SERIES *of* CUTS *of* QUITTING TIME *at the* PLANTATION
COTTON FIELD

*Slaves at work plowing furrows. The quitting bell is heard faintly.
One of the slaves,* ELIJAH, *stops.*

ELIJAH: Quittin' time.

*Another huge black slave, known as* BIG SAM, *turns on* ELIJAH
*sharply:*

BIG SAM: Who said?

ELIJAH: I sez.

BIG SAM: You can't sez. I'se de foahman. I'se de one dat sez when
it's time to quit. [*He calls to the other slaves.*] Quittin' time.

*The other slaves stop work. The bell stops ringing.* JONAS WILKER-
SON *draws up on a horse.*

WILKERSON: How much plowin' you got done today, Sam?

BIG SAM: More'n yesterday, Mistah Wilkerson.

WILKERSON: I want more than that tomorrow.

*The distant sound of horse's hooves on soft soil.* BIG SAM *looks off:*

*LONG SHOT*—GERALD O'HARA *on his finely bred, big white horse
riding at breakneck speed toward direction of the cotton field.*

*CLOSER SHOT*—GERALD *rides by, waves in greeting to the slaves
as he passes.*

GERALD: Hi, Sam!

SAM [*raises his hand in half-salute*]: Howdy, Marse Gerald!

*SWING CAMERA to FOLLOW* GERALD *as he gallops away into
the distance into a pasture of blooded cattle.*

PASTURE—*CLOSER SHOT*

*The grazing cattle look up, startled as* GERALD *whirls through them
on his horse at a full gallop. MOVE CAMERA to follow* GERALD *as his
horse jumps across a narrow stream to a glade where a half-dozen fine
saddle horses are pastured. They stampede as* GERALD *gallops in and out
of the scene, ducking expertly under the low-hanging branch of a tree
as he passes.*

THE GATE

SCARLETT *enters to the gate, running and looking back shiftily over
her shoulder. She is evidently well pleased with her escape. Then her
ear is caught by the sound of a horse's hooves galloping over ploughed
ground. This is evidently what she has been waiting for and she peers
excitedly around the gate post.*

ROADSIDE FENCE—*CAMERA SHOOTING ACROSS ROAD
TOWARD FENCE*

*The fence is a snake fence made of split logs. On it there is a sign:*

TARA

POSTED. NO HUNTING

GERALD O'HARA, OWNER

THE ROAD

*From* SCARLETT's *angle,* GERALD *is riding through the field across the road, just opposite the gate. His hunter jumps the fence directly into or over the CAMERA. Then* SCARLETT *steps into the scene.* GERALD *reins in and stiffens.*

GERALD: Well, missy, and what are you doing out here without your shawl?

SCARLETT: I was waiting for you, Pa.

GERALD: And you'll be telling your mother I've been jumping again!

SCARLETT: I'm no tattletale. I was waiting to ask you how they all were over at Twelve Oaks.

*Relieved, he bends to kiss her. Then he is riding up the avenue of cedars,* SCARLETT *accompanying him, her hand on the back of his saddle.*

GERALD: They're in the stew you'd expect with a barbecue on them tomorrow. Miss What's-her-name—Ashley's cousin—Miss Melanie Hamilton, that's the name. . . .

SCARLETT: Oh, she did come!

GERALD: She did. And a sweet, quiet little thing she is, like a woman should be.

SCARLETT: She's a mealy-mouthed, pale-faced nitwit, and I hate her!

GERALD: What's this?

SCARLETT: Was Ashley there with her?

GERALD, *already at the steps of the house, reins in.*

GERALD: He was. And if that's why you came out to wait for me why didn't you say so without beating around the bush? [*He sees that his daughter is weeping. He dismounts and turns his horse over to the waiting Groom, who leads the horse out of the scene.*] Have you been making a spectacle of yourself and all of us, running after a man who never gave you a thought beyond friendship?

SCARLETT's *head comes up.*

SCARLETT [*violent*]: He did give me a thought! I can tell!

GERALD: Has he been trifling with you? Has he asked you to marry him?

SCARLETT: No.

GERALD: Nor will he. I had it from John Wilkes this afternoon that Ashley's going to marry Miss Melanie. It's to be announced tomorrow.

SCARLETT's *head falls.*

SCARLETT: So it's true. [*Then desperately*] Oh, if only the Wilkeses didn't always have to marry their own cousins! If I'd had just a little longer it's me he'd have married!

GERALD: You'd never be happy with him.

SCARLETT: Oh, I would! I would!

GERALD: That you would not. Only when like marries like can there be any happiness. And the Wilkeses are different from us. They're queer folk. Let 'em marry their cousins and keep their books and poetry and music and oil paintings and such foolishness to themselves.

SCARLETT: Oh, Pa, if I married him I'd change all that!

GERALD: Oh, you would, would you? No wife has ever changed a husband yet. [*Then*] I'm sorry, daughter. I want to see pride in you tomorrow at Twelve Oaks. I'll not have the county gossiping about you. For a woman, love comes after marriage. And what does it matter whom you marry so long as he's a gentleman and a Southerner? My daughter can have any young buck in the county! [*He is leading her up the steps.*] Take one of the Tarleton twins for your husband and we'll run the two plantations together and I'll build you a fine house in the pines where they join.

*But* SCARLETT *is outraged.*

SCARLETT: Stop treating me like a child! I don't want a house! I don't want Tara or any old plantation! And I don't want to marry anybody but . . .

*Now it is* GERALD's *turn at indignation.*

GERALD: You stand there, Katie Scarlett O'Hara, and tell me you don't want Tara? Look at it, child! Look!

*And from the top step he forces her to look out over the landscape.*

THE PLANTATION—DAY

*From the steps of the house—that is, from* GERALD's *and* SCARLETT's *angle—the CAMERA looks out over the landscape to take in its full panorama of rich, agricultural land, made to look richer now by the long shadows of approaching evening.*

*PROLONGED PANNING SHOT—TARA from THEIR VIEW-POINT*

*This shot should take in not alone the blossoming dogwood trees, the slaves trailing in from the fields after work, the rich, red cotton land, but also the yard back of the house itself with its outbuildings, stable, toolshed, corral, row of great oaks by the slave cabins, the scuppernong arbor, the smokehouse, the cotton gin and the press, and all the real activities of the plantation which center there. In conclusion, CAMERA PANS to a distant plowman topping a distant hill silhouetted against the sunset, the ploughed earth red as a wound along the furrows. Over it:*

GERALD's VOICE: Land's the only thing in the world that matters!

The only thing worth working for, fighting for, dying for! Because it's the only thing in the world that lasts!

*And, as though to answer in the land's behalf, the Negroes are heard SINGING in the slave quarters.*

*BACK to TWO SHOT*–GERALD *and* SCARLETT

SCARLETT [*disgusted*]: Oh, Pa, you talk like an Irishman.

GERALD: 'Tis proud I am that I'm Irish, and don't be forgettin' that you're half-Irish, Miss—

*BACK to PANORAMIC SHOT*

GERALD's VOICE [*continues*]: —And to anyone with a drop of Irish blood in them, the land they live on is like their mother—But there, you're just a child and bothered about your beaux. When you're older, you'll be seeing how it is. 'Twill come to you, this love of the land—There's no getting away from it if you're Irish.

*REVERSE SHOT—ON the BACKS of* GERALD *and* SCARLETT

*Looking at the land.* GERALD *puts his arm around her. CAMERA RETREATS BACK, BACK, BACK, until we have the tiny silhouetted figures of* GERALD O'HARA *and his daughter gazing over the lands of Tara, beautiful in the sunset, to the thematic musical accompaniment which we will use for Tara throughout the picture.*

*FADE OUT*

*FADE IN:*

INTERIOR–TARA–STAIRCASE–MAMMY–NIGHT

MAMMY *is discovered on the landing looking out of the window. Off-screen we hear the girls quarreling.*

SUELLEN's VOICE: I *am* going to wear your green dress—

SCARLETT's VOICE: Oh, no you're not!

CARREEN's VOICE: Oh, do let her wear it, Scarlett!


*FADE IN:*

EXTERIOR–TARA–*LONG SHOT*–NIGHT

ELLEN O'HARA's *carriage drives up the driveway approaching the house.*

MAMMY: Yon she come! [*She turns and calls up the stairs.*] Miss Scarlett—Miss Suellen—Miss Carreen—yo' ma's come home!

*Voices together:*

SUELLEN's VOICE: Now we'll see if I'm going to wear it.

SCARLETT's VOICE: Shut up—I'm sick of hearing about it.

CARREEN's VOICE: All right, Mammy.

MAMMY: . . . A–acting lak a wet nurse fo' dem no-good, low-down w'ite trash Slatterys 'stead o' bein' here to eat her supper! [*She leans a little over the banister and calls out of scene.*] Cookie, stir up de fiah! Miss Ellen home. [*Then she goes immediately into her muttering again as she continues down the stairs.*] Miss Ellen got no business wearin' herself out—[*She breaks off as she crosses the hall to yell to someone off scene.*] Pork! Bring dat lamp to de do'—Miss Ellen home!—[*again starts muttering*]—wearin' herself out waitin' on folks dat did dey be wuth shootin' dey'd have darkies to wait on dem. An ah has said—[*She breaks off.*] Oh, Mist' Gerald—

PORK *enters the scene, holding high a candle in a round, low, silver saucer.*

*DISSOLVE TO*

THE VERANDAH–NIGHT

PORK *comes eagerly down the steps to welcome* ELLEN *as her carriage drives up to the steps. She descends.*

PORK: We wuz gittin' wuh'ied 'bout you, Miss Ellen. Mist' Gerald he tuk on terrible at you runnin' out ter hulp dem w'ite trash Slatterys 'stead of eatin' yo' supper!

ELLEN: I'm home again, Pork.

*As she advances up the steps,* JONAS WILKERSON *steps from behind a column to meet her.*

WILKERSON: You sent word you wanted to see me, Mrs. O'Hara.

ELLEN *pauses to regard him briefly with acid distaste, then:*

ELLEN: I've just come from Emmy Slattery's bedside, Mr. Wilkerson. I thought you should know that your child's been born. [*And, as* WILKERSON *starts to protest,*] Has been born and, mercifully, died. Good night, Mr. Wilkerson. [*She goes on into the house.*]

REVERSE ANGLE

*Featuring* WILKERSON's *silhouetted head in the f.g., a look of hatred on his face as* ELLEN *passes by him through the open door into the house.* PORK *follows her, carrying the lamp. The door closes.*

INTERIOR–MAIN HALL

ELLEN *inside the front door.* MAMMY *has come back into the hall and is taking* ELLEN's *hat and coat.* PORK *sets the lamp down on the opposite end of the hall table from its mate. They start down the hall towards* ELLEN's *study.*

MAMMY: Ah'll fix yo' supper for yo' mahseff.

ELLEN: After prayers, Mammy.

MAMMY: Ah gwine fix yo' supper mahseff an' you eats it. Ah has said time an' again it don' do no good weahin' yo'seff out waitin' on folks dat don' have niggers ter wait on dem! An' Ah has said . . . [*But* ELLEN *has gone on into the drawing room.*]

## THE DRAWING ROOM

ELLEN *entering,* GERALD *advances to meet her.*

ELLEN: Mr. O'Hara, you must dismiss Jonas Wilkerson.

GERALD: And where will I get another overseer?

ELLEN: He must be dismissed tomorrow morning!

GERALD: So the worthy Jonas sired the Slattery girl's brat, did he? Well, what can you expect from a Yankee and white trash?

*But the three daughters,* SUELLEN, CARREEN, *and* SCARLETT *have come into the room and* ELLEN *stops her husband with a gesture.*

SUELLEN: Mother, why can't I wear Scarlett's green dress tomorrow? I look a fright in pink!

ELLEN: Your pink gown is lovely, Suellen, and you may wear my garnets with it tomorrow. You look tired, Scarlett. I'm worried about you. Carreen, you should be in bed. Fetch me my beads. The lamp, please, Pork.

*She continues on into the living room for prayers.* SUELLEN *comes near to* SCARLETT.

SUELLEN: I don't want to wear your tacky green dress anyhow, stingy!

SCARLETT's *hand darts out and she gives* SUELLEN's *hair a vicious yank.*

SCARLETT: Oh, hush up!

SUELLEN *gasps, but before she can retaliate* ELLEN's *voice calls:*

ELLEN [*off screen*]: Prayers, girls.

SUELLEN *assumes a demure expression and goes toward the parlor.* SCARLETT *follows slowly.*

*DISSOLVE TO*

## PARLOR

*A circle of yellow light.* ELLEN *is on the floor on her knees, the open prayer book on the table before her and her hands clasped upon it.* GERALD *is kneeling beside her;* SCARLETT *and* SUELLEN *on the opposite sides of the table, their voluminous petticoats in pads under their knees;* CARREEN *kneeling facing a chair, her elbows on the seat. The house servants are kneeling by the doorway:* MAMMY; PORK, *straight as a ramrod; two maids, graceful in spreading, bright calicoes; the cook, gaunt and yellow beneath her snowy head rag;* PRISSY; *and a little colored houseboy, very sleepy. Their dark eyes are gleaming expectantly.*

ELLEN's *eyes are closed, her voice rises and falls, lullingly and soothingly. The Negroes sway as they respond.*

ELLEN: —and to all the saints that I have sinned exceedingly in thought, word, and deed through my fault, through my fault, through my most grievous fault—

ELLEN AND ALL: —therefore I beseech Blessed Mary, ever Virgin—

CLOSE SHOT—SCARLETT

*Her face has come up as though to show the Deity the depths of her suffering. She does not respond with the others.*

ALL [*except* SCARLETT] [*off-screen*]: —Blessed Michael the Archangel, Blessed John the Baptist—

*Then a bright light seems to turn on suddenly within* SCARLETT *and an ecstatic smile spreads over her face.*

SCARLETT [*as she looks up with sudden revelation, gasps to herself*]: But Ashley doesn't know I love him. [*a sudden thought*] I'll tell him. And then he *can't* marry her!

CLOSE SHOT—ELLEN

*She looks over severely at* SCARLETT *as she continues the prayer.*

ELLEN AND ALL: —the holy Apostles, Peter and Paul—

CLOSE SHOT–SCARLETT

*She realizes her mother's eyes are on her and bows her head with the others.*

SCARLETT [*joining with others*]: "—and all the Saints, that I have sinned exceedingly in thought, word and deed, through my fault, through my fault, through my most grievous fault—"

SCARLETT's *smile is even lighter and brighter as, along with the others, she performs the prescribed gesture of beating her breast.*

FADE OUT

FADE IN:

EXTERIOR–TARA–DAY

*The O'Hara carriage and* GERALD's *horse are waiting in the drive in front of the house.* GERALD *is on the verandah staring impatiently through the open door to the house.*

REVERSE CLOSE SHOT–GERALD

*He strides in a rage toward the door, bawling at the top of his lungs:*

GERALD: Mrs. O'Hara! Mrs. O'Hara!

PULL BACK CAMERA BEFORE GERALD *as he passes into the main hall.*

GERALD: Will you females never be ready to start?

INTERIOR–HALL–LONGER SHOT

GERALD *exits out of scene as* PRISSY *comes into the hall from direction of the kitchen, carrying a tray full of food. As she reaches the foot*

MGM, © 1939, 1967. Collection of Yvette Curran.

*of the stairs, she encounters* PORK *coming from the dining room.* PRISSY *is wearing slippers.*

PORK: Whut you doin' wearin' slippers, chile? Jus' 'cause I'm your Pa, don't think you kin go takin' on no airs.

PRISSY [*with extremely respectful fright*]: Yessuh!

*She quickly kicks off her slippers and starts up the stairs in her bare feet.*

FADE IN:

SCARLETT'S BEDROOM–DAY

SCARLETT *stands in her underwear, admiring her figure in a long glass, as* MAMMY *enters.*

SCARLETT [*over her shoulder*]: You can take all that back to the kitchen. I won't eat a bite.

MAMMY: Yas'm, you will! You is gwine ter eat eve'y moufful of dis.

SCARLETT *has picked up her stays.*

SCARLETT: No, I am not. So come here and lace me, because we're late already.

MAMMY *sees that she must proceed more deviously.*

MAMMY: Hole on an' suck in. [SCARLETT *catches firm hold of one of the bedposts.* MAMMY *pulls and jerks the laces vigorously.*] Ain' nobody got a wais' lak mah lamb. Eve'y time Ah pulls Miss Suellen littler dan twenty inches, she up an' faint.

SCARLETT *is breathing with difficulty.*

SCARLETT: I never fainted in my life.

MAMMY: 'Twoundn' do no hahm ef you wuz ter faint now an' den. Effen you want ter ketch a husban'. . . .

SCARLETT: I'll catch a husband. Put on the dress.

MAMMY *draws back.*

MAMMY: Whut mah lamb gwine wear?

SCARLETT *points to a fluffy mass of green sprigged muslin.*

SCARLETT: That.

MAMMY *is in arms.*

MAMMY: No, you ain'! You kain show yo' buzzum befo' three o'clock! Ah sho gwine speak ter yo' Ma 'bout you!

SCARLETT: If you say one word to her I won't eat a bite.

MAMMY *has to admit defeat and carefully drops the twelve yards of green sprigged muslin over the mountainous petticoats and hooks up the top of the tight, low-cut basque.*

MAMMY: You keep yo' shawl on yo' shoulders. Ah ain' figgerin' on you gittin' freckled affer de buttermilk Ah been puttin' on you all dis winter, bleachin' dem freckles you got on de beach at Savannah. [*The*

*dress on—and to* SCARLETT's *satisfaction—*MAMMY *turns back to the tray.*] Now, Miss Scarlett, you be good an' come eat jes' a lil.

SCARLETT: I'm going to have a good time today and do my eating at the barbecue.

MAMMY *squares off.*

MAMMY: Effen you don' care 'bout how folks talks 'bout dis fambly Ah does! Ah has tole you an' tole you dat you kin allus tell a lady by dat she eat lak a bird! An' Ah ain' aimin' ter have you go ter Mist' John Wilkes's an' eat lak a fiel' han' an' gobble lak a hawg!

SCARLETT: Mother's a lady and she always eats at parties!

MAMMY: When you git mah'ied you kin eat, too.

SCARLETT: Fiddle-dee-dee! Ashley Wilkes told me he *liked* to see a girl with a healthy appetite.

MAMMY *shakes her head.*

MAMMY: Whut gempmums says an' what dey thinks is two diffunt things. An' Ah ain' noticed Mist' Ashley axin' fer ter mahy you. [*This stops* SCARLETT *and she sits down to the tray.*] But don' eat too fas'! No use havin' it come right back up agin.

SCARLETT, *eating, discovers that she can take nourishment after all, but her tone of complaint continues.*

SCARLETT: Why is it a girl has to be so silly to catch a husband? I don't think Yankee girls have to act like such fools. When we were at Saratoga last year I noticed plenty of 'em acting like they had right good sense and in front of men, too!

MAMMY *snorts.*

MAMMY: Yankee gals! Yes'm, but Ah din' notice many of dem gittin' proposed ter at Saratoga.

SCARLETT: Yankees must get married. They don't just grow.

MAMMY: Men mahys dem fer dey money.

GERALD's VOICE [*off-screen*]: Scarlett! Scarlett O'Hara!

SCARLETT *is on her feet and makes for the door.*

*DISSOLVE TO*

EXTERIOR–THE VERANDAH STEPS–DAY

*The carriage stands waiting.* SUELLEN *and* CARREEN *are already installed. The Coachman is on the box and* GERALD *and* GROOM *are mounted like outriders alongside.* GERALD *is bawling:*

GERALD: If you're not here before I count ten, Katie Scarlett, we'll be going without you! One, two . . .

*The door opens and* SCARLETT *emerges, bonnet, shawl and parasol added to the blooming loveliness of her dress. She runs down the steps.*

SCARLETT: I'm here, Pa! But, oh, dear, my stays are so tight I know I shall never get through the day without belching!

*She gets into the carriage.* MAMMY *enters, carrying the enormous box which contains the girls' ball dresses and clambers into the carriage.*

*DISSOLVE TO*

COUNTRY ROAD–TWELVE OAKS IN DISTANCE–EXTREME LONG SHOT

*The O'Hara carriage and* GERALD *on horseback. In the distance ahead of the O'Haras, we see other carriages on the road going toward Twelve Oaks.* PORK *is driving the O'Hara carriage.* MAMMY *is on the seat beside him.* SUELLEN, CARREEN, *and* SCARLETT *sit in back.* GERALD, *riding alongside, pays little attention to his daughters. He is singing: "Peg in a Low-Backed Car."*

*BACK TO*

*CLOSE SHOT—*SCARLETT *and others in carriage*

SCARLETT *hiccups.*

SUELLEN: You wouldn't do that if mother were here. Pig!

SCARLETT *slaps her.* SUELLEN *slaps her back.* SCARLETT *slaps* SUELLEN *again.*

MAMMY [*turns around and glares at them*]: Miss Scarlett! [*in scandalized tone*] Miss Suellen! Behave yo'se'ves! Actin' lak po' w'ite trash chillun! If y'all is old enough to go to parties, you're old enough to ack lak ladies.

*The girls stop and glare at each other.*

*LONG SHOT–THE CARRIAGE*

GERALD *rides gaily beside the carriage, his voice rising in a high note of the song.*

*DISSOLVE TO*

TWELVE OAKS–THE GATE

*The O'Hara carriage is driving through the gate.* GERALD *is now accompanied by a dozen other Gentlemen Riders. The drive to Twelve Oaks is blocked with other carriages filled with other ladies.*

THE FRONT OF HOUSE

*In a Long Shot the Crowd at the barbecue may be seen swarming over the broad lawns. The guests as they arrive dismount from their carriages and are welcomed on the steps by* JOHN WILKES, *his son* ASHLEY, *and the ladies of the family.*

THE VERANDAH STEPS

JOHN WILKES, *tall, handsome, erect, silver haired, advances to meet the ladies of the O'Hara family as their carriage stops at the steps. He leaves behind him his daughters,* INDIA *and* HONEY, *and* CATHLEEN

*The camera crews film Scarlett and other guests arriving at Twelve Oaks for the Wilkeses barbecue. The next photograph is a publicity still from the same sequence.*

CALVERT, *who is just being made welcome to the party. A confusion of talk in which only* JOHN WILKES's *voice is clear.*

JOHN WILKES [*to* GERALD]: And why isn't Mrs. O'Hara with you today?

GERALD: She's after settling accounts with the overseer. She'll be along for the ball tonight.

*CAMERA PANS SLIGHTLY to the O'Hara girls and* INDIA, *John Wilkes's somewhat colorless daughter, who are standing a little apart.*

SCARLETT: India Wilkes, what a lovely dress!

SUELLEN: Perfectly lovely, darling!

CARREEN: Just *lovely!*

SCARLETT [*not looking at the dress, but looking around for* ASHLEY]: Can't take my eyes off it.

*She moves on into the HALL, CAMERA FOLLOWING HER IN, still looking around anxiously for sight of* ASHLEY.

*The hall is crowded with guests, most of the young belles and bloods of the County being present. The girls in crinoline and the laughing young men in fawn and gray trousers. Colored maids are hurrying up the stairs bearing the long boxes containing their mistresses' gowns for the evening. The Wilkeses' butler and his assistants hurry through the halls, bowing and grinning and offering tall, mint-topped, frosted glasses.*

*Young men greet* SCARLETT *eagerly as she moves through the crowd, scarcely noticing their greetings, her mind on* ASHLEY *alone.*

FEMININE VOICES: Scarlett, honey! Miss Scarlett, good mornin'. Where you goin', Scarlett?

MASCULINE VOICES: Miss Scarlett, your servant, ma'am. Good mornin', ma'am. Wait a minute, Scarlett!

SCARLETT [*scarcely turning her head*]: Good mornin'. . . . Mornin'. . . . Mornin'. . . .

INTERIOR–THE BEDROOM–DAY

*The two girls enter,* CATHLEEN *still chattering, but in whispers now, as they go to the mirror.*

CATHLEEN: . . . late in the afternoon without a chaperon. But he wouldn't marry her because he said he hadn't done anything to her, so her brother challenged him and he killed the brother and had to leave Charleston and now, well you can imagine!

SCARLETT, *busy biting her lips to make them red and patting her cheeks to make them pink, is not as attentive as she might be.*

SCARLETT: Well, I hope I can! Did the girl have a baby?

CATHLEEN: Oh, I don't think so! She was ruined, though.

*Kathleen Calvert (Marcella Martin) tells Scarlett that the handsome stranger at the Wilkeses' barbecue is Rhett Butler.*

SCARLETT: She sounds like a fool and I'm glad he didn't marry her. [*and she adds grimly and half to herself*] There's too many fools catching husbands these days! [*A final pat to her cheeks and she goes out.*]

EXTERIOR–THE VERANDAH–DAY

*A crowd of Young People and* SCARLETT *on her way through them, in spite of the greetings they call after her.*

VOICES: Hey, Scarlett! . . . Katie Scarlett O'Hara, you come here to us! . . . Can't you say good morning, Scarlett? . . . Scarlett, where are you off to in such a hurry? . . .

*But* SCARLETT *has gone.*

DISSOLVE TO

THE LAWN

*Another group of Young People, all milling about, and* SCARLETT *on her way through them as before, looking to right and left. Again Voices call her.*

VOICES: Scarlett, where's the fire? You're going the wrong way, Scarlett! . . . Barbecue's this way!

Then:

A SINGLE VOICE: Hey, Ashley!

SCARLETT *turns to look in the direction of this call.*

ASHLEY'S VOICE: Hey yourself!

*For a moment* SCARLETT'S *too bright smile fails her. Then she starts again in the direction of* ASHLEY'S *call.*

THE LAWN–*TRUCK SHOT*

*The Guests are moving across the lawn toward the barbecue tables,* ASHLEY *and* MELANIE *with them. Sound and dialogue ad lib as* SCARLETT, *filled with dignity, but walking just a shade too fast, catches up.* ASHLEY *turns, sees her and holds out his hand.*

ASHLEY: Welcome, Scarlett!

SCARLETT *is all but struck dumb with surprise.*

SCARLETT: Why, Ashley! I was wondering where you were keeping yourself, and to think of just running into you! [*She turns so brightly to* MELANIE.] Isn't this your cousin, Miss Hamilton from Atlanta?

ASHLEY: Melanie, you remember Scarlett O' . . .

MELANIE: Indeed, we're old friends from last . . .

*But* SCARLETT'S *plan of attack does not permit of* MELANIE'S *completing any sentence.*

SCARLETT: I didn't expect you'd remember me, Melanie! You don't mind me calling you Melanie? We all call each other by our first names out here in the country! I expect that seems just terribly countrified to you!

*And they are all continuing on their way toward the barbecue tables.*

MELANIE: It seems charm . . .

SCARLETT: My, but it's a treat for us to see visitors from the city! I expect it's just the latest thing wearing grey to a barbecue! And will you look at the way she's got that sash tied, Ashley? Isn't that just the cleverest way to tie a sash? Don't you let your city cousin monopolize you now, or we country girls will be jealous of her!

*They are passing the barbecue pits, where vast pieces of meat are turning on spits under the supervision of white-capped Negro Cooks, and the tables, on which other House Servants are carving and serving.*

SCARLETT: My, doesn't that smell delicious! Doesn't it look . . .

ASHLEY: Aren't you going to wish us happiness, Scarlett?

*The slightest flicker before* SCARLETT *can answer.*

SCARLETT: I always wish you happiness, Ashley. [*And to* MELANIE, *her tone the least bit drier than she means it to be.*] And you, too, Melanie, I'm sure. [*They have come up to where* HONEY WILKES *is standing by the barbecue table with* CHARLES HAMILTON.] Why, Charles Hamilton, you handsome old thing, you! [*Back to* MELANIE *as* CHARLES *attempts in vain to stammer a reply.*] Do you think it was kind of you to bring this good-looking brother of yours down here just to break our poor, simple, country hearts? [*She has extended her two hands to* CHARLES *in a manner that is neither poor nor simple.*] I want to eat barbecue with you, Charles Hamilton, and don't you dare go off philandering with any other girl, because I'm mighty jealous!

CHARLES: Oh, I won't, Miss O'Hara! How could I?

HONEY WILKES'S *jaw drops, but* SCARLETT *only flashes a look at* ASHLEY *to ascertain if he has observed her success. Finding him occupied with* MELANIE, *she pitches her next conquest a trifle higher, her attack aimed at* STUART *and* BRENT TARLETON, *whom she catches across the table just in the act of seating* INDIA WILKES *and* CARREEN.

SCARLETT: You come here to me, Stu Tarleton! And you, too, Brent! Didn't I promise you yesterday I'd eat barbecue with you? I never expected you'd be untrue to me! And India's so busy being hostess and all she won't hardly have any time for beaux today! [*The two boys have risen.* INDIA's *face is thunderous. But, with another glance at the still unobservant* ASHLEY, SCARLETT *attacks* FRANK KENNEDY, *who enters at this moment with* SUELLEN.] Why, Frank Kennedy! If I haven't just been looking everywhere for you! It just seems like years since we've had a visit together! [*She has taken his arm.*] Let's get away from this crowded old table and go off by ourselves!

*She leads him out of the scene, to* SUELLEN'S *intense fury, and the four girls:* HONEY, INDIA, SUELLEN, *and* CARREEN, *all find themselves stranded without beaux.*

INDIA [*pure nitric acid*]: I don't care if she is your sister! I think she's fast!

SUELLEN *nods vigorously, biting her lips to keep back the tears. Then the* CAMERA, *withdrawing from the table, finds* RHETT BUTLER *where he is standing with* CADE CALVERT.

CADE: There's the hardest hearted girl in the state of Georgia, Mr. Butler. Don't you want to meet her?

RHETT: No, thanks. I'd rather watch her.

INTERIOR–HALL OR ROOM AT TWELVE OAKS

*Opening on CLOSE SHOT OF A DOOR which is being opened by* ASHLEY'S *hand.*

*PULL BACK to show that* ASHLEY *is opening the door for* MELANIE.

EXTERIOR–BARBECUE–*THROUGH OPEN DOOR FROM THEIR ANGLE*

*Through the door lies a scene of gaiety and wild charm. The barbecue—a furbelow feast—is spread over the lawn. Children run under the trees. Black Mammies tag after them. Gallants and their ladies are eating, drinking, laughing—and Negroes, grinning and shiny-eyed, wander over the grass holding aloft great trays of food and drink.*

*There is a long table stretching down the center of the lawn at which many guests sit.*

*BACK TO* ASHLEY *and* MELANIE

MELANIE'S *lips part as if overcome for a moment by a sense of rapture as she and* ASHLEY *look at the scene.*

MELANIE: Ashley!

ASHLEY: Happy?

MELANIE: So happy.

ASHLEY: You seem to belong here—as if it had all been imagined for you.

MELANIE [*tenderly*]: I like to feel that I belong with the things you love.

ASHLEY: You love Twelve Oaks as I do.

MELANIE: Yes, Ashley—I love it as more than a house. It's a whole world that wants only to be graceful and beautiful.

ASHLEY [*with a sad smile*]: It's so unconscious that it may not last—forever.

MELANIE [*takes his arm, her voice grows softer*]: You're afraid of what may happen if the war comes, aren't you? But we don't have to

ABOVE: *Scarlett runs into the Tarleton twins on the stairs at Twelve Oaks.*
BELOW: *She also meets her future husband, Frank Kennedy, at the Wilkeses'
party. These are out-takes from GWTW cast aside before the film was put
together. One of the Selznick staff may be noticed at the lower left of the
scene with the twins.*

be afraid—for us. No war can come into our world, Ashley. Whatever comes, I'll love you—just as I do now—until I die.

ASHLEY *raises her hand and kisses it as we*

CUT TO

BARBECUE–*GROUP SHOT UNDER A TREE–Where* SCARLETT *on a high rosewood ottoman is surrounded by a circle of young men.* SCARLETT *is laughing.*

SCARLETT: Now isn't this better than sitting at an old table? A girl has only two sides to her at a table!

*Laughter and hearty approval as* SCARLETT *beams around her at the circle.* BRENT *and* STUART TARLETON *and* CHARLES HAMILTON *jump to their feet.*

BRENT: I'll get her dessert.

STUART: She said me.

CHARLES: Allow me, Miss O'Hara.

SCARLETT *looks the three over judiciously and makes her selection.*

SCARLETT [*as a great favor*]: I think that Charles Hamilton may get it for me.

CHARLES: Oh, thank you, Miss O'Hara! [*He hurries away.*]

*GROUP SHOT–*SCARLETT *and* BEAUX

SCARLETT [*laughing*]: I don't see why everybody's so excited about going to war. It's just riding horses, same as hunting.

STUART TARLETON: There's a lot more to it than hunting, Scarlett. You've got to know about sabres and strategy, don't you, Brent?

BRENT: Yes, you do—all kinds of things.

SCARLETT: I'd just love to drill a cavalry troop. And I'd only expect 'em to know one thing—how to kill Yankees very fast.

*They all laugh.* SCARLETT's *face suddenly falls as she sees:*

*LONG SHOT–*[*FROM* SCARLETT's *ANGLE*]–MELANIE *and* ASHLEY

*Arm in arm, walking across the lawn under the trees, absorbed in each other, coming from direction of the house.*

*CLOSE-UP–*SCARLETT

*Watching, jealous.* CHARLES HAMILTON's *face comes into the Close-Up, bending over to whisper to* SCARLETT. *He has returned with her dessert.*

CHARLES [*whispers in* SCARLETT's *ear*]: Miss O'Hara, I love you!

SCARLETT *looks at the food, shakes her head, distracted.*

SCARLETT: I don't guess I'm as hungry as I thought.

FADE OUT

*FADE IN:*

INTERIOR–A BEDROOM–DAY

MGM, © 1939, 1967. UGa Libraries, Marsh Papers.

*The blinds are closed and the young ladies of the party are resting, their frocks cast aside and standing upon the stiff, crinoline petticoats. The girls' stays are loosened, their hair is let down. Three of them—* MELANIE, HONEY *and* INDIA—*lie on the bed and two more—* SUELLEN *and* CARREEN—*have disposed themselves on the two sofas.* MAMMY *is spreading a coverlet over those on the bed.*

MAMMY: You young ladies be good now an' res' yo'seffs affer all de eatin' you done or you won' look fresh an' pretty w'en de ball starts. [*She draws back, looking around her.*] Whar's Miss Scarlett? [*She goes into the next room, muttering.*] Miss Scarlett, is you in hyah?

*The coast being clear,* SCARLETT, *fully dressed, slips out from behind the window curtain, tiptoes to the hall door and goes out.*

THE STAIR

*From below stairs* VOICES.

GERALD'S VOICE: God's nightgown, man! What do we want with peace after we've fired the first shot at the Yankees?

VOICES: Of course we'll fight! . . . We'll lick 'em in a month! . . . One Southerner can lick twenty Yankees! . . . Let the Yankees ask us for peace! Didn't they haul their flag down at Fort Sumter? . . . What else could they do? Our cannon blew it down! . . .

*In the meanwhile,* SCARLETT *has entered.*

SCARLETT [*bored as usual with war talk*]: Oh, fiddle-dee-dee! [*But she leans over the banister.*]

THE DINING ROOM–DAY

*The Wilkeses' punch bowl has been placed on the table and a group of a dozen Men, which includes* RHETT, ASHLEY, GERALD, JOHN WILKES, CHARLES HAMILTON, *the* TARLETON TWINS *and many other familiar faces, is suffering from various, milder degrees of intoxication.* RHETT *sits sardonically apart, smoking a cigar.* GERALD *is holding forth.*

GERALD: We've borne enough insults from the meddling Yankees! It's time we made them to understand we'll keep our slaves with or without their approval! 'Twas the sovereign right of the sovereign state of Georgia to secede from the Union! The South must assert herself by force of arms! She's not leaving the Union by the Union's kindness, but by her own strength, gentlemen!

*Hearty APPLAUSE to this. Through the door, however,* SCARLETT'S *figure has been visible on the stair landing.* CHARLES HAMILTON *has seen her there and risen, and gone out, closing the door after him, even before* GERALD *rolled out his final sonorous periodic.*

JOHN WILKES: Oh, if they won't let us go without fighting, I suppose . . .

GERALD: What's Ashley say? Aren't you ready to fight, Ashley?

ASHLEY: Well, no, Mr. O'Hara, to be frank, I'm not! If Georgia fights, I fight with her, of course. Like Father, though, I could wish that we hadn't fired the first gun.

RHETT BUTLER *leans forward.*

RHETT: Gentlemen, may I say a word? [*There is contempt in his manner, but the group turns toward him.*] Has any one of you ever thought that there's not a cannon factory in the whole South, and scarcely an iron foundry worth considering? Have you thought that we wouldn't have a single warship and that the Yankee fleet could bottle our harbors up? I've seen the North. All we have is our cotton and our slaves and our arrogance. The Yankees have everything and they'll lick us in a month.

*A tense silence;* STUART TARLETON *steps forward, with* BRENT *close at his heels.*

STUART [*heavily*]: Sir, what do you mean?

RHETT: I mean what Napoleon—perhaps you've heard of him?—meant when he remarked that God's on the side of the strongest battalion. [*He rises, turning to* JOHN WILKES.] You promised to show me your library, sir. Would it be too great a favor to ask to see it now? I seem to be making myself unpopular here.

JOHN WILKES *bows and turns out of the scene with* RHETT. ASHLEY *turns to* STUART TARLETON, *restraining him from following* RHETT.

ASHLEY: Arrogant devil, isn't he? Looks like one of the Borgias.

STUART: Borgias? Don't think I know them. Are they Charleston people?

ASHLEY *smiles.*

ASHLEY: They were a Spanish family who lived in Italy.

STUART: Oh . . . foreigners.

ASHLEY *nods gravely.*

THE STAIR

SCARLETT *is listening to* CHARLES HAMILTON *with half her attention.*

CHARLES: Miss O'Hara, I've already decided that if we do fight I'll join Mr. Wade Hampton's cavalry troops.

SCARLETT: What am I supposed to do, give three cheers?

CHARLES: If I go, will you be sorry, Miss O'Hara?

SCARLETT: I shall cry into my pillow every night.

CHARLES: Miss O'Hara. . . . I must tell you something. . . . I love you.

SCARLETT [*absently, her ear cocked towards the dining room*]: Hmm?

CHARLES: I love you. You are the most . . . the most beautiful girl I've ever known. You are like a shining hummingbird and all other girls seem sparrows beside you. I cannot hope that you could love me, my dear Miss O'Hara, but I want to marry you.

SCARLETT [*automatically reciting the formula*]: Mr. Hamilton, I am not unaware of the honor you have bestowed on me in wanting me for your wife, but this is so sudden I do not know what to say.

CHARLES: Please, Miss O'Hara, tell me that I may hope!

SCARLETT [*herself again*]: Oh, hush!

*She turns again to watch the dining room door as it opens and the* VOICES *from within are suddenly loud again.*

VOICES: They want war! We'll cure 'em of it! . . . States' rights, by . . . We'll lick 'em in one battle! . . . Gentlemen always fight better than the rabble! . . .

*From* SCARLETT's *angle,* ASHLEY *is seen to emerge from the dining room and cross the hall.*

SCARLETT: Ashley!

*He turns.* SCARLETT *starts down the stair,* CHARLES *following her.*

THE HALL

SCARLETT *enters to* ASHLEY, CHARLES *attending her. Breathing is difficult for her, but she manages a beaming smile for* CHARLES.

SCARLETT: Charles Hamilton, I left my best lace handkerchief under that tree where we ate barbecue. I was just on my way to fetch it. Won't you fetch it for me?

CHARLES: Oh, gladly, Miss O'Hara!

SCARLETT: I'll be waiting here.

CHARLES *goes by the front door. Her eyes burn at* ASHLEY, *who is completely nonplussed by her behavior.*

ASHLEY: Scarlett, what is it?

*She looks desperately round her, then goes quickly into the library. He follows, puzzled.*

THE LIBRARY

*A dim room, the walls completely lined with dark books, the blinds of the windows closed against the sun.* SCARLETT *backs away from the door as* ASHLEY *enters. He sees that she is trembling.*

ASHLEY: What is it, Scarlett? A secret?

SCARLETT: I love you.

*Silence. A well-trained mask comes down over* ASHLEY's *face and he smiles.*

ASHLEY [*he laughs in some embarrassment, then*]: Isn't it enough that you've gathered in every other man's heart today? Must you have mine, too? You cut your teeth on it!

*She takes a step towards him, her hands clenched, her young face turned desperately up to his.*

SCARLETT: Oh, don't tease me now, Ashley! I do love you! I do!

*His gesture stops her.*

ASHLEY: You mustn't say such things, Scarlett. You'll hate me for hearing them.

SCARLETT: I could never hate you! And I know you must care about me because . . . you do care, don't you?

*Her vehemence sobers him and, in spite of himself, he says more than he intended.*

ASHLEY: Yes. I care. [*Then*] Scarlett, can't we go away now and forget that we have ever said these things?

SCARLETT: How can we do that? Don't you want to marry me?

ASHLEY: I'm going to marry Melanie.

SCARLETT: But you can't! Not if you care for me, you! . . . [*Her hands are gripping his arms—he frees himself to hold her hands in his.*]

ASHLEY: Must you make me say things that will hurt you? You're so young you don't know what all this . . .

SCARLETT: I know I love you and want to be your wife! And you just now told me you cared for me!

ASHLEY: How could I help caring for you? You, who have all the passion for life that I lack! But marriage isn't for people as different as you and I! You'd want all of a man. I couldn't give you all of me. You'd hate the books I read and the music I love . . .

SCARLETT: If you care for me you can't love Melanie!

ASHLEY: She's like me, Scarlett. She's part of my blood and we understand each other. And I'm going to marry her, because . . .

SCARLETT: But you just said you care for me!

ASHLEY: I shouldn't have said it.

SCARLETT: Having been cad enough to say it, though! . . .

ASHLEY: I was a cad. I did you a wrong and Melanie a wrong. . . .

SCARLETT *strikes out in fury.*

SCARLETT: You're afraid to marry me! You'd rather live with that stupid little fool who can't open her mouth except to say yes and no and raise a passel of mealy-mouthed brats just like her!

ASHLEY: You mustn't say those things about Melanie!

SCARLETT: I "mustn't" be damned to you! Who are you to tell me I mustn't! You made me believe you wanted to marry me!

ASHLEY: Now, Scarlett, be fair! I never at any time . . .

SCARLETT: It's true! You did! And I shall hate you till the day I die! And I can't think of any name bad enough to call you! [*And with all her might she slaps his face. Then she draws back, horrified. He bows, indulges in a little gesture of regret, turns and walks out of the room. Then fury possesses her.*] Oh! Oh! Oh!

*A pair of little china vases—rosebuds and cupids—adorns the table before her. In her rage she seizes one in either hand and hurls first one and then the other at the fireplace. As they crash she is horrified to see* RHETT BUTLER *rise up out of the deep high chair beside the hearth.*

RHETT: It's bad enough to have an afternoon nap interrupted, but when I find my life endangered . . .

SCARLETT *grasps at dignity as best she can.*

SCARLETT: Sir, you should have made your presence known.

RHETT: I wakened too late to do so tactfully. Have no fear, however. Your guilty secret is safe.

SCARLETT: Sir, you are no gentleman!

RHETT: And you, Miss, are no lady.

SCARLETT: Oh!

RHETT: Don't think I hold that against you. Ladies have seldom held any charms for me.

SCARLETT: First you take a low, common advantage of me; then you insult me!

RHETT: I didn't mean to do that. You're a girl of admirable spirit, Miss O'Hara, and I hope to see more of you when you're free of the spell of the elegant Mr. Wilkes. He doesn't strike me as half good enough for a girl of your . . . what was it? . . . your passion for living.

SCARLETT: You aren't fit to wipe his boots!

RHETT: And you were going to hate him for the rest of your life!

*She sees that he is laughing at her and gives up, turning miserably away and saying as she goes out:*

SCARLETT: I don't know what I'm going to do for the rest of my life! I must get home! I must get home to my mother! [*She is gone.*]

DISSOLVE TO

THE LANDING

SCARLETT *enters, broken in body and soul. She is just opening the bedroom door. She stops, hearing whispers from within.*

SUELLEN'S VOICE: But, Melanie, you saw how she was carrying on with every man she could get her hands on!

MELANIE'S VOICE: Oh, no, Suellen! She's just high-spirited and vivacious!

THE BEDROOM

*The girls are sitting up now, enjoying the venom of gossip to the utmost. Only* MELANIE *is distressed, and* INDIA, *withdrawn a little from the others, seems to brood vengeance on poor* SCARLETT's *head.*

SUELLEN: Well, she certainly was going after your brother, Charles!

HONEY: And you know Charles and I . . .

CARREEN: Honey Wilkes, are you really! . . .

HONEY: Well, don't tell anyone yet, but I think we are! At least, I did till Scarlett . . .

MELANIE: Oh, I don't think that Scarlett meant . . .

SUELLEN: And what about my Mr. Kennedy, who's always been my beau? And I'm her sister! I think Scarlett acted as fast as a girl could act today!

MELANIE: Suellen, don't be unkind!

SUELLEN: Well, if you ask me, there's only one person she does give a rap about and that's Ashley!

MELANIE: You know that isn't so, Suellen!

SUELLEN: It is too so! And if you weren't always so busy looking for good in people that have no good in them . . .

INDIA: I hate Scarlett O'Hara and I shall hate her till the day I . . .

*But* SCARLETT *bursts in upon them. Sensation.*

SCARLETT: Go right ahead and hate me, India Wilkes! And you don't need to stand up for me, Melanie Hamilton! I heard every word you . . .

*But from the distance a man's voice is heard, half Indian war whoop, half a shout of triumph. The girls spring from the bed and run to the window.*

EXTERIOR–THE DRIVE IN FRONT OF THE HOUSE–DAY

*FROM THE GIRLS' ANGLE the* TARLETON BOYS *and* GERALD, *with plenty of others, surround a newcomer on a foaming horse. A battle of voices.* BRENT TARLETON *lets go another war whoop.*

GERALD: Now there can be no more holding back!

*Turmoil.*

THE DRIVE

*Confusion continues from ground level.*

STUART [*shouting*]: Jeems! Saddle our horses, Jeems!

JEEMS: Yassir, Mist' Stuart!

BRENT [*shouting*]: We're off to the war!

*A woman screams. The turmoil continues.*

THE VERANDAH STEPS

*Great excitement in the crowd as it mills about, and the older ladies*

*are hurrying from the house and down the steps. They jostle* SCARLETT
*as she comes through the door.*

SCARLETT *leans against a column, looking dazedly down.* CHARLES
HAMILTON *comes up to her.*

CHARLES: You don't know what's happened, Miss O'Hara? [SCARLETT
*shakes her head miserably.*] Mr. Lincoln has called for volunteers!
Seventy-five thousand of 'em!

SCARLETT: Don't you men ever think about anything interesting?

CHARLES: You don't grasp what I say. This means fighting, of course.
[*Then*] I'm so clumsy. I should have told you more gently. I'm sorry
if I've upset you. You don't feel faint, do you?

SCARLETT: No.

CHARLES [*pleadingly*]: Will you wait for me, Miss Scarlett? It would
be heaven just to know that you were waiting for me until after we've
licked 'em.

*More of the tumult as* SCARLETT *looks down at him. Then her face
sets. She forces a smile.*

SCARLETT: You'd take me to live in Atlanta, wouldn't you? [*Open-
mouthed, not daring to believe his ears, he nods excitedly, but she
continues almost as though he did not exist.*] And you could give me
everything I want? [*and, as the girls, now dressed, hurry past down
the steps*] And they'd never dare laugh at me again!

CHARLES [*completely bewildered*]: Laugh at you, Miss Scarlett?

*She forces a smile.*

SCARLETT: I wouldn't want to wait . . . Charles.

CHARLES: Can you possibly love me? Will you marry me now?

SCARLETT [*a gulp—then*]: Yes. I will marry you, Charles, if my
father permits.

CHARLES: Will we make it a double wedding with Melan . . .

SCARLETT [*sharply*]: No!

CHARLES: No. We want our own wedding, don't we? [*He kisses
the palms of her hands. Her eyes close. She turns her head away.*]
When may I speak to your father?

SCARLETT: The sooner the better.

CHARLES: Oh, Scarlett, I'll speak to him now!

*One more pressure on her two hands and he hurries out of the
scene. THE CAMERA GOES CLOSE TO* SCARLETT, *still against her
column, her eyes closed in misery.*

*THE CAMERA, meanwhile, has STARTED TO MOVE UP
SLOWLY TO A CLOSER SHOT OF* SCARLETT. *In her eyes we see
mixed emotions: a little fear as to what she has done, then determina-*

tion, and then sorrow as she turns and takes a step or two closer to the window so that we have her large silhouetted profile in the foreground, as beyond, we see ASHLEY gallop into scene. SCARLETT gives a little involuntary gasp as she sees him. Her hand goes to her mouth and tears start to fill her eyes as MELANIE runs in to join ASHLEY.

CLOSER SHOT—ASHLEY and MELANIE
(FROM SCARLETT'S ANGLE)
The most romantic shot possible of the White Knight of Georgia—ASHLEY WILKES—romantically and gallantly astride his rearing horse.
SHOT THROUGH WINDOW WITH SCARLETT IN PROFILE IN FOREGROUND
SCARLETT sees ASHLEY lift MELANIE off the ground to kiss her. He lowers her gently to her feet again, raises his hat in farewell, wheels his horse and dashes off—leaving the sorrowful figure of MELANIE gazing after him, her hands over her mouth.

SCARLETT [her heart breaking—a forlorn whisper]: Oh, Ashley—Ashley—

FADE OUT

FADE IN:
INTERIOR–PARLOR AT TARA–NIGHT
The reception after CHARLES and SCARLETT's marriage. The room is lighted by many candles. SCARLETT, in her mother's wedding dress and veil, stands in the receiving line in front of the mantlepiece between CHARLES on one side and her mother and father on the other, receiving congratulations from the guests. CHARLES is in the uniform of his troop.

The impression of a great many guests should be gained from a babble of voices, from silhouetted figures on the wall behind the receiving line—and from the people immediately ahead of and immediately behind ASHLEY and MELANIE who, as we pick up the scene, are the ones congratulating SCARLETT and CHARLES.

[Some of the men we see are in uniforms of their troops—ASHLEY, too, in uniform.]

MELANIE [kissing SCARLETT]: Scarlett, I thought of you at our wedding and hoped yours would be as beautiful. And it was.

SCARLETT [like a sleepwalker]: Was it?

MELANIE [nods emphatically]: Now we're really and truly sisters.

MELANIE moves a step forward to CHARLES. ASHLEY, coming up behind her, bends to kiss SCARLETT on the cheek without a word. He is embarrassed and avoids SCARLETT's gaze. He takes MELANIE's arm and moves off with her. SCARLETT turns to look after them, tears coming to

MGM, © 1939, 1967. UGa Libraries, Marsh Papers.

*her eyes.* CHARLES *sees this, but mistakes the cause. He looks at her lovingly, presses her hand, and whispers:*

CHARLES: Don't cry, darling. The war will be over in a few weeks and I'll be coming back to you.

SCARLETT *now really starts to cry and sob as she looks at him, and we*

DISSOLVE TO

SCARLETT'S BEDROOM

CHARLES, *in his dressing gown, approaches the bed in which* SCARLETT *is lying. She looks up at him in almost comic bewilderment. He smiles pathetically and turns his head toward the table beside her pillow, evidently reminding her of a document lying there. The CAMERA GOES CLOSE to this document to read that "Corporal Charles Hamilton is summoned to report to his Cavalry Troop. Signed, Wade Hampton, Commander."*

DISSOLVE TO

SCARLETT'S BEDROOM–TARA–CLOSE SHOT FROM HIGH ANGLE–BEDROOM TABLE–DAY

*On the table lies a sword in its scabbard and beside it an open, handwritten letter.*

FADE IN:

SWORD ON TABLE–CAMERA SHOOTING FROM ABOVE

*A sword in its scabbard lies beside an open, handwritten letter. CAMERA MOVES DOWN into CLOSE-UP of letter. The paper is of an inexpensive type of Confederate gray, faintly ruled. CAMERA IRISES DOWN to the lines:*

> Head Qrs.
> Hampton's Legion
> Columbia, S. C.
> 14 June, 1861

My dear Madam:

I would have advised you of Capt. Hamilton's illness had he not requested otherwise.

Herewith I send you his sword. May it console you that Captain Hamilton made the great sacrifice for our glorious Cause.

CAMERA PANS DOWN

Though he was not vouchsafed a
hero's death upon the field of
glory, he was nonetheless a hero,
dying in camp here of pneumonia,
following an attack of measles.

I am, Madam, very respectfully

Your obt. servt.
Wade Hampton
Col. Cmdg.

SCARLETT's VOICE: Send the sword to Melly.
SCARLETT'S BEDROOM
SCARLETT *and* MAMMY *stand by the table. The sword lies on the
table beside them.* SCARLETT *is in mourning.* MAMMY *is regarding her
indignantly.*

MAMMY: Ain't you any sentiment a–tall?
SCARLETT [*impatiently*]: He never even used it. Measles! Just like
Charles.

MAMMY: An' yo' husband fresh in his grabe! You didn't cry one
drap when you heard it. I'se ashamed of you, Miss Scarlett. 'Deed I
is—plumb ashamed.

SCARLETT [*angrily*]: Look what he did to me. Made me a widow—
so I've got to wear black the rest of my life—[*She turns away,
CAMERA PANNING WITH HER, to a mirror, and regards her reflection sourly.*] I look terrible in black. [*She makes a face at herself.*]
I hate mourning.

MAMMY's VOICE: Miss Scarlett, don't you talk dat way.
SCARLETT [*turning from the mirror to face* MAMMY, *with genuine
despair*]: I don't care. It's true. Widows can't do a single thing—go
anywhere—to parties or anything. It's worse than being a matron.
And matrons never have any fun. Widows might as well be dead.

*She starts to cry with self-pity, turns away, and flings herself face
down on the bed. The hall door opens, and* ELLEN *and the family doctor
enter.*

ELLEN [*anxiously*]: Scarlett, dear. [*crosses toward the bed*] Try not
to cry. Poor darling. You must keep your strength up. [*turning toward
the doctor*] She's been inconsolable since she got the news about
Charles.

DOCTOR [*sympathetically*]: Yes—yes. A change will do her good.
*TWO SHOT BY THE BED*—ELLEN *and* SCARLETT
SCARLETT *continues to sob.*

ELLEN: Did you hear what the doctor said, Scarlett?—You can go for a trip—a long trip. To Charleston. Wouldn't you enjoy that?

SCARLETT [*without looking up*]: I don't want to go to Charleston.

ELLEN: Then to Savannah. You can visit your Uncle Andrew.

SCARLETT [*still not looking up*]: I don't want to go to Savannah.

ELLEN: New Orleans. It's lovely there, I'm told. [*as* SCARLETT *doesn't answer*] Or Atlanta.

SCARLETT [*sits up eagerly, tear-stained*]: Atlanta?

ELLEN [*pleased with favorable results*]: Yes, dear. You could stay with Melanie and Aunt Pittypat.

SCARLETT [*drops her eyes, tries to sound hesitant*]: Well, I suppose—if you think I should—of course, Melly really needs me.

ELLEN [*smiles unsuspiciously*]: Yes, dear. You'll be such a comfort to each other.

SOUND *of doors closing.* SCARLETT *dabs at her eyes with a handkerchief.* MAMMY *enters scene, eyeing her shrewdly.*

ELLEN [*rises and turns to* MAMMY]: Start packing Miss Scarlett's things, Mammy. I'll go write the necessary letters. [*She exits.*]

SCARLETT [*sitting on the bed, staring rapturously ahead of her—whispers*]: Atlanta. . . . !

MAMMY [grimly]: Savannah would be better for you. You'll jus' git in trouble in Atlanta. . . .

SCARLETT [*guiltily*]: What trouble are you talking about?

MAMMY: You know what trouble Ah's talkin' about. I'se talkin' about Mistuh Ashley Wilkes. He'll be comin' to Atlanta when he gets his leave—and you sittin' there waitin' fo' him—[*hisses it*]—jes' like a spider. He belongs to Miss Melanie and . . .

SCARLETT [*who has risen and walked slowly to* MAMMY. *She speaks grimly and icily.*]: You go pack my trunks like Mother said.

*FADE OUT*

# Second
# Sequence

*ADE IN:*
EXTERIOR–ATLANTA–RAILROAD STATION–DAY
*A brick shed swarming with the activity of a railroad station in war time. Soldiers in uniform are all over the place as the little local from Jonesboro pulls in. CAMERA GOES CLOSE, as the train comes to a stop and* SCARLETT, *pale and pretty in her black mourning dress, her crêpe veil fluttering almost to her heels, her eyes shining with excitement, stands on the step.* PRISSY, *behind her, holds the infant, Wade Hampton.* UNCLE PETER, *an elderly, upright Negro coachman, steps forward to meet her.*

UNCLE PETER: Dis Miss Scarlett, ain't it? Dis hyah Peter, yo' Aunt Pitty's coachman.

SCARLETT: Oh, I've heard about you, Uncle. . . .

*She is stepping down, but* UNCLE PETER *stops her.*

UNCLE PETER: Doan' step down in dat mud! Lemme cahy you.

SCARLETT: Oh, no, Uncle Peter!

*But he picks her up with ease, despite his apparent frailness and age.*

UNCLE PETER: Miss Scarlett, you doan' weigh nuthin'! An' Miss Pitty she won't nebber fergive me eff you gits yo' feets wet.

PRISSY, *with* WADE HAMPTON, *has also descended.*

UNCLE PETER: Is dat air chile yo' nuss? Miss Scarlett, she too young ter be handlin' Mist' Charles' onlies' baby! [*He carries* SCARLETT, *CAMERA FOLLOWING, across the platform, talking as he goes.*] Ah come nigh on tyin' Miss Pitty an' Miss Melly in dey cah'rige. Ah tell dem dey jes' gits splashed wid mud an' ruin dey new dresses.

*They have come to a part of the platform outside the shed where* MISS PITTY *and* MELANIE *are waiting in* MISS PITTY'S *carriage, the horse's head held by a young Negro urchin. A babble of voices as* UNCLE PETER *deposits* SCARLETT *on the seat of the carriage.*

MELANIE: Here she is, Aunt Pitty!

MISS PITTY: Oh, my dear!

SCARLETT [*at the same time*]: Aunt Pitty! Melanie!

MELANIE: Oh, Scarlett, Scarlett! We're so glad you've come!

MISS PITTY: And to think I saw you last on your wedding day! My dearest, Scarlett, I shall weep!

MELANIE: Don't, Aunt Pitty! Make Scarlett welcome instead!

MISS PITTY: Oh, I do make her welcome, but I can't help weeping! [PRISSY *enters, carrying* WADE HAMPTON.] And here's my dear, dead nephew's baby son, who never knew his father! I shall have to weep, Melly! If I don't weep, I shall faint! Here, let me have him! [*She takes the child from* PRISSY.]

UNCLE PETER [*to* PRISSY]: You git up in front, gal, an' we drives home ter Miss Pitty's house!

*He is climbing up on the box. But* WADE HAMPTON *is crying.*

SCARLETT [*to* PRISSY]: Give him a sugar tit to make him hush!

*A column of young soldiers is marching into the station to entrain, their uniforms new, their equipment shining.* SCARLETT *views them with pleasure.*

SCARLETT: I'm going to like it here! It's alive and exciting!

*DISSOLVE TO*

EXTERIOR–THE BAZAAR–NIGHT

*Torches illuminate the scene and a sign, stretched across the wide door of the armory in which the bazaar is being held, describes the function's purpose as* SECOND ANNUAL MONSTER BAZAAR, FOR THE BENEFIT OF ATLANTA'S OWN MILITARY HOSPITAL. *Carriages are depositing ladies and gentlemen—most of the latter in uniform—at the door. The music of a military band sounds from within. The angle is from above, and the CAMERA DRAWS BACK presently to a first-story balcony, where* RHETT BUTLER *and* BELLE WATLING *are seated. CAMERA stops when their figures are silhouetted in the f.g.*

RHETT: Here we sit in peace and comfort, my dear Belle, while the quality of Atlanta makes its supreme contribution towards winning the war.

*CAMERA has drawn back to show the two silhouettes:* RHETT, *in civilian clothes of the smartest, languidly smoking a thin cigar, while, with his other hand, he toys with a stack of twenty-dollar gold pieces, and* BELLE *looking every inch the buxom but well-groomed leader of her profession.* BELLE *laughs.*

BELLE: I've been sitting here noticing how many of those contributors owe me money. [*She points at the scene below.*] There's Hugh Elsing now. He was drunk here last night. On champagne. And not a bean in his pockets when I went through them. That's my contribution to winning the war. Free drink for heroes.

RHETT [*smiles*]: As your financial advisor, Mrs. Watling, I must warn you against carrying that patriotic policy too far.

BELLE [*she eyes him sagely*]: Those who aren't heroes pay my bills, my friend.

RHETT *smiles and slips the gold pieces back into his pocket. To do so he has to lean a little forward. Someone in the crowd below catches his eye and he sits up sharply.*

RHETT: Hello! I didn't know she'd come to Atlanta.

BELLE: Now you've found a friend. [*She leans forward as well.*] Let's see if I can guess which one. [RHETT *has risen, smiling. She notices this.*] It's the little widow. She would be your type. Irish, isn't she?

RHETT: To judge by her name she must be. [*But he smiles with mock sanctimoniousness.*] But we don't bring up ladies' names in this place, do we?

BELLE: Don't look at me that way. I can see she's a lady.

RHETT *turns from the balcony and the CAMERA, retreating before him, comes into the room of gilt mirrors and barroom art.*

BELLE: I can see more. Just by the way she walks I can see she's a hard, fast, cruel little . . .

RHETT: I know her better than you, my dear Belle. For all that, I think I may look in on the bazaar for a little.

BELLE [*shrugs, then*]: Shall I see you later?

RHETT: Who knows?

BELLE: Don't forget who pays for the heroes' champagne, will you? [*For answer,* RHETT *counts five of his twenty-dollar gold pieces out on the table. She rises to take them.*] About your little Irish widow, though. I know who she is. She's me, without my heart of gold. And she'll never be any good for any man.

*But* RHETT *is already on his way to the door.*

                                        *DISSOLVE TO*

INTERIOR–THE BAZAAR–NIGHT

*The band is playing "The Bonnie Blue Flag" and the whole assembly is singing. There is a chorus of:*

> Hurrah! Hurrah! For the Southern rights, hurrah!
> Hurrah for the Bonnie Blue Flag
> That bears a single star!

*Then CAMERA, centering first on the draped portraits of Jefferson Davis and Alexander Stephens, backs away to take in first the musicians' platform—the booth occupied by* SCARLETT *and* MELANIE *just adjacent—and then the whole assembly. The entire gathering being established, CAMERA moves along a line of booths, passing first a group of young officers, all a little intoxicated and all intensely patriotic.*

AD LIB:

Lee's got 'em on the run! . . .

Oh, there's no doubt about it! . . .

They'll be yelling for peace! . . .

One more big victory and the war'll be over! . . .

*Through this crowd comes the trio of* SCARLETT, MELANIE, *and* MISS PITTY. MELANIE *is in a frightened but excited frame of mind.* MISS PITTY *is downright beside herself with panic.* SCARLETT, *in mourning, but minus her widow's veil, is riding high, wide, and handsome.*

MISS PITTY: But, Scarlett, darling! You know Melanie and you shouldn't be here! Appearing in public and poor Charles only dead a year!

SCARLETT: Oh, fiddle-dee-dee, Aunt Pitty! I think it's the least we can do for the hospital to take on our share towards making this bazaar a success! And it does look much better for me to be in the booth with Melanie and there's the chaperons' corner where you belong!

*They are in truth passing the upholstered corner where the older ladies are seated, and* MISS PITTY *stops, her mouth open with horror at* SCARLETT'S *dismissal.* SCARLETT, *however, pushes* MELANIE *forward.*

SCARLETT: I'm at a party again!

MELANIE: Aunt Pitty's right, we shouldn't be here! But it *is* exciting!

SCARLETT: It's too good to be true!

*Then the dancing begins, and* SCARLETT *and* MELANIE *seek refuge from the polka-ing couples in their booth.*

THE BAZAAR–THE DOOR

RHETT BUTLER *enters, surveys the crowd, smiles and moves slowly forward.*

THE BAZAAR–SCARLETT'S AND MELANIE'S BOOTH

MELANIE *has just concluded the sale of a sofa pillow with the Stars and Bars embroidered on it.* SCARLETT, *however, bends over the counter, leaning on her elbows, her chin in her hands, and stares out at the crowd as it dances by. As* MELANIE *turns away to another customer,* SCARLETT'S *eyes close, her body sways, and her feet go in time to the polka. Then, suddenly, she is staring off-screen in horror. Seeing* RHETT'S *approach, she attempts to flee. Her dress catches, though, on a nail in the booth's exit and, before she can disentangle herself:*

MELANIE: What is it, Scarlett? What's the . . .

RHETT [*saunters up to the booth*]: I hardly hoped you'd remember me.

SCARLETT [*a gulp, then*]: It's Mr. Rhett Butler, isn't it?

MELANIE *is as delighted as* SCARLETT *is appalled.*

MELANIE: Captain Butler now, Scarlett! And the famous blockade runner the whole Confederacy's talking about. [RHETT *kisses her hand, or the equivalent.*] I expect all the girls here are wearing dresses you've brought through, Captain Butler. Except Scarlett and me. What are you doing so far from the seaports?

RHETT: I'm in and out of Atlanta a good deal, Mrs. Wilkes. The wares I bring in have to be sold, you know.

SCARLETT *has sat down on her stool suddenly and not too steadily.*

MELANIE: What's the matter, Scarlett? Are you faint?

SCARLETT *shakes her head vigorously, fanning herself the while.*

RHETT: It's warm. May I lead you to a window, Miss O'Hara?

MELANIE: Oh, but she isn't Miss O'Hara any more! She's Mrs. Hamilton and my sister now!

RHETT [*bows*]: I'm sure that's a great gain to two charming ladies. [*But there is something about his tone that* SCARLETT *does not relish.*] Are your husbands here tonight for this happy occasion?

MELANIE *simply cannot understand his clumsiness in the very face of* SCARLETT's *widow's weeds.*

MELANIE: My husband is in Virginia, but Charles . . .

*Her voice breaks, but* SCARLETT *puts her fan aside.*

SCARLETT [*flat*]: Charles died in camp of the fever.

RHETT *is overwhelmed. He takes up* SCARLETT's *fan and operates with it.*

RHETT: Permit me to say that to die for one's country is to live forever.

SCARLETT *does not know what to make of this.*

MELANIE [*genuinely moved*]: What a beautiful thing to say!

SCARLETT [*furious*]: There's no need to blow my hair all out of place!

MELANIE *finds this rudeness shocking.*

MELANIE: Scarlett, darling! [*then to* RHETT] She just isn't herself when she hears poor Charlie's name spoken.

RHETT: Oh, I can believe that! [*But he adds quite seriously to* MELANIE] I think *you're* a courageous lady, Mrs. Wilkes.

SCARLETT: Don't you think I'm? . . . [*She stops herself.*]

RHETT: What?

SCARLETT: Nothing.

*More customers come to distract* MELANIE, *leaving* RHETT *free to continue his conversation with* SCARLETT.

RHETT: Your husband has been dead long?

MGM, © 1939, 1967. Collection of Yvette Curran.

SCARLETT: Almost a year.

RHETT: Had you been married long?

SCARLETT: Two months.

RHETT: A tragedy. For him. [*Her eyes flash, but she says nothing.*] In India, when a man dies he's burned. And his wife is burned with him.

SCARLETT: How dreadful! Don't the police do anything about it?

RHETT: For myself, I think it's a more merciful custom than our Southern way of burying widows alive.

SCARLETT: You don't think I'm buried alive?

RHETT: Aren't you? Of course you are! In crêpe. I take it this is your first public appearance?

SCARLETT: I know it looks odd. But no sacrifice is too great.

RHETT [*smiles*]: It's such sacrifices as yours that hearten our brave boys in gray.

SCARLETT: I'm never quite sure whether you're serious or . . .

RHETT: Serious, Mrs. Hamilton? I'm reverent!

SCARLETT: Perhaps I shouldn't have come. Perhaps it does look to some people as if I hadn't loved my husb . . .

RHETT: Go on. I'm waiting breathlessly.

SCARLETT's *eyes flash and her nostrils distend and her whisper has the venom of a rattlesnake's hiss.*

SCARLETT: I wish you'd go away! If you'd had any raising you'd have known I never wanted to see you again! But you think because your stupid little boats can run away from the Yankees you've got a right to jeer at the brave men and women who are sacrificing everything for the Cause!

RHETT [*holds up both hands*]: Stop! Stop! You started off very nicely. But I'm sick of hearing about "the Cause," and so are you!

SCARLETT: How did you know . . . [*She stops herself just in time.*] I've nothing more to say to you, Captain Butler. Just because you're conceited over being the great blockader doesn't give you the right to insult us patriots.

RHETT [*smiles*]: I shouldn't want so charming a little patriot as yourself to overestimate my contribution to the Cause.

SCARLETT: I don't care to listen to your brags.

RHETT: Blockading's a business with me and I'm making money out of it. When I stop making money I'll quit. What do you think of that?

SCARLETT: I think you're a nasty, ill-bred, mercenary creature, just like the Yankees!

RHETT: Exactly. Since I'm not such a fool, though, as to subscribe to this folly of fighting, why shouldn't I take the intelligent man's advantage of those who . . .

SCARLETT: Will it be necessary for me to call my carriage and go home to get rid of you?

RHETT: A red-hot little rebel!

*But a roll of drums distracts both of them, and the CAMERA, looking up with them, sees* DR. MEADE *on the musicians' platform. Many voices cry "ssh!" as* DR. MEADE *spreads out his arms for quiet.*

DR. MEADE: We must all give grateful thanks to the charming ladies who have made this bazaar possible tonight. [*shouts of approval*] We have with us tonight the intrepid mariner who has so successfully run the blockade for a year and who will run it again to bring us the drugs we need. Captain Rhett Butler!

*CAMERA MOVES BACK to see* RHETT's *graceful bow in response to the cheers of the crowd.*

RHETT [*sotto voce to* SCARLETT]: Pompous goat, isn't he?

SCARLETT *is at first horrified, then stifles a giggle.*

THE MUSICIANS' PLATFORM

DR. MEADE: We need gold, however, and I am asking you for it! I'm asking a sacrifice small compared with the sacrifices our gallant men in gray are making! Ladies, the Confederacy wants your jewelry! There will pass among you some of our gallant wounded with baskets and . . .

*The rest of his speech is lost in the storm and tumult of clapping hands and cheers. CAMERA picks out* HUGH ELSING, *a split-oak basket over his unwounded left arm, as he makes his rounds, and the women and girls give up their bracelets, brooches, rings, and earrings. General Ad Libs.* MAYBELLE MERRIWETHER *runs in to him.*

MAYBELLE: There! There! Wait, Hugh! I've got them unfastened now!

*She surrenders her twin gold bracelets from above and below her elbow. CAMERA goes to* FANNY ELSING *as she cries out to her mother.*

FANNY: Mamma, may I?

*She delivers. The gathering up of the jewelry continuing,* HUGH ELSING *comes up to* RHETT *and* SCARLETT *with his basket. A glance at* SCARLETT, *then* RHETT *throws a handsome gold cigar case into it.*

RHETT: For the Cause.

HUGH: Mrs. Hamilton?

SCARLETT's *right hand is seen as it reaches none too eagerly for her right earring. But the earring has been left off as unsuitable to her*

*mourning and she heaves a sigh of all too apparent relief and throws wide her hands to show that she is wearing no jewelry. Then she sees her wedding ring on her finger, looks at it, hesitates a moment, then:*

SCARLETT: Yes, I have something for you, after all.

*She wrenches the ring from her finger and tosses it into the basket.* RHETT *smiles.*

MELANIE: Oh, my brave, brave girl! Wait, please, lieutenant! I have something, too!

*She pulls off her own wedding ring. For a brief instant she clutches it tightly in her palm, then, biting her lip, lays it gently on the pile of jewelry in the basket, turning to* SCARLETT *as she does so.*

MELANIE: If you hadn't been brave enough to do it, I should never have been!

HUGH *passes on with the basket.*

RHETT: That, Mrs. Wilkes, was a beautiful gesture.

SCARLETT, *turning, is surprised to see that he is not sneering. Another roll of drums again distracts her.*

THE MUSICIANS' PLATFORM

DR. MEADE: And now, ladies and gentlemen, I've an innovation to propose that may shock not a few of you! [*a general edging forward on the part of crowd*] The dancing is about to begin and the first number will be a reel. Gentlemen, if you wish to lead the reel with the lady of your choice you must bid for her. I will be auctioneer.

*Sensation. General Ad Libs.*

THE BOOTH

MELANIE: Don't you think it's . . . it's just . . . it's just a little like a slave auction?

SCARLETT: I don't care if it is! I wish I could be one of the slaves!

*Her eyes are glittering.* RHETT *notes this, smiles, steps out of scene. Off-screen* HUGH ELSING's *voice rings out.*

HUGH's VOICE: Twenty dollars for Miss Maybelle Merriwether!

*The bid is raised to twenty-five dollars by another buck, to thirty by a third and to thirty-five again by* HUGH, *in a state of mingled fury and excitement.*

THE BAZAAR

MAYBELLE MERRIWETHER *being knocked off to* HUGH ELSING *amid great applause, she collapses blushing against* FANNY ELSING's *shoulder and the two girls hide their faces. An* OFFICER *calls out off-screen.*

THE OFFICER: Twenty-five dollars for Miss Fanny Elsing!

*Now it is* FANNY's *turn to collapse.*

### THE MUSICIANS' PLATFORM

DR. MEADE *is leaning over to receive the excited bids from the young officers, three or four of these mounting to less than fifty dollars. Then* RHETT *steps coolly into the scene.*

RHETT: For Mrs. Charles Hamilton. One hundred and fifty dollars in gold.

*A sudden silence, then murmurs, the bystanders being aghast.*

### THE BOOTH

SCARLETT *is rigid with mingled astonishment and anger.* MELANIE's *arm goes 'round her.*

MELANIE: Scarlett! Oh, Scarlett, how awful of him!

SCARLETT *would answer but she cannot catch her breath.*

### THE MUSICIANS' PLATFORM

DR. MEADE [*bends over to* RHETT]: Mrs. Hamilton is in mourning, Captain Butler. Another of our belles, perhaps?

RHETT: No, Dr. Meade. [His glance sweeps the crowd coldly.] Mrs. Hamilton.

DR. MEADE [*he is annoyed*]: I tell you it's impossible! Mrs. Hamilton would not consider.

### THE BOOTH

SCARLETT *steps forward to lean eagerly out across counter.*

SCARLETT: Oh, yes, I would, Dr. Meade! What's more, I will!

*She walks out of booth into CAMERA, leaving* MELANIE *incredulous behind her.*

### CHAPERONS' CORNER

MISS PITTY *rises. So do* MRS. MERRIWETHER *and* MRS. MEADE. *But sudden faintness overcoming* MISS PITTY *at the shock of* SCARLETT's *behavior, the other two ladies are prevented from interfering.*

### BELOW MUSICIANS' PLATFORM

*Continued sensation as* SCARLETT *advances to meet* RHETT.

SCARLETT [*beaming*]: How dare you make me so conspicuous, Captain Butler?

RHETT: Well, you wanted to dance and, widow or not, I'm blest if I see why you shouldn't.

*The orchestra breaks into that best of all reel tunes: "Dixie."* RHETT *and* SCARLETT *go to their places as the reel forms.*

RHETT: You aren't committing any crime, are you?

SCARLETT: I'll think about that tomorrow.

*The dance begins.*

*QUICK DISSOLVE TO*

*LONG SHOT, the reel concluding and the band striking into a waltz—"When this Cruel War Is Over"—the various figures breaking up into waltzing couples.*

THE BAZAAR–*CLOSE SHOT*

RHETT *is waltzing with* SCARLETT. *She looks into his eyes, singing to him the last lines of the song:*

SCARLETT [*singing*]:

> Weeping and sad and lonely
> Sighs and tears how vain!
> When this cruel war is over,
> Pray that we meet again!

[*She concludes*] Oh, you waltz so well, Captain Butler! Most big men don't.

RHETT: I'm going to bid you in for the next reel. And the next and the next.

SCARLETT: You do talk scandalous, but I'm not going to stop you! I'm tired of sitting at home! I'm going to dance and dance now, and I wouldn't mind dancing with Abe Lincoln himself!

*DISSOLVE TO*

*CLOSE TWO SHOT*–RHETT *and* SCARLETT *(WAIST FIGURES)–WALTZING*

RHETT: You're the most beautiful dancer I've ever held in my arms.

SCARLETT [*coquettishly, with something of her old manner from her barbecue scene*]: Oh, Captain Butler, you shouldn't hold me so close. I'll be mad if you do! [RHETT *holds her even closer and whirls her around.*]

*MEDIUM SHOT–DANCERS WALTZING*

*CLOSE TWO SHOT*–RHETT *and* SCARLETT–*WALTZING*

SCARLETT: Another dance and my reputation will be lost forever.

RHETT: If you've enough courage, you can do without a reputation.

SCARLETT: Oh, you do talk scandalous!

*LONG SHOT–DANCERS ON FLOOR–LOW CAMERA SETUP*

*CLOSE TWO SHOT*–RHETT *and* SCARLETT

SCARLETT: You do waltz divinely, Captain Butler.

RHETT: Don't start flirting with me. I'm not one of your plantation beaux. I want more than flirting from you.

SCARLETT [*coquettishly*]: What *do* you want?

RHETT: I'll tell you, Scarlett O'Hara, if you'll take that Southern belle simper off your face. [*She drops her expression and looks at him, embarrassed.*] Some day I want you to say to *me* the words I heard you say to Ashley Wilkes . . . [*She looks up at him, gasping with fury at the shamelessness of the reminder.*] "I love you."

SCARLETT, *aghast at his brazen attack and at the revelation of his interest, narrows her eyes when she realizes that at last she has the upper hand over this man whose insults she has been unable to cope with in their two meetings.*

SCARLETT [*triumphantly*]: That's something you'll never hear from me, Rhett Butler, as long as you live! You shouldn't hold me so tight, Captain Butler.

*He holds her even tighter.*

*FADE OUT*

# Third
# Sequence

*ADE IN:*

INSERT OF WALL MAP OF VIRGINIA, WEST VIRGINIA, MARYLAND, AND PENNSYLVANIA—with the names of the major cities in large, distinct print: RICHMOND, WASHINGTON, BALTIMORE, PHILADELPHIA.

*An old man's hand, from off-screen, draws a heavy line marking the route of march of General Lee's Army of Virginia, in its invasion of the North in the campaign of 1863, showing the crossing of the Potomac many miles above Harper's Ferry, the passage across Maryland and into Pennsylvania to the furthest point reached by the Confederates, during the war, amongst the mountains of Pennsylvania. The name, Gettysburg does not appear on the map.*

LAWYER RANDOLPH'S VOICE [*as his hand draws a line on the map*]: Right there—in the heart of Pennsylvania—is where Lee's Army is at this minute. If that don't prove Lee's out to capture Philadelphia, not Washington, I don't know what does.

OLD MR. MERRIWETHER'S VOICE: He's foolin' the Yankees just like he's fooled you. It's Washin'ton he's after.

INTERIOR–*FULL SHOT* OF LAWYER RANDOLPH'S OFFICE –*CAMERA ON BOOM*–DAY–MAP ON WALL IN BACKGROUND

*The office is on the ground floor of a building at the corner of Marietta and Peachtree Streets. The two old gentlemen [*MERRIWETHER *is over seventy and* RANDOLPH *only a few years his junior*] *are gazing at the map on the wall.* RANDOLPH *is standing, with a pencil in his hand.* MERRIWETHER *is seated, a Panama hat on one knee while he smokes a stogie.*

RANDOLPH: No, sir. Philadelphia. And he'll beat the Yankees again like he did at Fredericksburg and Chancellorsville and the war'll be over.

MR. MERRIWETHER: Well, I hope you're right, John. But it appears to me like we keep on winnin' battles and losin' the war. The Yankees are like the hairs on your face. The more you get rid of, the more grow in.

*The distant beat of a drum growing louder invades the quiet room.*

RANDOLPH: You're always cawin' like an old crow, Merriwether. [*The beat of the drum grows louder.*] Listen to that. The heartbeat of the South, sir—the spirit of our people. We can't lose.

*These snapshots by Wilbur G. Kurtz were taken on the GWTW set while preparations were being made to film the wartime street sequences in Atlanta. Mr. Kurtz, as historian on the film, had caused the names of actual Atlanta merchants of the period to be used on the storefronts constructed for the film. The firm in the upper picture is "Lawshe & Haines."*

*CAMERA PULLS BACK through open window which overlooks Marietta Street.* RANDOLPH *crosses to the window and looks out. He is joined there by* MR. MERRIWETHER. *The drum beat is even louder.*

RANDOLPH [*gazing off toward the marching troops out of view*]: Look at 'em come. Uniforms not so clean as they were. Buttons not so bright. But hearts stout as ever.

MERRIWETHER [*gravely*]: Boys of seventeen and men past forty. They keep gettin' younger and older. We'll get our chance to tote a gun yet, John.

RANDOLPH: Not us. Before the week's out Lee will have whipped the Yankees and we'll be celebratin' the Fourth of July as the Independence Day of the Confederacy.

*Now the drumbeat is very close. CAMERA PULLS BACK FURTHER over the heads of the marching troops, and shows that the window where the two old gentlemen are standing is in the corner of the building at the junction of Marietta and Peachtree Streets. The troops are a small detachment, with a young boy acting as drummer. They make a sharp, right turn at the intersection, going out of scene, down Peachtree Street, toward the station. As a military force they are none too prepossessing. They include boys and middle-aged men. Their uniforms are a bizarre mixture. Their guns vary in size and type. CAMERA PANS FURTHER so that it is SHOOTING across Peachtree Street and down Decatur Street. There, in front of Belle Watling's house,* RHETT BUTLER *is just mounting his horse.*

EXTERIOR–IN FRONT OF BELLE WATLING'S HOUSE–DAY

RHETT *is just settling himself in the saddle, preparatory to riding away when* BELLE WATLING *comes out of the front door fully dressed, but without a hat and with her hair somewhat disordered. She has a woman's hatbox in her hand.*

BELLE [*calling*]: Rhett, wait! [*She approaches the horse, holding out the hatbox.*] You forgot something.

RHETT [*taking the box, smiles*]: You haven't even asked who it's for.

BELLE [*tartly*]: I didn't have to. No use my tellin' you you're a fool.

RHETT: Jealous?

BELLE: She ain't your sort.

PEACHTREE STREET–DAY–BRIEF TRUCKING SHOT OF MRS. MERRIWETHER *and* MRS. ELSING–*as they walk along.*

MRS. ELSING: Did you notice? It was a lady's hatbox.

MRS. MERRIWETHER: And he'll probably give it to some nice young girl.

MRS. ELSING: Disgusting! Going directly from a—from a woman like that into some decent home.

MRS. MERRIWETHER: You don't suppose—?

MRS. ELSING [*eyes the other woman understandingly*]: I wouldn't put it past her.

INTERIOR–MISS PITTY'S HOUSE–THE DINING ROOM–DAY

SCARLETT, MELANIE, *and* MISS PITTY *are seated around the table.* MISS PITTY *is in tears,* MELANIE *is tense, and* SCARLETT, *though defiant, has an excellent appetite and eats heartily throughout the scene.*

SCARLETT: I don't care what that old buffalo—I mean Mrs. Merriwether—says! I'll bet I made more money for the hospital than any girl there! More than all the messy old stuff we sold, too!

MISS PITTY: Oh, dear, what's the money matter? I couldn't believe my eyes! And poor Charles hardly dead a year! That awful Captain Butler!

MELANIE: I can't believe he's so bad! When you think how brave he is!

SCARLETT [*her mouth full*]: He isn't brave! He does it all for money. He doesn't care a thing for the Confederacy. But he dances divinely.

*She continues eating, but* MELANIE *rises and moves behind her to put her arms around her neck.*

MELANIE: At least, it was a brave thing you did last night. And I'm not going to let anyone say a word against you! Don't cry, Aunt Pitty. It's been hard on Scarlett, not going anywhere.

MISS PITTY: What will her mother say, though, when she hears?

SCARLETT'S *eating is again interrupted, this time by a sudden loss of appetite.*

SCARLETT: Why should Mother hear?

MISS PITTY: Child, I'm responsible for you in Atlanta!

SCARLETT *rises and runs 'round to drop on her knees at* MISS PITTY'S *side.*

SCARLETT: Oh, Aunt Pitty, you mustn't tell Mother! Please! I couldn't bear for her to think of me as a vulgar show-off with no dignity! I promise, Aunt Pitty, I'll never, never speak to that man again! Oh, please, Aunt Pitty!

UNCLE PETER *has entered.*

UNCLE PETER: Gempmum jes' brung dis, Miss Melly.

MELANIE: For me? [*She rips open the envelope, looks into it, gasps.*]

SCARLETT: What is it?

UNCLE PETER: Gempmum say sumpin' 'bout Majah Wilkes.

MISS PITTY [*a squeal*]: Ashley's dead!

*Her head falls back and her arms go limp. A hoarse sound from* SCARLETT. *She rises, her hand clutching her throat.*

MELANIE: No, he's not dead! It's nothing. Her smelling salts, Scarlett! [*As* SCARLETT *goes to sideboard for them,* MELANIE *supports* MISS PITTY.] There, there, now! [SCARLETT *returns with salts.*] Breathe deep. No, it's not Ashley. I'm sorry I scared you. I was so happy, though . . . I *am* so happy! [MISS PITTY revives. MELANIE *empties the envelope onto the tablecloth.*]

MELANIE'S WEDDING RING–*CLOSE SHOT*

*Melanie's wedding ring lies on the tablecloth.*

MELANIE [*off-screen*]: I told you he was a gentleman, didn't I?

THE DINING ROOM–DAY

*The company as before. Then* MELANIE *slips the wedding ring back on her finger.*

UNCLE PETER: Whut answer does Ah give de gempmum?

MELANIE: I'll give the answer myself, Uncle Peter.

*She goes quickly into the hall. The CAMERA stays on* SCARLETT *and* MISS PITTY.

THE PARLOR

MELANIE *stands holding* RHETT's *hand.*

RHETT: The Confederacy may need the life blood of its men, Mrs. Wilkes, but it doesn't yet ask the heart's blood of its women. I've redeemed your ring at many times its value.

MISS PITTY *and* SCARLETT *enter.*

MELANIE: No one but a gentleman of refinement and thoughtfulness would have understood. [*She bursts into tears.*]

MISS PITTY: Melanie, my dear!

MELANIE: It's all right. It's only because I'm happy that I'm crying. Excuse me. . . . [*She goes out of the room.*]

MISS PITTY [*almost tearfully to* RHETT]: I don't know what it is about you, but I do think you'd be a nice, attractive man if I could just feel that you respected women. [*She follows* MELANIE *out.*]

SCARLETT: You aren't giving my wedding ring back to me.

RHETT [*his look is quizzical*]: Have you been married?

SCARLETT: You know I have.

RHETT [*smiles*]: War, marriage, and childbirth have all three passed over you and left you quite untouched.

SCARLETT: I'm sure I don't know what you mean by that. [*Coyness rears its ugly head.*] I'm prettier than she is and I hate the Yankees just as much as she does, and I don't see why you're so much nicer to her!

RHETT: If I'm nicer to Mrs. Wilkes than I am to you, it's because she's one of the few great ladies I've ever been privileged to know.

SCARLETT: I know why you gave Melanie back her ring! It was so my Aunt Pitty would have to invite you here and give you a chance to see more of me!

RHETT [grins at her]: I've brought *you* this. [Turning, he picks up a bandbox which he offers her.] It's part of my last cargo from overseas. There's Rue de la Paix on the lid, if that means anything to you. [She takes the box, wondering, opens it and with an involuntary cry of delight extracts a most beautiful green bonnet.] Put it on.

She flies across the room to the mirror, pops the bonnet on her head, ties the ribbons under her chin, and turns.

SCARLETT: I'll buy it! I'll give you every cent I've got! I've only got fifty dollars now, but next month . . .

RHETT: That bonnet would cost about two thousand dollars in Confederate money at the present rate of exchange.

SCARLETT is not unnaturally taken aback.

SCARLETT: Oh, dear!

RHETT: I don't want any money for it. It's a gift.

SCARLETT [draws herself up]: Candy and flowers and perhaps a book of poetry or a small bottle of Florida water are the only gifts a lady can accept from a gentleman or the gentleman will try taking liberties. [Then, however, she is herself again.] But I simply can't give you back this bonnet! I'd almost rather you took a liberty!

RHETT: Oh, Scarlett, you're so young you break my heart! But I shall bring you presents whenever I see things that enhance your charms. I shall bring you a green watered silk for a frock to match the bonnet.

SCARLETT [is alarmed]: If you think I'll marry you for the bonnet, I won't.

RHETT: You flatter yourself. I'm not a marrying man.

SCARLETT: I don't even intend to kiss you for it, either!

RHETT: Then why is your mouth pursed up in that silly way?

SCARLETT: Oh!

RHETT: Since you seem to expect it . . . [he bends down and kisses, not her lips but her cheek, carelessly.] Now, stamp on the bonnet and show me what you think of my presents and me.

SCARLETT decides quickly what she thinks of them.

SCARLETT: I shall do no such thing! I shall cover the bonnet with black crêpe and wear it! [He steps to her, unties the bow under her

*Rhett and Scarlett in the "Paris Bonnet" scene that gave the writers on
the screenplay so much trouble.* ABOVE: *This version of the scene is a still as
filmed by George Cukor.* BELOW: *Victor Fleming's version of it.*

*chin, and drops the bonnet back into the box.*] What are you doing? You said it was mine!

RHETT: Not to change into a mourning bonnet, my dear.

SCARLETT: You're a black-hearted scoundrel!

RHETT: Aren't we both scoundrels, Scarlett?

SCARLETT: You're the horridest men I've ever known! Give me back that bonnet! I shall tell Aunt Pitty it cost a hundred dollars and she'll tell everybody in town and everybody will be green with envy and talk about my extravagance! I won't wear it, though, till you bring me the green silk.

*Music.* RHETT *smiles, hands her the bonnet, but retains hold of one of the ribbons. With measured grace, he produces a gold pocket knife and opens it.*

RHETT: I shall need a sample to match the color on my next block-ade runner's visit to Paris. [*He grins.*] In behalf of our brave boys in gray. [*He cuts a bit off the end of the ribbon.*]

FADE OUT

FADE IN:
EXTERIOR–ATLANTA–A STREET–DAY

*Music: like a distant and ominous military march. A column of Infantry is passing. Uniforms are shabbier than before, and among the rifles a good many have been brought from home, not issued by an arsenal. The ages of the men have changed perceptibly. There are more older men and boys among them.*

*CAMERA advances, through a space between companies, to the curb of the sidewalk, where it picks up* MRS. MEADE *and* MRS. ELSING *and follows them steadily and at a slow walk as they go along the street. The sidewalk is moderately crowded with pedestrians moving in both directions.* MRS. MEADE, *who is reading aloud from a letter, has just collided with one of these.*

MRS. MEADE: I'm very sorry! [*then, to* MRS. ELSING] I must look where I'm going.

MRS. ELSING: Don't stop, Mrs. Meade. I'll guide you.

MRS. MEADE [*resumes reading*]: "Lee's been holding us here in Maryland, but we all know we're going right up into Pennsylvania. So the Yankees will soon learn what it's like to be invaded. . . ."

MRS. ELSING [*with all possible fervor*]: I hope he teaches them to suffer as we've suffered!

MRS. MEADE *looks fearsomely at her friend.*

MRS. MEADE: They must be in Pennsylvania now! Lee may be fighting his greatest battle now!

MRS. ELSING: Go on! Go on! We're so hungry for news, and your Darcy writes such marvelous letters!

MRS. MEADE [*resumes reading*]: "Could Pa manage to get me a pair of boots? I've gone barefoot for two weeks now. . . ."

*The two ladies have reached the intersection of a side street down which the column of Infantry is turning.*

COMMAND: Squads RIGHT! MARCH!

*CAMERA leaves the ladies on the curb waiting for their opportunity to cross, slips through another space between companies to encounter* MR. MERRIWETHER *and* MR. RANDOLPH. *They turn, CAMERA following, to proceed along the sidewalk.*

MR. RANDOLPH: Lee's in Pennsylvania. Taking the war right into Yankeeland. Forcing battle. [*Then, as their eyes meet*] He won't lose.

MR. MERRIWETHER [*grimly*]: He'd better not.

*They are passing a corner mansion set apart from the street by a cast-iron fence. Workmen are wrecking the fence and carrying the iron across the sidewalk to a horse dray which is backed up against the curb. As the two old gentlemen reach the steps of the mansion, an elderly lady—*MISS BLESSINGTON—*comes down to them in intense agitation. They lift their hats.*

MISS BLESSINGTON: Good morning, Mr. Merriwether! Mr. Randolph, good morning! May I walk along the street with you? [*Without waiting for their permission, she joins them, chattering to keep back the tears.*] I thought I could watch them wrecking our fence, but I can't! Oh, I know the army needs the iron for cannon, just like it needed our jewelry, but my father brought that fence from New Orleans. . . .

MR. MERRIWETHER [*grim as before*]: One more victory and the war's over, Miss Blessington. [*And he points.*] And there are those who have lost more than cast-iron fences.

*The three pause to look and CAMERA, leaving them, comes at once to where a ramshackle buckboard is backed up against the curb. It is disgorging a haggard and ragged group of refugees into the welcoming arms of ladies of Atlanta. CAMERA picks up what they are saying to one another.*

A MAN: I had a good farm home in Tennessee. Twenty acres in corn and sixty hogs. Till Streight's raiders come. . . .

A WOMAN: Lee'll show 'em what for in Pennsylvania now! If he don't burn every farm and kill every hog . . .

ANOTHER MAN: 'D'ruther he spared the hogs and killed the Yankees! Like my woman died comin' from Tennessee, and left her young uns to live off charity or starve or . . .

*An old man behind him suddenly collapses in the act of climbing out of the wagon. There is a commotion as the refugees bend over him. One of the young ladies of Atlanta leaves the wagon to run to a second street corner. the CAMERA following her. She calls out to an army ambulance which is coming towards CAMERA up this second side-street.*

THE YOUNG WOMAN: You in the ambulance! Here's an old man's fainted.

*Voices from the sidewalk as the ambulance pulls up and the attendant climbs down from his seat beside the driver. CAMERA, crossing this second street, catches a glimpse of a wounded man on a stretcher.*

WOUNDED MAN: Yankees! Dirty Yankees!

*CAMERA, leaving this second street, comes at once to a corner grocery of the medium class and encounters* MISS PITTY *and* MRS. MERRIWETHER *as they come out, each lady carrying a very small parcel.*

MRS. MERRIWETHER: It's only lately I've taken to visiting the stores myself. And only because I couldn't believe such prices were possible.

MISS PITTY [*enviously*]: I saw you buying tea, Mrs. Merriwether.

*They are walking along, CAMERA FOLLOWING.*

MRS. MERRIWETHER: I saw you buying sugar, Pittypat Hamilton. That's a far worse extravagance.

MISS PITTY *is covered with confusion.*

MISS PITTY: Oh, not really it isn't! Sometimes I feel a craving for sweets that molasses won't satisfy. And Uncle Peter makes our tea for us, you see, out of some herbs he finds in the garden and dries. It's quite delicious once one gets accustomed to it, but it does need sugar!

MRS. MERRIWETHER [*breaking out*]: Why should we get accustomed to dried herbs? What good are these glorious blockade runners doing if they can't bring through a simple thing like tea, at a price decent people can afford to pay?

*They have come to a building before which other horse drays are unloading crates, and* DR. MEADE's *voice rings out.*

DR. MEADE: Speculators you are! Wicked, greedy speculators! [*The ladies hurry forward.*] Sucking the life blood of the Confederacy! Scoundrels! Scavengers! I demand to see Captain Butler!

*The CAMERA and the two ladies have caught up by now and* MELANIE *is dragging the furious doctor out of the scene.*

MELANIE: It's no use, Dr. Meade! You know Captain Butler won't see you! Come back to the hospital!

DR. MEADE [*shouts back over his shoulder*]: You may tell your precious Captain Butler in his den of brigands that once Lee's won his battle in Pennsylvania and ended this war, we'll . . . [*to* MELANIE] We'll ride Mr. Rhett Butler out of town on a rail and strip him of every last cent of his ill-gotten millions! [*He strikes a crate with his cane.*] What's in these boxes? Chloroform? Morphine for our wounded? No! Trash for wastrels! Because it's trash Rhett Butler makes his profit on! [*They are passing a shop window in which silks and velvets are displayed.*] Silks and velvets! Can I run a hospital on silks and velvets?

MELANIE: I know! I know! But you mustn't get so angry! You're tired enough without that.

*They have reached the entrance to the hospital and the CAMERA pauses at last.*

DR. MEADE: If I had more nurses like you, Melanie Wilkes, I shouldn't be tired and lose my temper so easily. I shall write to the papers, though, and make a stench of the very name of Butler! [SCARLETT, *in her nurse's uniform, comes out of the hospital just in time to hear this.*] And you may tell your Aunt Pitty I want to hear no more of him in her house! Do you understand, Melly?

SCARLETT *makes a face as she steps out of the doorway. He goes into the hospital.*

MELANIE: Oh, dear! Oh, dear!

SCARLETT [*stops her*]: Aren't you coming home with me, Melly? There's Uncle Peter waiting, and I've had enough of nursing for one day. [*Two orderlies pass them, carrying a wounded man on a stretcher into the hospital. A second pair with a second stretcher follows.*] I'm sick of nursing! And men with lice and without any legs and . . .

MELANIE: You don't mean that, Scarlett.

SCARLETT: Yes, I do so mean it! [*She takes* MELANIE's *arm to force her across the sidewalk to the carriage.*] Here's Aunt Pitty toddling up the sidewalk now. And she's got old lady Merriwether with her. Get in the carriage so the old buffalo'll see there isn't room for her! [*She has pushed* MELANIE *into the carriage ahead of her. Just as she herself is climbing in, however,* BELLE WATLING *appears from the side street.*] Good heavens!

BELLE: I wanted a word with Mrs. Wilkes if there's no objection.

*The two girls fairly cower away from her, but* MELANIE *manages to stammer:*

MELANIE: No! Oh, no!

BELLE: Mrs. Watling's my name.

MELANIE: How do you do?

BELLE: I expect you think I've got no business even speaking to you.

MELANIE: Hadn't you best tell me what your business is?

BELLE: First time I came here I volunteered as a nurse. One of the ladies—Mrs. Meade I think—told me they don't want my kind nursing here. She may have been right. This time I waited for you. From what I hear, you're human and sensible. I've come this time to give the hospital money.

*She holds out a knotted handkerchief to* MELANIE, *who takes it because she can think of nothing better to do.*

MELANIE: You're very kind.

BELLE: I'm not kind. I'm a Confederate like you, that's all.

*Nervously fumbling the handkerchief, the money falls out of it: five ten-dollar gold pieces, some of which roll off* MELANIE'S *lap onto the floor.*

SCARLETT: Look, Melly! [*She stoops greedily to pick up the fallen pieces.*] It's a great deal of money! Ten, twenty, thirty . . .

BELLE: There's fifty dollars in gold.

MISS PITTY *and* MRS. MERRIWETHER *have just arrived, and* MISS PITTY'S *horror is acute.*

MISS PITTY: Scarlett, who is this woman? Who is this woman, Melly?

MELANIE: She's just given the hospital fifty dollars in gold.

BELLE: I'll be back to see Mrs. Wilkes every week with more. You'll be needing all you can get after today, no matter where it comes from.

MELANIE [*starts*]: "After today?" What do you mean by "after today," Mrs. . .

SCARLETT: Let me see that handkerchief!

*She takes it.* CAMERA *goes with her to read the initials R.B. embroidered in the corner.*

MRS. MERRIWETHER: Throw away the horrible creature's handkerchief, Scarlett!

SCARLETT: It isn't her handkerchief! It's Rhett Butler's handkerchief! Oh, if I weren't a lady wouldn't I tell that varmint what I think of him!

MRS. MERRIWETHER: Need anything surprise you about Captain Butler? Haven't we all learned . . .

*But* BELLE *has gone, and* MRS. MEADE *enters breathless.*

MRS. MEADE: The news! It's come! General Lee's fought his battle! Darcy and Ashley were both in it, Melly!

*A wail from* MISS PITTY.

MELANIE: Is Ashley all right? . . . [*She corrects herself.*] I mean, did Lee win the battle?

MRS. MEADE: There's nothing yet. Nothing but the name of the town where the battle was fought. [*She is going.*]

SCARLETT: What is the name of the town?

MRS. MEADE: Gettysburg.

MELANIE: Climb in, Aunt Pitty! Drive to the depot, Uncle Peter! To the telegraph office at the depot!

MISS PITTY *clambers in, and* UNCLE PETER *is driving out of the scene. Now the CAMERA goes back down the street along which it has just come. Miss Pitty's carriage and others are now elements in a mob which presses toward the depot. Augmented from every side street, every house and shop on the way, the mob speaks as it goes, the word "Gettysburg" crackling through the tension.*

AD LIBS: Gettysburg! Gettysburg! . . . No Gettysburg on any map I ever saw! . . . Mark by words, this battle of Gettysburg will be one of the most famous fights in history! . . . Gettysburg will be the turning point of the war! . . . Met the whole Yankee Army at Gettysburg! . . . Met 'em at Gettysburg and licked 'em there! . . . We'll make a national holiday to remember Gettysburg! . . . Heard Lee's called Abe Lincoln to Gettysburg and made him surrender, too! . . . Lee won't stop at Gettysburg! . . . Wonder how far Gettysburg is from Philadelphia? . . . He's left Gettysburg now! He's half way to New York! . . . Fredericksburg, Chancellorsville, and now Gettysburg! . . . I'll say to my son: My father fought at Gettysburg! . . . [*Etc., etc., the word repeated over and over.*]

THE SQUARE IN FRONT OF THE DEPOT

*The place is filled with a vast crowd of people, but the voices now have dimmed to a low hum, for the crowd in the square is silent with anxiety. In the foreground, an old man wipes the sweat from his brow, turns to his wife as he does so.*

OLD MAN: They must know inside! They must have news! Why don't they tell us?

*His wife silences him, a trembling finger to her lips.*

THE GLASS WINDOWS OF THE TELEGRAPH OFFICE

*In the foreground, the heads and shoulders of the anxious crowd. Through the windows the operator can be seen clicking his instrument and straining in vain for an answer. The operator's partner turns to hold up a sign against the window. The sign reads:* NO NEWS FROM THE NORTH. *A kind of whimper of disappointment runs through the crowd,*

*then in the distance voices and some heads turn in the direction of the
sound.*

THE SQUARE IN FRONT OF THE DEPOT

RHETT *is forcing his horse through the crowd.*

RHETT: Gangway, please! If you don't mind . . . I want to get
through to those ladies over there.

*Voices hoarse with strain snap at him.*

A VOICE: Where's your uniform?

ANOTHER VOICE: Why ain't you with the army?

RHETT *smiles and forces his horse forward.* MRS. MERRIWETHER *and
her daughter,* MAYBELLE, *see him from their carriage.* MRS. MERRI-
WETHER *stands.*

MRS. MERRIWETHER: Speculator! Scavenger!

*The crowd takes up the cry, but* RHETT *rides on. He pulls up alongside Miss Pitty's carriage and doffs his hat.*

RHETT: Ladies, good morning. [*Seeing* MRS. MEADE, *he adds, low,
to* SCARLETT] Wouldn't this be a perfect time for Dr. Meade to give us
his speech about victory perched like an eagle on our banners?

SCARLETT: I'd just made up my mind I'd never speak to you again!
Though I've got to admit you've got nerve coming here with this mob
just hungry to tear you to pieces!

RHETT: I came to tell you ladies that the first casualty lists are being
printed at the "Examiner" office now.

*The crowd around the carriage, hearing this—for it is spoken loudly
so that they will hear it—becomes restless.*

VOICES: The "Examiner." . . . That's where we ought to be! . . .
Come on! . . . Down Whitehall Street! . . . 'Tisn't far! . . .

*And they are off in a tumult, Miss Pitty's and the other carriages
with them,* RHETT *leading the way on his horse.*

DISSOLVE TO

IN FRONT OF "EXAMINER" OFFICE

*The tumult increases, for the mob, another portion of it, is now
jammed against the open windows of the Examiner office, where long
galley sheets are being handed out.* RHETT *shoulders his way through
the crowd to snatch a handful and leaves,* CAMERA FOLLOWING
*him, to bring them to Miss Pitty's carriage. He tosses one set to* MELANIE
*and moves away to distribute the others among the other carriages.*
MELANIE'S *hands are trembling so that she cannot read the list.*

MELANIE: You take it, Scarlett!

SCARLETT [*as she takes it*]: The W's! Where are the W's! [*She finds
them and reads.*] White . . . Wilkins . . . Wynn . . . Young . . .

ABOVE: *The truncated "prop" locomotive* Swiftsure *is shown as a background for historian Wilbur G. Kurtz, himself an All-American railroad buff. This snapshot was taken by Rudy De Saxe on March 31, 1939.* BELOW: *The photograph of Hattie McDaniel was taken on the same set the next day by Mr. Kurtz.*

Atlanta Historical Society, Kurtz Collection.

ABOVE: *Extras outside the Atlanta* Examiner *office on April 1, 1939, the day the sequence showing the receipt of news from Gettysburg was made.* BELOW: *A publicity still from the same day's filming.*

ABOVE: *Clark Gable was not working the day this picture of him talking to Vivien Leigh on the set was made, but just visiting while Scarlett's scene with Big Sam and other Atlanta street scenes were filmed.* BELOW: *Vivien Leigh is resting between takes. The man standing in front of the window is Harry Wolf, camera assistant. Snapshots by Wilbur G. Kurtz.*

Yerkes . . . He's not on it! Oh, Melly, he's not on it! . . . There's no Wilkes on it!

MISS PITTY *faints.*

SCARLETT: Oh, Auntie, for heaven's sake! Melly, pick up the salts! Hold her up, Melly!

MELANIE, *weeping with happiness, steadies* MISS PITTY's *head and holds the smelling salts to her nose.* MAYBELLE MERRIWETHER, *frantic with joy, runs to the side of the carriage.*

MAYBELLE: Oh, Melly! Hugh's safe! He's all right, Melly!

MELANIE: Maybelle, I'm glad! And Ashley's safe! [*Turning, she sees something off-screen which frightens her.*] Look! Mrs. Meade!

*They all turn.* MISS PITTY *is coming to.*

MRS. MEADE'S CARRIAGE

*FROM* MELANIE's *ANGLE,* MRS. MEADE *is sitting quietly in the back seat, her young son,* PHIL, *beside her, the casualty list lying on her knees, her head bowed.*

PHIL MEADE [*helplessly*]: There, there, Mother!

MRS. MEADE [*looks up*]: He won't be needing those boots now.

MELANIE [*enters scene*]: Oh, Mrs. Meade!

MRS. MEADE [*nods*]: Yes. Darcy.

PHIL MEADE: Mother, you've still got me! And if you'll just let me, I'll go kill all the Yankees!

MRS. MEADE *clutches his arm as though she would never let him go.*

MELANIE: Phil Meade, you hush your mouth! Do you think it'll help your mother to have you off getting shot, too? I never heard anything so silly! [*She calls out.*] Aunt Pitty! [MISS PITTY *enters.*] Darcy Meade's killed.

MISS PITTY [*to* MRS. MEADE]: Oh, my poor darling!

MELANIE: We'll take Mrs. Meade home to her house together. Uncle Peter can look after Scarlett.

MELANIE *and* MISS PITTY *climb into the Meade carriage.*

MISS PITTY'S CARRIAGE

*The tumult around is now lessening somewhat as* SCARLETT, *with wide and terrified eyes, studies the list.* RHETT *returns.*

RHETT: I'm sorry, Scarlett. [*She looks up at him.*] Many of your friends?

SCARLETT [*her voice choking*]: Just about every family in the county. [*She points to the list.*] "Calvert, Raiford, Lieutenant." Raif! I grew up with Raif! "Monroe, Joseph." Little, bad-tempered Joe! And both of the Tarleton boys! Both of them, Rhett! [*Even* SCARLETT *breaks.*]

## MILLEDGEVILLE AND MACON TELEGRAPH LINE.
### CONNECTING WITH ALL LINES, EAST, WEST, NORTH AND SOUTH.

OFFICE HOURS—From 7 A. M. to 10 P. M.
SUNDAYS—From 8 to 9 A. M., and from 7 to 9 P. M.

### LIST OF RATES FOR TEN WORDS OR LESS

| | | | | | |
|---|---|---|---|---|---|
| MACON | 50 & 5 | SAVANNAH | 100 & 9 |
| ATLANTA | 110 & 9 | AUGUSTA | 110 & 9 |
| COLUMBUS | 90 & 9 | CHARLESTON | 125 & 9 |
| MOBILE | 130 & 10 | RICHMOND | 200 & 18 |
| MONTGOMERY | 110 & 9 | COLUMBIA | 145 & 10 |
| WILMINGTON | 180 & 11 | PETERSBURG | 200 & 13 |
| GRIFFIN | 100 & 9 | MARIETTA: | 150 & 11 |
| DALTON | 170 & 12 | CHARLOTTESVILLE | 200 & 16 |

Dated *Martinsburg, Va. July 14* 186 3

*To Dr. J. A. Meade, Atlanta*

*Your son Darcy died today of wounds received on the third, instant.*

*Capt. B. C. McCurry*

Two properties picked up on the GWTW sets. The telegram above was
not used in the film. The form was copied from a Confederate telegram. The
wording of Ashley's leave was by Wilbur G. Kurtz. In both cases the hand-
writing set out to achieve readability, not authenticity.

*Head Qrs. Cav. Corps*
*Nr Orange Court House, Va.*
*23 Dec. 1863*

*In consideration of meritorious services performed
during the late campaign in Pennsylvania, a four
days furlough is hereby granted to Maj Ashley Wilkes
of Cobb's Legion.*

*E. V. White*
*Maj & A. A. Genl*

*Approved*
*J. E. B. Stuart*
*Maj. Gen. Comdg.*

RHETT: There'll be longer lists tomorrow and again the day after. And maybe for weeks to come.

*He takes the reins of his horse from* UNCLE PETER.

SCARLETT [*miserable*]: Oh, Rhett, why do wars have to be?

RHETT *swings himself savagely into his saddle, so that he towers over* SCARLETT *and the crowd around them.*

RHETT: Because men love 'em! [SCARLETT *looks up, startled.*] Yes, Scarlett, they do, the fools! And let 'em say what they like about me for making my fortune out of their folly! I know nothing on earth can be worth what this war's going to do to the South we've loved!

*During this, a pair of old people—not "quality folks"—have gone hopelessly past Rhett's horse, so blinded by their tears for their dead grandson that they have to duck under Rhett's horse's head, and all this that follows up to the very end should be played against the background of the suffering commoner.*

RHETT: When the war ends, though, and our South is gone forever, I shall be alive and well, with a million dollars!

SCARLETT: You are a varmint!

RHETT [*he laughs*]: You won't have to wait much longer to see that I'm right. General Lee's lost this battle of Gettysburg. They've heard at headquarters he's retreated on Maryland. [SCARLETT's *jaw drops.*] Don't you be downcast. They'll have to give Ashley Wilkes his home leave now to visit awhile with the women who love him. Both of 'em. [*He doffs his hat, bowing ironically.*]

*DISSOLVE TO*

THE RAILROAD STATION–ATLANTA–THE PLATFORM

*The leave train has just come in. The engine is puffing. A multitude of embraces: mothers and sons; husbands and wives; lovers and sweethearts; and of all social classes and conditions. There is much calling of the familiar phrase: "Merry Christmas!"*

MELANIE—*incoherent sobs and babblings of happiness—clings to* ASHLEY, *unconscious of anything else.* MISS PITTY, JOHN WILKES, HONEY *and* INDIA WILKES *crowd around. Only* SCARLETT *is missing, and* MELANIE *turns to look for her.*

THE STATION–*CLOSE SHOT*–SCARLETT

*CAMERA finds* SCARLETT *alone in the crowd, her eyes burning up* ASHLEY's *reunion with his wife.* MELANIE *calls from off.*

MELANIE's VOICE: What makes you so shy all of a sudden, Scarlett?

SCARLETT *steps forward, her face upturned to show all that a child's heart can hold of agony.*

SCARLETT: I knew I'd be glad to see you, Ashley. I just didn't have any notion of how glad. [ASHLEY *bends over to kiss her lightly on the cheek.*] Wherever did you get that uniform? It's nothing but rags.

ASHLEY [*laughs*]: My dear, I'm the Beau Brummel of the regiment. Look at my boots. Aren't they splendid. I had to shoot a Yankee to get them.

SCARLETT [*eagerly*]: Did you really shoot one? Tell me!

MELANIE: There! We're ready to go home now.

*She takes his arm, hugging it close to her.* HONEY *or* INDIA—*or both —cling to him, too, and they lead him out,* JOHN WILKES *following with* MISS PITTY. SCARLETT *starts after them, her fingers just touching her cheek where* ASHLEY *kissed her.*

*DISSOLVE TO*

OUTSIDE THE TRAIN SHED–ROW OF WOUNDED ON STRETCHERS

*Some are being loaded into wagons. Others are still being brought from the train shed and placed in the long line, awaiting their turn to be transported to the hospital.* DR. MEADE *is superintending the work.*

DR. MEADE [*loudly, addressing no one in particular*]: More wagons! I have to have more wagons! I must get these men to the hospital. We can't let 'em lie out here in the cold.

*CLOSE SHOT*–STRETCHER

*A man, both legs crudely bandaged, lies on his back motionless. CAMERA MOVES INTO CLOSE UP. He is evidently dead.*

DR. MEADE'S VOICE: It's an outrage. A disgrace to the fair name of the South.

OUTSIDE TRAIN SHED–ROW OF DRAYS

*They are being loaded with crates of merchandise.* RHETT BUTLER, *on a sleek horse, smoking a cigar, directs the work.*

DR. MEADE'S VOICE [*continuing, loudly*]: Not enough horses and wagons for the wounded, but always plenty to carry silks, laces, and such gee-gaws for the speculators and profiteers.

RHETT BUTLER *turns his horse around so that he faces* DR. MEADE, *who is out of scene.*

RHETT [*without taking the cigar from his mouth*]: Referring to me, Doctor?

DR. MEADE *strides into scene, gazing up indignantly at the man on the horse.*

DR. MEADE: Yes! To *you*, Captain Butler. And others like you—who line your pockets while the South starves.

RHETT [*mockingly*]: Tut, tut, Doctor. I thought I was the scourge of the Yankee fleet. The will-o-the-wisp of the bounding main.

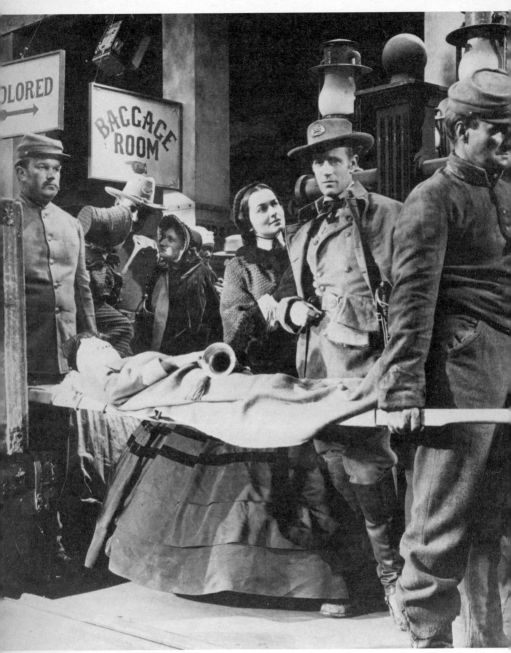

MGM, © 1939, 1967. UGa Libraries, Perkerson Collection.

DR. MEADE [*hotly*]: I said that before I knew you for what you are. A raven, sir. A human vulture who speculates in food, raises prices. A vampire sucking the life blood of our soldiers. . . .

RHETT: Our brave lads in gray.

DR. MEADE: If you weren't a thorough scoundrel, you'd let me use those drays of yours to take these men to the hospital.

RHETT [*coolly*]: You may use my wagons as soon as I'm through with them [*indicates the boxes being loaded onto the drays*]. That stuff's just as perishable as yours—and more valuable. [*He turns away. Evidently sees someone out of scene for he smiles, bows and raises his hat.*]

CAMERA PANS *in that direction, REVEALING* MELANIE *and* ASHLEY, *followed by* AUNT PITTY, *with* SCARLETT *bringing up the rear, issuing from the train shed and approaching Aunt Pitty's carriage.*

THE GROUP–BY AUNT PITTY'S CARRIAGE

ASHLEY *is gazing off curiously toward* RHETT.

ASHLEY: Who's that?

MELANIE [*with a pleased smile*]: Captain Butler. Don't you remember? You met him at Twelve Oaks.

AUNT PITTY [*with a distressed air*]: I wish he wouldn't speak to us. I never know what to do. People say the most terrible things about him.

MELANIE: I don't care what they say. I don't believe it.

SCARLETT [*tartly*]: You never believe anything bad about anybody. [*To* ASHLEY] Everybody knows what Rhett Butler is. He thinks we're going to lose the war.

ASHLEY [*gravely, noncommittal*]: Does he?

SCARLETT: He calls it a rich man's war and a poor man's fight.

ASHLEY: I've heard that expression before. I'm not so sure it isn't true.

MELANIE [*shocked*]: Ashley!

TWO SHOT–ASHLEY *and* MELANIE–BY THE CARRIAGE

*He smiles down at her soberly.*

ASHLEY: There's so much I have to tell you—and such a little time to tell it.

CLOSE-UP–SCARLETT–*unhappy, jealous.*

DISSOLVE TO

EXTERIOR–BARNYARD–AUNT PITTYPAT'S HOUSE–DAY

UNCLE PETER *is in the yard, hatchet in his hand. He is in pursuit of a large frightened rooster.*

UNCLE PETER [*during the chase*]: Come on, ol' gentleman . . . we'se et all yo' wives. We'se et all yo' little chicks. You'se got nobody to worry yer head about fer leavin'. Come on. . . . Now you jus' stand still so you can be Chris'mus gif' fer dey w'ite fo'ks. Now hol' on . . . hol' on . . . don't go gettin' so uppity even if yo' is the las' chicken in Atlanta. . . . [*He pounces on the rooster.*]

*QUICK DISSOLVE TO*

INTERIOR–DINING ROOM–AUNT PITTYPAT'S–CHRISTMAS DAY

*Open on CLOSE-UP of CARCASS—the remains of the poor old rooster. We hear* SCARLETT's *voice as CAMERA STARTS TO PULL BACK:*

SCARLETT'S VOICE [*petulantly*]: Oh, let's not hear about the war. It's Christmas. . . . [*softly and reminiscently*] Let's talk about Twelve Oaks and Tara and the times before there was any old war. . . . Can we have the wine, Aunt Pittypat?

*Now CAMERA has pulled back to reveal* AUNT PITTYPAT, SCARLETT, MELANIE, *and* ASHLEY *about the table. In background a sad little holly wreath and holly decorating the table.* AUNT PITTYPAT *is carefully dividing the contents of a Madeira bottle among four glasses.* UNCLE PETER *stands at her side.*

AUNT PITTYPAT [*pouring the wine*]: Why did you say there wasn't enough, Uncle Peter? There's plenty. [*She takes the tray from* UNCLE PETER *and carries it to the others.*] This is the last of my father's fine Madeira that he got from his uncle, Admiral Wilbur Hamilton of Savannah, who married his cousin, Jessica Carroll of Carrollton, who was his second cousin once removed and kin to the Wilkeses, too. And I saved it to wish Ashley a Merry Christmas. But you mustn't drink it all at once, because it *is* the last.

*DISSOLVE TO*

MELANIE: Shall we make the great presentation, Scarlett?

SCARLETT: The great presentation? You make it, Melly. I guess it's your place.

ASHLEY: What presentation?

*Now the CAMERA FOLLOWING,* MELANIE *goes to the Christmas tree, under which a new Confederate tunic lies carefully folded.*

MELANIE: Take off your coat! You take it off him, Aunt Pitty!

MISS PITTY *proceeds.*

ASHLEY: Go gently, Aunt Pitty! This uniform has to have very delicate treatment!

MGM, © 1939, 1967. UGa Libraries, Perkerson Collection.

MELANIE: No, it doesn't, Ashley! It doesn't matter now!

*She returns to him, displaying the new tunic in proud triumph.*

ASHLEY: Melanie!

MELANIE *nods through proud tears.*

MISS PITTY: Do let's see if it fits!

ASHLEY: Did she make it herself?

SCARLETT *backs slowly and tragically away from the group till she comes up against the desk.*

MELANIE: A tailor cut it. But I sewed it for you, Ashley!

ASHLEY: It's too beautiful, Melly! I didn't know any tunic could fit so well.

*His arm goes around her. He kisses her with the deepest and most tender devotion.* SCARLETT *is stricken.*

JOHN WILKES: I think Ashley's seen enough of us for one evening. I think we should all say good night.

*FADE OUT*

*FADE IN:*

INTERIOR–AUNT PITTY'S HALLWAY–NIGHT

*CLOSE-UP–*SCARLETT*–as she turns her head slowly, her eyes following the upward movement of someone out of scene. Tears gather in her eyes.*

*CAMERA MOVES BACK TO REVEAL* SCARLETT *standing with a candle in her hand at foot of stairs, looking up.*

STAIRS–SCARLETT *IN FOREGROUND*

*Mounting to the second floor are* MELANIE *and* ASHLEY, *arm in arm.* UNCLE PETER *is lighting the way for them, holding aloft a fine, silver candelabra. At the head of the stairs,* MELANIE *pauses and looks down at* SCARLETT.

*LONG SHOT (from their angle)–shooting diagonally across the stairs.*

SCARLETT *standing in the doorway to the living room, her hand on the drape, watching* ASHLEY *and* MELANIE *off-screen. The scene is lighted by a candle on a table beside* SCARLETT *and by* UNCLE PETER'S *candle off-screen.*

*TWO SHOT–*ASHLEY *and* MELANIE*–looking back at* SCARLETT.

*On* ASHLEY's *face we read his realization of* SCARLETT's *emotions. His eyes flicker a little and he glances quickly again at his wife's hand on his new sleeve. But immediately he forces a smile and calls to* SCARLETT.

ASHLEY [*abrupt and crisp*]: Goodnight, my dear.

MELANIE *tenderly throws a kiss to* SCARLETT.

MELANIE: Goodnight, Scarlett darling.

*CLOSE-UP–*SCARLETT

*Still gazing upward after* MELANIE *and* ASHLEY. *She opens her lips to mumble a wretched goodnight to them, but fails, and closes her lips again with a long breath. Standing there completely motionless for a moment, she hears their footsteps going into their bedroom, a slight embarrassed cough from* ASHLEY *and then the sound of the door closing softly but decisively. At that, her fingers, holding the drape, clench into a fist for an instant, and then slowly and hopelessly relax and slip down the drape. The light effect on* SCARLETT's *face has been changing for the past moment or two as* UNCLE PETER's *candle vanishes, but her face remains lit by the wan light of the candle beside her.*

*DISSOLVE TO*

EXTERIOR–MISS PITTY'S HOUSE–DAY

*It is misting and a day of thaw. The eaves of the porch are dripping drearily. The front door opens, and* UNCLE PETER *enters, carrying Ashley's knapsack and bedroll.* UNCLE PETER *starts down the steps.* SCARLETT *appears in the door behind him.*

SCARLETT [*in a whisper*]: Is it time? Is it time, Uncle Peter?

UNCLE PETER: Pretty quick now, Miss Scarlett.

SCARLETT: Miss Melly—will she be driving down to the depot with him?

UNCLE PETER: In dis wet an' cole, Miss Scarlett? Ah heerd Majah Wilkes tellin' Miss Melly he din' want her even comin' downstairs. Said he couldn't git away no how eff she even done dat much.

SCARLETT: Oh! Well . . . you go right along with his luggage, Uncle Peter.

UNCLE PETER *goes down the steps. She turns again into the house, closing the door after her.*

INTERIOR–THE HALL

SCARLETT *leaves the door and walks to the foot of the stair to listen. A second's pause, then, in an agony of impatience, she looks at the grandfather's clock. Then she whispers up the stair.*

SCARLETT: Oh, Ashley! Please come down, Ashley! Please leave me a minute to tell you goodbye!

*Again a pause, then, as though in answer, the sound of a door opening above.* SCARLETT *gasps. The door closes again.* SCARLETT *backs away from the stair as* ASHLEY *comes down. He does not see her until he reaches the bottom step. Then she goes to him swiftly. He tries to smile, but his face is drawn.*

SCARLETT: Ashley, may I go to the depot with you?

ASHLEY: I'd rather remember you saying goodbye to me here.

SCARLETT: Then I won't go. See, Ashley! I've got a present for you, too!

*She runs to a table for a sash of yellow silk which she presents to him.*

ASHLEY: Scarlett, it's beautiful! Tie it on me, my dear. [*She wraps the bright lengths about his waist and ties the ends in a knot.*] Did you make it yourself? [*She nods.*] Then I'll value it all the more.

SCARLETT: You know there's nothing I wouldn't do for you!

ASHLEY: Is that true, Scarlett? Then there's something you can do for me.

SCARLETT: What is it?

ASHLEY: Will you look after Melanie for me?

SCARLETT is dashed.

ASHLEY: She's so frail and so gentle. And she loves you so much. If I were killed and she had . . .

*But this possibility is more than* SCARLETT *can bear.*

SCARLETT: You mustn't say that! It's bad luck to speak of death! Oh, say a prayer quickly!

ASHLEY [*he smiles*]: You say it for me. And light some candles, too. We shall all need candles now that the end is coming.

SCARLETT [*draws back*]: The . . . the end?

ASHLEY: The end of the war. And the end of our world, Scarlett.

SCARLETT: You, too, Ashley? You think the Yankees are beating us? All this week you've talked about how strong General Lee . . .

ASHLEY: All this week I've talked lies. The Yankees have beaten us. Gettysburg was the end, only people back here don't know it yet. They can't realize how things stand with us, Scarlett. My men are barefoot now, and the snow in Virginia's deep. When I see them, and see the Yankees coming and coming, always more and more . . . [*He finishes with a gesture.*] When the end does come I shall be far away. Even if I'm alive. Too far to look out for Melanie. It'll be a comfort for me to know that she has you. You will promise, won't you?

SCARLETT [*nods dully*]: Yes. Is that all, Ashley?

ASHLEY: All except goodbye.

SCARLETT [*now she really breaks down*]: Ashley! Ashley! I can't let you go away!

ASHLEY: You must be brave! [*His voice has changed subtly.*] You must. How else can I stand going? [*He leans down to take her face in his hands.*] Scarlett, you're so fine and strong and beautiful. Not just your sweet face, my dear, but all of you.

SCARLETT: Kiss me. Kiss me goodbye.

*He bends his head to her forehead. But she turns her face so that his lips meet her lips and her arms are about his neck in a strangling grip. For an instant he presses her body close to him, all his muscles hard. Then, suddenly, he reaches up, detaches her arms from his neck and stands holding her crossed wrists in his two hands.*

ASHLEY: No, Scarlett. No.

SCARLETT: I love you! I've always loved you! I've never loved any-one else! I just married Charlie to hurt you! Oh, Ashley, I love you so much I'd walk every step of the way to Virginia to be near you! Ashley, tell me you love me, and I'll live on it all the rest of my life!

*He looks at her almost stupidly for a moment; then in his face she sees his love for her and his joy that she loves him and, battling with both, his shame and his despair. Then he turns to take up his hat.*

ASHLEY: Goodbye.

*He goes out. A sob and she runs to the door to look after him. CAMERA, looking over her shoulder, watches him as he goes quickly down the snow-bordered walk.*

SCARLETT [*a whisper*]: When the war's over, Ashley! When the war's over!

FADE OUT

FADE IN:

EXTERIOR–A STREET IN ATLANTA–DAY

*Soldiers are maching along, a fife and drum corps at the head of the column. There are more elderly men now than before and more younger boys and the members of the fife and drum corps are scarcely better than children. Their spirit is, if anything, higher than ever. As they march, they are singing "When this Cruel War Is Over" [if that melody can be altered to march time]. Two citizens of Atlanta stand on the curb watching the soldiers pass.*

FIRST CITIZEN: Who'd ever thought we'd see fighting on the soil of Georgia?

SECOND CITIZEN: We drove them out once. We'll drive them back into Tennessee again.

FIRST CITIZEN: I hope you're right. I believe you're right. This man, Sherman, though . . . [*He shakes his head.*]

RHETT BUTLER *comes driving along the street.*

FROM RHETT's ANGLE—*the singing continues, the sound of the marching audible, and the shadows of the passing troops on the pavement beneath his horse's hooves—show cheering groups of citizens at the curb. Their faces are strained and their enthusiasm is forced.*

RHETT *sees* SCARLETT *in one of these groups, reins in his horse and lifts his hat.*

RHETT: Good morning.

SCARLETT: Oh, it's you, is it?

RHETT: You look like a ragpicker's child.

SCARLETT: That isn't polite. You can take me in and drive me some place where nobody will see me. I won't go back to that hospital! I'd rather be hanged! The wounded are coming in faster than ever now, but I didn't start this war and I see no reason why I should be worked to death. Don't look shocked.

RHETT: I was shocked when I saw you cheering. You, of all people!

SCARLETT *has climbed into the buggy. They drive away.*

SCARLETT: Why wouldn't I cheer? Aren't they going out to drive the Yankees back?

RHETT: At least they're going out to do what they can to keep the Yankees from taking Atlanta.

SCARLETT: You mustn't say such things!

RHETT: Kennesaw Mountain's only twenty-two miles away.

SCARLETT: But our troops aren't going to retreat from there! One of our captains told me so last night! He says the lines around Kennesaw Mountain are impre . . . well, he meant the Yankees can't take 'em! They've got cannon planted all over the mountainside and the Yankees can't possibly get by!

RHETT: General Johnston's preparing to make his final stand here.

SCARLETT: A siege! Oh, turn the horse around! I'm going back to Tara!

RHETT: Running away? I'm ashamed of you, Scarlett! I wouldn't miss this siege for anything. New experiences enrich the mind, you know.

SCARLETT: My mind's rich enough!

RHETT: You know best about that. Perhaps I'll be staying to rescue you. Who knows?

SCARLETT: I can take care of myself, thank you.

RHETT: Never say that to a man, or you might be left to take care of yourself some day.

SCARLETT: You know the Yankees will never get to Atlanta!

RHETT: I'll bet you they'll be here before summer's over. I'll bet you a box of bonbons against a kiss.

SCARLETT: I'd as soon kiss a pig!

RHETT: I've always heard you Irish are partial to pigs. Keep 'em under your beds, don't you? You should be kissed by somebody who

knows how. Some day I'll kiss you and you'll like it. But not yet. I'm waiting for the memory of the estimable Ashley Wilkes to fade.

SCARLETT: Will you kindly turn your horse around? I think I'll go to the hospital after all.

RHETT: Then lice and slops are preferable to my conversation?

SCARLETT: You go to Halifax! And let me out of this buggy before I jump! [*In her anger she has reined in the horse herself. Now she stands.*] And I don't ever want to speak to you again!

SCARLETT *jumps, but her hoop catches in the wheel and for a moment there is a flashing view of petticoats and pantalettes. But she goes on without looking back, leaving him to laugh softly as he clucks to his horse.*

*DISSOLVE TO*

INTERIOR–THE HOSPITAL–THE NURSES' RETIRING ROOM –DAY

*A little closet cluttered with the paraphernalia of nurses. The wraps and bonnets of those on duty hang from hooks on the wall, likewise the uniforms and caps of those off duty. There are boxes of stores, piles of sheets and pillowcases and hampers for dirty linen. A door at the back, standing open, shows the ward beyond with its double line of cots, all occupied.* MELANIE *can be seen walking down the aisle. She is walking on air, as the saying goes. Elation shines in her even at this distance.* SCARLETT, *still in a fury, is tying her apron over her dress.*

SCARLETT [*muttering to herself*]: Waiting for Ashley's memory to fade! How dare he even mention Ashley to me? As though Ashley's memory could ever fade!

MELANIE *enters, closes the door behind her, and stands leaning against it, beaming.*

SCARLETT: Melly, what in heaven's name's come over you?

MELANIE: I'm going to have a baby. [SCARLETT *is stunned.*]

MELANIE [*coming to her*]: Dr. Meade just told me, not an hour ago! He says it will be here in late August or September. I wasn't sure till today. Oh, Scarlett, isn't it wonderful?

SCARLETT [*numb*]: Wonderful? You having Ashley's baby wonderful? [*She sits suddenly on a pile of bed linen.*]

MELANIE: You don't know how I've envied you having Wade! [*She sits beside* SCARLETT *and takes her hand.*] I've wanted a baby so! And I was afraid I mightn't ever have one! [*A sound from* SCARLETT, *a sound only, but* MELANIE *does not rightly read the wild dismay of her look.*] I know you're surprised! Oh, Scarlett, how shall I ever write Ashley?

BELOW: *Another out-take from Selznick's cutting-room rejects. Sam Wood is shown in the center of the picture. At the left is Pearl Adams, stand-in and sometime double for Hattie McDaniel. At the right is Harry Davenport.*

It wouldn't be so embarrassing if I could tell him! Did you write Charlie when you found out about Wade Hampton? [SCARLETT *rises suddenly.*] Darling, don't look like that!

SCARLETT [*violently*]: Hush up! Will you hush up?

MELANIE [*rises, stricken with remorse*]: Oh, Scarlett, I'm so stupid! I guess all happy people are stupid! I forgot about Charlie!

SCARLETT: I tell you, hush up! [*She sits weakly on the dirty clothes hamper.*]

MELANIE [*goes to her*]: Don't try working today. [*She reaches to a shelf for a bottle of lotion.*] Let me rub your head for you.

SCARLETT: You leave me alone! Go away and leave me alone!

*Baffled and hurt,* MELANIE *backs away towards the window.*

MELANIE: It's hot in here. I'll . . . I'll just open . . .

*Suiting the action to the word, she opens the window. A chord of music, and she stands transfixed by what she sees outside.*

EXTERIOR–THE HOSPITAL–DAY

*FROM* MELANIE'S *ANGLE show* MISS PITTY *in her carriage at the curb outside, while* DR. MEADE *stands beside her, holding in his hand a telegraph blank.* MISS PITTY *is weeping bitterly, so is* UNCLE PETER. DR. MEADE *is seen to urge her to calm herself and to wave* UNCLE PETER *to drive off. Then* DR. MEADE, *still studying the telegram and deeply troubled, turns back toward the hospital.*

INTERIOR–THE NURSES' RETIRING ROOM

SCARLETT *and* MELANIE *as before.* MELANIE *turns from the window. A giddy pause, then, forgetting* SCARLETT'S *existence, she runs out through another door, not into the ward, but into an adjoining room.* SCARLETT *stares after her, dumbfounded.*

THE HOSPITAL–DR. MEADE'S OFFICE

*An improvised office: a desk and chair, doctor's equipment of the period, and an operating table which, presumably, the doctor uses for examinations.* DR. MEADE, *entering by one door, finds himself face to face with* MELANIE, *who has just entered by the other.*

DR. MEADE: Melanie, my dear!

MELANIE [*close to him*]: You don't have to beat about the bush, Dr. Meade. [*She points to the telegram in his hand.*] Isn't that meant for me?

DR. MEADE: You're a brave girl, Melanie. You must be brave now. [*He hands her the telegram.*] It might be worse, you know. He's only missing. Here, I'll get you a glass of water.

MELANIE [*stupendous self-control*]: I'm all right, Dr. Meade. I'm all right.

DR. MEADE: I was a fool to let your aunt's carriage go. I'll get mine to take you home. [*He goes out.*]

*Neither of them has seen that* SCARLETT *has followed* MELANIE *into the room. Now she steps forward.*

SCARLETT: Missing? Missing?

MELANIE [*shakes her head*]: I know my darling is dead.

*Then* SCARLETT *breaks completely. She flings herself sobbing across the operating table.* MELANIE *goes to her to comfort her.*

MELANIE: You mustn't cry, Scarlett! I've got to be calm. I've got to take care of myself for the baby's sake! [*But her knees are none too steady and she drops with the weeping* SCARLETT *at the foot of the table.*] At least I've got his baby!

SCARLETT: And I've got nothing! Nothing! . . . Nothing!

*FADE OUT*


*FADE IN:*

Atlanta prayed while onward
surged the triumphant Yankees. . . .

Heads were high but hearts were
heavy, as the wounded and the
refugees poured into unhappy Georgia. . . .


HOSPITAL NIGHT SCENE

INTERIOR–HOSPITAL IN CHURCH–NIGHT

*THE CAMERA, TRUCKING, enters the front door of the church, and, as a worshiper would in times of peace, comes slowly down the center aisle: toward a light which burns at the far end of the aisle, illuminating the altar and two women's figures who are bending, motionless, over an indistinct vagueness in the shadows under the altar. Their attitudes are queerly religious—macabre and pitiful in that place.*

*Slowly we reveal that the center aisle of the church is lined and crowded with beds now: beds of all descriptions commandeered from the homes of Atlanta—from the sagging, ugly iron bedsteads with cracked and peeling paint taken from the shacks of Negroes and poor white trash to one enormous and baronial canopied bed from a mansion. This magnificent bed has in it a bearded and ugly common*

*soldier, smoking a corncob pipe whose intermittent glow lights his*
*suffering face at lonely, painful intervals in the darkness. Next to him, a*
*busted, sagging cot holds a thin form, and a fine, aristocratic face is*
*on the pillow, with closed eyes—and the hat and sword of an officer*
*have been dumped on the foot of the cot.*

*The whole scene of the beds is dimly lit from unseen sources, and*
*enormous, looming shadows move vaguely on the walls. From some-*
*where, a man's voice, high-pitched and terribly tense, is saying—almost*
*chanting—words which, as the CAMERA enters and trucks slowly, are*
*indistinct. And from the beds, continuously, come the awful night*
*sounds of that place, running underneath that one voice in a litany of*
*pain.*

*As CAMERA comes steadily down the aisle, nearer and nearer to*
*the pulpit, the light there is revealed as the wavering flame of an old*
*kerosene lamp, the figures become* MELANIE *and* SCARLETT; *and they*
*are bending over a bed, from which that high-pitched, chanting voice*
*is coming.* SCARLETT *is busy with bandages.*

[*NOTE:* MELANIE *has a towel pinned around her head, like a coif.*]

THE VOICE [*gradually becoming more and more distinct*]: —and
there's a place there where a wild plum tree comes to flower in the
springtime. Down by the creek, you know. And at sundown you can
stand there and see the little rings the fish make when they come up
to feed, and maybe if you're real quiet, you'll see a white-tail buck
come out of the woods to drink. And then, pretty soon, when you
smell the woodsmoke comin' across the fields, you pick up your creel
and sling it over your shoulder and go home to supper. You . . . go
home . . .

MELANIE [*soothingly, like trying to quiet a fretful child in the*
*night*]: Yes, I know—I know . . .

*THE CAMERA is now there and has stopped, very close, making*
*a TWO SHOT of* MELANIE *and* SCARLETT *against the altar. Their*
*shadows are enormous against the altar. They look at each other as the*
*voice goes on.* MELANIE *bites her lip, and then looks down again at the*
*unseen man in the bed.* SCARLETT *is watching* MELANIE's *face curiously.*

THE VOICE [*beginning to wander a little in delirium*]: When we
were little, it was there that my brother Jeff and I used to . . . I told
you about my brother, Jeff, didn't I, ma'am? . . . I *know* I did. He
. . . we don't know where Jeff is, now, ma'am. Since Bull Run, we
haven't heard anything and . . . but, when we were little, Jeff and I
used to play down there and . . .

MELANIE: Please, major . . . We *must* have your temperature now.

Please do just take this in your mouth and not talk any more. Not just now.

*She stoops, with the thermometer in her hand, and finally straightens up, looking again at* SCARLETT.

THE VOICE [*mumbling over the thermometer*]: . . . we played we were knights of the Roundtable, Jeff and I . . . and we went a-dragon-slaying . . .

*With this, the voice trails off into an awful, stertorous breathing.*

SCARLETT [*finishing ravelling the bandages*]: Melanie—I'm so tired. I've *got* to go home. Aren't you tired, Melanie?

MELANIE [*smiling a little with anguish*]: No . . . I'm not tired. This could be . . . Ashley. And only a stranger here to comfort him. I'm not tired, Scarlett.

*Tears come to* SCARLETT'S *eyes.* MELANIE *turns and looks out, over all the beds, from which the night sounds are coming.*

MELANIE: They could all—be Ashley, Scarlett . . . and . . .

*The two women look at each other for a moment. Then* MELANIE *stoops again, followed by her shadow on the altar and takes the thermometer from the mouth now silent except for the breathing.*

*As she straightens up, holding the thermometer in both hands to read it, bowing her head a little to read it, CAMERA PANS UPWARD, and her shadow on the pulpit's face is like that of a saint, bowing its head over folded hands.*

FADE OUT SLOWLY

INTERIOR–HOSPITAL IN CHURCH–NIGHT (JULY 1864)–*CLOSE SHOT*–STAINED GLASS WINDOW OF A RELIGIOUS TABLEAU

*A shell bursts outside, lighting up the sky. The reverberation shakes the window, cracks it, and a piece of glass with one of the religious figures on it falls out.*

*CAMERA PANS DOWN to* DR. MEADE, *with* SCARLETT *and a Medical Corps* SERGEANT *behind him, in the main room of the church which has been turned into a hospital. The* SERGEANT *is in full uniform with a blood-stained apron over him and his sleeves turned back from his wrist. Beds, almost touching each other, are crowded together—almost more than the church can hold. In them lie the wounded and dying, who scream out in terror, frightened by the explosion:*

AD LIBS FROM MEN: The Yankees! . . . The Yankees are coming! . . .

SCARLETT [*trembling*]: Dr. Meade! [*Another explosion heard from outside.*] The Yankees! They're getting closer!

DR. MEADE [*wearily, but very calm*]: They'll never get into Atlanta. They won't get through old Peg-Leg Hood.

*CAMERA TRAVELS WITH* MEADE, SCARLETT, *and the* SERGEANT, *as they walk through the wounded and dying men toward the nave of the church. Unkempt and staring men are tossing, moaning, and crying out. The place swarms with flies. Bandages and rags lie beside the beds. The room is lighted by smoking kerosene lamps. Only a few doctors and orderlies and women volunteer nurses are in attendance. Huge and grotesque shadows of the patients line the walls. As they pass, we pick up some of the background action and hear en route, the lines indicated below:*

DR. MEADE *stops at one bed, lifts up the man's bandaged arm and briefly instructs the nurse standing by:*

DR. MEADE: Have this tourniquet loosened.

*A man's voice is heard crying, ghastly and ghostly:*

SOLDIER [*crying out*]: Gimme somethin' fo' the pain! Somethin' fo' the pain!

DR. MEADE *calls back to the man who is obviously in agony—his neck bandaged with bloodstained cloths as if he had been shot through the throat.*

DR. MEADE: Sorry, son. We haven't anything to give you.

*A man in one bed—his head swathed in bandages. From under these wrappings a thin stream of blood flows down his cheek. He tosses his head from side to side, trying to shake off the flies and mosquitoes. A nurse at his bedside waves a wisp made of newspaper over his head. A soldier with bandaged and bound arms, scratching his back against a pillar, like an animal.*

SOLDIER: These animules are driving me crazy.

*An Episcopalian Chaplain, his own arm in a sling, sits at a bedside next to the pillar, giving a man a glass of water. A young soldier dictating a letter to a woman who sits beside him writing on a block of paper with a lead pencil, her work lit by a kerosene lamp around which moths are fluttering. With one hand she brushes them away from the soldier. As* DR. MEADE, SCARLETT, *and* SERGEANT *pass, we hear some of the soldier's words:*

DYING SOLDIER: —that I will never see you nor Pa again—

*A grave-faced, bearded man reading quietly from a prayerbook— undisturbed by two battered veterans sitting up in the next beds playing seven-up.*

CARD PLAYERS: What luck, you've got my Jack! . . . Give me an ace, and I'll start another war. . . . I'll bid the Moon! . . .

SCARLETT, DR. MEADE, *and the* SERGEANT *have reached the nave of the church.*

SERGEANT [*as they approach a bed*]: This man just came in, Doctor. His leg.

*THE CAMERA STOPS BEHIND A FOREGROUND PIECE of a pulpit which hides the wounded man. We see only the heads and shoulders of* MEADE, SCARLETT, *and the* SERGEANT *as* MEADE *bends over to make his examination.*

MEADE [*to the wounded man, looking up*]: That leg'll have to come off, soldier.

SCARLETT, *horrified, steps a little aside.*

SOLDIER'S VOICE [*terrorized*]: No . . . no . . . Lemme alone!

MEADE: Sorry, soldier.

SERGEANT [*frightened*]: We're all run out o' chloroform, Dr. Meade.

MEADE: Then we'll have to operate without it.

*CLOSE-UP–*SCARLETT–*Reacting in disgust and horror.*

SOLDIER'S VOICE [*moaning*]: No. No. Lemme alone. You can't do it! I won't let you do it to me!

MEADE *and* SERGEANT

MEADE: Tell Dr. Wilson to take that leg off immediately. It's gangrene. [*Wearily passes his hand over his forehead.*] I haven't seen my family in three days. I'm going home for half an hour.

*As the Sergeant steps forward to lift the soldier from the bed,* DR. MEADE *turns out of scene.*

*CLOSE SHOT–*SCARLETT

*A soldier who is very young with a boyish face, calls out to* SCARLETT *as she passes:*

SOLDIER: Where's ma' mammy? You said you was goin' to bring ma' mammy.

SCARLETT [*dully*]: She's on her way. She'll be here.

SOLDIER'S VOICE [*as* SCARLETT *passes on*]: I want her. I want her.

CUT TO

*TRUCKING SHOT with* DR. MEADE–*nearer the other end of the room, on his way out. His attention is attracted by the attitude of a patient in a bed. He steps over, lifts the eyelids of the unconscious man. He is dead.*

MEADE: You can free this bed, nurse.

*FOLLOW WITH* DR. MEADE *as he goes out the door into the ENTRY VESTIBULE.*

*There, approaching a table at one side, is a line of men—the walking wounded—men with bandaged arms and heads, on crutches, in nightshirts of various degrees of uniform undress. As each man comes up to the table a young boy in butternut with a flour-sacking apron gives him a spoonful of medicine from a big bowl. The same spoon is used for all.*

DR. MEADE *pauses at another makeshift table in the center of the vestibule at which an old colored woman stands rolling bandages.*

DR. MEADE [*picking up a roll of gray-looking cloth*]: Do you call these bandages?

NEGRESS: Yessah—leastways we pulled the buttons off 'em.

MEADE *shakes his head, shrugs, and continues on toward door.*

CUT BACK TO

SCARLETT–*standing by two beds with a pan of water. In one of the beds lies an unkempt, ugly looking man. In the other, a youngish soldier lies moaning.*

FIRST SOLDIER [*the ugly one*]: Make him stop moanin', will you, Miss? I'm tryin' to sleep. . . .

SCARLETT: I've got to wash your wound.

FIRST SOLDIER: What for? Ye can't keep them lice off me. They come crawlin' out o' nowhere like the Yankees. [*The other soldier moans.*] Make him stop moanin', I tell you. I wanna sleep.

SCARLETT: Lie still.

*She starts uncovering his shoulder to unbandage and wash the wound.*

FIRST SOLDIER: Vomitin'—that's all he's been doin'! Vomitin' and moanin'. I wanna sleep.

SCARLETT *is busy with the bandage. The Second Soldier speaks softly.*

SECOND SOLDIER [*the boyish one*]: Put yo' hand on ma face fo' just a bit, lady . . . on ma face here, where it hurts. . . . [*He moans.*] [SCARLETT *turns around. She puts her hand on his face.*]

SECOND SOLDIER [*faintly*]: Thank you, ma'am. Goodnight, lady. . . . [*He closes his eyes and is silent.*]

*The Medical Corps* SERGEANT *seen previously with* DR. MEADE *and* SCARLETT *comes up. He looks at the young man who has stopped moaning now.*

SERGEANT: I guess he's out of the war—fo' good. [*draws the sheet over his face*].

SCARLETT *starts to scream out when she realizes the man is dead— puts her hand over her mouth and stops herself.*

FIRST SOLDIER: That's mo' like it. Now I can git some sleep. I ain't slept since the fight at Peachtree Creek.

*FOLLOW* SCARLETT *as she passes to the next bed and automatically stoops to put down the water bowls and begin washing the wounded man lying in it. We see it is* FRANK KENNEDY. *A bandage around his jaw partially obscures the Burnside whiskers, now ragged and dirty; but we see clearly that his face is lined and his hair and beard, such as we see of it, have thin streaks of gray. The war has taken a terrible toll from him.*

*Looking up at* SCARLETT, FRANK *speaks with difficulty:*

KENNEDY: Miss Scarlett—

SCARLETT [*recognizing him*]: Why—Frank Kennedy—!

KENNEDY: Miss Suellen—is she well?

SCARLETT: Oh, fine, Frank, fine—and she'll be so glad to hear I've seen you.

*She wets a rag in the water and brings it toward his face. He weakly pushes her hand away.*

KENNEDY: I can't—can't let you wash me, Miss Scarlett—

SCARLETT: Fiddle-dee-dee, Frank, why I've—

*The* SERGEANT *comes into the scene.*

SERGEANT [*to* SCARLETT]: Dr. Wilson needs you in the operating room, Mrs. Hamilton. He's going to take off that leg. Better hurry. . . .

SCARLETT *turns away.*

*FOLLOW* SCARLETT–*to the door outside the small adjacent room which is used as the operating room.*

*As she comes to the door she hears piercing cries from inside.*

OPERATING ROOM [*FROM* SCARLETT'*s ANGLE*]

*The operation is in progress, but we see it only in tremendous shadows on the wall: the doctor with scalpel in hand and the screaming patient.*

SOLDIER'S VOICE [*howling*]: No! . . . No . . . lemme alone! No! No . . . I can't stand it! No, no!

*The doctor adjusts the shade on the hanging lamp and the whole scene goes green.*

*CLOSE SHOT*–SCARLETT

*She hesitates an instant, stands in the doorway looking. The agonized cries of the man sweep over her. She stands frozen with the horror of the picture.*

MAN'S VOICE: Don't cut. Don't cut. No. No. . . . Don't cut. . . . Don't! Don't. . . . Oh, my God. . . . My God!

SCARLETT *lets out a bloodcurdling scream. She turns and begins to run. Another explosion reverberates. The* SERGEANT *appears again, running after her:*

SERGEANT: Mrs. Hamilton, hurry! Dr. Wilson is waiting!

SCARLETT [*grimly—and with terror and disgust edging her voice*]: Let him wait. I'm going home. I've done enough. I don't want any more men dying and screaming. I don't want any more! [*She runs out.*]

# Fourth
# Sequence

*ADE IN:*

INTERIOR–MISS PITTY'S HOUSE–THE DINING ROOM–
RAIN–DAY

*Music and an explosion of artillery, and the three women—*SCAR-
LETT, MELANIE, *and* MISS PITTY—*at the table, sit listening.* COOKIE, *in
the act of passing some breakfast dish, also stands listening. The door
from the kitchen opens, and* UNCLE PETER *and* PRISSY *enter. They pause
there and listen. Then the sound comes again. Another distant detonation of artillery.* WADE HAMPTON *begins to cry.* SCARLETT *rises and goes
out.*

THE HALL

*Music and* SCARLETT *enters, opens the front door, and looks out.
Troops are marching by along Peachtree Street.*

EXTERIOR–PEACHTREE STREET

*CAMERA, from* SCARLETT'S *angle, is closer to the troops and shows
them now as they are: old men and boys, and all of them ragged. A
group of old men passes last.*

PEACHTREE STREET IN FRONT OF MRS. MERRIWETHER'S
HOUSE

*From* SCARLETT'S *angle,* GRANDPA MERRIWETHER *comes through the
gate of the house across the street, in an oddly assorted ancient and
modern uniform.* MRS. MERRIWETHER *fastens a shawl around his
shoulders. He walks forward into the CAMERA, his jaw set. She stands
looking after him.*

PEACHTREE STREET IN FRONT OF MRS. MEADE'S HOUSE

MRS. MEADE, *forcing back the tears, bids young* PHIL MEADE, *also
in uniform, goodbye. He walks joyously toward CAMERA, his mother
looking after him.*

PEACHTREE STREET IN FRONT OF MISS PITTY'S HOUSE

*The soldiers are marching by in front of Miss Pitty's house.* SCAR-
LETT *enters.*

SCARLETT [*to an older officer on a horse*]: Excuse me, sir . . .
[*Another detonation of artillery.*] That's not cannon, is it? It can't be
cannon! [*The older officer, reining in his horse, looks down at her. She
recognizes him.*] Mr. Wilkes!

JOHN WILKES: *HALT!* Company *HALT!* [*His detachment halts.*]
I had hoped to see you, Scarlett. I was charged with so many messages
from your people. But they're rushing us out.

SCARLETT *has seized his hand and clutches it desperately.*

SCARLETT: Oh, Mr. Wilkes, are things so bad we've got to send old men out to fight for us?

JOHN WILKES [*he smiles*]: What better way could an old man die than doing a young man's work? Let me kiss your pretty face. [SCARLETT *turns her face up to his. He kisses her lightly.*] And you must deliver this kiss to Aunt Pittypat and this to Melanie.

*Two more kisses, but* SCARLETT *draws back.*

SCARLETT: Wait! Wait! I'll call Melly out! [*She runs toward the house out of scene, calling:*] Melly! Melly!

*But already the troops are crowding up behind John Wilkes's detachment, and the officer in command of them rides up to* JOHN WILKES.

THE OFFICER: What's holding things up?

JOHN WILKES: Nothing, Captain. [*He smiles again.*] I should have liked to see my daughter-in-law. But then I should like to see my first grandchild, too. [*and to his detachment*] Company, *FORWARD MARCH!*

*The detachment resumes its progress out of the scene,* JOHN WILKES *riding out with them.*

MISS PITTY'S HOUSE—THE FRONT DOOR

SCARLETT *and* MELANIE *come out of the house.* MELANIE *runs down the steps calling:*

MELANIE: Mr. Wilkes! Mr. Wilkes!

SCARLETT *follows her, and the CAMERA follows* SCARLETT.

SCARLETT: Stop, Melly! Melly, you mustn't run!

MELANIE *turns to the gate as* SCARLETT *comes up to her.*

MELANIE: He's gone!

*She bursts into tears on* SCARLETT's *shoulder as* SCARLETT *holds her close. More troops are passing and the CAMERA PANS along the street to Dr. Meade's house, where a group of men are standing on the curbstone, among them* DR. MEADE *and* RHETT BUTLER.

DR. MEADE [*to the crowd*]: They'll stop the Yankees! They'll stand as the Spartans stood at Thermopylae!

*Murmurs of assent, then:*

RHETT: The Spartans died to the last man at Thermopylae.

DR. MEADE *glares at him. Among the troops that are passing through the rain show one old gentleman walking with a cane, unarmed, his Negro servant trotting beside him, holding an umbrella over his head.*

*DISSOLVE TO*

PEACHTREE STREET IN FRONT OF MISS PITTY'S HOUSE

UGa Libraries, Kurtz Photographs.

ABOVE: *Extras play the rag-tag, bob-tailed soldiers called into the Georgia Militia to help defend Atlanta against Sherman and his Federal troops. Mr. Kurtz's photograph of them is undated but was probably taken early in April 1939.* BELOW: *His snapshot of Clark Gable with his back to the camera was made April 1.*

UGa Libraries, Kurtz Photographs.

*The rain has ceased.* WADE HAMPTON *crouches on the porch, peering through the balustrade at the scene beyond. Artillery and munitions are rattling past Miss Pitty's house down the street. In the opposite direction a line of wounded straggles along the sidewalk. Music and detonations of artillery.*

*CAMERA MOVES FORWARD. The lawn is covered with prostrate men, too tired to walk further, too weak from wounds to move.* SCARLETT, MELANIE, MISS PITTY, PRISSY, COOKIE, *and* UNCLE PETER *work among them, tearing sheets into bandages with which to tie up wounds, dipping out water from buckets to quench desperate thirst. In the street itself, the marching of the outward bound troops is complicated by the passage, also from the opposite direction, of farm wagons, ox carts and even private carriages, commandeered by the medical corps to carry the wounded. At the sight of buckets and dippers the conveyances halt and a chorus goes up in cries and whispers:*

VOICES: Water. . . . Water, for the love of heaven! . . .

SCARLETT *is picked up, fairly shaking a wounded man.*

SCARLETT: What's the news? Can't you tell us the news?

WOUNDED MAN: News, Miss? What news?

SCARLETT: The battle? How's it going? Are we driving 'em back?

WOUNDED MAN: Now it's hard to be sartin of that, lady.

ANOTHER WOUNDED MAN: Can't tell nothin' much about battles, when you're in 'em.

SCARLETT *moves away distracted, through the crowding wounded.*

VOICES: Yes'm, them Yankees is comin' all right. . . . Shut up, you fool! Do you want to scare the ladies? . . . Don't fret, Miss, they can't take Atlanta. . . . No, ma'am, we got a million miles of breastworks round this town. . . . Whyn't you ladies go ter Macon or somewheres that's safer . . . It ain't goin' ter be so healthy for ladies here. . . . There's goin' ter be a powerful lot of shellin'. . . . We've got to fall back. . . . They outnumber us by thousands. . . .

*The CAMERA concentrates upon a* SOLDIER *who is supporting an exhausted comrade.*

THE SOLDIER [*to* SCARLETT]: Missy, I got a pardner here who I was aimin' ter git ter the horspittle, but looks like he ain't goin' ter last that fer.

SCARLETT: I don't know where we can put him!

*CAMERA concentrates on another group, consisting of* MELANIE *and a* SECOND SOLDIER.

SECOND SOLDIER: Lady, I shore could do with some vittles. I'd shore relish a corn pone if it didn't deprive you none.

MELANIE: I'll see what I can find. [*She turns toward the house. An* OFFICER *accosts her.*]

OFFICER: Madam, forgive my intrusion, but . . . [*He smiles and crumples on the lawn in a dead faint.*]

MELANIE: Oh!

*But* MISS PITTY *is there to kneel beside him.*

MISS PITTY: Melanie, it's the queerest thing, but I've quite forgotten that the sight of blood always makes me faint!

SCARLETT *is passing.*

THE STREET IN FRONT OF MISS PITTY'S HOUSE

*An ox cart is drawn up at the curb. It is piled with bodies. One of them—not the uppermost—is the handsome young captain who accosted* JOHN WILKES.

VOICES: Water! . . . Water! . . .

SCARLETT [*she enters*]: Can any of *you* tell me how the battle's going?

YOUNG OFFICER: Water! Water!

SCARLETT: Why, it's Captain Randall!

YOUNG OFFICER: Water! . . . Get me out! . . .

SCARLETT *reaches to his shoulders to pull him, but the bodies above make it impossible to extract him. Then his head falls back. She sees that he is dead. She shrinks back in horror. The ox cart drives on out of the scene.*

SCARLETT: Oh, Ashley! Ashley! [*She drops on the curb, her head between her hands, sobbing.*]

*DISSOLVE TO*

THE STREET IN FRONT OF THE "EXAMINER" OFFICE–NIGHT

*It is early evening, and the streets are still filled with people. A shell screams overhead. The crowd runs in panic. The shell explodes, felling three or four.*

*DISSOLVE TO*

A HOUSE IN THE RESIDENCE DISTRICT

*The scream of another shell. It strikes the roof of the house, destroying the chimney. CAMERA PANS quickly down the wall of the house to show the father and mother of the family with their children, just out of bed, struggling down into the cellar.*

*DISSOLVE TO*

PEACHTREE STREET–DAY

*Again the scream of a shell. This one strikes a large tree, which is felled. Out of the cloud of dust a line of Negro troops appears march-*

*ing toward the CAMERA. As they pass, one of the Negroes*—BIG SAM—
*breaks ranks, shouting:*

BIG SAM: Lawsy, Miss Scarlett! You, 'Lige! 'Postle! Prophet!

SCARLETT *has entered to meet* BIG SAM *and three other big Negroes.
An officer rides in.*

OFFICER: Better get back in line, you boys.

SCARLETT: Oh, Captain, don't scold them! They're our people. This
is Big Sam, our foreman, and Elijah and Apostle and Prophet from
Tara! [*and back to the Negroes:*] What are you boys doing so far from
Tara? Why aren't you home taking care of Father and Mother?

*She is shaking hands all around, her small, white hand disappear-
ing into their huge, black paws.*

BIG SAM: Dey done sont an' tuck us, Miss Scarlett! 'Kase us wuz de
fo' bigges' an' stronges' han's at Tara!

SCARLETT: Took you, Sam?

BIG SAM: Yass'm, Miss Scarlett! Dey tuck all dey han's!

SCARLETT: Took the hands from Tara? Who's working the plantation?

BIG SAM: Ain't nobuddy lef' ter work de plantation, Miss Scarlett.
Ain't nobuddy lef' in de house but Pork an' Dilcey an' Mammy!

SCARLETT: You shouldn't have left Mother now, Sam!

BIG SAM: Us is ter dig de ditches fo' de w'ite gempmums ter hide
in w'en de Yankees comes.

SCARLETT [*she turns to the Captain*]: Captain, what does he mean?

CAPTAIN: We have to strengthen the fortifications of Atlanta. The
general can't spare any men from the front to do it. Keep moving, men!

*Cries of "Goodbye, Miss Scarlett," from the Negroes as they rejoin
their ranks and the detachment moves out of the scene. But* SCARLETT
*runs a step or so after the* CAPTAIN.

SCARLETT: They're not falling back again!

CAPTAIN: Don't you worry, Miss. General Johnston says he can hold
Atlanta forever.

*The street, cleared, shows* MRS. MERRIWETHER *and her daughter,*
MAYBELLE, *as their house servants are piling them and their luggage
into a two-horse carriage.*

MRS. MERRIWETHER: Goodbye, Scarlett. Say goodbye to Pitty for
me! I'm glad to see she has come to her senses and is leaving, too! If
there's going to be a siege, we've all got to get out while we can!

*A shell exploding, much nearer, frightens* MRS. MERRIWETHER'S
*horses and the carriage lurches out of the scene in the direction oppo-
site to that taken by the Negroes. A low sound from* SCARLETT. *Turning*

*back to the house, she passes* PRISSY *and* UNCLE PETER *and her aunt's carriage.* UNCLE PETER *is quieting the single horse with an assortment of the soothing sounds usually employed, while* PRISSY, *in a dither, heaps bundles and hampers into the carriage.* SCARLETT *breaks into a run at the walk to the house, the* CAMERA *following her.*

SCARLETT: If they're all going, I'm going too! I'm going back to Tara where I belong! I'm going back to my mother! [*She disappears through the front door.*]

INTERIOR–MISS PITTY'S HOUSE–MELANIE'S BEDROOM–DAY

MELANIE *sits in a big chair.* DR. MEADE *stands beside her.* MISS PITTY *stands nearby. Her agitation is intense.*

DR. MEADE: It's out of the question for her to go with you, Pitty. You go alone and leave the young ladies here!

MISS PITTY: Without any chaperon?

DR. MEADE: Good heavens, woman, this is wartime! And haven't they got Mrs. Meade next door?

MISS PITTY: Oh, I know, but it hardly seems the judicious thing to do!

*Another shell, nearer this time, and* MISS PITTY *squeals with terror.* DR. MEADE *pushes her through the door.*

DR. MEADE: Get along with you now! You're only upsetting Melly!

MISS PITTY *stammers goodbyes as* SCARLETT *appears in the hall outside.*

SCARLETT: But if I were to take Melly to Tara with me! They need me at Tara! My mother needs me, doctor! And I need my mother!

DR. MEADE: Would you want her to have her baby in a buggy? She stays right here where I can watch her! [MISS PITTY *has disappeared below stairs. He calls back to* MELANIE.] And in bed, too! No running down stairs to cellars! Not even if shells come right in the window!

*He goes.* SCARLETT *is following.*

MELANIE: Oh, Scarlett! [SCARLETT *comes distractedly back to her.* MELANIE *catches her hand.*] Don't you go to Tara and leave me, Scarlett! I'll die if you aren't with me when the baby comes! You promised Ashley you'd take care of me!

SCARLETT *jerks her hand free roughly and stares down at* MELANIE *with all the dislike of which she is capable.*

SCARLETT: I know I did. And I don't go back on my promises to Ashley. [*She goes out.*]

THE HALL

SCARLETT, *entering from Melanie's room, encounters* PRISSY.

PRISSY: You don' have ter be askeered fo' nothin', Miss Scarlett. Ah knows all 'bout birthin' babies. Ain' mah ma a midwife? Ain' she raise me ter be a midwife, too?

SCARLETT: It's a great comfort to hear that, Prissy. A great comfort. *She starts for the stair. The front door slams below. She stops. CAMERA looks down the stair with her into the empty hall, strewn with the litter of departure.* WADE HAMPTON *stands whimpering at the foot of the stair.*

SCARLETT [*to* PRISSY]: Go down and shut Wade Hampton up. And clean up that litter.

PRISSY: Yass'm, Miss Scarlett. [*She starts down the stair.*] Don' you be troubled fer nothin'. [*A few steps and she stops—then*] It's empty, Miss Scarlett. Dis house shure is empty!

SCARLETT [*on edge*]: Go on, Prissy! Do as I tell you!

*A few more steps—the pause filled by* WADE HAMPTON's *whimpering—and* PRISSY *looks up again.*

PRISSY: We all alone, Miss Scarlett! [*And her wails augment* WADE HAMPTON's.]

SCARLETT: We are alone. [*She turns savagely towards Melanie's door.*] And it's your fault, and I hope you die for it! [*Then, suddenly penitent, frightened and superstitious all at once*] Oh, I didn't mean that! [*She looks up to heaven for forgiveness.*]

FADE OUT


FADE IN:

# SIEGE

The skies rained Death. . . .

For thirty-five days a battered
Atlanta hung grimly on, hoping
for a miracle. . . .

Then there fell a silence . . .
more terrifying than the pounding
of the cannon. . . .

*FADE IN:*

EXTERIOR–PEACHTREE STREET–NIGHT

*The cannonade, if any, is only faintly audible. The street is now completely deserted except for* RHETT BUTLER, *who saunters along toward Miss Pitty's house—wide-brimmed Panama hat and long cigar, more than usually debonair.*

MISS PITTY'S HOUSE–THE PORCH

SCARLETT *sits in a rocker, her hands clenching the arms, clearly under a more than usually heavy strain. The porch is lighted from the windows of the drawing room behind. The gate clicks off-screen. She looks up sharply and sees* RHETT *as he speaks.*

RHETT: Good evening.

SCARLETT: Oh, it's you, is it? [*He comes up the steps into the scene.*] Yes, I've stayed. And I'm so lonely I'm even glad to see you. [RHETT *has perched himself on the porch rail opposite her. She continues with a shudder.*] Are all sieges as quiet as this?

RHETT: I don't know that there's any rule about sieges. The enemy doesn't camp under the city walls in a modern war. Sherman might have taken Atlanta by storm of course. But that would have been costly and Sherman's no fool. So he's surrounding the city at a comfortable distance. When his circle's closed, the city will fall and our troops will surrender. Unless, that is, they can forget their Southern gallantry in time to get out before he's cut off their last road of escape. [*He swings round to seat himself beside her.*] Why didn't you go? All the best people have gone. To be sure, there are still several thousand ordinary residents of the less aristocratic parts of town. . . .

SCARLETT: I wanted to go! I wanted to go home to Tara to my mother! [*She concludes desperately.*] I couldn't leave Melanie!

RHETT, *on his feet, is horrified.*

RHETT: You don't mean to tell me that Mrs. Wilkes is still here? I never heard of such idiocy! This is no place for her in her condition!

SCARLETT: A nice bachelor wouldn't speak about her condition, and if the Yankees do come, she won't be in any worse danger than me!

RHETT: I'd back you against the Yankees any day.

SCARLETT: I'm not sure that's a compliment.

RHETT: It isn't. When will you stop looking for compliments?

SCARLETT: On my deathbed.

RHETT, *leaning against an upright post of the porch, inspects his long cigar, pulls on it once or twice to revive it, then glances quizzically in* SCARLETT's *direction.*

RHETT: So you've stayed with Mrs. Wilkes! This is the strangest situation I've ever encountered. I couldn't believe it when I heard it today.

SCARLETT: I see nothing strange about it. She's Charlie's sister and like a sister to me.

RHETT: She's Ashley Wilkes's widow, you mean. But even that . . .

SCARLETT *is on her feet in anger.*

SCARLETT: I was almost on the point of forgiving you for your former boorish conduct, but now I shan't! And you've no right to conclude that Ashley's dead just because he's . . .

*But he has reached out to take her hand and force her back into her chair.*

RHETT: Sit down, Scarlett, and settle your ruffled fur. [*He looks about him.*] What luck to find you with neither protector nor chaperon in the house! [*She giggles nervously but makes no effort to withdraw her hand.*] Don't giggle. [*He turns her hand over and kisses its palm. Then he kisses her wrist.*] Don't pull away. I won't hurt you.

*In spite of herself,* SCARLETT *tastes his caresses with relish.*

SCARLETT: I'm not afraid of you, Rhett Butler! Nor of any man in shoeleather!

RHETT: The sentiment does you credit. But speak a little more softly. You don't want Mrs. Wilkes to hear you, I hope? [*then*] You do like me, don't you?

SCARLETT: Yes—when you aren't acting like a varmint.

RHETT: I think you like me because I am a varmint.

SCARLETT: I like nice men that I can depend on to be gentlemanly.

RHETT: You mean men you can bully. Could you ever love me?

*Her eyes blaze with triumph.*

SCARLETT: No. Not unless you mend your manners.

RHETT: I've no intention of mending them. And it's just as well. Because I don't love you and it would be tragic for you to suffer the pangs of unrequited love twice over.

SCARLETT *has drawn back in some amazement.*

SCARLETT: You dare to tell me you don't love me!

RHETT: Did you hope that I would?

SCARLETT: Don't be so presumptuous!

RHETT: You did hope, of course. I'm sorry to disappoint you. I might love you, but I realize that you still cherish the memory of the godlike and wooden-headed Mr. Wilkes. Still, there should be room in your heart for me. [*But* SCARLETT *is restive.*] Scarlett, do stop wriggling. I'm making a declaration. I've wanted you since the first time I laid eyes on you at Twelve Oaks. I want you more than I've wanted any woman and I've waited longer for you than I've ever waited for any.

*Now* SCARLETT *is really triumphant.*

SCARLETT: Well, I won't marry you! I wouldn't marry you, Rhett, if you were the last . . .

RHETT: Haven't I told you I'm not a marrying man?

SCARLETT: Well, then, what are you driving . . .

RHETT: Why should you and I carry things to the extreme of the marriage service?

SCARLETT [*gasps, then*]: Well, if you mean what I think you do, let me tell you right now there'd be nothing in that for me!

RHETT [*He is delighted.*]: There! That's what I like about you! Any other woman would have shown me the door, but you . . .

*Now* SCARLETT *is on her feet and furious.*

SCARLETT: Well, I will show you the door! I can't put you out because you're out already, but I can go in and slam the door in your face! [*She has opened the front door and faces him from the threshold.*] Go away from this house! And don't you ever come back with your piddling papers of pins and ribbons, thinking I'll forgive you! I won't!

*He picks up his hat and bows; and she sees, in the light from the hall, that he is grinning. Inarticulate with rage, she goes to slam the door in his face. It catches on the edge of the hall rug. He steps forward.*

RHETT: May I help you?

*With his walking stick, he pokes the rug straight.*

SCARLETT: You!

*She does close the door, but her fury has lost a good deal of its force. He stands smiling still and smoking his cigar.*

FADE OUT

FADE IN:

INTERIOR–SCARLETT'S BEDROOM–DAY

*Music.* SCARLETT *lies on her bed asleep. Again the booming of cannon, but this time more distant.* SCARLETT *awakens and sits up uneasily at a distant report. Then,* CAMERA *going close, she is seen to be suddenly terrified. She springs out of bed and, the* CAMERA *following her, runs to the window, struggling into her wrapper as she goes. She stands listening to the distant artillery.*

UPPER HALL

PRISSY *comes up the stair carrying Melanie's breakfast tray. She is singing to herself.*

PRISSY [*singing*]:
>Jes' a few mo' days for ter tote de weary load!
>No matter, 'twill never be light!
>Jes' a few mo' days, till we totter in de road . . .

SCARLETT, *emerging from her bedroom, encounters* PRISSY *at the head of the stair.*

SCARLETT: Shut up that singing, Prissy! And give me that tray. I'll take it in to Miss Melly.

*She has taken the tray from* PRISSY. *The guns again. She knocks on* MELANIE'S *door.*

MELANIE [*from within*]: Come in.

SCARLETT *goes into* MELANIE'S *room.*

MELANIE'S BEDROOM

SCARLETT *is entering.* MELANIE *lifts her head weakly from the pillow.*

MELANIE: Oh, it's you, Scarlett!

*The guns again hold* SCARLETT *listening at the door.*

MELANIE: I'm sorry about the cannon. They're down Tara way now, aren't they?

SCARLETT: Umm.

MELANIE: I know how worried you are. You'd be home with your mother now if it weren't for me, wouldn't you?

SCARLETT: Umm.

MELANIE: Why don't you take Wade Hampton and go back to your mother and just forget about me?

SCARLETT *is tempted, let there be no doubt of that. Then, however:*

SCARLETT: No.

MELANIE: I love you for being so good to me.

SCARLETT: Do you? Well . . . [*She proffers the breakfast tray.* MELANIE *shakes her head.*] What's the matter?

MELANIE *reaches up to lay her hand on* SCARLETT'S.

MELANIE: If I die today, will you take my baby?

*The guns again, and* SCARLETT *turns in agony toward the window.*

SCARLETT: Aren't things bad enough without you talking about dying?

MELANIE: I wish you'd promise me, Scarlett. Because I'm going to have my baby today.

SCARLET [*turning back*]: What makes you say that?

MELANIE: It began at daybreak.

SCARLETT [*terrified*]: Why didn't you call me? [*She sets down the tray and goes back to* MELANIE.] I'll send Prissy right out for Mrs. Meade! She'll know what's going on! [*She goes out.*]

DISSOLVE TO

## THE DINING ROOM

SCARLETT *is feeding* WADE HAMPTON. *Then, because the child's wide, frightened eyes upset her:*

SCARLETT: Stop staring at me like a frightened goat! [PRISSY *enters the hall by the front door.* SCARLETT *turns.*] You're as slow as molasses in January! Where's Mrs. Meade?

PRISSY: Mis' Meade done got wud early dis mownin' dat young Mist' Phil done been shot.

SCARLETT: Oh, no!

PRISSY *nods happily.*

PRISSY: An' Mis' Meade she tuck de cah'ige an' gone ter fetch him home.

SCARLETT: Phil, too!

PRISSY: Mis' Meade ain' gwine ter be studyin' 'bout comin' up hyah today. An' Mis' Meade's Cookie say effen Miss Melly's pain git too bad, jes' you put a knife under her bed an' it cut de pain in two.

SCARLETT: Don't stand there talking like a ninny! Put on a clean apron and go over to the hospital. I'm going to give you a note to Dr. Meade. And if he isn't there give it to one of the other doctors. And if you don't hurry back this time I'll skin you alive!

PRISSY: Yass'm.

SCARLETT *goes into the parlor.*

## PARLOR

SCARLETT *sits at the desk to scribble a note, speaking the while to* PRISSY *in the hall.*

SCARLETT: And ask any of the gentlemen for news of the fighting down Tara way.

PRISSY [*panic-stricken*]: W'at you sayin', Miss Scarlett? De Yankees ain' at Tara, is dey?

SCARLETT: I told you to ask for news!

*She blots the note and rises. But* PRISSY *begins to bawl loudly.*

SCARLETT: Stop bawling! Do you want Miss Melly to hear you? [*Then, as* PRISSY *subsides*] Go change your apron! [*She pushes* PRISSY *out into the dining room and herself starts up the stairs.*]

DISSOLVE TO

## MELANIE'S BEDROOM

MELANIE *as before.* SCARLETT *enters.*

SCARLETT: Mrs. Meade's gone! She's just got word . . . [*She stops herself.*] She's gone over to the hospital, so I sent for the doctor.

MELANIE *smiles.*

ABOVE: *Prissy stands on the set for light and color tests while preparing for never-used scenes of packing for the exodus from Atlanta. A technician may be seen in the left background.*

MELANIE: How long did it take Wade Hampton to get born?

SCARLETT: Less than no time. I was outside and I didn't any more than just get in the house. Mammy said it was scandalous. Like one of the darkies, she said.

MELANIE: I hope I'll be like one of the darkies, too. [*She smiles again.*]

SCARLETT: You'll be all right. I'll get dressed and fetch some cold water and sponge you off. It's going to be hot today. [*And with a rough and impatient efficiency she pats Melanie's pillows into shape.*] Don't worry. We've still got plenty of time.

*DISSOLVE TO*

MELANIE'S BEDROOM

MELANIE'S *eyes are closed and her lips are white.* SCARLETT, *now fully dressed, stands beside her holding her hand tightly, sponging her arm.*

SCARLETT: Don't try to be brave. Yell all you want to. There's no-body to hear. [MELANIE'S *grip relaxes.* SCARLETT *draws back her hand and flexes the cramped fingers. She looks anxiously toward the clock.*] This room's an oven already and it isn't noon yet. [*She goes to close the blinds.*] If I don't take a strap to that Prissy when she gets back! If she gets back! If she hasn't run off and . . .

MELANIE: Please, Scarlett! [SCARLETT *turns.*] The flies.

SCARLETT *picks up a fan and walks back to the bed to fan the flies from* MELANIE'S *face.*

MELANIE: On my feet, too.

*She kicks restlessly.* SCARLETT *pulls the sheet back over* MELANIE'S *feet. Then a sound from out of doors catches her ear. She crosses again to the window.*

MELANIE'S BEDROOM

SCARLETT *stands at the window. From her angle, through the blinds,* PRISSY *is coming down the street, this time at a panic-stricken run.* SCARLETT *turns from the window.*

SCARLETT: I'll . . . I'll go get you some cooler water and bathe you again. [*She darts out through the door.*]

HALL

SCARLETT *is coming down the stairs.* PRISSY *enters, frantic with terror.*

PRISSY: Dey's fightin' at Jonesboro, Miss Scarlett! Dey say our gempmums is gittin' beat! Whut'll happen ter Maw an' Paw effen dey gits ter Tara? Whut'll happen ter us effen dey gits hyah?

SCARLETT: Hush up, will you? Where's Dr. Meade?

PRISSY: Ah ain' nebber seed him, Miss Scarlett!

SCARLETT: Why not?

PRISSY: He ain' at de horspittle! A man tole me de doctah's down by de depot wid de wounded sojers jes' come in from Jonesboro, but, Miss Scarlett, Ah wuz skeered ter go down dar! Dey's folkses dyin' down dar! Ah's skeered of daid folkses! . . .

SCARLETT: All right. I'll go to the depot! And you sit by Miss Melly and do whatever she wants. But if you so much as breathe where the fighting is I will skin you alive. [*She has clapped her green bonnet on her head and is tying the strings as she turns to the door.*] And don't tell her the other doctors won't come, either! [*She goes out, slamming the door after her.*]

*DISSOLVE TO*

EXTERIOR–PEACHTREE STREET IN FRONT OF MISS PITTY'S HOUSE–DAY

*As* SCARLETT *runs down the path from the front steps, a* DESPATCH RIDER *comes galloping along the street. She calls out to him.*

SCARLETT: Oh, stop! Please stop!

*He reins in so suddenly that the horse goes back on his haunches.*

DESPATCH RIDER: Madam?

SCARLETT: Is it true that the Yankees are coming?

DESPATCH RIDER: I'm afraid so, Madam.

SCARLETT: Do you know so?

DESPATCH RIDER: Yes, Madam, I do. The despatch came into headquarters half an hour ago. From the fighting to the south.

SCARLETT [*aghast*]: From the south! Oh, dear!

DESPATCH RIDER: The message said: "We have lost the battle and are in full retreat."

SCARLETT: What shall I do?

DESPATCH RIDER: I can't say. The army will be evacuating Atlanta tonight.

SCARLETT: Going off and leaving us to the Yankees?

DESPATCH RIDER: I'm afraid so. [*He touches his hat and goes.*]

SCARLETT *turns desperately back to the house, hesitates for a moment of agony, then turns and runs down the street.*

*DISSOLVE TO*

ATLANTA–A STREET

*It is a place of shops. The populace is looting. Many women and children carry all manner of goods in their arms and over their shoulders.* SCARLETT, *panting and sweating, forces her way through the crowd. She is almost run over by a woman in her carriage. The woman*

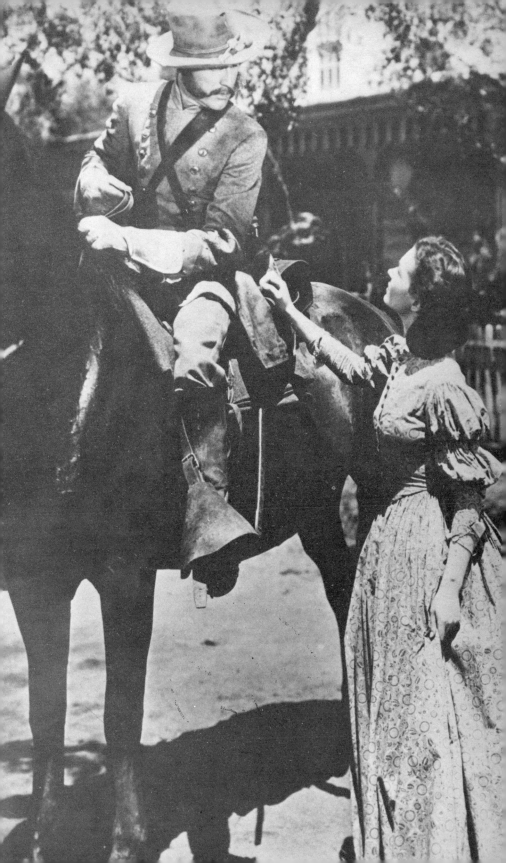

*stands on the coachman's box, whipping her horse through the crowd, while a Negro servant in the backseat tries to hold loot from spilling out. Over all this, like a refrain, the cry Ad Lib:*

VOICES: The Yankees are coming! . . . Let's get it before the Yankees! . . .

DISSOLVE TO

A STREET–THE FRONT OF A SALOON

*Looting by the more disreputable classes is in progress. Prostitutes reel drunkenly out through the door of the saloon and* SCARLETT *barely escapes the crash of a window as she forces her way past them.*

VOICES: The Yankees are coming! . . .

DISSOLVE TO

STREET AT INTERSECTION PEACHTREE AND DECATUR– *CAMERA TRUCKING with* SCARLETT

*The atmosphere of the whole is of terrific heat and sweat.*

*CAMERA IS SET UP to shoot over a pile of fallen timbers and other debris of the siege which blocks the lefthand side of the road.* SCARLETT *comes toward the CAMERA, sees the obstruction, climbs over it or goes around it.*

*A commissary wagon with a torn canvas cover has been crowded out of the road half way up onto the sidewalk. Coming south down Decatur Street, to cross Peachtree Street come troops, both foot and horse, ragged, defeated, but still carrying their arms, still retaining some semblance of military formation and well under the control of their officers. These are "the matchless infantry" in defeat; retreating without panic.*

SCARLETT, *now on the side of the road, has to break through their ranks to go toward the depot. She worms her way through the men who stumble around her as she breaks their ranks.*

*CAMERA STILL MOVES with* SCARLETT *as she continues down Peachtree Street, crossing Decatur, pushing her way through a small crowd of people on the sidewalk. These people are the poor, the hooligans and the riffraff who either have no means or no desire to quit the besieged city. They stand watching the departure of the troops. They are quiet now but when we see them again after the army has left they will be the howling, ravening crowd of looters* SCARLETT *and* RHETT *encounter on their flight from the burning city. As* SCARLETT *comes on the edge of the crowd, a group of people come left, up Decatur Street from the warehouse to the south, bearing all sorts of edibles and supplies and babbling excitedly. In the confusion, above*

*the cracking of whips, the thudding of horses' hoofs, and the march-*
*ing feet of the infantry, we can still distinguish their cries:*

AD LIBS: Go and get it, boys! . . . The warehouse—they've opened
the warehouse—They're giving out food. . . . Get it! . . . Hurry up!
. . . Free food!

*Some of the people surrounding* SCARLETT *turn in the direction from*
*which this rabble is coming, run off to get food. In the stream coming*
*up Decatur Street we see an* OLD MAN *with a wheelbarrow loaded with*
*flour, some* PICKANINNIES *staggering past with overflowing buckets of*
*molasses, two ragged* WHITE BOYS *dragging a sack by its ears, the sack*
*lumpy with potatoes.*

PICKANINNIES: Free 'lasses!

OLD MAN: Flour!

WHITE BOY: Free 'taters!

*Peachtree Street is choked with the troops going south on Decatur*
*across the intersection—wagons, cavalry detachments and guns.*

*Artillery of every description is being hauled out of town. It is a*
*scene of frantic haste. Men and horses subordinate themselves to the*
*need of the guns; infantry and cavalry have to wait their turn. They*
*are less precious to the Confederacy than these irreplaceable cannon.*
*In the course of this, at intervals, two ambulances [can double on the*
*same one] come up Peachtree Street in the opposite direction from*
SCARLETT, *coming from the depot. They make a sharp turn south on*
*Decatur, in same direction as the troops. Guns, caissons, and limbers*
*rattle past. Whips crack, men shout and curse. A battery standard*
*bearer goes flashing past. The only break in the fast moving tide is an*
*ox-drawn stone sledge on which a potbellied siege howitzer has been*
*loaded; a weapon too heavy to be transported on wheels. Its progress*
*across the intersection is slow as men push and strain to help the*
*plodding train of oxen with their load.* SCARLETT, *poised on the curb-*
*ing, thinks she sees her chance to cross, begins to run.*

*MEDIUM SHOT*–SCARLETT

*Just as she crosses in front of the oxen, a light cannon comes thun-*
*dering up on the other side of the oxen. The lead horse on the offside*
*just misses her as the gunner pulls its head over toward his own mount.*
*She gains the opposite curb.*

PEACHTREE STREET BELOW DECATUR

*The street is lined with horse and mule-driven ambulances and men*
*work quickly but silently carrying the wounded on stretchers along*
*the sidewalks and loading them into the lines of ambulances and carts.*

*Extras enact scenes of the evacua-tion of Atlanta. Snapshots taken April 4, 1939. Extra footage of street scenes similar to these were eventually used in* Raintree County. *Snapshots by Wilbur G. Kurtz.*

*Vivien Leigh directs Assistant Director Stacey while Assistant Cameraman Wolf looks on. Property man Arden Cripe tests the driver's seat of a Confederate ambulance. Extras get ready for the scene of the wounded at the Atlanta depot. Cameraman Arthur Arling prepares to ascend in boom. Snapshots taken May 20 and 22, 1939.*

UGa Libraries, Kurtz Photographs.

We see SCARLETT *come down the street. As she nears the depot there is a growing sound of overwhelming pain, a composite tone of anguish; cries, moans, shrieks and terrified curses.*

PEACHTREE STREET

*CLOSE MOVING SHOT–CAMERA SHOOTING TOWARD* SCARLETT *as she walks–TRUCKING AHEAD OF HER*

*We see her puzzlement at the ever-increasing noise. Her steps become slower and slower and a worried frown creases her brow.*

END OF PEACHTREE STREET

*CAMERA SHOOTING toward rear of two ambulances parked almost wheel to wheel. Through this gap comes* SCARLETT *into close foreground and stops aghast. The noise we have heard has reached its height.*

*REVERSE SHOT ON* SCARLETT'S *FACE*

*All the horror and the misery of what we are about to see is reflected in her face.*

PLAZA AND DEPOT

*BIG PULL-BACK SHOT* [Boom]–*in which the CAMERA, DRAWING FARTHER AND FARTHER BACK AND UPWARDS, reveals the vast expanse of the railway yards, close to the depot—completely covered with the bodies of wounded Confederates lying under the hot sun.*

*The CAMERA STOPS on the Confederate flag, hanging limply from the top of the flag pole. Only a handful of male orderlies and women attendants move amongst the wounded, some of whom lie stiff and still—others writhing under the hot sun, moaning and crying out. Everywhere swarms of flies and thin puffs of dust blow over the men.*

*TRUCKING SHOT–CAMERA PULLING BACK BEFORE* SCARLETT

*Involuntarily her hand rises to her mouth as she fights back the quick nausea that hits her. Then, fighting her own desire to flee, to get away from this appalling scene, she forces herself to start through the rows of wounded to look for* DOCTOR MEADE. *The men are of all ages— some are boys not more than fifteen or sixteen years old. Others, old men in their sixties and seventies. Flies creep contentedly and undisturbed over bloodstained faces. CAMERA TRUCKS AHEAD of her as she moves first between two* WOUNDED MEN, *one on his back, arm flung across his eyes to shield them from the sun, feebly moving his head to keep the flies away. Because of his wounded face, his constant cry for water has a strange, inhuman sound, like the cry of a bittern. . . .*

WOUNDED MAN: Wa'rrr—wa'rrr. . . .

The other man lies on his side, head pillowed on his arm, coat un-buttoned to allow bloodstained linen from a stomach wound to hang out on the ground. Everywhere the men are crying for water in a steady, low moan of voices.

WOUNDED MEN: Lady—water! Please, lady, water! . . . Water! . . . Please . . .

SCARLETT changes her course a little to reach an orderly who is binding a tourniquet about a soldier's arm, which has not merely been shot, but which has obviously been shattered. Blood is streaming from the arm. He works with fast, feverish movements.

SCARLETT: Where's Doctor Meade?

ORDERLY [too busy to even touch his hat]: Sorry, Ma'am, I ain't got no time to know.

CAMERA CONTINUING TO PULL BACK IN FRONT OF SCAR-LETT HALTS as she stops short as she is about to step over the body of a wounded officer.

SCARLETT [gazing down in horrified recognition]: Mr. Wilkes! [She kneels beside him.]

TWO SHOT—SCARLETT and JOHN WILKES

He is evidently pretty far gone, but he recognizes her and tries to smile.

MR. WILKES: Scarlett—

SCARLETT: Oh, Mr. Wilkes, what can I do? Can't I do something?

CLOSE-UP—JOHN WILKES

His eyes close wearily, lips barely form the words.

JOHN WILKES: Tell me—Melanie—how is she?

CLOSE-UP—SCARLETT

SCARLETT [momentarily taken aback]: Melly—oh, Melly—why she's —Oh, Mr. Wilkes, didn't you know?

CLOSE-UP—JOHN WILKES

His face muscles suddenly relax as he dies.

SCARLETT goes on, CAMERA following her. Lifting her skirts, she steps over dead men, over men who lie dull-eyed, with hands clutched to bellies where dried blood has glued torn uniforms to wounds, over men whose beards are stiff with blood and from whose broken jaws come sounds. . . .

VOICES: Water! Water! . . .

SCARLETT reaches a group of men under the car shed and cries out loudly.

SCARLETT: Dr. Meade! Is Dr. Meade here?

MGM, © 1939, 1967. UGa Libraries, Marsh Papers.

*One of the men points.*
CAR SHED
DR. MEADE, *with two exhausted orderlies, is crouching over a stretcher.* SCARLETT *enters to him.*
SCARLETT: Dr. Meade!
DR. MEADE [*looking up*]: Thank heaven you're here! I can use every pair of hands!
*She stares at him bewildered, dropping her skirts. They fall over the face of a wounded man, who feebly tries to turn his head to escape their smothering folds.*
DR. MEADE: Wake up, child! Get to work!
*She bends over the doctor to clutch his arm.*
SCARLETT: I can't work here! Melly's having her baby! Doctor, you've got to come!
DR. MEADE: A baby? Are you crazy? I can't leave these men for a baby! They're dying! Hundreds of 'em! Get some woman to help you! Get my wife!
SCARLETT: Mrs. Meade can't come! She's just gone to . . . [*Then she stops herself.*] You must come, doctor! She'll . . . Melanie might die!
DR. MEADE: Die? Yes, they'll all die! All these men! No bandages! No chloroform! No morphine! Oh, God, for a little morphine. Damn the Yankees! Oh, God damn the Yankees!
*A* SOLDIER *grins up at him from a stretcher.*
THE SOLDIER: Give 'em hell, doctor!
SCARLETT: Doctor, please!
*The violence of her despair recalls him to himself. He looks up at her out of haggard eyes.*
DR. MEADE: Child, I'll try. I can't promise, but I'll try. When we get these men 'tended to. The Yankees are coming and our troops are moving out. I don't know what we'll do with these men. There aren't any trains. The Macon line's been captured. But I'll try. Only run along now! Don't bother me now! There's nothing to bringing a baby! [*He turns to his work.*]
*She realizes that he has forgotten her. She goes.*

DISSOLVE TO

A STREET
SCARLETT *is running wildly through the crowd.*

DISSOLVE TO

SCARLETT, *crossing the street, is all but run down by an artillery train.*

*DISSOLVE TO*

*Almost fainting for lack of breath,* SCARLETT *collapses on the steps of a church. Soldiers are marching by. She gets to her feet and forces her way through them.*

*DISSOLVE TO*

PEACHTREE STREET IN FRONT OF MISS PITTY'S HOUSE

SCARLETT *comes up to the front of Miss Pitty's house.* WADE HAMPTON *is swinging on the gate.*

SCARLETT: Go out in the backyard and make mud pies and keep out of my way! [*She passes him.*]

*He follows her, sobbing.*

WADE HAMPTON: Wade hungry!

SCARLETT [*over her shoulder*]: I don't care! Go into the back yard, or I'll . . . [*She goes into the house.*]

INTERIOR–MISS PITTY'S HOUSE–THE HALL

SCARLETT *enters.* PRISSY *meets her.*

PRISSY: Is de doctah come?

SCARLETT: He can't come.

PRISSY: Oh, Miss Scarlett, Miss Melly bad off!

SCARLETT: The doctor can't come. There's nobody to come. You've got to manage without the doctor, Prissy. I'll help you. [PRISSY's *mouth falls open and her tongue wags wordlessly.*] Don't look so simple-minded!

PRISSY [*backing away*]: Lawsy, Miss Scarlett . . .

SCARLETT: Well?

PRISSY: Lawsy, we's got ter have a doctah! Miss Scarlett, Ah don' know nuthin' 'bout birthin' babies! Maw din' nebber let me 'roun' w'en folkses was havin' dem!

*All the breath goes out of* SCARLETT's *lungs in a gasp of horror.* PRISSY *makes a lunge past her, but* SCARLETT *grabs her.*

SCARLETT: You black liar, what do you mean? You've been saying you knew everything about it!

PRISSY: Ah don' know huccome Ah tell sech a lie! Ah jes' see one baby birthed an' Maw she lak ter wo' me out fer watchin'!

*But* SCARLETT *loses her temper completely and slaps the black face with all the force of her tired arm.* PRISSY *screams. Then, from above,* MELANIE's *voice is heard crying:*

MELANIE [*off-scene*]: Scarlett, is it you? Scarlett, please come quickly! Scarlett!

SCARLETT [*turning to* PRISSY]: Build a fire in the stove and keep hot water boiling in the kettle. Bring up all the towels you can find. [*Then, loud*] I'm coming, Melly! [*She goes up the stairs.*]

*DISSOLVE TO*

SHADOW EFFECT

MELANIE'S VOICE: Oh, Scarlett, you'd better go before the Yankees get here.

SCARLETT'S VOICE: I'm not afraid. You know I won't leave you.

MELANIE'S VOICE: It's no use. I'm going to die.

SCARLETT'S VOICE [*firmly and authoritatively*]: Don't be a goose. Hold on to me, hold on to me!

*Throughout above scene,* SCARLETT'S *voice and attitude are those of such confidence and assurance as to try to dismiss* MELANIE'S *fears.*

MELANIE'S VOICE: Talk to me, Scarlett! Please! Keep talking to me!

*DISSOLVE TO*

EXTERIOR–AUNT PITTY'S HOUSE–NIGHT

*The house is dark except for the light coming from Melanie's open bedroom window.*

OUTSIDE–OPEN LIGHTED WINDOW

*CAMERA SHOOTING through the window excludes the bed from view, revealing only that portion of the room close to the hall door. The SOUND of an infant's crying is heard. Then* SCARLETT *appears within, crossing to the hall door and going out.*

INTERIOR–AUNT PITTY'S HOUSE–DOWNSTAIRS HALLWAY

SHOOTING TOWARD STAIRS

SCARLETT *comes down the stairs slowly, utterly exhausted, her hair disordered, her face drawn. As she reaches the foot of the stairs,* PRISSY *appears from the direction of the kitchen with a pan full of steaming water and fresh towels.*

SCARLETT: Don't mind that. It's all done now.

PRISSY: Yas'm.

SCARLETT: Well, I guess everything's all right—in spite of you. The next thing for us is to get out of here. The Army's goin' tonight. I don't aim to stay and let the Yankees catch us.

PRISSY: The Yankees? Is dey comin'? Oh, Miss Scarlett!

SCARLETT: You run down town. Run all the way. And find Captain Butler. I don't care if you have to look in every barroom in town. You find him. Tell him I want him—that I said for him to come right away and bring a horse and carriage.

PRISSY [*aghast*]: Lawsy 'Mighty, Miss Scarlett, I'se skeered. S'pose de Yankees gets me?

SCARLETT [*sharply*]: Go—do you hear? If you don't want me to sell you down the river so you'll never see your mother again—sell you for a field hand—you drop that and go. [PRISSY, *terrified, literally drops the pan of hot water and towels, and runs out of scene toward the door.*]

SCARLETT [*angrily*]: You fool—you black fool!

*She stoops and picks up the pan and the towels.*

HALLWAY

REVERSE ANGLE–SHOOTING TOWARD OPEN FRONT DOOR–SCARLETT *in foreground*

PRISSY *has vanished outside. A distant flash of light is seen through the doorway, then the c-c-crumph of a heavy explosion.* SCARLETT *runs to the door and looks out.*

CLOSE SHOT OF SCARLETT–AT FRONT DOOR–CAMERA OUT-SIDE

*The* SOUND *of another heavy explosion. A flash of light on* SCAR-LETT'S *face.*

SCARLETT [*in terror*]: The Yankees! Oh God, please, please, make Rhett come! [*She turns back into house.*]

# Fifth
# Sequence

*ADE IN:*

INTERIOR–A BARROOM IN DECATUR STREET–NIGHT

*The place is filled with a tumultuous mob of Atlanta's lower classes, all men, all chattering the rumors and news of the day and almost all very drunk. The phrase: "The Yankees are coming!" crackles on every lip except* RHETT's. *He stands in the foreground, laughing, turned out as always, a little drunk, his mirth tinged with something not entirely mirthful, almost a horror of the crowd around about him. Then* PRISSY *calls him from the tumultuous street beyond the swinging, half-door of the barroom.*

PRISSY: Capt'n Butler! Capt'n Butler! [*He turns.*] Capt'n Butler, you come out hyah in de street ter me! [*He is amazed. He sets his drink down unfinished, pays for it and goes to* PRISSY, *CAMERA FOLLOWING HIM, as* PRISSY *continues in the wildest agony:*] De Yankees is comin'! Dey'll kill us all! Dey'll run bay'nits in our stummicks!

RHETT: Why are you telling all this good news to me? I seem to have heard something very like it inside.

PRISSY: Ah'm Miss Scarlett's Prissy . . . [*He recognizes her.*] An' she done sent me fer you! You tell Capt'n Butler ter come quick, she say, an' bring his hawse an' cah'rige! Or an amb'lance eff he can git one!

RHETT: What does she want with an ambulance?

PRISSY: Miss Melly! . . . [*He remembers.*] She done have her baby today! A fine baby boy an' Miss Scarlett an' me we brung him!

RHETT [*astounded*]: Miss Scarlett and you! Do you mean to tell me that Scarlett! . . .

PRISSY: Well, it was mostly me, but Miss Scarlett helped me! An' Ah don' expec' no doctah could have done no better! Only Miss Melly she feel po'rly now it's all over!

RHETT: I can believe that!

PRISSY: An' de Yankees is comin' an' Miss Scarlett say . . . [*The night is suddenly split wide open by a terrific explosion, the flash of which blazes over the street outside and the force of which knocks part of the wooden awning down behind* PRISSY.] De Yankees is hyah!

RHETT *reaches for her.*

RHETT: Better come inside, Prissy. The Yankees aren't here, but . . .

*He is pulling her through the door. In spite of her terrors, she resists him.*

PRISSY: Capt'n Butler, mah Maw'ud wear me out wid a corn stalk eff Ah goes into a barroom!

*The crowd from the barroom, rushing for the street, ends the argument between* RHETT *and* PRISSY *by forcing them both out of the door and along the sidewalk.*

EXTERIOR–DECATUR STREET–NIGHT

*The crowd is running along the street in wild panic. More explosions and the sky is filled with soaring brands and sparks.* RHETT *and* PRISSY *are washed along with the crowd. CAMERA FOLLOWS THEM.*

RHETT: You're entirely right, Prissy. Keep out of bars and you'll keep out of a great deal of trouble. Only that isn't the Yankees. It's our own soldiers blowing up the munitions trains, so the Yankees won't get 'em when they do come. Why didn't they get 'em out of here this morning? Come around the corner here, away from this mob! [*They turn the corner into a side street. He mops his brow.*] It's a terrible thing to be in at the death, Prissy. A terrible thing. Though I don't suppose that means too much to you. Now, then! [*But a column of soldiers passing, he forgets* PRISSY *and steps forward to the curb to speak to one of the officers.*] Are you going? Are you leaving us, Lieutenant? [*And he walks along the sidewalk beside the* LIEUTENANT.]

LIEUTENANT: That's what we're doing. We're the last from the north breastworks. They'll have the south and east cleared out before daybreak.

RHETT: Then we can expect General Sherman for breakfast. Oh, it's all right, Lieutenant! I don't see what else you can do. [*He touches his hat. The* LIEUTENANT *passes on.* PRISSY *is tugging at his sleeve to attract his attention. He turns to her with a bitterness wholly unlike his usual manner.*] You won't have to wait long for emancipation now, Prissy.

PRISSY: It was a hawse Ah was askin' fer.

RHETT: So it was! And it's just as well you don't know what the other word means. Tell Miss Scarlett to rest easy. They've taken my horse and carriage, but I'll steal a horse out of the army corral if there's one left. I've had to steal horses before this night and I'll steal her one if I get shot for it. Now cut and run home. [PRISSY *starts to speak, but he cuts her off rudely.*] Go on!

*Another explosion.* PRISSY *goes in terror.* RHETT *turns slowly, his face toward the CAMERA, dark and terrible.*

EXTERIOR–AUNT PITTY'S HOUSE–FULL SHOT–*with only one lighted window on the second floor.*

DISSOLVE TO

*SAME SHOT AS ABOVE*

*Now many windows are lighted.* SCARLETT's *figure may be glimpsed, moving from room to room gathering things in her arms, blowing out the lights as she goes.*

EXTERIOR–MISS PITTY'S HOUSE

SCARLETT *comes out through the front door, her arms full of clothes. Hurrying down the steps in an animal panic, she drops a good many of them. Then she hears the sound of a horse in the street, throws the balance of them over the open gate and forgets them completely as she runs out to welcome* RHETT. RHETT *drives into the scene on the seat of a more than rickety buckboard which is pulled by a more than rickety old horse.*

SCARLETT: Rhett! Is that you, Rhett?

RHETT: Whoa! [*He reins in.*] Good evening. Fine weather we're having. I hear you're taking a trip.

*He jumps down from the wagon: in his belt two ivory-handled, long-barrelled duelling pistols.*

SCARLETT: If you make jokes now, I'll kill you!

RHETT: Don't tell me you're frightened!

SCARLETT: I'm frightened to death, and if you had the sense God gave a goat, you'd be frightened, too! [RHETT, *meanwhile, has tied the horse to the hitching post in front.*] We've got no time to talk! We must get out of here!

RHETT: Where are we going? There's just one road left open out of this town. The Yankees have got all the others.

SCARLETT: I'm going home.

RHETT *is astonished.*

RHETT: You don't mean to Tara?

SCARLETT: To Tara, yes.

RHETT: You little fool, you can't go to Tara!

*But* SCARLETT's *obsession turns hysterical.*

SCARLETT: I will go home! You can't stop me! I want my mother! I'll kill you if you try stopping me!

RHETT: But the Yankees may be at Tara now! Don't you know they fought around there all day? If you got there, you'd probably find it burned! I won't let you go! It's insanity!

SCARLETT: I'll go if I have to walk every step of the way!

*Her exhaustion breaks her down to tears. Suddenly she is in his arms and he is comforting her.*

RHETT: There, there, my dear, don't cry. We'll get you home some-how. Only, as you said, we must move quickly. We must get Mrs. Wilkes into the wagon. Now blow your nose like a good child.

*They start toward the house.*

*DISSOLVE TO*

AUNT PITTY'S HOUSE–VERANDAH

RHETT *and* SCARLETT *enter scene past* CAMERA *and go into the house, followed by* PRISSY.

SCARLETT [*as they go*]: PRISSY, you can put my dresses in the wagon.

RHETT: No. We've got to save all the weight we can. You'll have to forget your vanity for once.

*They vanish inside. A moment after they have disappeared inside, CAMERA PANS UP to the open, lighted window to* MELANIE's *bed-room.*

INTERIOR–MELANIE'S BEDROOM–MELANIE *in bed*

*Above the bed is a photograph of* ASHLEY *in uniform.* CHARLES HAMILTON's *sword is on the wall beside it.* MELANIE *lies, eyes closed, breathing gently, one arm about the bundled infant beside her. CAMERA PANS to the hall door as* RHETT *and* SCARLETT *enter, fol-lowed by* PRISSY.

RHETT: We're taking you home to Tara, Mrs. Wilkes.

*CAMERA PANS with him to the bed.*

MELANIE [*her eyes open; faint voiced*]: Tara—

SCARLETT *enters to the bed.*

SCARLETT: The Yankees are comin', Melly.

*Deftly* RHETT *hands the baby to* SCARLETT *and tucks the sheet about* MELANIE.

RHETT: Do you think you can put your arms around my neck?

MELANIE: I think so.

*She tries, but the arms fall weakly back.*

RHETT: I'll try not to hurt you. [*Then, with the deft steadiness of hard muscles and strong shoulders, he picks* MELANIE *up from the bed, speaking to* SCARLETT *as he does so.*] Bring the blanket, too.

SCARLETT *obeys and starts after* RHETT *toward the door.* RHETT *stops.*

MELANIE: Please—

RHETT: What is it?

MELANIE: Ashley—Charles—

RHETT: What's that?

SCARLETT [*impatiently*]: His picture—Ashley's picture—and Charles' sword—she thinks she can't live without them.

RHETT: Bring them—and the lamp—I don't want to stumble on the stairs. [*He goes out of scene toward the door.*]

SCARLETT *turns to* PRISSY, *out of scene.*

SCARLETT: Here, take this.

PRISSY *enters scene; goes.* SCARLETT *picks up the* and *removes* ASHLEY'S *picture and* CHARLES' *sword from the wall above the bed. CAMERA PANS with her as, holding the lamp high, she follows* PRISSY *out the door.*

### THE HALL

WADE HAMPTON *is standing at the foot of the stair.* PRISSY, *on her knees, buttons his coat about him.* RHETT *carries* MELANIE *down,* SCARLETT *following. The lamp throws uncertain shadows on the wall.*

PRISSY: Ah got de bed fixed in de wagon good as Ah knows how.

SCARLETT: Take the baby.

PRISSY *relieves her of the baby and she takes* WADE HAMPTON'S *hand.* RHETT *carries* MELANIE *out through the front door.* PRISSY *follows with the baby.* SCARLETT, *still carrying the lamp, leads* WADE HAMPTON *out after them.*

### FRONT OF MISS PITTY'S HOUSE AT FRONT DOOR
### MEDIUM SHOT

RHETT BUTLER *comes out the door with* MELANIE *in his arms.* PRISSY, *carrying the baby, is at his heels. Bringing up the rear is* SCARLETT. RHETT *pauses, glances off down Peachtree Street, the others grouping behind him.*

SCARLETT [*from the rear*]: What is it, Rhett?

### FULL SHOT OF PEACHTREE STREET AND THE CITY IN THE DISTANCE–*From their point of view–Shooting over* RHETT'S *shoulder holding portion of him in foreground*

*The glow of fire above the trees of the distant town is seen for the first time.*

RHETT: They must have set fire to the warehouses down by the depot.

### GROUP SHOT–ON THE VERANDAH OF MISS PITTY'S HOUSE–RHETT *in foreground*

*Beyond him may be seen* SCARLETT'S *white, anxious face.*

SCARLETT: The Yankees? Already?

RHETT: No. Our people. Burning up the supplies like the ammunition. We'll have to hurry if we want to get across the tracks.

SCARLETT: But we can't go that way.

RHETT: We have to. The McDonough Road's the only one the Yankees haven't cut yet. [*sardonically*] Still want to go to Tara?

SCARLETT: Yes—yes—hurry.

*He goes down the steps out of scene, the others following.*

PEACHTREE STREET IN FRONT OF MISS PITTY'S HOUSE

*As* SCARLETT *enters to the wagon,* RHETT *is installing* MELANIE. *Then he takes the baby from* PRISSY *and places it tenderly in* MELANIE'S *arms and hoists* WADE HAMPTON *up beside her.* PRISSY *clambers in to cover* MELANIE *and the baby with a blanket.* RHETT *turns to* SCARLETT.

RHETT: Not much of a horse, is he? Looks like he'll die in the shafts. He's the best I could do, though. Some day I'll tell you, with embellishments, just where and how I stole him. In front with me.

*He has untied the horse and climbed up to the driver's seat.*

SCARLETT *hesitates a moment, confused to know what to do with the lamp. She sets it on the sidewalk and is climbing in beside him. He takes the reins.*

SCARLETT: Wait! I forgot to lock the door. [*He laughs.*] What are you laughing at?

RHETT: At you, locking the Yankees out.

SCARLETT: Hurry! Hurry!

*He flaps the reins on the horse's back. They drive away, disappearing into the dark distance. In the foreground the lamp, still burning, sheds its little circle of yellow light on the pavement.*

*DISSOLVE TO*

PEACHTREE STREET

*Toward CAMERA comes the horse at a lope, the wagon swaying behind it as it bumps over the ruts. The horse and the wagon and the people in it are only dim figures in the semi-darkness under the trees, the only moving objects to be discerned on the street. There are a number of distant detonations as the wagon passes CAMERA which PANS with it revealing once again at the far end of the street the fire glow and smoke rising above the distant rooftops.*

A STREET IN THE CITY

*In MEDIUM CLOSE SHOT the wagon sways along, throwing* PRISSY *and* WADE HAMPTON *about "like corn in a popper." The baby wails.* PRISSY *and* WADE HAMPTON *cry out as they are bruised against the side of the wagon. From the front seat,* SCARLETT *reaches back to impose silence on* PRISSY *by pinching.* MELANIE *lies still and gives no sound. The detonations continue.*

*DISSOLVE TO*

TWO SHOT–RHETT *and* SCARLETT *on the WAGON–as the light of the fire at the far end of Peachtree Street is reflected on their faces for the first time. At this point, between their two figures and behind them,*

MGM, © 1939, 1967. UGa Libraries, Marsh Papers.

*appears* PRISSY'S *black face, utterly terror-stricken, the light reflected on her as well.*

SCARLETT: I never dreamed it would end like this—

RHETT: I did. I always saw those flames.

SCARLETT: It's like the whole world was turned into a bonfire.

RHETT: It is. That's more than Atlanta burning.

BUSINESS SECTION OF PEACHTREE STREET

*LONG SHOT from their viewpoint—CAMERA holding horse's head in foreground*

*Flames are visible at the far end of the street for the first time. Beyond the burning building an explosion shoots flames and sparks high in the air.*

*TWO SHOT—*RHETT *and* SCARLETT *on wagon*

PRISSY *ducks out of view.* SCARLETT *shrinks closer to* RHETT, clinging to his arm.

*Seated beside* RHETT, SCARLETT'S *teeth chatter with terror and she shrinks closer to him, clutching his arm and looking to him for something reassuring. At her touch he turns to her, his eyes gleaming.*

SCARLETT: Do we have to go through the fire?

*The wagon is struggling through the panic-stricken mob. Embers from the conflagration shower over both street and wagon.*

*The glare of the fire is brighter here and its crackle audible. Throngs of women surge along past the "Examiner" office, away from the CAMERA, carrying hams across their shoulders. Little children hurry by their sides, staggering under buckets of streaming molasses. Young boys drag sacks of corn and potatoes. An old man struggles along with a small barrel of flour on a wheelbarrow. Men, women and children, black and white, lug packages and sacks and boxes of food. Our wagon, coming toward the CAMERA, cleaves the crowd.*

DISSOLVE TO

*LONG SHOT SHOOTING AWAY from fire across intersecting street toward approaching WAGON in background*

*As the wagon approaches the intersection, it is forced to halt by a detachment of weary, slipshod, Confederate troops who appear in foreground, crossing Peachtree Street and heading down the intersecting thoroughfare. An officer counts "One—Two—Three—Four" in a pathetic effort to count the step and keep up the morale of his men.*

*TWO SHOT—*RHETT *and* SCARLETT *on WAGON*

*Impatiently, they watch the troops pass.*

SCARLETT: Oh, dear! Why can't they hurry?

RHETT [*smiles grimly*]: With them goes the last semblance of law and order. Now the Decatur Street roughs will stand the town on its head.

*As the last of the Confederates in foreground straggle off down the intersecting street,* RHETT *slashes at the horse with the reins. The wagon lurches forward, going past CAMERA down Peachtree Street. For a moment HOLD on empty Peachtree Street, SHOOTING toward the church. The sound of more explosions and bright flashes of light follow.*

*VERY LONG SHOT STILL SHOOTING AWAY from fire toward approaching WAGON*

*The street is completely empty except for the distant wagon. The reflection of the flames [which are behind the CAMERA] against the buildings should give a weird, frightening effect. For a protracted moment the wagon clatters down the street toward CAMERA as if through an abandoned city. Only sound at the moment is the clop-clop of the horse.*

SCARLETT: Faster, Rhett, faster!

RHETT: He's making all the speed he can.

SCARLETT: No, no! Faster!

*Suddenly there is a crash of breaking glass.*

MUSIC SHOP WINDOW–CAMERA INSIDE

*Silhouetted in foreground are one or two instruments of the period. One pane of glass has already been broken. Outside the window, a Decatur Street tough flings a huge missile, smashing the rest of the window so that it seems to splinter directly past the CAMERA. Through the gaping hole we get a glimpse of the horse and wagon passing in the background. An instant later, three or four other toughs join the one who threw the missile outside the window. They start grabbing instruments from inside the shop window. Intersperse with this action the sound of more explosions accompanied by bright flashes of light.*

CORNICE OF A BUILDING

*The light of the fire is reflected on the building. The whine of projectiles going through the air is heard, followed by a sharp explosion. A part of the cornice blows off.*

PEACHTREE STREET–HORSE AND WAGON *approaching CAMERA–as the falling masonry crashes to the street in foreground between horse and CAMERA.* RHETT *pulls up the horse sharply which rears in panic.*

PEACHTREE STREET–CAMERA SHOOTING FROM NARROW, DARK ALLEY

*Beyond the entrance of the alley, the horse and wagon may be seen, their passage blocked by the debris. Past the CAMERA, out of the alley, run a number of hooligans.*

CLOSER VIEW–HORSE AND WAGON–*blocked by debris.* RHETT *is trying to urge the horse forward over the fallen masonry but the horse balks, refusing to go any further. In both the foreground and background appear figures of looters running, bursting into shops, some of them already laden with spoils. The whole has an atmosphere of disorder and drunkenness—a city falling into chaos as it nears its death.*

*A hooligan with a woman's hat on his head, his arms full of billowing dresses goes by in front of the wagon.*

*A thin, white-faced tough with a tremendous haunch of beef clutched to his chest, his pockets in his coat stuffed with loaves of bread, shuffles past.*

*Two men with a demijohn of liquor, both drunk, both struggling for it as they run.*

CLOSE SHOT–RHETT *and* SCARLETT

RHETT *frantically urges the horse forward.* SCARLETT *sits beside him, taut and silent.*

*A horse and wagon swings sharply to avoid a delicate, thin-legged settee which has been dragged into the street. Perhaps the rear wheel of the wagon touches it as it goes by.*

CLOSE SHOT–OUTSIDE A SALOON DOOR–*as the end of a battering ram strikes it. The door gives but doesn't burst open. The battering ram is hauled back out of view for another blow.*

INSIDE THE SALOON DOOR–[BLACK SCREEN]–[CRASHING SOUND]

*The entire door falls inward, revealing the red light of the fire outside. Against the red glare silhouetted figures drop the battering ram and storm into the saloon. One carries a flaming pine knot torch, which lights up the interior, showing a portion of the bar and rows of bottles, disclosing that it is a saloon. The mob starts fighting for the bottles.*

PEACHTREE STREET–AT FIVE POINTS

SILHOUETTE SHOT OF LOOTERS AGAINST BACKGROUND OF FIRE

*This shot should be designed to give a Dante's Inferno effect, with riotous figures of men and women silhouetted against the flames. Some of them are drunk, others laden with loot. More and more figures join the others. There are sounds of breaking glass, splintering wood, women's cries, the yelling of men.*

*CLOSE SHOT–*GROUP IN BACK OF CART

*The baby squawls and* PRISSY *cowers beside* MELANIE's *still form.*
EXTERIOR–STREET

*Five looters pass the wagon. They carry dressed carcasses of hogs on their shoulders, the heads of the swine swaying up over their own craniums, giving a weird effect of half-human, half-animal figures, the white cadavers pale against their flanks.*

*A man in silhouette against the flames tilts back his head to drink from a bottle.*

*A man, arms about two women with streaming hair, goes reeling past, the whole party drunkenly lurching and screaming.*
DEBRIS IN STREET–BURIED CAMERA SHOT SHOOTING AWAY FROM FIRE

*The decrepit horse stumbles over the top of the debris, the wagon teetering dangerously as if about to go over at any moment,* RHETT *lashing the horse. Horse and wagon pass directly over* CAMERA.
CAMERA IS SHOOTING UP PEACHTREE STREET AWAY FROM FIRE–LONG SHOT–HORSE AND WAGON

*In foreground is the intersection of Marietta Street. The wagon is coming toward* CAMERA. *Four* TOUGHS *appear, from behind* CAMERA, *all four of them straining to roll a hogshead barrel. One of them sees the horse, points.*

FIRST TOUGH: A horse!

SECOND TOUGH: Grab him!

*The* FOURTH TOUGH *stays with the barrel. The others start forward.*
HIGH ANGLE–FOLLOW SHOT OF WAGON–[CAMERA TRUCKING]–SHOOTING ACROSS SCARLETT's *and* RHETT's BACKS

*The fire at the end of the street is no longer in view because this is a high, sharply angled shot. The* TOUGHS *run into scene obviously intending to stop the wagon.*

FIRST TOUGH [*yelling*]: Give us that horse!

*CLOSE-UP–*SCARLETT–*Terrified*

*CLOSE SHOT–*TOUGH *hanging onto horse*

RHETT *jumps on horse's back, pulls his arm back.*

*CLOSE SHOT–*RHETT–*On horse's back.* TOUGH's *head in foreground.* RHETT *brings his fist down and knocks* TOUGH *out of scene. Starts back to wagon seat.*

*LONG SHOT–Group of* TOUGHS–[*Running to foreground*]

*LONG SHOT–STREET–*HITCHING POST *in foreground* [*Low Setup*]

RHETT's *wagon turns at intersection, rides out of scene.*

CLOSE-UP–*Group of* TOUGHS

TOUGH: Down the alley. Cut 'em off!

LONG SHOT–ENTRANCE TO ALLEY

*Wagon appears, rides down alley. CAMERA PULLS BACK.* TOUGHS *run in, stop wagon. Horse rears.*

MEDIUM CLOSE SHOT–RHETT *and* SCARLETT

RHETT *pulls reins, reaches out of scene to hit* TOUGH. *Gets back on seat. Hits at another tough who jumps into scene, knocks him out. He whips the horse and the wagon starts out.*

LOW ANGLE SHOT–TOUGHS

*They leap at the horse.*

TOUGHS: Get out of that wagon! . . . Come on, get out of there! . . . Get out of that wagon! . . .

RHETT *fights them off.* SCARLETT *and* PRISSY *scream.*

TOUGH: Give us that horse!

RHETT *knocks the last tough off the wagon, whips the horse, and the wagon drives off. The horse and wagon go out of scene PAST CAMERA.*

REAR VIEW OF WAGON–SHOOTING DOWN ALLEY TO-WARD FLAMES IN BACKGROUND

*The wagon bounces about from side to side dangerously, as it rocks down alley away from CAMERA. A burning building is at the far end of the alley.*

CLOSE SHOT–MELANIE

*Lying face up on the mattress, one limp arm about the bundled baby. They are being roughly tossed about.* MELANIE *is biting her lip to keep from crying out.*

HORSE AND WAGON IN A BRIGHT GLARE OF FLAMES

*The horse abruptly stops without being pulled in and rears back.* SCARLETT *cries out.*

TWO SHOT–RHETT *and* SCARLETT

*She is clinging to him desperately. Even he looks alarmed. Behind them* PRISSY's *frightened face appears from the back of the wagon. She screams.*

BURNING BUILDING AND BOXCAR–FROM THEIR ANGLE

*Only a few feet beyond the box car is a flaming building. Sparks, embers, and bits of burning wood are showering the boxcar. Carry over this SOUND of* PRISSY's *scream.*

CLOSE THREE SHOT–SCARLETT, RHETT, PRISSY

PRISSY *screams.* SCARLETT *is terrified.*

PRISSY: Oh, Miss Scarlett! Miss Scarlett!

SCARLETT: Hush up! Hush up!

PRISSY: Oh, Miss Scarlett! Oh!

RHETT: They haven't left much for the Yankees to take, have they?

SCARLETT: Rhett, how are we going to get through?

RHETT: We'll have to make a dash for it before the fire reaches that ammunition!

*On hearing this line, PRISSY hurls herself to the floor of the wagon, screaming with terror. RHETT decides what to do—looks around frantically, then decides on his course which is to the left, veers horse around, strikes him with whip and exits left.*

HORSE AND WAGON–BOXCAR AND BURNING BUILDING IN VIEW

RHETT *lashes at the animal, pulling him around to make a half-turn away from the burning building and the boxcar and across the open freight yards. The panic-stricken horse finally starts forward.*

GRANDEUR SCREEN – FULL SHOT – BURNING WAREHOUSES

RHETT *drives the horse on a slanting course toward CAMERA away from the burning buildings and the long row of boxcars. As the wagon approaches CAMERA, a huge burning beam drops directly in foreground. The horse rears back, giving the impression that exit by that route is cut off. At the same time, flames appear in immediate foreground at the right hand side of screen. A moment later more flame appears in foreground at left of wagon. RHETT jumps down and seizes the horse's head. He struggles with the animal a moment, trying to turn the horse away toward the left hand end of the screen. In the extreme left corner of the GRANDEUR SCREEN is an opening between the boxcars and the buildings that is not yet closed by flame.*

RHETT [*tugging at the horse*]: Easy, boy, easy. Come along, now. [*The horse doesn't budge.*]

RHETT [*calls to SCARLETT*]: Give me your shawl! Quick!

SCARLETT [*bewildered and frightened, her face half-hidden by the shawl*]: Why? What are you going to do?

RHETT: Don't ask questions. Do as I tell you. And quick!

*She flings her shawl at him. Swiftly, he wraps it around the horse's head. The first boxcar on the right of the screen blows up. RHETT starts to pull the horse toward the tunnel of safety at the left corner of the screen.*

SCARLETT: Rhett! Rhett! Not that way!

RHETT [*pointing toward the opening*]: It's our only chance. Between those cars. Before they all blow up.

MGM, © 1939, 1967. UGa Libraries, Marsh Papers.

MGM, © 1939, 1967. UGa Libraries, Marsh Papers.

*Slowly, pulling the reluctant horse, he heads away from CAMERA toward the spot still clear of flame. A moment after they have disappeared through the opening, the flames reach their climax, the boxcars start to blow up, the largest building at the left end of the screen collapses and the screen becomes a mass of flames.*

LAP DISSOLVE TO

EXTERIOR–ROAD ON EDGE OF TOWN

*LONG SHOT OF HORSE AND CART AND TROOPS–HOT, DUSTY NIGHT*

*The foreground sky is red, trailing off into darkness. The horse and wagon are careening down the road away from the CAMERA, toward the rear of retreating troops headed in the same direction.*

[NOTE: *The soldiers in this scene are walking tiredly, dispiritedly, heads down, too weary to hurry, too weary to care, dragging their rifles. Many are barefooted, some in dirty bandages, so silent that they might all be ghosts.*]

RHETT *is forced to slow up.*

*REVERSE ANGLE–TROOPS AND WAGON*

*Burning buildings in the not-too-distant background. Along the road past CAMERA go the disorganized retreating Confederates, their figures highlighted by the flames. For the most part they are foot soldiers, but amongst them are mounted officers in the last stage of fatigue.*

*GROUP SHOT–RETREATING CONFEDERATES ON THE ROAD–Horse and Cart in background*

A YOUNG SOLDIER, *sixteen years old at the most, dragging his rifle which is almost as tall as he is, and stumbling along like a sleepwalker, stops, wavers, and falls. Without a word, two men fall out of the last rank and walk back to him. One, a tall, spare man with a long, black beard, silently hands his own rifle and the boy's to the other. Then, stooping, he jerks the boy to his shoulders. He starts off slowly after the retreating column, his shoulders bowed under the weight.*

YOUNG SOLDIER [*in feeble fury*]: Lemme alone. Put me down. I can walk.

*The bearded soldier, without replying, plods on after the others, still carrying him.*

TWO SHOT–RHETT *and* SCARLETT *on the wagon–HIGH ANGLE FROM SIDE OF THE ROAD–Retreating troops in BACKGROUND*

*The dispirited shadows of Hood's army continue to shuffle past silently.*

RHETT [*softly*]: Take a good look, my dear. It's a historic moment.
You can tell your grandchildren how you watched the Old South
disappear one night.

SCARLETT *looks around as she hears a wail from the baby in the cart.*

INTERIOR–CART [*Over* SCARLETT'*s shoulder*]

MELANIE *stretched out as if dead, the wailing baby in her arms.*

PRISSY, *terrified, crouched in a corner, coughs from the smoke.*

*TWO SHOT*–RHETT *and* SCARLETT *on the seat*

SCARLETT *turns back to* RHETT.

SCARLETT [*impatiently*]: Oh, Rhett, please hurry!

RHETT [*his eyes still on the passing soldiers*]: They were going to
lick the Yankees in a month . . . the fools . . . the poor, gallant
fools. . . .

SCARLETT [*bitterly*]: They make me sick—all of them. Getting us
all into this with their swaggering and boasting.

RHETT [*with a sad smile—sits still, the reins in his hands, a curious
moody look on his swarthy face*]: That's the way I felt once—about
their swaggering and boasting.

SCARLETT: Oh, Rhett, what would we ever have done without you?
I'm so glad you aren't with the army! [*He turns to give her one look
that makes her drop his arm and shrink back. She stammers:*] Oh, yes,
I know! I haven't forgotten Charles, who's dead, and Ashley, who may
be dead, and all the fine young men! But I can't help wanting you to
hurry! [PRISSY *and* WADE HAMPTON *begin coughing from the smoke.*]
Oh, name of heaven, Rhett! Are you crazy? Hurry! Hurry!

RHETT, *recalled to himself, brings the tree limb down on the horse's
back with a cruel force that makes the animal leap forward. Smoke
engulfs them.*

*DISSOLVE TO*

EXTERIOR–A COUNTRY ROAD–NIGHT

RHETT: We're out of town now. [*He reins in the horse.*] Let the
horse blow a bit.

SCARLETT: Oh, yes, yes! Please, Rhett, let's hurry! The horse isn't
tired!

*TWO SHOT*–RHETT *and* SCARLETT *on cart*

SCARLETT: Why did you stop?

RHETT [*indicating fork in road*]: This is the turn to Tara . . . let
the horse breathe a bit. [*He turns to her.*] Scarlett, are you still determined to do this crazy thing?

SCARLETT: Oh, yes, yes! Rhett, let's go on!

RHETT: It's suicide. It probably means driving right through the Yankee army—and even if you miss 'em, the woods are swarming with deserters.

SCARLETT: But I know a wagon track a little farther on. Pa and I used to ride it. It winds all over, but it comes out right back of Twelve Oaks. [*eagerly*] We can get through—I'm sure we can.

RHETT: Not *we*, my dear—*you*. I'm leaving you here.

SCARLETT [*aghast*]: You're what? [RHETT *laughs, hands the reins to her, calmly jumps clear of the wagon wheel down to the ground.*] Rhett!

*CLOSE SHOT*–RHETT [*From* SCARLETT's *point of view–Holding her in foreground*]

SCARLETT's VOICE [*terrified*]: Where are you going?

RHETT [*smiles, looks at her for a moment, then speaks*]: I'm going, my dear girl, to join the army. . . .

SCARLETT [*relieved*]: Oh, you're joking. I could choke you for scaring me so.

RHETT [*smiling*]: I'm very serious, Scarlett. I'm going to join up with our brave lads in gray.

SCARLETT: But they're running away!

RHETT: No, Scarlett. They'll turn around and make a last pathetic stand—if I know anything about them. And when they do, I'll be with them. I'm a little late, but "better late than—"

SCARLETT [*looks down at him with genuine horror*]: Rhett, you *must* be joking!

RHETT: Selfish to the end, aren't you? Thinking only of your own precious hide and not of the gallant Confederacy.

SCARLETT [*wailing desperately*]: Oh, Rhett, how can you do this to me? . . . Why should you go now—after it's all over . . . and I need you . . . Why? Why?

RHETT [*with self-irony*]: Why? Perhaps because of the sentimentality that gets all Southerners in the end. Now that our brave bullies are done for, I find them strangely appealing. Perhaps I'm ashamed of myself after all—who knows?

SCARLETT: I thought you were smart. . . . I thought you were just above everything like—like that . . .

RHETT: Nobody can stay smart forever, my dear—if they're human. There's always something turns a man into a fool. A cause, or a woman, or sometimes just nothing at all but having to stand up where he belongs . . .

SCARLETT: You can't go off and leave me all alone . . . [*as he laughs*] . . . abandon helpless women.

RHETT: Helpless! Heaven help General Sherman and all his Yankees if they run into you! . . . Now climb down here. I want to say goodbye.

SCARLETT: No!

RHETT *climbs up on the wheel hub, roughly catches her under the arms, and swings her to the ground. He drags her several paces from the wagon,* SCARLETT *screaming as he does:*

SCARLETT: Rhett, please! Don't go! You can't—please—I'll never forgive you. . . .

RHETT [*taking her by the arm*]: I'm not asking you to forgive me. I'll probably never understand or forgive myself. And if a bullet gets me, so help me, I'll laugh at myself for being an idiot [*drawing her closer*]. But there's one thing I do know—and that's that I love you, Scarlett. In spite of you and me, in spite of the whole silly world going to pieces around us—I love you. Because we're alike. Renegades, both of us . . . selfish and shrewd and able to look things in the eyes and call them by their right names.

SCARLETT: Don't hold me like that . . . let me alone. . . .

RHETT: You asked me to stay . . . [*mockingly*] "I could not love thee half so well, loved I not honor more." Isn't that worthy of the noble Ashley Wilkes? [*He kisses her, bending her body back, kissing her again and again on the neck and mouth and on the throat.*] Sweet, Scarlett. Sweet girl . . . [SCARLETT *ceases struggling. He looks into her eyes.*] Here's a soldier of the South loves you, Scarlett—and nobody else. Wants to feel your lips and arms. Wants to take the memory of your kisses into battle with him. [*He grasps her more firmly and grins into her face.*] Never mind about loving me. You're a woman sending a soldier to his death with—with a beautiful memory. . . . Kiss me, Scarlett—kiss me, once. . . .

*She is overwhelmed. But from the wagon behind* WADE HAMPTON *cries out:*

WADE HAMPTON: Muvver! Wade fwightened! [*Cukor will coach the child actor in this pronunciation.*]

SCARLETT *wrenches free.*

SCARLETT: You low-down, cowardly, nasty thing! [*She draws back her arm and slaps him across the mouth with all the force she has left. He steps backward, his hand going to his face.*] Soldier! You're worse now than you ever were. That's all you can be—a cad! A rotten, nasty cad! They were right. Everybody was right—you aren't a gentleman. . . .

RHETT [*quietly and with a cynical smile*]: A minor point—at such a moment. . . . [*He hands her a dueling pistol.*] Here. Use this if you need it. But don't shoot the nag in your excitement.

SCARLETT *looks at him for a second in doubt, then the shrewd practical* SCARLETT *seizes the gun.*

SCARLETT [*waving the pistol*]: Go on. Go on get killed. I'm glad. I hope a cannonball lands right slap on that grinning head of yours. [*She starts to cry.*] I hope it blows you into a million pieces! I—

RHETT *laughs. He is amused, half bitter.*

RHETT: Never mind the rest. I follow your general idea. When I'm dead on the altar of my country, I hope your conscience hurts you. [*He doffs his hat.*] Goodbye, Scarlett.

*He turns and disappears into the darkness.*

SCARLETT *stands watching his figure retreating into the darkness. As his figure disappears, the sound of his footsteps is still heard for a moment or two.* SCARLETT *turns, her shoulders drooping, back to the wagon, her knees shaking. She walks a few steps farther toward the horse.*

*Sobbing, she buries her face against the neck of the horse, clinging to it. She is alone with the wagon and its helpless load on the road. The horse's head droops a little lower, and* SCARLETT'S *stormy sobs gradually die away into strangled gasps of utter weariness. With a long, shaken breath, she lifts her head and draws the back of her hand across her eyes, wiping the tears away like a tired child. Then, in a characteristic little way, she lifts her chin with determination. But as she takes hold of the horse's bit, her whole form is sagging from emotional letdown; and when she speaks, her voice is dull in contrast with her tempestuous words to Rhett a moment ago.*

SCARLETT [*dully*]: Come on, you. We're going home. . . .

*Pulling at the bit, she starts leading the horse off. As the old nag stumbles abjectly forward, drawing the wagon with its pitiful load, we hear the baby's pitiful wail, and—*

*DISSOLVE TO*

EXTERIOR–A COUNTRY LANE–NIGHT

*A battery of Yankee artillery drives along the lane. CAMERA sees the passing artillery through a screen of willows. Following them, it comes to a foreground where the wagon stands,* SCARLETT *clutching a blanket over the horse's head.* WADE HAMPTON *whimpers.* SCARLETT *gesticulates frantically to* PRISSY, *who clamps a hand over his mouth.*

*DISSOLVE TO*

A FIELD–NIGHT

*A campfire around which a detachment of Yankee cavalry is sleeping, a* SENTRY *on guard. The* SENTRY *challenges.*

SENTRY: Who goes?

*A* SOLDIER *wakens, sits up beside the campfire.*

SOLDIER: Hear something?

SENTRY: Horse and wagon.

*He cocks his rifle. They both listen. Silence.*

SOLDIER: You're dreaming! [*He falls back.*]

*The* SENTRY *relaxes.*

*DISSOLVE TO*

LONG SHOT

BRIDGE NEAR WAGON ROAD

*The bridge is near a narrow wagon track, deeply rutted and torn by the wheels of gun carriages. The scene is desolate and barren. In the ditch is a little of the impedimenta abandoned by the retreating Confederate army . . . this wreckage only dimly seen, a dull gleam of metal here and there; but mostly just shapeless lumps of junk.*

*The wagon bearing* SCARLETT *and her charges is in the ditch immediately under the bridge.* SCARLETT *cowers in the seat—*PRISSY, MELANIE, *and the baby in back. Yankee artillery passing overhead on the bridge. We hear the voices of some of the* ARTILLERYMEN *bawling, rather drunkenly, in song:*

ARTILLERYMEN [*singing on sound track*]: We're coming, Father Abraham, three hundred thousand strong . . .

*In continuous movement, CAMERA NOW TILTS UPWARD until it includes the lower portion of artillery wheels passing overhead on the wooden bridge.*

SCARLETT's *face hardens, and by her expression we read that she knows the troops are Yankees by the song. The song is interrupted on a dolorous note by the shout of an officer:*

OFFICER'S VOICE: You artillery teamsters! You're taking up all the road. Pull aside and let the cavalry through!

*As the wheels roll off the bridge, there is a momentary pause, during which we hear a thin wail from the baby in the bed of the wagon.*

SCARLETT [*turning—in a fierce whisper*]: Shut up!

*Now the lighter sound of the cavalry horses trotting over the bridge.*

CLOSE SHOT–SCARLETT–BRIDGE OVERHEAD IN VIEW

*On the bridge there is no sound except the trampling of hoofs on*

ABOVE: *Clark Gable, Vivien Leigh, and Butterfly McQueen ride in the wagon used in the scenes of the escape from Atlanta and the trip to Tara. Taken July 1, 1939.* BELOW: *Scarlett hides the wagon under a bridge. Taken at Big Bear Lake, June 15, 1939.*

the planks and the faint jangle of equipment. SCARLETT crouches deeper into the shadows. As the last of the cavalry goes out of view, a soft whinny comes from the horse in the ravine.

SCARLETT [jerking on the reins, her voice low and venomous]: Stop —stop it, you!

RAVINE AND BRIDGE–WIDER ANGLE

Horse and wagon are only faintly discernible in the deep shadows of the ravine. Now the horse lets loose a full-voiced whinny. But at the same instant the Yankee artillery drivers whip up their horses and the guns rumble on their way.

DISSOLVE TO

EXTREME LONG SHOT
COUNTRYSIDE–NIGHT–MOONLIGHT

Against the night sky, the wagon is silhouetted. Beneath it and in a little distance is water, and in it we see the reflection of the silhouetted horse and wagon.

Framing the shot in the foreground is the silhouetted, grotesque figure of a dead soldier.

CLOSE SHOT–MELANIE–asleep in the back of the wagon, the baby in her arms. Off-scene we hear PRISSY, singing weakly, "whistling in the dark," to keep up her courage.

PRISSY [singing weakly]: "Jus' a few mo' days fer to tote de weary load—"

During the above, the CAMERA HAS PANNED OVER TO A CLOSE SHOT OF PRISSY and SCARLETT on the wagon seat.

SCARLETT [snaps at PRISSY]: Shut up!

PRISSY [quavering]: I din' know dis country could be so still! Ain' dere nuthin' lef' livin' nowheres aroun' hyah? . . . Ah's skeerd, Miss Scarlett!

SCARLETT: I'm scared, too—But we'll get home to Mother and then everything will be all right.

BACK TO

LONG SHOT

Again the silhouette and again the reflection in the water. [Similar shot but a different setup, without the dead soldier.]

DISSOLVE TO

EXTERIOR–FIELD–DAWN–A TREE TOP AGAINST A DAWN SKY

The tree top is just faintly washed with early morning light, and a mockingbird is singing. CAMERA PANS DOWN to show the morning

*mist rising through the branches* . . . PANS DOWN FARTHER, dis-
*closing the dead body of a Confederate sharpshooter, hanging head
downward, his foot caught in a crotch of the tree. CAMERA PANS
DOWN STILL FARTHER to the woebegone horse lying as if dead
. . . then PANS OVER revealing the wagon.* SCARLETT *is lying asleep
among the others in the back of the wagon.*

*The four refugees are asleep on the floor of the wagon:* SCARLETT
*with* MELANIE'S *bare feet almost in her face,* PRISSY *curled up like a
cat under the wagon seat, the baby wedged in between her and*
MELANIE.

CLOSE SHOT–SCARLETT *ASLEEP IN WAGON*

*She stirs and wakens, opening her eyes. The mockingbird is greet-
ing the dawn with the song of the cardinal. For a moment* SCARLETT
*blinks sleepily. Suddenly she gasps in horror—sits upright, staring.*

DEAD SHARPSHOOTER HANGING IN TREE [FROM SCAR-
LETT'S VIEWPOINT] [CAMERA SHOOTING OVER HER
SHOULDER]

*The mockingbird is still singing—long trills.*

BACK TO SCENE AT WAGON

SCARLETT *turns her head, glancing at those in the wagon.* MELANIE
*is lying, eyes closed as if dead.* SCARLETT *screams, reaches out a hesitant hand to touch* MELANIE'S *face.*

MELANIE'S *eyes flutter. She speaks with an effort:*

MELANIE [*distractedly*]: . . . Water . . . [*her eyes open fully now.
She looks up at* SCARLETT.] Scarlett, please. Water.

SCARLETT: There isn't any.

MELANIE *turns weakly, and with a great effort, puts her arm around
the baby.*

MELANIE: Oh, my poor baby! My poor baby!

SCARLETT: Don't worry—Mother will take care of him when we
get home.

PRISSY *crawls out from under the wagon seat.*

PRISSY [*forlornly*]: Oh, Miss Scarlett, I'se powerful hongry.

SCARLETT [*irritably*]: I'm hungry, too, and I'm thirsty, and I feel like
crying. But I have to do everything. The least the rest of you can do is
hush up. [*She rises painfully and gets down from the wagon. She
approaches the fallen horse and tugs him by the bridle.*] Get up! Get
up—I say! [*The horse moves but still refuses to rise.* SCARLETT *shakes
his head furiously—kicks him.*] You get up! I'll kick you until you do.

*The horse starts to struggle to its feet.*

DISSOLVE TO

*BUZZARDS AGAINST A HOT NOON SKY*
*They circle ominously.*
OPEN FIELD–LITTERED WITH DEAD–HOT DAY
*CAMERA SHOOTS PAST a distorted limb of a dead man in*
*foreground*
*The field has been pitted by the cannon and is also marked with*
*tracks left by a great deal of troop movement, artillery wheels, etc.*
*The horse and wagon are in a LONG SHOT coming toward*
*CAMERA. The weary nag, close to collapse, picks its way slowly*
*amongst the corpses, the wagon bumping behind it.* SCARLETT *and*
PRISSY *are seated on the driver's plank.*
PAN SHOT–HORSE AND WAGON
*As it jolts across the field of dead.*

DISSOLVE TO

THE MALLORY PLACE–DAY
*The CAMERA PANS past the brick post of a gate pitted with rifle*
*fire, the gate itself hanging loose and a field cannon, one wheel shot*
*to splinters, lolling beside it. In the foreground, a dead horse and its*
*rider. In the background, the burned ruins of the plantation mansion,*
*only the chimneys standing.*
THE FIELD
*Music. The wagon as before.*
PRISSY [*a whisper*]: You think we gwine ter find Tara lak dis, Miss
Scarlett?
SCARLETT'S *look is eloquent, then:*
SCARLETT: I'm not thinking about how we're going to find Tara.
Get down and we'll go to the well and fetch some water.
PRISSY: Oh, no, Miss Scarlett! Dere mout be hants up dar!
SCARLETT: I'll make a hant out of you if you don't come with me!
*She walks away.* PRISSY *is climbing down.*

DISSOLVE TO

THE MALLORY PLACE
*A trough below the stables.*
*Spring water flows into the trough and overflows into a bucket on*
*the ground below.* SCARLETT *enters and falls on her knees to drink*
*deeply, burying her face in the water.* PRISSY *stands looking on, then,*
*unable to maintain the attitude of slave to mistress another moment,*
*she touches* SCARLETT'S *shoulder.*
PRISSY: Ah's thusty, too, Miss Scarlett!

SCARLETT: Take the bucket down to the wagon and give them some. Give the rest to the horse and get him harnessed. I'm going to try to find something to eat.

*She goes out as* PRISSY *drops on her knees to drink.*

THE MALLORY PLACE–THE ORCHARD

SCARLETT *stoops to pick up a few apples from the ground. She rejects some rotten ones and bites into one good one. The taste of the apple turns her stomach. She spits out her mouthful and goes on out of the scene, her skirt held up and moderately filled.*

THE COUNTRY LANE

PRISSY *is watering the horse, which is already harnessed. The baby is wailing.* SCARLETT *enters, carrying her apples.*

SCARLETT [*to* PRISSY, *about the horse*]: Take more than water to do him any good. [*She dumps her apples into the wagon.*] The Yankees must have taken everything else. [*She looks dully down at* MELANIE.] Hadn't Miss Melly ought to be feeding the baby? He'll starve if she doesn't.

PRISSY, *the horse watered, moves aft.*

PRISSY: Miss Melly kaint feed no baby. She too far gone.

SCARLETT: Well, I guess if they're going to die they're going to die. [*She climbs heavily into the wagon seat, unties her bonnet and pulls it off.*] Better put this over Miss Melly's face. [*She throws the bonnet back to* PRISSY.] I'll be freckled as a guinea hen, but I don't guess freckles matter like they used to. Get in, Prissy.

PRISSY *climbs in.*

SCARLETT: We'll be going on to Tara now. Tara . . . [*In terror* SCARLETT *looks once more toward the Mallory place. Her face contracts.*]

SCARLETT: Tara! [*She smites the horse with Rhett's bough. The wagon lurches forward.*] I could walk faster than this horse! If only I didn't have you and Miss Melly and the baby and Wade, I could run every step of the way home to Tara!

PRISSY *creeps forward to clutch her from behind.*

PRISSY: Don' you go off an' leave us now, Miss Scarlett!

SCARLETT: If only I could! [*Her face contracts again.*] Oh, Mother! Mother! Will I ever get through to you? [*Then, looking off to the roadside across from the Mallory place, her face contracts once more with horror.*]

THE MACINTOSH PLACE

*Another plantation house, burned: these ruins still smoking.*

PRISSY [*off-screen*]: Whut makes it so quiet, Miss Scarlett? I din' know dis country could be so quiet! Ain' dere nuthin' lef' livin' nowheres aroun' hyah?

*DISSOLVE TO*

A COUNTRY LANE–DUSK

*Music and the clump of the horse's hooves on the road. The wagon is now pulling through a place of burned woods. CAMERA aimed at the road ahead of the horse.*

PRISSY [*off-screen*]: Ah's skeered, Miss Scarlett!

*CAMERA pulls back, halting behind their backs,* SCARLETT *still driving,* PRISSY *crouched as before.*

PRISSY: Dey's been fightin' aroun' hyah in dese woods! Dey's daid men hyah!

SCARLETT: Prissy, hush up!

*The horse stops to blow. CAMERA retreats still further to show* MELANIE *and the two children on the floor of the wagon,* WADE HAMPTON *asleep, the baby wailing faintly.*

MELANIE: Are we home, Scarlett?

SCARLETT: We soon will be. This is Twelve Oaks now. That's their mock orange hedge you smell. [PRISSY *sits up as the wagon moves forward.*] Here's the gate ahead. [*She calls.*] Hello!

PRISSY: Don' holler, Miss Scarlett! Dere ain' no tellin' *whut* mout answer!

SCARLETT: I know that! I've got to see, though, Prissy! I've got to see!

*She clambers down out of the wagon,* PRISSY *following her. CAMERA remains on* MELANIE. *A weak, meaningless smile comes over her face.*

MELANIE [*low*]: Twelve Oaks! Twelve Oaks!

SCARLETT: Oh—no!

PRISSY [*her face peering fearfully over* SCARLETT's *shoulder*]: Y-you see a ghost?!

SCARLETT [*in low voice of horror*]: Look, you fool! Look at what they've done to Twelve Oaks.

*REAR VIEW OF TWELVE OAKS–*SCARLETT *and* PRISSY *in foreground.*

*Only the burned wreck of the lovely old house is still standing. Its two tall chimneys, ". . . like gigantic tombstones towering above the ruined second floor. And broken, unlit windows blotching the walls like still, blind eyes . . ."*

*CLOSE-UP*–SCARLETT

SCARLETT [*angry tears in her eyes; softly, but all her hatred in her voice*]: The Yankees—the dirty Yankees!

*PAN SHOT*–SCARLETT

*She drops the horse's bridle and runs forward toward the house, CAMERA PANNING AFTER HER.* PRISSY *lurches along beside her, trying to keep up.*

*FRONT VIEW OF TWELVE OAKS–LOW ANGLE*

*CAMERA PANS DOWN the smoke-stained chimneys, past gutted second floor to the charred verandah and the remnants of the front hallway. One of the great columns lies half burned across the driveway where it fell. At the far end of the ruined hallway, entering from the rear,* SCARLETT *appears—*PRISSY *at her heels. Halfway down the hallway,* SCARLETT *pauses.*

INTERIOR–HALLWAY TWELVE OAKS–*CLOSE SHOT*–SCARLETT

*She looks about her, aghast.*

SCARLETT: Oh, I could kill 'em! I could kill every Yankee there is!

PRISSY [*haunted*]: Ah don't lak it here. I'se gwine back to de wagon.

SCARLETT *pays her no attention.* PRISSY *pads off to the rear door, CAMERA PULLING BACK, revealing more and more of the ruined interior.*

SCARLETT *moves to the window, broken now, where on the afternoon of the barbecue* ASHLEY *and* MELANIE *had stood, looking out upon the crowded scene of gaiety on the spacious lawns.*

EXTERIOR–TWELVE OAKS GROUNDS–[*OVER SCARLETT'S SHOULDER*]

*The awful desolation which the Yankees have left there. The once smooth lawns have been gouged and dug and pitted by trampling feet and hooves and by wagon wheels: the trunks of the trees are charred and blackened by the campfires whose mounds of ashes are scattered about, and overhead the leaves have been withered by the heat of the fires.*

*All about are scattered the junk and litter of a camping army: rags, some bottles, a broken caisson wheel, bits of metal, and splintered wood.*

*An old and ragged shirt hangs desolately on a bush; and all the garden furniture is smashed or overturned in a dreadful vista of disorder.*

SCARLETT [*softly*]: And this was Twelve Oaks—Oh, Ashley—I hope you never see this.

*As she turns and goes back toward the charred remnants of the house,*

DISSOLVE TO

HORSE AND WAGON AT EDGE OF WOODS ROAD–DUSK

SCARLETT *enters to the wagon, pauses, looking about her.*

SCARLETT [*calling*]: Prissy! Prissy! What's happened to you?

PRISSY [*crawling from under wagon*]: Don' go to Tara, Miss Scarlett. Dey's all done gone. Ah knows. Dey's all daid. Ah can feel it . . . [*points to her stomach*] . . . in hyah.

SCARLETT: Hurry, you fool!

*Suddenly, very near, out of the darkness of the surrounding underbrush, a cow moos.* PRISSY *jumps and shrieks.*

PRISSY: It's a ghos'!

*She throws herself on the ground.*

UNDERBRUSH

*A placid cow peers out, lowing plaintively.*

BY THE WAGON

SCARLETT [*laughs shakily*]: Sit up, you fool! It's nothin' but a cow. [PRISSY *sits up—the cow lows again.*] Is that cow hurt?

PRISSY: Soun's ter me lak she need milkin' bad.

SCARLETT: We can use that milk for the baby.

PRISSY: You don't 'spec' me to milk that cow, Miss Scarlett! Ah nebber had no truck wid cows. Ah's house help.

SCARLETT: You idiot! We're not going to stop to milk her now. We're taking her with us. If Tara is—I mean—

PRISSY: How all we gwine ter tek a cow wid us, Miss Scarlett? Cows ain' no good effen dey ain' been milked. De bags swell up an' bust. Dat's why she hollerin'.

SCARLETT: Since you know so much about it, take off your petticoat and tear it up and tie her to the back of the wagon.

PRISSY: Miss Scarlett, you knows Ah ain' had no petticoat fer a month an' ef Ah did have one, Ah wouldn't put it on her fer nuthin'. Ah's skeerd of cows.

SCARLETT *looks at her disgustedly, then picks up her own skirt, unties the waist tape from her petticoat and slips it down over her feet. She puts one end between her teeth, clutches the hem in her hand and jerks, gnawing until the material starts to rip into shreds.*

EXTERIOR–THE COUNTRY LANE–DUSK

*The wagon as before.* MELANIE *calls faintly.*

MELANIE: Scarlett! Scarlett!

SCARLETT *answers from off-screen.*

SCARLETT [*off-screen*]: We're coming, Melly! We've found a cow! We'll have milk for you and the baby!

*She enters, leading the cow by the halter she has improvised out of the petticoat and looped about its horns.*

MELANIE: Poor baby! [*Then, as* SCARLETT *is making the cow fast to the rear of the wagon*] Is Twelve Oaks all right?

SCARLETT *stops. She cannot answer. Then:*

SCARLETT: We're going on to Tara. [*She is climbing back into the wagon seat.*]

DISSOLVE TO

THE COUNTRY LANE–DUSK

*Another hill and the horse is balking.* SCARLETT *tugs, then calls out:*

SCARLETT: Get out, Prissy, and make Wade Hampton get out! If he can't walk you'll have to carry him.

*But* PRISSY'S *voice is again raised in violent protest.*

PRISSY: Miss Scarlett, I kain' walk! Mah feets done blister an' dey's thoo' mah shoes an' Wade an' me don' weigh 'nuff ter mek no diffrunce!

SCARLETT [*furious*]: Get out or I'll pull you out and leave you here in the dark! [PRISSY *has clambered down and lifts* WADE HAMPTON *after her.* WADE HAMPTON *begins crying.*] And make Wade hush! I can't stand it!

*The procession starts forward up the hill.*

DISSOLVE TO

A HILLTOP

*Music.* CAMERA *is backing away before the last exhausted effort of the strange procession. The music reaches its climax.*

TARA–THE GATE

*Music.* SCARLETT *leads the horse through,* PRISSY *following with* WADE HAMPTON *tottering beside her. The music ceases abruptly.*

SCARLETT: I can't see! I can't see!

PRISSY: Ah dassn't look!

CLOSE TWO SHOT–PRISSY *and* SCARLETT

SCARLETT [*turning back to* MELANIE]: Melly! Melly! We're home! We're at Tara!

MELANIE'S VOICE [*very weak*]: Oh, Scarlett! Thank goodness!

SCARLETT *rises to her feet and lashes at the horse. He doesn't move.*

SCARLETT [*striking at him vehemently and clucking*]: Hurry! Move, you brute!

*The horse's legs buckle and he goes down. A shiver passes over him and his muscles relax.*

PRISSY [*terrified*]: Miss Scarlett! He's daid!

SCARLETT *leaps down from the wagon paying no attention to the horse and, talking as she does, runs toward the CAMERA at right angles to the wagon, through the gate and up the driveway. Her hand to her head, she peers ahead as she runs.*

SCARLETT: I can't see the house! Is it there? I can't see the house! [*with rising terror*] Have they burned it? [*She stops.*]

CLOSE-UP–SCARLETT

*As she searches the darkness* [*looking straight into CAMERA*] *her face is gradually and slightly lighted by the moon.*

SHOT OF THE SKY

*Clouds moving and baring the moon.*

CLOSE-UP–SCARLETT–[*Her face lighted by the moon*]

*The anxiety on her face changes to joy as she sees the house. Her face lighted by the changing light of the moon across which the clouds are still moving.*

SCARLETT [*her voice raised in a wild cry*]: It's all right! It's all right! They haven't burned it! It's still there!

LONG SHOT–TARA–[*From* SCARLETT's *angle*]

*As the clouds uncover the moon and the house is plainly revealed in the moonlight.*

MEDIUM LONG SHOT–TARA

SCARLETT *runs across the lawn toward the house, screaming:*

SCARLETT: Mother! Mother!

*She runs slightly left to right to match the angle of her run in succeeding scene.*

TARA–FRONT OF HOUSE

*Out of the darkness,* SCARLETT *comes running toward the verandah steps. She is almost staggering with weariness, and her breath is coming in spent, sobbing gasps. She runs up those familiar steps, she goes to the front door and starts to open it. It is locked. She knocks; and when there is no answering sound or movement, she knocks again—more loudly and more loudly in a gathering crescendo of hysteria until finally she is hammering frantically on the door with both fists, screaming:*

SCARLETT: Mother! I'm home. Mother, let me in! It's me—Scarlett!

*The door opens slowly, silently, and* GERALD *is there—in the dark hallway.* SCARLETT, *with both quivering hands upraised where she has been pounding at the door, stares for a second at his terribly changed face and then throws herself forward, clinging to him. Slowly, with a curious effect of dazed fumbling, his arms go about her.*

SCARLETT [*AS CAMERA MOVES CLOSER*]: Oh—oh, Pa! I'm home . . . I'm home. . . .

GERALD, *holding her in his arms, stares at her dazedly, blinking heavily once or twice. He begins to tremble "as if he had been awakened from a nightmare into a half-sense of reality. The eyes that looked into hers had . . . a fear-stunned look. He was only a little old man and broken."*

GERALD: Katie—Katie Scarlett—Oh, darlin'!

INTERIOR–HALLWAY

MAMMY *appears behind* GERALD *in the hallway.* SCARLETT *turns to her and is engulfed in her arms.*

SCARLETT: Mammy! Mammy! I'm home! I'm home!

MAMMY: Honey—honey chile—

*Clinging,* SCARLETT *rests her head wearily on* MAMMY's *bosom.*

SCARLETT [*with a long sigh*]: Oh, Mammy, I'm so—so—Where's Mother? [*looking up suddenly into* MAMMY's *face*]

MAMMY [*after an instant's pause, obviously avoiding a direct reply*]: Why . . . Miss Suellen and Miss Carreen—dey was sick wid de typhoid. Dey had it bad but dey's doin' all right now . . . jus' weak lak li'l kittens. . . .

SCARLETT [*impatiently*]: But . . . but . . . where's *Mother?*

MAMMY [*again hesitates; avoids* SCARLETT's *eyes*]: Well, Miss Ellen . . . she tuk down wid it, too. An' las' night she—

*CAMERA MOVES CLOSER TO* SCARLETT's *FACE. Drawing back in* MAMMY's *arms,* SCARLETT *stares at her for a long moment—blankly at first, then her eyes begin to dance with anguish and her lips part, as little by little is mirrored on her face the dawning of full realization. Until finally her face is frozen in a mask of horror. With that perfectly immobile face, she "swallows and swallows but a sudden dryness seems to have stuck the sides of her throat together," and when she speaks at last it is in a ghastly, harshly whispering travesty of her voice.*

SCARLETT [*the word long drawn-out, almost with a curious effect of wonder*]: Mother! . . .

*Slowly she pulls back from* MAMMY; *breaks the clinging hold of her arms. She starts running, staggering a little on her feet, calling:*

SCARLETT: Mother! [*She turns to look into* ELLEN's *office, still calling:*] Mother! [*She runs out of the office, turns, and runs toward the parlor, still calling:*] Mother!

*Until she stops before the open doorway of the parlor from which candlelight comes.*

CLOSE SHOT–SCARLETT–OUTSIDE LIGHTED DOORWAY
*As she goes in, her face a mask.*
INTERIOR PARLOR–*From* SCARLETT's *viewpoint–Holding her in
foreground*
*On a table, with candles at her head and feet,* MRS. O'HARA's *body
lies, covered with a sheet except for her face.*
REVERSE ANGLE–MRS. O'HARA'S BODY *in foreground*
SCARLETT *enters slowly, like a sleepwalker, her eyes fixed on the
figure of her mother. In this trancelike state, she moves into a CLOSE-
UP, staring at her mother's face. But all her suffering, and now this
shock, have numbed her mind in a cold hell of unreality; have frozen
her mind into an immobility which is reflected in her face. She can't
come to her mother now; her grief can't break through in tears nor
even in a gesture. Slowly, as in a dream of suspended motion,* SCARLETT
*draws back.*
*As she does, far in the background, in the door, are revealed*
MAMMY *and* PORK, *peering in wide-eyed, with loving but morbid
interest.*
MAMMY *is holding a dish of hog grease, with a rag smoking evilly
in it, giving off a sick brown light.*
TARA–JUST INSIDE THE DOOR OF THE PARLOR
*CAMERA TRUCKING AHEAD OF* SCARLETT
*Walking in this dreamlike state,* SCARLETT *comes out of the parlor
into the hallway. At the door, she is joined for just a moment by the
two Negroes, who hover about, partly in front of her as she walks, staring straight ahead, at nothing.* MAMMY, *holding the light-dish high,
flutters solicitously.*
MAMMY: Honey—Chile, let Mammy he'p you, an' . . .
PORK: Miss Sca'lett, Ma'am, kain' Ah—
SCARLETT *pays utterly no attention, does not pause in her slow,
hypnotic walk. The Negroes' voices sink into concerned and worried
murmurs, and they look at each other. Then they drop back, behind
her, and out of the scene.*
*The shadowy figure of* GERALD *appears, and is passed, in the
macabre gloom of the hallway. In a vague and wandering gesture, he
touches his mouth with fumbling fingertips; but is silent. And his
haunted face is left behind as* SCARLETT *walks on.*
*The dreamlike unreality of this whole scene is intensified by the
sick light, casting huge and grotesque shadows which walk with* SCAR-
LETT. *The CAMERA CONTINUES TO TRUCK in front of* SCARLETT,
*and as she comes farther and farther away from the light in* MAMMY's

*hands the shadows loom and stir, larger and more dreamlike all around her.*

*Walking like a somnambulist,* SCARLETT *crosses the hallway of her childhood, where she has been happy and frivolous, long ago. Once she touches, with wondering fingers, the dim surface of the console table: and again, she lets her fingers trail along the smooth curve of the banister, which once her darting hand had touched so lightly.*

*And as if the touch of these things, known so well in childhood, had power to break through into her mind, her breath starts coming faster and faster—finally there is a catch in it—the mask of her face begins to crumple a little—she begins to walk faster and faster—the catch in her breath becomes a little jerky noise, almost like a small animal might make in pain. And then, it is a strangled sob—and she starts running. Through the door of the parlor again, running.*

*CAMERA ON* SCARLETT *AS SHE COMES RUNNING IN*

*Stumbling, sobbing,* SCARLETT *comes across the room. Her face is wildly alive again now with a vivid agony of grief and horror. As she sees her mother again, her eyes dilate enormously, and with both fists pressed against her mouth, she gives a strangled, prolonged and piercing scream [Her face is very close to the CAMERA and WE HOLD ON IT for its full effect.]*

*LONGER SHOT*

SCARLETT *throws herself down on her knees beside the table at her mother's feet.* SCARLETT's *face is buried against the sheet, her hands, writhing and twisting in agony, are knotted above her head. [Her face between her rigid elbows.] As the CAMERA MOVES CLOSER, the twisting hands writhe more and more slowly until they are motionless, clenched.*

*A wind blows the candle flame gently, almost as if a quiet presence were passing there. . . .*

*SLOW FADE OUT*

# Sixth
# Sequence

ADE IN:

INTERIOR–HALLWAY AT TARA–DAWN–[*SHOOTING AT THE CLOSED DOOR OF THE LIVING ROOM*]

MAMMY *and* PORK *are wearily and anxiously watching the closed door. Slowly it opens and beyond the body of* MRS. O'HARA *may be seen a window, gray with the early morning light. The dish of grease which has served as a candle has burned out but is still sending up a thin spiral of smoke in the dawn.*

SCARLETT *comes out of the parlor. She is beyond grief. Her face, tear-stained and agonizingly tired, shows what she has been through during the entire night. No tears are left. She is drained of emotion. As she marches slowly into the hall, the* CAMERA RETREATS IN FRONT OF HER.

PORK *and* MAMMY *glance at each other.* MAMMY *tentatively extends an arm as though to touch* SCARLETT, *and then withdraws it.*

MAMMY [*seeking to control the emotion in her voice*]: Miss Scarlett honey—

PORK [*same*]: If they's anything Ah can do, Miss Scarlett—

SCARLETT *starts slowly down the hall.* PORK *picks up a primitive candle like the one over* ELLEN's *body, and he and* MAMMY *anxiously follow* SCARLETT, CAMERA TRUCKING WITH THEM.

SCARLETT: What did you do with Miss Melly?

MAMMY: Don' you worry yo' pretty haid 'bout Miss Melly, chile. Ah done slapped her in bed a'ready 'long wid de baby.

SCARLETT [*nods, then says*]: Better put that cow I brought in the barn, Pork.

PORK: Dere ain' no barn no mo', Miss Scarlett. De Yankees buhned it fo' fiahwood.

SCARLETT: In the stable then!

MAMMY: Dey buhned the stables, too, Miss Scarlett.

SCARLETT [*bitterly*]: Why didn't they burn the house?

MAMMY: 'Cause dey used de house fo' dey haidqua'ters, Miss Scarlett.

SCARLETT *stops.*

PORK: Dey camped all aroun' de place. De pastures wuz blue wid 'em.

SCARLETT [*this is the last sacrilege*]: Yankees . . . in Tara! [*She looks around the hall, sick at heart. She starts down the hall again.*

*Suddenly she is aware of a gnawing pain in her stomach.*] Pork—I'm starving. Get me something to eat.

MAMMY: Dere ain' nothin' to eat, honey. Dey tuck it all.

SCARLETT [*incredulous*]: All the chickens—everything?

PORK: Dey tuck dem de fust thing. And whut dey didn't eat dey cah'ied off 'cross dey saddles.

SCARLETT: No dried peas? No corn?

PORK: Lawsy, Miss Scarlett, dey pastured dey hosses in de co'n . . . an dey druv dey cannons and wagons 'cross de cotton till it wuz plum ruint, 'cept a few acres over on de creek bottom. Not more'n 'bout three bales.

SCARLETT [*wild*]: Don't tell me any more about what "they" did!

MAMMY [*propitiatingly*]: I got some apples buh'ied under de house. We'se been eatin' on dem today.

*They have by now reached the open door to* ELLEN'S *study.* SCARLETT *doesn't comment because she suddenly sees her father.*

STUDY

*He sits, a broken and distracted figure, neither awake nor asleep, neither alive nor dead. He is a weird sight, sitting in the half darkness —the dawn which is creeping in through the window just lighting his face.*

*As we get close to him we realize he is shuffling papers, obviously only going through the motions of examining them.* SCARLETT *goes to him and strokes his head silently. Suddenly she sees something next to him. It is a bottle of locally made corn whiskey and next to it a gourd.*

SCARLETT: What's that, Pa? Whiskey?

GERALD [*even his voice is vague*]: Yes, daughter.

SCARLETT *pours some of the whiskey into the gourd and gives it to* GERALD, *as to a child.*

SCARLETT: Drink this, Pa.

*He gulps it down, obediently. She takes the gourd back from him, her nostrils wrinkling in distaste at the reek, and holds it to her mouth.*

GERALD, *again aimlessly shuffling his papers, follows her movements with his eyes, a vague stirring of disapproval in them.* SCARLETT *draws a deep breath and drinks swiftly, the hot liquid burning her throat, choking her and bringing tears to her eyes.*

*She pours another terrific slug into the gourd and raises it to drink again.*

GERALD: Katie Scarlett! That's enough. You're not knowing spirits. You'll be making yourself tipsy.

MGM, © 1939, 1967. UGa Libraries, Marsh Papers.

SCARLETT [*bitterly*]: I hope it makes me *drunk*. I'd like to be drunk. [*She finishes her drink, sees* GERALD's *puzzled, hurt face and rises, approaches Gerald and pats him on the knee.*] What are those papers?

GERALD [*vaguely*]: Papers?

SCARLETT: Yes. Those in your hand.

GERALD: Oh . . . Oh . . . [*Looks at them as if seeing them for first time.*] Bonds—all we have left—all we've saved—bonds.

SCARLETT [*hopefully*]: What kind of bonds, Pa?

GERALD [*shuffling them*]: Why, Confederate bonds, of course, daughter.

SCARLETT [*sharply*]: Confederate bonds! What're *they* good for?

GERALD [*with a flash of his old peremptory manner*]: I'll not have you talkin' like that, Katie Scarlett!

SCARLETT [*dismayed*]: Oh, what'll we do, Pa? What'll we do without money—or *anything*?

GERALD [*confused and hurt like a small boy*]: We must ask your mother. [*as though he's made a discovery*] That's it! . . . We must ask Mrs. O'Hara.

SCARLETT [*startled*]: Ask . . . Mother?

*A look of horror comes over her face as she realizes for the first time that her father's mind is gone.*

GERALD *looks up at her with a gentle smile and pats her hand.*

GERALD: Yes—yes. . . . Mrs. O'Hara will know what's to be done. Now stop crying and go out for a ride. I'm busy.

SCARLETT [*in a hushed voice, her arms going around the seated figure and standing behind him where he cannot see her trembling lips*]: Yes, Pa . . . but don't worry about anything. Katie Scarlett is here . . . so you needn't worry.

*She turns her head sharply, bites her lip, and with supreme effort controls her tears. She leaves* GERALD *and walks into the hall.*

DISSOLVE TO

SUELLEN'S AND CARREEN'S BEDROOM–DAY

SUELLEN *and* CARREEN *lie, wan with sickness, each in her own bed. All the accoutrements of the Victorian sickroom meet* SCARLETT's *gaze as she looks, dressed now, through the open door. The closeness of the room sickens her. She crosses quickly to the window and opens it. The sisters stir.* CARREEN *lifts her head weakly.*

CARREEN: Scarlett, can that be you?

*Before* SCARLETT *can answer, however:*

SUELLEN: Tell Mammy to bring some water up and bathe us.

SCARLETT: I'll tell her. [*She bites her lip and is going.*]

DISSOLVE TO

### THE BACK COMPANY ROOM

MELANIE *lies in the big bed asleep. As* SCARLETT *opens the door,* DILCEY *is just rising from a chair by the window. She goes to lay* MELANIE's *baby beside* MELANIE. *She looks up.*

DILCEY: Nuthin' wrong wid this chile 'cept he hongry, and whut it take to feed a hongry chile I got.

SCARLETT: It was good of you to stay, Dilcey. [*She is going.*]

DISSOLVE TO

### THE HALL–TRUCK SHOT

*Holding her father's arm closely,* SCARLETT *opens the big front door; and they step together,* CAMERA *following them, onto the verandah. The music swells as they stand silhouetted against the landscape of the plantation and in mathematically the same composition as when they looked out over the lands of Tara. Now, however, the lawns are knee-deep in wild mustard, the gravel drive is rutted and blotched with weeds, the borders are broken down and dead, the walls tumbled and the fences broken, and the statue of the Three Graces lies overturned upon its circlet of cannas. The musical accompaniment reaches a tragic climax and subsides somewhat as* SCARLETT *turns to her father.*

SCARLETT: Pa, do you remember the last time we stood here?

GERALD: We must have stood here many times, Katie Scarlett.

SCARLETT: There was one night, though. The night before the barbecue at Twelve Oaks. The night before they all went off to war. And you said . . .

GERALD [*breaks out wildly*]: Mrs. O'Hara is dead, Katie Scarlett! Your mother is dead!

SCARLETT *has to swallow before she can answer; then she seats her father in a chair—broken, and some of the window panes behind it broken.*

SCARLETT: You sit here, Pa, till I come back for you. [*She leaves him so.*]

DISSOLVE TO

### KITCHEN

MAMMY *turns from the stove, where she is heating water, as* SCARLETT *enters and sits on a kitchen chair.*

SCARLETT: Mammy, I want you to tell me about Mother. I couldn't bear to hear Pa talk about her.

MAMMY: Miss Scarlett, it wuz dem Slatterys, dem trashy, no-good, low-down po'–w'ite Slatterys dat kilt Miss Ellen.

SCARLETT *looks up, bewildered.*

MAMMY: Dey wuz sick wid disyere thing. Ole Miss Slattery's gal, Emmy, come down wid it an' Miss Slattery come hotfootin' it up hyah affer Miss Ellen, jes' lak she do de night Emmy had dat no good Yankee Jonas Wilkerson's baby. Miss Ellen had mo'n she could tote anyways, but she went down dar an' she nuss Emmy through. Yas'm, dat's how Miss Ellen ketch de typhoid. An' den Miss Carreen an' Miss Suellen . . .

SCARLETT [*stifling a sob*]: Don't I can't hear any more!

MAMMY, *weeping too, takes* SCARLETT's *hands in hers, but immediately a change comes over her.*

MAMMY: Honey, yo' han's! Ain' yo' maw tole you an' tole you dat you can allus tell a lady by her han's?

SCARLETT [*She is on her feet.*]: What good are ladies now? What good are gentleness and breeding now? I came home for Ma's comfort and guidance and she isn't here! And nothing she ever taught me will help me now! Better I'd learned to pick cotton like a darky! Mother was wrong! We were all wrong, Mammy!

MAMMY: Honey chile!

*But Scarlett is already on her way out of doors.*

INTERIOR–COVERED WAY

SCARLETT *walks down the covered way and stands looking out onto the grounds.*

EXTERIOR–GROUNDS OF TARA–[*From* SCARLETT's *viewpoint or over her shoulder*]–EARLY MORNING

"*Deep ruts and furrows were cut into the road where horses had dragged heavy guns along it and the red gullies on either side were deeply gashed by the wheels. The cotton was mangled and trampled where cavalry and infantry, forced off the narrow road, had marched thru the green bushes, grinding them into the earth. Here and there in road and fields lay buckles and bits of harness leather, canteens flattened by hooves and caisson wheels, buttons, blue caps, worn socks, bits of bloody rags, all the litter left by a marching army.*"

CLOSE SHOT–SCARLETT [IN COVERED WAY]

*In reaction to the desolation, she is nearing the end of her rope. She exits from the covered way and starts across the grounds.*

LONG SHOT–DESOLATE FIELDS

*As* SCARLETT *walks away from the* CAMERA *toward the vegetable garden which is on a knoll to the right, passing the well, the ruined orchard and the cottonfield with only a few miserable patches of white remaining. In the background, we see charred slave quarters and barn, the paddock, the scorched trees, the skeleton of the cotton press and the ruins of the split rail fence which had been around the kitchen garden.*

CLOSE SHOT–VEGETABLE GARDEN–RUINED OUTHOUSES IN BACKGROUND

*The soft earth, scarred with hoofprints and heavy wheels—the vegetables mashed into the soil.*

SCARLETT *wearily comes into the garden and looks down at the earth. As she stoops to pick some radishes from a short row, CAMERA PANS DOWN WITH HER.*

*She kneels and eats several as fast as she can get them into her mouth, not bothering to remove the dirt. Suddenly she gets ill at her stomach—and slowly, miserably, she retches as she falls face forward on the ground and sobs.*

*CAMERA HOLDS on the portrait of the defeated, prostrate and sobbing figure. This is the lowest moment in* SCARLETT O'HARA's *life— and we should feel that she is completely defeated.*

*After we have held this portrait, the sobs slowly stop—and CAMERA MOVES DOWN to* SCARLETT's *head. Her head moves somewhat so that we see her face—and we see her expression change slowly into bitter determination. Ever so slowly, and with grim determination, she pulls herself up on her hands, and as CAMERA STARTS TO DRAW BACK she rises first to one knee—and finally straight up. This is the crucial moment of* SCARLETT O'HARA's *life. And it is the most magnificent moment of her life. Out of this complete defeat a new and mature* SCARLETT O'HARA *is born. She stands there, fist clenched, her dress soiled, face smudged with dirt, and speaks slowly with grim determination—measuring each phrase carefully. Before speaking she raises her clenched fist and looks up, delivering her speech to the sky:*

SCARLETT: As God is my witness . . . As God is my witness . . . They're not going to lick me! . . . I'm going to live through this and when it's over I'll never be hungry again . . . no, nor any of my folks! . . . If I have to lie—or steal—or cheat—or *kill!* As God is my witness, I'll never be hungry again!

*She stands, her fist still clenched, as CAMERA DRAWS BACK on the determined figure outlined against the devastation of the plantation.*

*CAMERA PULLS BACK FARTHER AND FARTHER—revealing* SCARLETT *standing near an enormous ruined oak, backgrounded only by the sky.*

THE CAMERA FINALLY PULLS BACK TO AN EXTREME LONG SHOT

*A puff of early morning wind stirs the trees and bushes—like a harbinger of a new day.*

*FADE OUT*

*FADE IN:*

And the Wind swept through Georgia. . . .

## SHERMAN!

To split the Confederacy, to leave it crippled and forever humbled, the Great Invader marched . . . leaving behind him a path of destruction sixty miles wide, from Atlanta to the sea. . . .

Tara had survived . . . to face the hell and famine of defeat. . . .

*DISSOLVE TO*

EXTERIOR–PADDOCK–*TRUCK SHOT*–DAY

PORK *is milking in the late afternoon sun. Two or three final pulls at the cow's teats and he rises to carry his milk pail back to the house. CAMERA follows him along the path and past the creek bottom cotton patch where* SCARLETT *is picking cotton. Her back is bent double with exhaustion, her dress soaked with sweat. She straightens to ease her back and to glance out toward* DILCEY *and* PRISSY, *where they are picking a few rows beyond her. Then she sees* PORK *and calls him.*

SCARLETT: Pork, you come here to me! Let me see that pail! [*Startled, guilty even,* PORK *carries the pail over for her inspection.*] Call that milking? How do you expect me to keep Miss Melly and her baby and Wade Hampton alive? That cow's got more milk in her than that! You go back and strip her down like I told you this morning. And last night and yesterday and . . . [MAMMY *has entered.*] And you, Mammy, go dig those yams like I told you!

MGM, © 1939, 1967. UGa Libraries, Marsh Papers.

LEFT: *Snapshot of Oscar Polk as Pork.* RIGHT: *Snapshot of Isabel Jewell as Emmy Slattery. Taken on the Tara set, June 9, 1939, by Wilbur G. Kurtz.*

COTTON PATCH

SCARLETT, DILCEY, *and* PRISSY *as before. CAMERA CUTS to a new angle as* PRISSY *slips her bag from her shoulders, straightens, throws back her pig-tailed head for all the world like a dog baying the moon.*

PRISSY: Mah feets pains me an' mah back pains me an' Ah got de misery so bad all obber me Ah kain' pick no mo' cotton!

*But* DILCEY, *bag and all, has stepped across to* PRISSY's *row. She raises the cotton stalk in her hand and brings it down sharply across* PRISSY's *shoulders. A wail of pain from* PRISSY.

DILCEY: You pick!

PRISSY *resumes her labors.*

SCARLETT: Pa used to have a hundred hands to pick Tara's cotton. I've only got you and Prissy.

DILCEY: Ah ain' fergit how yo' Paw bought me so's mah Po'k wouldn' grieve an' how he bought mah Prissy so's Ah wouldn' grieve an' how good yo' Maw allus wuz ter me. Ah'm part Injun, Miss Scarlett. Injuns don' never fergit.

SCARLETT [*she smiles*]: Dilcey, when good times come back, I'm not going to forget how you've stood by and helped me.

*She bends over and begins picking again, but* DILCEY *stops her.*

DILCEY: You picked enuff fer one day, Miss Scarlett. Effen you wuk too hard, you'll tek sick, too.

SCARLETT *cannot deny her exhaustion.*

SCARLETT: All right, Dilcey [*her face sets*]. But we won't be alone in this cotton patch tomorrow.

*She shoulders her cotton bag and starts grimly towards the house.*

INTERIOR—SUELLEN'S AND CARREEN'S BEDROOM

*The girls are sitting up in bed, talking mournfully.*

CARREEN: What will the South be like without all our fine boys? There'll never be anyone to take their place.

SUELLEN: What's going to happen to Southern girls, that's what I want to know! There'll be no one to marry us! With all the boys dead, there'll be thousands of girls all over the South who'll die old maids!

SCARLETT [*off-screen*]: Too bad about you!

*Both sisters turn, startled, as* SCARLETT *enters to them.*

SUELLEN: You can talk because you've been married, and everyone knows somebody wanted you!

SCARLETT: Well, old Ginger Whiskers Kennedy isn't dead! He'll come back and marry you. He hasn't got any better sense. Though personally I'd rather be an old maid than marry him! [*She tears the coverlet from* CARREEN'*s bed and turns to perform the same service for* SUELLEN.] Get out of those beds, you two, and go down and chop Mammy's kindling for her!

*The girls are aghast.*

CARREEN: We couldn't chop kindling!

SCARLETT: Why not?

SUELLEN: It would ruin our hands!

SCARLETT: Look at mine!

*She shows them as they are now: cracked and scratched, bleeding, and blistered.*

SUELLEN: I think you're hateful to talk to Baby and me like this when we're still so sick! If Mother were here . . .

SCARLETT: You're not sick! You'll both be out in that cotton patch with Dilcey and me first thing tomorrow morning!

SUELLEN: I won't work in the fields like a darky! You can't make me! Oh, if Mother could hear you!

SCARLETT: You just mention Mother's name again, Suellen O'Hara, and I'll slap you flat! Mother worked harder than any darky on the place and you know it!

MELANIE *enters from her room by the communicating door. She is barefoot and clad in night dress and tattered wrapper.*

CARREEN: Scarlett, you've changed so you just don't seem real!

SCARLETT: Well, you two haven't changed! You go right on thinking and acting and complaining like the war hadn't happened and we were still rich as Croesus with food to burn! And you're living off what I do for you without lifting a finger!

MELANIE: Scarlett! Dear Scarlett!

*She puts her thin arm around* SCARLETT'*s shoulder to quiet her. But* SCARLETT *breaks free.*

SCARLETT: So they are, Melly! So are you, too! I've got you all on my neck for the rest of my life!

MELANIE *draws back, hurt, and* SCARLETT *is briskly penitent.*

SCARLETT: No, I didn't mean you. You come back to your room to bed. You're really sick.

*She goes with* MELANIE *into* MELANIE'*s room. The two girls look after her.*

EXTERIOR–TARA CREEK BOTTOM COTTON PATCH–LATE AFTERNOON–(NOVEMBER 1864)–*LONG SHOT*

*The stalks and leaves of the cotton are withered. Only scattered bolls still cling to the plants, many having already fallen to the ground: for this is autumn. Scattered over the field are all that are left of the*

*people of Tara: The shot is framed on the side with the foreground
figure of* GERALD *[in profile] sitting aimlessly playing with a blade of
grass or something of the sort. The next nearest the CAMERA are*
MAMMY *and* PRISSY; *then a little farther away* SUELLEN *and* CARREEN;
*and* SCARLETT, *the farthest away, pulling desperately at a well rope and
swinging the bucket clear of the well brim. Next to her on the ground
are two pails. [*PORK *is not in the field as the scene opens, as he is off-
screen milking the cow.]*

CLOSE SHOT–SUELLEN *and* CARREEN
*In ragged soiled dresses, they are picking cotton in sullen silence.
Both girls look weary and ill.*

SUELLEN *[straightening up]*: Oh, my back's near broken . . . *[with
a sob]* Look at my hands! *[holds them out]* Mother said you could
always tell a lady by her hands.

*Her hands are scratched and grubby.*

CARREEN *[sweetly]*: I guess things like hands and ladies don't matter
so much any more . . . You rest, Sue. You're not well yet and I can
pick cotton for both of us.

SUELLEN: Scarlett's *hateful*—making us work in the fields like—
*[She starts to sob.]*

SCARLETT'S VOICE: Too bad about that!

*Both sisters turn startled and frightened as* SCARLETT *enters to them.
She is carrying two large buckets of water, which she deposits on the
ground.*

SCARLETT: Now get back to work! I can't do *everything* at Tara
all by myself.

SUELLEN: What do I care about Tara! I hate Tara!

SCARLETT *looks at her for a moment in rage, then slaps her as hard
as she can so that* SUELLEN *almost collapses with sobbing.*

SCARLETT: Don't you ever dare to say you hate Tara again! That's
the same as hating Pa and Ma! *[She picks up water buckets and walks
out of scene.]*

LONG SHOT–FIELD
*As* SCARLETT *crosses, walking toward* PORK *who is approaching with
a milk pail*—MAMMY *a little behind him.* PRISSY *can be seen working
in the distance in the background.*

INTERIOR–MELANIE'S BEDROOM–DAY
SCARLETT *and* MELANIE *enter.*

SCARLETT: Get back into bed, I tell you, or you'll have a relapse.
I can't have that when you're just getting better. *[She is helping*
MELANIE *into the bed. She sees* WADE HAMPTON.] What are you doing

in your Aunt Melly's room? Trot out in the yard and play and don't let me catch you in here again! [WADE HAMPTON *bursts into tears.*] And don't sniffle! I can't stand to hear sniffles when I . . .

*Near the breaking point, she turns to the window and buries her face in the curtain.* MELANIE *draws the sobbing child to her and quiets him. He stops crying at her touch. A moment, then* SCARLETT's *sobs subside.*

MELANIE: Why did we fight? What was the good of it all?

SCARLETT: I'm not going to think about that now. I'm not interested in anything but just holding body and soul together.

*CAMERA has gone close to her as she dries her eyes on the white window curtain. Then:*

SCARLETT: The war can't last forever. We'll get through.

*Then her face sets at something she sees beyond the window.*

MELANIE'S BEDROOM

SCARLETT's *head in the foreground. From her angle a* YANKEE CAVALRYMAN *rides up the drive; slouched in his saddle, a long pistol at his hip.*

SCARLETT [*She turns from the window.*]: Stay where you are, Wade Hampton. Melanie, lock your door.

*She goes out,* MELANIE *looking in wonderment after her.*

EXTERIOR–FRONT OF THE HOUSE

*The* YANKEE CAVALRYMAN *dismounts easily and, pistol in hand, comes up the steps to the front door.*

INTERIOR–UPPER HALL

SCARLETT *crouches over the banister. From her angle—her head and shoulders in the foreground—the front door opens and the* YANKEE *comes in, his pistol drawn. He stands looking about him. He smiles and, feeling himself secure in what seems to be an uninhabited house, slips his pistol back into the holster, looks about him and slouches into the dining room.* SCARLETT *draws back trembling with fury, steps out of her slippers and disappears.*

SCARLETT'S BEDROOM

SCARLETT *stands over her bureau drawer, loading the pistol* RHETT *gave her on the night of the flight from Atlanta.*

HALL

*The* YANKEE *enters from the dining room,* ELLEN's *sewing box in his left hand. He is admiring her gold thimble, which he has placed on the little finger of his right hand. He looks up.*

YANKEE CAVALRYMAN: Halt! Or I'll shoot!

STAIR

SCARLETT *stands on the stair, the pistol hidden in the folds of her skirt. The* YANKEE *enters below her, the sewing box tucked under his arm, his revolver in hand. Seeing that he has only a girl to contend with, his face breaks into a half-contemptuous smile.*

YANKEE CAVALRYMAN: So there is somebody home! [*He slips pistol back into its holster.*] All alone, little lady?

CLOSE SHOT–SCARLETT

*Her hands clutching the pistol, she stares down at him silently.*

LONGER SHOT

SCARLETT *glaring down furiously at the* YANKEE—*the* YANKEE *grinning up at her.*

YANKEE: Y'ain't very friendly, are you? . . . [*He opens the sewing box and holds up the earbobs.*] Y'got anything else besides these earbobs?

SCARLETT [*with hatred and fury*]: You Yankees have been here before.

YANKEE [*looks around the hall, laughs*]: Regular little spitfire, ain't you? . . . [*He suddenly notices that* SCARLETT *is holding something behind her skirts.*] What've you got hidden in your hand?

*He starts up the steps toward her, eyeing her mockingly.* SCARLETT *stands without moving to stop him, letting him approach until he has nearly reached her.*

VERY LARGE CLOSE-UP–YANKEE's *face*

*Eyeing* SCARLETT, *his face comes closer and closer to the* CAMERA, *until* SCARLETT's *hand comes into the scene, pointing the pistol directly at his head. His eyes widen in horror, which we hold for a second as he looks at the muzzle. Then the pistol fires straight into his face.*

BACK TO SCENE

*The body rolls backward down the stairs and lands face up on the floor below. The face is terribly marked with powder smoke and burns —and blood streams from the pit where the nose had been. In the foreground a thin wisp of smoke from the pistol which* SCARLETT *still holds in her hand.*

SCARLETT *gazes down, her hatred giving way to horror at the realization of what she has done. She hears footsteps from the upper flight of stairs and turns to see* MELANIE *on the landing, clad only in her nightgown. She is holding out* CHARLES' *naked sabre.*

MELANIE *stops and looks down at the scene below.*

HIGH ANGLE SHOT FROM LANDING [*Over* MELANIE's *shoulder*]–*at* SCARLETT *on the stairs beneath her; and at the body of the marauder beneath* SCARLETT *in turn, lying on the hall floor.*

*CLOSE-UP*–MELANIE

*Standing with the sword in her hand. "There was a glow of grim pride in her usually gentle face, approbation and a fierce joy in her smile. . . ."*

*BACK TO SCENE*

SCARLETT *looks up at* MELANIE, *frightened. The sound of feet running outside, and* SUELLEN's *voice:*

SUELLEN's VOICE: Scarlett! Scarlett!

CARREEN's VOICE [*frightened*]: Scarlett! What happened? What happened?

MELANIE *thinks quickly, turns to the window and throws it open.*

EXTERIOR–[*Over* MELANIE's *shoulder through the window*]

SUELLEN *and* CARREEN, GERALD *with them, are running toward the house.*

MELANIE [*with teasing gaiety*]: Don't be scared, chickens. Your big sister was trying to clean a revolver and it went off and nearly scared her to death. [*She laughs.*]

SUELLEN, CARREEN *and* GERALD—OUTSIDE

CARREEN: Oh, thank goodness.

SUELLEN [*crossly*]: Haven't we got enough to frighten us?

GERALD [*reprovingly*]: Tell Katie Scarlett she must be more careful. *They turn and exit.*

*BACK TO SCENE*

SCARLETT [*admiringly*]: What a cool liar you are, Melly.

MELANIE *runs down the few steps to* SCARLETT.

MELANIE: We must get him out of here, Scarlett, and bury him. If the Yankees find him here—they'll—[*She steadies herself on* SCARLETT's *arm.*]

SCARLETT: I didn't see anyone else. I think he must be a deserter.

MELANIE: But even so we've got to hide him. They might hear about it and they'd—they'd come and get you.

SCARLETT *looks at her, then goes down the stair.*

LOWER HALL AND STAIRS

*The dead* YANKEE *lies sprawled across the foreground.* SCARLETT *comes down toward him from the stair, fascinated but revolted.*

SCARLETT: I could bury him in the arbor, where the ground is soft, but—[*then, up to* MELANIE]—but how will I get him out of here?

MELANIE: We'll both take a leg and drag him. [*She starts down.*]

SCARLETT: You couldn't drag a cat!

MELANIE *smiles and advances to* SCARLETT.

MELANIE [*as she joins* SCARLETT, *again clutching her for support*]:

Scarlett, do you think it would be dishonest if we went through his haversack?

SCARLETT: I'm ashamed I didn't think of that myself [*drops to her knees*]. You take his haversack. I'll search his pockets.

*Stooping over the dead man with distaste, she unbuttons the remaining buttons of his jacket and systematically begins rifling his pockets.* MELANIE *starts for the haversack, but is weak and sits abruptly on the floor, leaning back against the wall.*

MELANIE [*shakily*]: You look—I'm feeling a little weak.

SCARLETT [*pulling out a bulging wallet wrapped about with a rag— in a whisper*]: Melly, I think it's full of money! [*She tears off the rag and with trembling hands opens the leather folds.*] Oh, Melly, look— look!

MELANIE *looks and her eyes dilate. Jumbled together are a mass of bills, United States greenbacks mingling with Confederate money and, glinting from between them, a few gold pieces.*

SCARLETT: Ten . . . twenty . . . thirty . . . forty. . . .

MELANIE [*as* SCARLETT *starts fingering bills*]: Don't stop to count it now. We haven't time—

SCARLETT: Do you realize this means we'll have something to eat?

MELANIE: Look in his other pockets! Hurry! Hurry!

*She drags herself across the floor to the dead man's knapsack, dumping its contents out on the floor. The first item is a package of coffee. She smells it and displays it to* SCARLETT.

MELANIE: Coffee! Smell it!

SCARLETT *smells. Her eyes close in ecstasy. Then she points to the mess from the knapsack.*

SCARLETT: Oh, Melly!

*From the mess, she picks up quickly a pair of earrings.*

MELANIE: A thief! [*She recoils again from the dead body.*] He must have stolen those!

SCARLETT: Of course he did! He came here to steal more from us! First they ruin Tara and leave us to starve! And now they're back again to take what's . . .

MELANIE: I'm glad you killed him! Now get him out of here!

SCARLETT, *on her feet, surveys the problem.*

SCARLETT *bends over, catches the dead man by his boots and tugs. He is heavier than she realized, and she feels suddenly weak. Turning so that she backs the corpse, she catches a heavy boot under each arm and throws her weight forward. The body moves, and she jerks again. Tugging and straining, perspiration dripping from her forehead, she starts to drag him down the hall toward the front door, a red stain following her path.*

SCARLETT [*gasping*]: If he bleeds across the yard, we can't hide it. Give me your nightgown, Melly. I'll wad it around his head. [MELANIE'S *white face goes crimson.*] Oh, don't be silly. I won't look at you. If I had a petticoat or pantalettes, I'd use them.

*CAMERA PANS with* SCARLETT *as she turns back to the dead soldier.*

*CLOSE SHOT—*MELANIE

*Terribly embarrassed, she is crouching against the wall. As the CAMERA MOVES UP to a CLOSE-UP OF ONLY HER FACE AND SHOULDERS, she reaches down out of scene and pulls the ragged garment over her head—and, painfully embarrassed and shielding her naked shoulders as best she can with one arm, silently tosses it to* SCARLETT.

*CLOSE SHOT—*SCARLETT

*She catches the gown, throws a quick disgusted glance at* MELANIE, *and starts wrapping it around the man's head, muttering disgustedly.*

SCARLETT: Thank heavens I'm not that modest! [*Calls over her shoulder to* MELANIE.] Now go back to bed. You'll be dead if you don't. I'll clean up the mess after I've buried him. [*She wraps his head in the nightgown.*]

*CLOSE-UP—*MELANIE

*Still with one arm across her naked shoulder, she looks down at the pool of blood with a sick face.*

MELANIE [*in a sick whisper*]: No, I—I'll clean it up. I'll do it with one of the rag rugs.

SCARLETT: Well, kill yourself then and see if I care! [*She bends over the dead man's feet and picks up one boot under each arm.*] And if the girls come down, or Mammy or Pork come back, or Pa! . . . Keep 'em here in the house till I'm through with this! Then we won't have to think of it any more, but just spend the money! [*She jerks the door open.*] Look! We've got a horse to plough with out of this, too! Now we can send Pork off to Macon to buy food! And seed for the spring planting! Oh, I'd have been a ninny not to kill him!

*CLOSE SHOT—*SCARLETT

*She finishes wrapping the man's head and stands up.*

SCARLETT [*looking down at him*]: Well, I guess I've done murder. [*She draws the back of her hand across her eyes, throws out her chin.*] Oh, I won't think about that now. I'll think about that tomorrow.

*As she lifts up the soldier's legs and starts to drag him out, we—*

*FADE OUT*

*FADE IN:*

EXTERIOR–TARA–LATE AFTERNOON

*Rain, half sleet, is falling over the cape jessamine bush in front of the house. The twigs of the bush are all glazed with ice. CAMERA climbs slowly to a window against which the rain is beating. Through the window* MELANIE *can be seen, a cup of glue in her hand, trying to stick the loosened paper back in place across a broken pane.*

INTERIOR–DRAWING ROOM

*In the foreground,* SCARLETT *is working over the fire, which is burning badly.* MELANIE *comes toward her from the window.*

MELANIE: There isn't much I can do. The paper's wet and the glue won't hold it.

SCARLETT: This wood's so wet it won't burn. And there's no heat in it anyway.

*From upstairs comes the sound of* WADE HAMPTON *crying.*

WADE HAMPTON: Aunty! Aunty Melanie! I want you, Aunty!

*Then tears. The two girls listen for a moment. Then* SCARLETT *cannot endure the sound and cries out in a half-strangled voice.*

SCARLETT: Can't you make Wade hush?

MELANIE: You can't blame a sick child for being fretful.

SCARLETT *sinks back hopelessly on her knees.*

SCARLETT: No. He should have a doctor and medicine, and there's neither one to be had. And no neighbor to call in to help us, Melly. [*Then she rises and goes to* MELANIE *in terror.*] Doesn't it frighten you to be living this way? Like animals! Hungry and cold and alone!

MELANIE [*trembling*]: Scarlett, don't!

SCARLETT: Alone in this county that used to be chuckful of kin and friends!

MELANIE: Don't think about it, Scarlett!

SCARLETT: It's like being nailed up in a haunted barrel! [*She turns away to drop into a chair.*]

MELANIE: Yes, it is like that.

*Again* WADE HAMPTON *wails.*

SCARLETT: It isn't the sickness so much as just plain hunger. [*then wildly*] But I'm hungry, too!

MELANIE: He's too young to know that. I'll go up to him. I'll try to make him hush.

SCARLETT: Don't leave me alone!

MELANIE: I'll be back. [*She goes towards the door.* PORK *enters.*

*He carries a small, dead rooster in one hand. He is limping painfully.*]
Pork!

PORK *comes past her to* SCARLETT.

PORK: De traps wuz all empty fo' de third day, Miss Scarlett, but Ah ketched dis rooster runnin' wild in de woods. He ain' hardly big 'nuff ter feed eleven people, but he's all we got.

SCARLETT [*she is watching the Negro*]: Why are you limping, Pork?

PORK: Ah ain' limpin', Miss Scarlett.

SCARLETT: What's all that blood on your trouser leg?

PORK: Dat mus' hev come from dis bird.

SCARLETT: The bird's responsible all right. Melly, you take that rooster in to Mammy and fetch me back some bandages and hot water. [MELANIE *goes, taking the rooster.*] Now, pull up that trouser leg. [PORK *demurs.*] Go on! Pull it up! [*He obeys.*] Just as I thought. Your leg's all full of shot. Sit down now. Sit down and tell me where did you . . . [*She forces herself to say it.*] . . . where did you steal our supper.

PORK [*he tries to feel guilty*]: Ah dunno huccome Ah wander so far 'way as Fayetteville, but de traps wuz empty an' Ah jes' happen ter pass by a hen coop . . .

*A gesture from* SCARLETT *stops him. Then, from her kneeling position on the floor, she looks up at him.*

SCARLETT: You must be more careful. What would we do without you? You've been mighty good and faithful and when we've got plenty of money again, I'm going to buy you a big gold watch and engrave on it something out of the Bible: "Well done, good and faithful servant."

PORK [*he beams*]: Dat soun' mighty fine, Miss Scarlett! W'en you specktin' ter git all dat money?

SCARLETT *straightens, sitting back on her heels again.*

SCARLETT: I don't know, Pork, but I'm going to get it sometime! When this war's over I'm going to have lots of money and never be hungry or cold again! We'll all wear fine clothes and have plenty of fried chicken every day and . . . [MELANIE *enters with a basin of hot water and some strips of linen,* MAMMY *following.*] I'd forgotten! We don't talk about good things to eat, do we? [*Then suddenly she is on her feet.*] Miss Melly and Mammy will bandage your leg for you, Pork. I haven't time now. [*She is going out.*]

MELANIE: Scarlett, where are you going?

SCARLETT *is wrapping a ragged old cloak about herself.*

SCARLETT: I'm going to get on that horse of ours and get out of this barrel we're in! I'm going to take what's left of our eighty dollars and go to Jonesboro or Macon even, and buy this family enough to eat for once!

*The others are horrified.*

PORK: Miss Scarlett!

MELANIE: You mustn't think of it, Scarlett!

SCARLETT: Why mustn't I?

MAMMY: Honey chile, de Yankees!

SCARLETT: The Yankees may be a thousand miles away!

MELANIE: Or they may be just across the river. [*She shudders.*] We don't know. We don't know anything outside.

*A pause.* WADE HAMPTON *is crying again.*

WADE HAMPTON: Aunty! Aunty Melanie, please come!

SCARLETT: I'll hush Wade Hampton. And Mammy can make him some chicken broth from that rooster. I guess the war will be over some day. I hope we live to see the end of it. [*She goes out into the hall.*]

*FADE OUT*

# Seventh
# Sequence

*ADE IN:*

*EXTREME LONG SHOT–TARA–(MAY 1865)–DAY*

GERALD *is galloping like the wind toward Tara, approaching the fence.*

QUICK DISSOLVE TO

INTERIOR–HALL–TARA

*VERY LOW CAMERA SETUP, wide angle lens shooting the entire length of the hall.*

*The door flies open and* GERALD *bursts in, making a great clutter of noise.* MELANIE, SCARLETT, SUELLEN, *and* CARREEN *pour into the hall from all directions—*CARREEN *and* SUELLEN *together.*

*CAMERA MOVES UP TO CLOSE SHOT OF* GERALD, *as fast as the CAMERA can move. As the CAMERA reaches his mad face:*

GERALD: Katie Scarlett! Katie Scarlett! It's over! It's over! It's all over! The war! Lee surrendered!

*On the word "surrendered" swing the CAMERA to a TWO SHOT of* CARREEN *and* SUELLEN*—larger than waistsize.*

SUELLEN *and* CARREEN [*almost simultaneously*]: It's not possible!

CARREEN: Oh, why did we ever fight! . . .

*SWING CAMERA, as fast as it can move, to a LARGE CLOSE-UP OF* MELANIE.

MELANIE [*ecstatic*]: Now Ashley will be coming home to me! My beloved will be coming home to me now!

SCARLETT *starts.*

HALL–CLOSE SHOT

SCARLETT's *face is sombre, her lips barely move, her voice is barely audible as she echoes* MELANIE's *words.*

SCARLETT: My beloved will be coming home to me now! Yes. Ashley will be coming home. We'll plant more cotton. Cotton ought to go sky high next year. . . .

DISSOLVE TO

*LONG SHOT–ROAD–IN FRONT OF TARA–(SEPTEMBER 1865)–DAY*

*On the road is a weary procession of Confederate soldiers returning from the war, stretching back and dotting the road in small groups as far as we can see. Most are walking, barefoot. All are in ragged uniforms, about one-fourth of which wear blue coats which have been taken from Yankee prisoners or from the dead. At least half the men seen are wounded—some with a missing leg, some with a missing arm, some with bandages, etc. It is a pitiful portrait of the lame, the halt, and the blind that now constitute the largest part of what is left of Southern manhood. Some are on horses in even more wretched condition than their riders. Over this the title:*

Home from their lost adventure
came the tattered cavaliers. . . .

Grimly they came hobbling back
to the desolation that had once
been a land of grace and plenty. . . .

And with them came another
Invader . . . more cruel and vicious
than any they had fought . . . the
Carpetbagger. . . .

*As the TITLE FADES OFF, we hear a male voice singing "Marching Through Georgia," and a buggy appears in the background, coming toward CAMERA. In it is* JONAS WILKERSON, *the ex-overseer of Tara, and beside him sits a flashily dressed, Free-Issue Negro, who is doing the singing. The horse, at a gallop, bears down upon some of the returning foot soldiers, forcing them off the road. As the buggy comes abreast of the CAMERA, it almost strikes one man who has put up his arm and is standing in front of the buggy to stop it. He is supporting another soldier who is obviously very weak and wounded.* WILKERSON *pulls up sharply, having almost hit the man.*

WILKERSON [*standing up, in a rage*]: Get out of the road, Rebel! Get out of the way.

SOLDIER: Have you room in your carriage for a dying man?

WILKERSON: I got no room for any Southern scum, alive or dead! Get out of the way!

*He half-raises his whip threateningly. The* SOLDIER *just looks at him. For a moment the two men's eyes are locked, then* WILKERSON'S *eyes waver and glance away.*

SOLDIER [*quietly*]: I reckon he'd rather try and walk it, at that.

WILKERSON [*violently—whips his horse*]: Gid-ap! [*yells at soldiers*] Jump, you gray-backed beggars!

NEGRO: Hunh . . . Ack' as tho dey won de war!

*The horse starts through and the stragglers scamper away.* WILKERSON *spits on them as his buggy breaks through their ranks and passes on.*

EXTERIOR–VERANDAH–DAY

MELANIE *stands with* TWO SOLDIERS.

MELANIE: You see, it's my husband. We've had no word from him.

FIRST SOLDIER: I was in Rock Island prison camp, but I never got to know any Major Wilkes.

*The* SECOND SOLDIER *sees that* MELANIE *winces and hastens to add:*

SECOND SOLDIER: We privates didn't get to know majors, though, Ma'am, so . . .

*But* MELANIE, *biting her lip, has turned out of the scene.*

*DISSOLVE TO*

INTERIOR–MELANIE'S BEDROOM–NIGHT

MELANIE *sits on her bed, crying softly,* CARREEN *bending over her.*

CARREEN: But Ashley hasn't died in prison! I know he hasn't!

MELANIE: I can't help feeling discouraged.

CARREEN: Some Yankee chaplain would have written you!

MELANIE [*She only shakes her head.*]: Why hasn't Ashley written?

CARREEN: Melly, you know what the mails are now!

MELANIE: But how do I know he hasn't died on the way home?

CARREEN: Wouldn't some Yankee woman have written you that? [SCARLETT *enters.*] There must be some kind Yankee women! You remember we met a nice Yankee woman in Saratoga!

SCARLETT: Nice, my foot! She asked me how many bloodhounds we kept to chase our slaves! I never saw a nice Yankee man or woman! Don't cry, though, Melanie. Ashley'll come home. It's a long walk and maybe he hasn't got any boots.

MELANIE's *tears break out afresh.*

EXTERIOR–DRIVE

*More soldiers are coming up the drive to the house.*

INTERIOR–DRAWING ROOM

*The sofas are made up for beds and more beds are made up on the floor.* MELANIE *is working on one of them. Looking up from her knees, she sees the newcomers as they walk up the verandah steps. She rises and runs out.*

EXTERIOR–VERANDAH

MELANIE *enters to the soldiers. They take off their hats awkwardly.*

MELANIE: I wonder if you could tell me. . . . You see, my husband —Major Wilkes his name is—I haven't had any word except just "missing."

FIRST SOLDIER: Now, Ma'am, don't you bother about your husband. I was captured and they fed me on the fat of the land in prison.

MELANIE [*She smiles.*]: I think you're a liar. What do you think?

FIRST SOLDIER [*sheepishly*]: I think so, too. But don't worry.

EXTERIOR–TARA–DAY–(SEPTEMBER 1865)

*MEDIUM SHOT shooting at SCUPPERNONG ARBOR which is in back of the smokehouse at the side of Tara.*

*In the foreground on the lawn are three men wrapped in blankets —one lying peacefully stretched out, and two sitting playing cards. None of them speaks.*

*THE CAMERA STARTS TO MOVE UP TO A CLOSE SHOT AT THE ARBOR where, behind a screen of bushes and blankets draped over the structure, are the heads and shoulders of three scarecrow soldiers. One is* FRANK KENNEDY. *The other two men have been stripped and one is trimming his whiskers with a pair of shears. Sound of splashing from behind the bushes.* FRANK KENNEDY *seems reluctant.* MAMMY *stands determined on the lawn, a pitchfork in her hands.*

MAMMY: Now you come on. Gimme dem pants, Mr. Kennedy. Come on. [*He throws his uniform trousers over the hedge.* MAMMY *spears them on her pitchfork.*] Now you scrub yo'seff wid dat strong lye soap befo' Ah comes an' scrubs you mah-seff! Ah's gwine to put dese britches in de boilin' pot!

*She walks a few steps to the boiling pot and drops the trousers in, throws the pitchfork on the ground, and starts toward the covered way, muttering to herself:*

MAMMY [*muttering*]: The whole Confed'rut army got de same troubles—crawlin' cloe's an' dysent'ry!

NEAR THE END OF THE COVERED WAY

*As* MAMMY *enters scene she meets* SUELLEN *who has just come out.*

SUELLEN [*sputters*]: I think it's humiliating the way you're treating Mr. Kennedy!

MAMMY: You'd be a sight mo' humiliated effen Mr. Kennedy's lice gits on you!

SUELLEN *is indignant. FOLLOW* MAMMY *as she leaves her and passes the COVERED WAY on her way to the smokehouse. On the steps and the porch are seven to ten gaunt Confederate soldiers hungrily devouring food. A couple of the men are crippled and the others in various states of disrepair. Their clothing, recently boiled by* MAMMY, *is clean but ragged and unpressed. A table bearing food is set up on the porch at which* PRISSY *is cutting a watermelon.* PORK *is busying himself in the background seeing that the men are fed. As* MAMMY *approaches and turns to go toward the smokehouse, CAMERA SWINGS IN THE OPPOSITE DIRECTION to the steps of the covered way.* MELANIE *is sitting on the steps folding a pile of mended garments, her work basket beside her feet. A tired and footsore Confederate in washed and dried clothes is also sitting on the steps, eating. Little* BEAU *is toddling about on uncertain legs, sometimes falling forward, catching himself with both hands, and then straightening up again to toddle about the* SOLDIER. *Gurgling with delight, making little inarticulate noises, he is trying to play with the* SOLDIER; *pestering him, flirting with him, plucking grass with his baby fists and throwing the grass at the* SOLDIER, *etc.* MELANIE *looks up and sees what the baby is doing.*

MELANIE: Oh, come on, Beau. Leave this gentleman alone. Because he's tired and hungry.

SOLDIER: I don't mind, ma'am, it's good to see a youngster again. Nice little fellow. Another two years of war and we could have had him with us in Cobb's Legion.

MELANIE [*eagerly*]: Were you in Cobb's Legion?

SOLDIER: Yes, ma'am.

MELANIE: Why then you must know my husband, Major Wilkes!

SOLDIER: Oh yes, ma'am . . . he was captured at Spotsylvania, I think.

MELANIE [*horrified*]: Captured! [*then suddenly relieved*] Oh, thank heaven, then he isn't—[*She stops herself.*] Oh, my poor Ashley, in a Yankee prison!

SCARLETT'S VOICE: Melanie!

MELANIE *turns to see* SCARLETT *motion to her.* SCARLETT *stands just outside the door to the house.* MELANIE *goes to her. As she leaves,* MELANIE *glances back doubtfully at little* BEAU, *whom she is leaving behind. The* SOLDIER *pats the child's shoulder with his free hand.*

MELANIE: Yes, Scarlett. I—come along, Beau.

SOLDIER: I'll watch out for him, ma'am. We're good friends.

MELANIE: Oh, thank you.

*She rises and goes up the steps toward* SCARLETT.

TWO SHOT–SCARLETT *and* MELANIE

MELANIE *enters scene,* SCARLETT *talking as she does:*

SCARLETT [*scolding, in a low voice*]: Here I slave day and night just so we can have enough food to keep body and soul together . . . and you give it all away to these starving scarecrows. I'd as soon have a plague of locusts around the place!

MELANIE: Oh, don't scold me, Scarlett, please. I've just heard that Ashley was taken prisoner.

SCARLETT: Ashley a prisoner!

MELANIE: Yes . . . and maybe if he's alive . . . and well . . . he's on some Northern road right now . . . and maybe some Northern woman is giving him a share of her dinner and helping my beloved to come back home to me.

SCARLETT, *ashamed and abashed, lowers her eyes, touches* MELANIE *on the arm.*

SCARLETT [*quietly*]: I hope so, Melly.

*CAMERA PANS with* SCARLETT *as she turns from* MELANIE *to go into the house, moody, her thoughts on* ASHLEY.

KENNEDY'S VOICE: Miss Scarlett!

SCARLETT *stops and turns back.* KENNEDY *approaches her from direction of the covered way, embarrassed and breathless. He is wrapped in pinned up blankets and quilts.*

INTERIOR–TARA HALL

*Through the open door, as* SCARLETT *and* KENNEDY *enter, a few men seen in the background on the steps of the covered way.*

*During the following dialogue CAMERA TRUCKS with* SCARLETT *and* KENNEDY *as they turn and walk toward the front door,* FRANK *having difficulty with his blankets and quilts.*

KENNEDY: Miss Scarlett, I wanted to take up something with your Pa, but he doesn't seem to . . .

SCARLETT [*interrupting impatiently*]: Perhaps I can help you. I'm the head of the house now.

KENNEDY: Well, I—I—[*He claws at his beard.*] Miss Scarlett, I was aiming to ask him for Suellen.

SCARLETT [*simulating amazement*]: Do you mean to tell me, Frank Kennedy, you haven't asked for her after all these years that she's been *counting* on you?

KENNEDY [*grins in embarrassment and hems and haws, moving from one foot to the other*]: Well, the truth is . . . I'm so much older than she is—and—well, now I haven't a cent to my name.

SCARLETT [*encouragingly*]: Who *has*, nowadays?

KENNEDY [*with simple dignity*]: Miss Scarlett, if true love carries

any weight with you, you can be sure your sister will be rich in that.
. . . I'll go out somewhere and get myself a little business. And as soon
as I get on my feet again—we can—

SCARLETT [*kindly*]: All right, Frank. I'm sure I can speak for Pa.
You go ask her now.

KENNEDY: Oh, thank you, thank you, Miss Scarlett!

*By now they are at the front door.* FRANK KENNEDY *opens it in frantic
excitement and runs out onto the verandah.*

EXTERIOR–VERANDAH

*As* KENNEDY *bursts out the door and starts across, he almost knocks
over* MELANIE *and* MAMMY *who have come up onto the verandah from
the grounds.*

KENNEDY: Excuse me, Mrs. Wilkes, excuse me!

*He flutters off, as* SCARLETT *comes out from the hall.* MELANIE *and*
MAMMY *look after* KENNEDY, *astonished.*

MELANIE [*She turns to* SCARLETT.]: Scarlett, what seems to be the
trouble with Mr. Kennedy?

SCARLETT: More trouble than he guesses. He's finally asked for
Suellen's hand.

MELANIE: Oh, I'm so glad.

SCARLETT: It's a pity he can't marry her now. At least be one less
mouth to feed. . . .

*She looks at* MELANIE *who is looking down the driveway and follows* MELANIE's *gaze.*

DRIVEWAY [*From point of view of* SCARLETT *and* MELANIE]

*Up the driveway, under the trees in the distance, a solitary soldier
is walking from the road toward the house.*

BACK TO SCENE

SCARLETT [*grumblingly*]: Oh, another one! I hope this one isn't
hungry.

MAMMY: He'll be hongry.

MELANIE [*turns to go back across the porch*]: I'll tell Prissy to get
an extra plate and . . .

*She stops suddenly, her hand goes to her throat clutching it as
though it is torn with pain.* SCARLETT *comes to her, catching her arm.
After only a second* MELANIE *throws the hand off her arm and flies
down the steps.* MELANIE *is off, running as fast as her vast skirts will
permit.* CAMERA *is after her. As she runs, the little figure grows
larger and is seen to be* ASHLEY *and we see the wordless reunion of
husband and wife.*

*CLOSE TWO SHOT:* MAMMY *and* SCARLETT

SCARLETT, *realizing, reels back, then suddenly starts forward. But* MAMMY *stops her, seizing* SCARLETT'S *skirt.*

MAMMY: Don't spoil it, chile!

SCARLETT: Turn me loose, you fool! Turn me loose! It's Ashley!

*But* MAMMY *does not turn her loose.*

MAMMY [*quietly*]: He's her husban', ain' he?

FADE OUT

FADE IN:

INTERIOR–JONESBORO–BLACKSMITH SHOP–DAY

*The Yankee cavalryman's horse is being shod by a Negro* BLACK-SMITH. ASHLEY *and* PORK *stand by.*

BLACKSMITH: Yassir, Mist' Wilkes. Ain' no mo' plantations up our way. Ain' no mo' folks nor no mo' nuthin'. Now Ah'm freed Ah got ter mek mah livin' fo' mahseff. Ah wuz a blacksmith on de ole plantation. Now Ah'm de blacksmith hyah in Jonesboro.

ASHLEY: I can't see that we're being of much help to T-boy, Pork. I heard Miss Scarlett giving you errands to do. I should enjoy a stroll through the town myself.

PORK: Yassir, Mist' Ashley. [*He shuffles out.*]

BLACKSMITH [*looking up*]: Ah wouldn' go strollin' eff Ah wuz you, Mist' Wilkes. Things ain' lak dey used ter be roun' hyah.

ASHLEY: It never hurts a man to see for himself, T-boy.

EXTERIOR–JONESBORO–STREET

*An old house. A squad of Yankee soldiers storms up the steps, bursting through the front door.* ASHLEY *enters, stops appalled, then goes near to look in through the parlor windows.*

INTERIOR–THE HOUSE

*From* ASHLEY'S *angle the scene in the parlor can be seen. Two elderly ladies cower against a square piano. A Yankee officer stands over them. His men pull down the Confederate flag which is draped over the portrait of an officer, take with it the officer's sword and pistols. These last they surrender to the Yankee* SERGEANT *who examines them callously. One of the* SOLDIERS *opens the window.*

SOLDIER: Here's another house keeping up the old Rebel spirit! [*He throws the flag out.*]

EXTERIOR–THE STREET–DAY

*The street as before.* ASHLEY *is startled as the flag falls at his feet. He stoops indignantly to pick it up, but another Yankee* NON-COM *snatches it first and tosses it into a dump cart which stands at the*

*Postwar street scenes in Atlanta.* ABOVE: *Selznick International Pictures publicity still.* BELOW: *An undated photograph by Wilbur G. Kurtz.*

curb. The SERGEANT *in the window throws pistols and sword after the flag.*

SERGEANT: Weapons, too! Firearms!

*At the same moment two more soldiers come out of the house, leading a middle-aged man, who limps on a wooden leg, between them. They march him off up the street, The* NON-COM *who picked up the flag picks up the sword and pistols, watching* ASHLEY *closely.*

THE NON-COM [*to* ASHLEY]: What are you staring at, Rebel?

ASHLEY *goes out of the scene.*

JONESBORO–A STREET

*A sign:* FREEDMEN'S BUREAU, *is strung across the façade of a former store. Negroes lounge in the front, noisy and self-assured.* PORK *passes, eyeing them in alarmed dismay.*

JONESBORO–A STREET

PORK, *entering, finds himself in front of a polling place. A lorry, alive with Negroes, is drawn up at the door.* PORK *turns to one of the colored bystanders.*

PORK: Whut goes on inside dar?

*Before the Negro can answer a Yankee steps forward: a* CARPET-BAGGER, *cast to type, with a vengeance.*

CARPETBAGGER: Can't you read? No. Well, they're voting.

PORK: Niggers?

CARPETBAGGER: Don't you want to vote?

PORK: Whut fo'?

CARPETBAGGER: You're a citizen now.

PORK *is bewildered.*

INTERIOR–POLLING BOOTH–CLOSE SHOT

*A white hand can be seen guiding a black hand to make a cross under the Republican ticket.*

EXTERIOR–THE STREET

*Outside the polling place as before.*

CARPETBAGGER: You can go in and vote with the best of 'em. And that's more than the Rebels can do.

PORK: Ah'm a Rebel.

CARPETBAGGER: Will you fellows listen to the way this darky's talking? Says he's a . . .

JONAS WILKERSON *and another Yankee have already joined the group, also two or three Negroes. Now* ASHLEY *comes in to* PORK *and* PORK *turns to him, frightened.*

PORK: Mist' Ashley, let's us git outer disyere town. Let's us go home.

*But* JONAS WILKERSON *steps forward.*

WILKERSON: Never mind the darky. This is the man I want. Wilkes is the name, I believe? Ashley Wilkes once of Twelve Oakes? Now of . . .

ASHLEY: You have the advantage of me.

WILKERSON: I know I have. [*The Yankees and Negroes laugh.*] You're living at Tara now, where I used to be overseer in the good old days. [ASHLEY *remembers.*] Meet my friend the tax collector, Mr. Wilkes.

ASHLEY *turns to find himself facing another Carpetbagger.*

WILKERSON: Him and me was just having a little talk about Tara. Maybe you'd like to hear what we've decided.

*DISSOLVE TO*

# INTERMISSION

# Eighth
# Sequence

*I*NTERIOR–TARA–ELLEN'S OFFICE–DAY

SCARLETT *sits at the desk, writing, the CAMERA looking past her head and over her shoulder at the letter, the text of which reads:*

Dearest Aunt Pitty:—
We can't possibly come to live with you in Atlanta because we couldn't leave Tara. Things have gone rather better with us since Ashley . . .

*From off-screen* MELANIE's *voice is audible.*

MELANIE'S VOICE: Then we'll just have to put a new patch on the other pair, Wade.

*The CAMERA, still holding* SCARLETT's *head in the foreground, moves up from the desk to see* MELANIE *and* WADE HAMPTON *on the verandah just outside the open window.* MELANIE *is helping* WADE HAMPTON *to button on the trousers she has just patched for him, while, with her bare foot, she rocks her baby's cradle.*

MELANIE'S VOICE: Try to be more careful of these, though. They won't stand much more.

*From off-screen the sound of a horse's hooves on the gravel.* WADE HAMPTON *runs out, calling:*

WADE HAMPTON: Here's Uncle Ashley home again! Uncle Ashley!

THE VERANDAH

WADE HAMPTON *is running down to meet* ASHLEY, *who rides in to the foot of the verandah steps, mounted on the Yankee cavalryman's horse,* PORK *accompanying him on foot.* ASHLEY *dismounts as gracefully as he can with a sack of provisions which hangs over the front of the saddle.* GERALD, *seated apart, watches him; and* SCARLETT *enters from the front of the house.*

SCARLETT: You got back quickly.

ASHLEY: There wasn't anyone ahead of me at the blacksmith's.

SCARLETT *looks down at her feet. Her shoes are broken and split and tied together with rope.*

SCARLETT: It's a fine state of affairs when horses have shoes and humans haven't.

MELANIE *conceals her bare feet under her skirt.* ASHLEY *looks down at his own feet. His boots are bound together with strips of canvas.*

ASHLEY: I'll put the horse in the paddock.

*He passes the sack of provisions to* PORK, *who starts with it toward the kitchen.*

SCARLETT: I'll do it.

ASHLEY: Do you think I can't manage?

*He leads the horse out of the scene.*

SCARLETT: Ashley, I didn't mean! . . .

*She starts down the steps after him.*

MELANIE: I keep telling him he mustn't be so touchy. He wasn't brought up to be a farmer. He's got to learn.

SCARLETT: It's hard on him. I'll . . . I'll go make it right with him.

*She is following* ASHLEY *out of the scene.*

THE DRIVE

*The corner of the house.* SCARLETT *enters, passing* PORK, *where he stands with the sack of provisions.*

PORK: Miss Scarlett . . .

SCARLETT [*stopping*]: Yes, Pork. What is it?

PORK: Ah knows Ah ain' got no right ter ask you, Miss Scarlett, but jes' how much money hev you got lef'? In gol'?

SCARLETT: Ten dollars. Why?

PORK [*shaking his head*]: Dat won' be ernuf, Miss Scarlett.

SCARLETT: Enough for what?

PORK: Ernuf fo' de taxes.

SCARLETT: What are you talking about? I've paid the taxes.

PORK: [*The Negro's loving joy in catastrophe*]: Seems lak you din' pay ernuf. Dat's whut dey said over ter Jonesboro. You'd oughter hev paid lots mo' taxes, Miss Scarlett. Dey runnin' de taxes way up sky high on Tara.

SCARLETT: But they can't do that!

PORK: Ain't much dey kain' do effen dey's a mind ter, Miss Scarlett. You don' never go ter Jonesboro no mo', an' Ah'm glad you don', 'kase it ain' no place fo' a lady dese days. But seems lak some Yankee wants ter buy in Tara cheap at a sheriff's sale effen you kain' pay extra taxes an' everybody knows you kain' pay 'em. [*He heaves a sigh of delighted despair.*]

SCARLETT [*Her anguish is all too genuine.*]: I thought our troubles would be over when the war ended!

PORK: No'm, Miss Scarlett, looks lak our troubles is jes' gittin' started.

SCARLETT: How much taxes do they want us to pay?

PORK: Three hundred dollars. [SCARLETT *gasps.*] Dat's whut dey tol' Mist' Ashley an' me.

SCARLETT: Three hundred. . . . It might just as well be three million!

PORK: Yas'm. Mist' Ashley tol' me not ter say nuthin' ter you 'bout it an' he'd tell you hisseff, but Ah thought Ah mout as well.

SCARLETT: I'm glad you did. Don't speak of this to Pa. I don't want him upset. We've got to raise it, that's all.

PORK: Yas'm. How?

SCARLETT: I don't know. I'll ask Mr. Ashley.

PORK: He ain't got no three hundred, Miss Scarlett.

*But* SCARLETT *is irritated by his evident enjoyment.*

SCARLETT: I can talk to him about it if I want to, can't I?

*She goes out of the scene, leaving him shaking his head over his basket.*

PADDOCK

*The gate of the paddock is half broken loose from its hinges.* ASHLEY *has tied the horse to the paddock rail and with an axe is clumsily trying to repair the gate.* SCARLETT *enters to him. Her eyes fill with tears.*

SCARLETT: Ashley . . .

ASHLEY [*He smiles.*]: They tell me Abe Lincoln got his start splitting rails. Just think what heights I may climb to once I get the knack. [*But his arm slips and knocks the gate completely loose.*] Once! [*He looks at her. His smile fades.*] So Pork told you, did he? [*Then his head falls.*] And you come to me for help and I've no help to give you.

SCARLETT [*She takes a step toward him.*]: What's going to become of us, Ashley?

ASHLEY: What do you think becomes of people when their civilization breaks up? Those who have brains and courage come through all right. Those who haven't are winnowed out.

SCARLETT: For heaven's sake, Ashley Wilkes, don't stand there and talk nonsense at me when it's us who are being winnowed out!

ASHLEY: Not you. You can take life by the horns and twist it to your will. [*He takes her hands in his, smiling with all his old grace and charm.*] These are the most beautiful hands in the world, Scarlett. [*He kisses each palm lightly.*] They're beautiful because they're so strong. And every callous is a medal you've won working for us. For your sisters and Melanie and our baby and me. [*Then, shrugging his shoulders, he drops her hands.*] I don't see much hope for me, though. I don't see where I fit in the world any more. [*And his eyes stray off as to some remote star now extinguished.*] The world I belong to's gone. Every day I realize how helpless I am to cope with this world

that's taken its place. [*He looks back at her.*] I suppose that means I'm a coward!

SCARLETT: You, Ashley? What is it you're afraid of?

ASHLEY: Oh, nameless things. Mostly of life becoming too real for me, I expect. Not that I mind splitting rails. [*But his gaze shifts off again.*] But I do mind very much losing the beauty of the old life I loved. Before the war, Scarlett, life *was* beautiful. Living at Twelve Oaks was a beautiful thing. I see now, though, that it was only a shadow show. And I've always avoided everything but the dreams and shadows. [*He smiles again.*] I tried to avoid you, Scarlett, and here I am living on your charity.

SCARLETT: Not charity, Ashley!

ASHLEY: Oh, yes! [*And again he smiles.*] You see, you were too real for me.

SCARLETT [*She is puzzled.*]: No, I'm not.

ASHLEY [*He shakes his head sadly.*]: I can't make you understand, because you don't know the meaning of fear. So you'll never mind facing realities and never want to escape from them as I do.

SCARLETT: Escape? [*She turns a quick, guilty look toward the house, then*] I do want to escape, though! Oh, Ashley, I'm so tired of it all! I've struggled for food and money and I've weeded and hoed and picked cotton until I can't stand it another minute! The South's dead! The free niggers and carpetbaggers have got it! [*She clutches his arm suddenly.*] Ashley, let's us run away!

ASHLEY [*drawing away from her*] You and I run away? Where to?

SCARLETT: Anywhere! They want officers in the Mexican Army! We could be happy there! I'd work for you, Ashley! I'd do anything for you! You know you love me better than Melanie! She can't give you any more children! The doctor says she can't! but I can, Ashley!

*He is startled. His eyes fall. He bites his lip.*

ASHLEY: We agreed to forget that day at Twelve Oaks.

SCARLETT [*She is undaunted.*]: Have you forgotten it? Can you honestly say you don't love me, Ashley?

ASHLEY [*very steady*]: I don't love you.

SCARLETT: That's a lie!

ASHLEY [*He turns indignantly on her.*]: And if I did, could I go off and leave Melly and the baby? You couldn't leave the girls!

SCARLETT: Yes, I could leave them! Someone always looks out for those who can't look out for themselves! I'm sick and tired of 'em!

ASHLEY [*He tries to control her.*]: I know you're sick and tired. That's why you're talking this way now. But I'm going to help you. I'm beginning to learn.

*She will not be controlled.*

SCARLETT: There's only one way you can help me! Take me away!

*She has flung herself against him, her body pressing his, her arms around him and her face upturned to his.*

ASHLEY: Don't! Don't!

*His hands are gripping her shoulders, but she smiles her small, bright smile, and her face goes closer to his.*

SCARLETT: You love me, Ashley!

ASHLEY: We shall both be sorry, Scarlett!

*He kisses her, then, breaking free, suddenly shakes her till her hair tumbles down about her shoulders.*

ASHLEY: We won't do this, I tell you! We won't do it! [*And he fairly throws her clear of him.*] It won't happen again! I'll take Melanie and the baby and go!

SCARLETT: You love me! Say it! Say it! You love me!

ASHLEY: All right, I'll say it! I love your courage and stubbornness! How much do I love them? So much that a moment ago I could have forgotten the best wife a man ever had! But I'm not going to forget her, Scarlett!

SCARLETT [*Her head falls.*]: Then there's nothing left for me. Nothing to fight for. Nothing to live for.

ASHLEY: Yes, there is something. Something you love better than me, though you may not know it. [*He stoops quickly, scrapes up a handful of moist earth and presses it into the palm of her hand.*] Tara.

*She is looking at her handful of earth. Then her head comes up.*

SCARLETT: You needn't go. I won't have you all starve simply because I've thrown myself at your head. It won't happen again. [*She walks away from him.*]

*DISSOLVE TO*

VERANDAH

SCARLETT *enters, walking steadily, clutching the ball of red clay in her hand. As she turns up the steps, she sees* MELANIE *staring straight before her, clutching* WADE HAMPTON *against her chair.* MELANIE *points.*

MELANIE: We've got visitors, Scarlett.

*Surprised,* SCARLETT *turns to look down the drive.*

DRIVE

*From* SCARLETT'S *angle a shiny new buggy is driving toward the house.* MR. JONAS WILKERSON *holds the reins, his wife,* EMMY, *born* SLATTERY, *showily turned out, sits beside him.*

VERANDAH

*The verandah as before.*

SCARLETT: Who do we know with a brand new buggy?

*But the buggy pulls up at the steps and* EMMY *climbs out.*

SCARLETT: Why it's Emmy Slattery!

EMMY: Yes'm, it's me.

WILKERSON: Mrs. Wilkerson now. Don't guess you've forgotten your old overseer, have you?

*He is coming up the steps to the verandah, but* SCARLETT *explodes.*

SCARLETT: Get off those steps, you trashy wench! Get off this land! Get out!

EMMY *stops suddenly and glances back at* WILKERSON, *who joins her.*

WILKERSON: Now, I don't like you speaking that way to my wife.

SCARLETT: Wife? [*She laughs contemptuously.*] About time you married her! [*and to* EMMY] Who's baptized your brats since you killed my mother!

EMMY *gasps and would retreat down the steps, but* WILKERSON *stops her with a rough grasp on her arm.*

WILKERSON: We came out here to pay a call—a friendly call—and talk over a little business with old friends . . .

SCARLETT [*beside herself*]: Friends? When were we ever friends with the like of you? The Slatterys lived on our charity and Pa fired you and you know why! Friends! Get off this place before I call Mr. Wilkes!

EMMY *flees to the buggy, but her husband stands his ground.*

WILKERSON: Still high and mighty, are you? You want to be careful how you talk, young lady! The state of Georgia's under martial law now—or as good!

SCARLETT: If your soldiers were men they'd protect our rights and not . . .

WILKERSON: Rights? You Rebels got no rights!

SCARLETT: Get off this place!

WILKERSON: You won't sing that tune much longer. You're broke. You can't even pay your taxes. I came out here to offer to buy this place from you—to make you a right good offer. Emmy's got a hankering to live here. . . .

SCARLETT: I'd tear this house down stone by stone and burn it and sow every acre with salt before I'd see either of you put foot over this threshold!

WILKERSON: Well, by cracky, I won't give you a cent for it now! You high-flying, bog-trotting Irish'll find out who's running things

ABOVE: *A scene of Thomas Mitchell with Oscar Polk after Gerald had become deranged.* BELOW: *A camera crew preparing for one of Mitchell's postwar scenes. Snapshot by Wilbur G. Kurtz made June 5, 1939.*

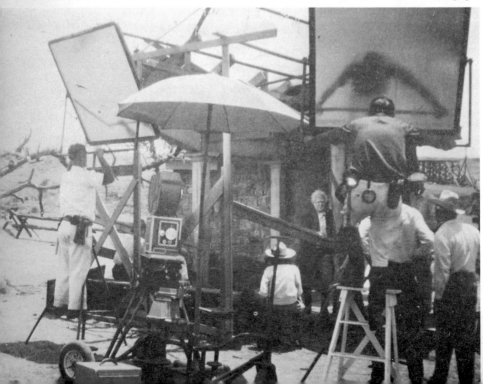

around here when you get sold up for taxes! I will buy this place, lock, stock and barrel, furniture and all, and I will live in it! But I'll wait for the sheriff's sale!

SCARLETT: Get out, I tell you! Get out!

*But* GERALD *has risen and joined her on the steps.*

GERALD: What did he say, daughter?

SCARLETT: Now, never mind, Pa! He can't do any of that!

WILKERSON: Oh, can't I?

GERALD [*crescendo*]: Sell out Tara, did he say?

SCARLETT: Now, don't get excited, Pa! [*then, back to* WILKERSON, *who has already clambered into his buggy*] Get out, I tell you! Get out!

WILKERSON: We're going, honey. But we'll be back. [*He drives his buggy out of scene.*]

GERALD [*frantic*]: Sell out Tara! Sell out . . .

SCARLETT: Pa! Please don't get excited! [*Then, however,* GERALD *straightens suddenly and with the low roar of an angry bull plunges down the steps on his way towards the paddock.*] Pa, where are you going? [*then, suddenly loud with terror*] Pa!

*She runs down the steps.* MELANIE *rises and totters after her.*

PADDOCK

GERALD *has already untied the Yankee cavalryman's horse from the paddock rail. Voices—*ASHLEY'S, MAMMY'S, PORK'S *and* SCARLETT'S—*ring out from the off-screen pursuit as he swings himself into the saddle.*

GERALD: Filthy Yankees! Preposterous Yankees! I'll show them who the owner of Tara is!

SCARLETT *reaches him first and snatches at the bridle. Jerking the horse's head out of her reach, he knocks* PORK—*who enters—to the ground.*

GERALD: Stand clear of my horse!!!

*He wheels and charges past* MELANIE, *who has run into the scene.*

SCARLETT: Pa!!!

DRIVE

GERALD *rides around the corner of the house, where* MAMMY, DILCEY, *and* WADE HAMPTON *stand terrified.*

MAMMY: Fo' de Lawd, Mist' Gerald!

GERALD *reins in, pulling his mount fairly back on his haunches, and shouts his purpose to the world.*

GERALD: That scum left the land of Tara without a thrashing! May the saints forgive me if he lives to boast of that!

And he kicks his horse and is off across lawn and garden. SCARLETT is after him first, as the others follow. MELANIE stops, her hand to her heart, but SCARLETT runs on, her skirts held up to her knees.

GARDEN–TRUCK SHOT

A place of trees, extending to a roadside hedge. CAMERA FOLLOWS the old man as he rides through the trees, urging his mount with shouts and kicks and blows of his hat about the withers. The cries of the pursuers grow fainter, then suddenly the hedge blocks GERALD's way. One final shout as the old man sets himself for the jump, but the horse refuses and throws his rider clean over his head, and GERALD lies on the ground—still. From the distance the wild shrillness of SCARLETT's scream.

FADE OUT

FADE IN:

INTERIOR–HALL–DAY

PORK, a heavy band of black crêpe tied to his arm, comes through the front door, closing it after him. He crosses the hall, sniffling. SCARLETT calls out sharply from the drawing room.

SCARLETT [off-screen]: Pork! Pork!

PORK stops.

PORK: Yas'm, Miss Scarlett. [He goes into the drawing room.]

DRAWING ROOM

SCARLETT stands alone, in heavy mourning. PORK enters.

SCARLETT: If you don't stop crying, I'll cry myself!

PORK: Yas'm. Ah tries but eve'y time Ah tries Ah thinks of Mist' Gerald an' . . .

SCARLETT: Well, don't think. I can stand everybody else's tears but yours. [Then] Blow your nose, Pork. I've got a present for you.

She goes to a desk, opens a drawer, takes out a large gold watch and chain with many fobs and seals. She holds it out to PORK, who gasps.

PORK: Fo' de Lawd! Dat's Mist' Gerald's watch!

SCARLETT: I'm giving it to you.

PORK [He retreats in horror.]: Oh, no'm! Dat's a w'ite gempmum's watch. Dat watch belong by rights ter lil Wade Hampton!

SCARLETT: What did Wade Hampton ever do for Pa? I know Pa'd approve. Here, take it.

PORK accepts the watch in reverent delight. Then one more misgiving overcomes him.

PORK: You got no bizness partin' wid dis watch now, Miss Scarlett, when you need all yo' valu'bles ter sell for' dat tax money!

SCARLETT: I wouldn't sell Pa's watch. [*Her face sets.*] And I've got my plans all made for that tax money. Send Mammy in here to me.

PORK *goes. She turns to a long pier glass. Her hands pat her cheeks and feel frantically at her collar bones.*

SCARLETT: I'm not pretty enough! I'm thin! I'm so thin!

MAMMY [*entering*]: Yas'm, Miss Scarlett?

SCARLETT *has turned to the window, where the long green portieres are still hanging. She takes them in her two hands and pulls them open to examine them. She holds them against her.*

SCARLETT: I'd forgotten these portieres were this shade of green.

MAMMY: Yass'm, dey's green, Miss Scarlett. Dey allus wuz green.

SCARLETT: Go up to my room and bring me down that green bonnet Captain Butler gave me years ago in Atlanta. And bring down Ma's old box of dress patterns, too.

MAMMY: Whut you wan' wid dress patt'runs, Miss Scarlett?

SCARLETT: I've got to have a new dress.

MAMMY: You don't need no new dress! Ain' no other ladies got new dresses. Dey weahs dey ole ones an' dey weahs dem proudfully! Ain' no reason why Miss Ellen's chile kain' weah rags effen she wants ter, an' eve'body respec' her lak she wo' silk. An' whut we got lef' ter mek a new dress outer?

*Scarlett jerks the portieres down, pole and all.* MAMMY *cries out.*

MAMMY: Whut you up ter wid Miss Ellen's po'teers?

SCARLETT: You're going to make my new dress out of them!

MAMMY [*She is horrified.*]: Not outer Miss Ellen's po'teers! Not w'ile Ah's got breaf in mah body!

SCARLETT *becomes metallic as a steel anvil.*

SCARLETT: They're my portieres now! I'm going to get me three hundred dollars in Atlanta! And I've got to go looking like a queen!

*An unspeakable suspicion grows in* MAMMY's *heart.*

MAMMY: Who gwine to 'Lanta wid you?

SCARLETT [*sharply*]: I'm going alone.

MAMMY: Dat's whut you thinks. Well, Ah's gwine wid you—wid you and dat new dress.

SCARLETT [*with fake sweetness*]: Now, Mammy darling. . . .

MAMMY: Don' do no good to sweet talk me, Miss Scarlett. Ah know'd you since Ah put de fus' pair of diapers on you. Ah said Ah's gwine to 'Lanta wid you and gwine Ah is.

SCARLETT: I'd as soon have a bloodhound after me, but I can't stop you.

MAMMY: Whut is you fixin' ter do dat you gotter go lookin' lak a queen, Miss Scarlett?

SCARLETT [*She flinches.*]: I won't think about that now. I'll think about that tomorrow.

DINING ROOM–NIGHT

*The patterns and portieres are spread over the table.* MAMMY *is fitting* SCARLETT'S *new dress on her.* MELANIE, SUELLEN, *and* CARREEN *look on.* ASHLEY *walks to and fro.*

CARREEN: Isn't it lovely just to see a new dress again?

SUELLEN: If Scarlett doesn't have to wear mourning for Pa, I don't! If Scarlett can make Ma's portieres into dresses, so can I! Wait till you get back and see what I'm wearing, Scarlett!

ASHLEY: Whom do you know in Atlanta who's got three hundred dollars, Scarlett?

MELANIE [*laughs*]: It must be Captain Rhett Butler. Scarlett and he parted such warm friends!

SCARLETT *does not laugh. Ashley sees this and sees the sharp glance* MAMMY *flashes at her.*

ASHLEY: Scarlett!

SCARLETT *lies her way out a bit too glibly.*

SCARLETT: I guess it's not hard to mortgage a good plantation. And three hundred isn't such a big mortgage either. Easy to pay off out of next year's cotton.

ASHLEY *goes suddenly.* MELANIE *rises.*

MELANIE: Ashley, what's the matter?

SCARLETT: Let me speak to him.

*She follows him out.*

HALL

SCARLETT *closes the door behind her as she enters.*

SCARLETT: Why are you angry, Ashley? Is it because I want to look the best I can in Atlanta?

ASHLEY [*turns to her heavily*]: I told you I was a coward. Now you can see for yourself what a coward I am. I shouldn't be letting you go to Atlanta at all. But I can't face your asking me why I don't do something myself instead of . . . instead of what you're planning.

SCARLETT [*a gulp, then*]: You . . . you don't know what you're talking about, Ashley Wilkes.

*QUICK DISSOLVE TO*

EXTERIOR–ATLANTA–THE STATION–DAY

*It is a windy, autumnal day of gray sky and scudding clouds over-head. The depot has not yet been rebuilt since the burning of the city. Only charred timbers and broken brick walls remain. The uniforms now are of Yankee soldiers who speak Yankee talk. The bustle of war-time has disappeared. This is not to say that the station is deserted, except by contrast to our previous glimpses of it. Its activities now are such as any small station's would be in time of peace. The train rolls in as before; and* SCARLETT, *now quite handsomely turned out in her new dress, descends,* MAMMY *following her.* SCARLETT *forthwith sees some-thing which both startles and appals her.* MAMMY, *behind her, is simi-larly disturbed.*

STATION

*A Yankee sentry in full Yankee uniform stands on the platform. We see him from* SCARLETT's *angle. Then* SCARLETT *and* MAMMY *enter, pass-ing him. He pays no attention to them; and* SCARLETT *goes by, staring straight before her.* MAMMY, *however, is unable to resist eyeing the Yankee.* CAMERA *follows the two travellers from Tara as they come out from the shed onto the sidewalk.* SCARLETT *looks up and is again appalled.*

*The American flag is flying from the flagpole above the station.*

MAMMY [*turns to Scarlett*]: Whut's come ove' disyere town, Miss Scarlett?

SCARLETT: What you'd expect. The Yankees have come over it.

*She hurries on to the curb, where she is accosted by an elderly* NEGRO COACHMAN, *who stands up on his box to hail her.*

NEGRO COACHMAN: Cah'ige, lady? Two bits fer anywhar in 'Lanta!

MAMMY *throws him an annihilating glance.*

MAMMY: Ladies don' never ride in hired hacks!

NEGRO COACHMAN: Dis ain't no hired hack! Dis hyah's Ole Miss Talbot's cah'ige! Ah belongs ter her whutebber dey say an' Ah's drivin' it ter mek money fer de both of us!

MAMMY: Whut Miss Talbot is dat?

NEGRO COACHMAN: Miss Suzannah Talbot of de Milledgeville Tal-bots.

MAMMY: Does you know her, Miss Scarlett?

SCARLETT: No. But then I know so few Milledgeville folks.

MAMMY: Den us'll walk. Drive on, nigger.

MAMMY *and* SCARLETT *go out of the scene.*

ATLANTA–A STREET

*This is merely a shot of a street in the burned area where rehabili-tation has not yet begun.* SCARLETT *and* MAMMY *enter,* SCARLETT *in the* lead, picking her way through the refuse which clutters the sidewalk, looking fearfully about her at the ruins.

ATLANTA–A STREET

A corner where a building has already been rehabilitated. Signs alongside the door attract SCARLETT's attention as she enters. She looks at them, reading the unfamiliar names with wonderment.

SCARLETT: "Jonathan Cushing, M.D. . . . Hezekiah Greene, Insurance . . . Caleb Adams, Attorney-at-Law . . ."

MAMMY [looks wonderingly]: Ah kain' read, but Ah can see dem ain' no 'Lanta names.

SCARLETT: No.

Some passing Yankees obliterate the pair from the scene.

ATLANTA–THE MAIN STREET–LONG SHOT

Here all is rebuilding activity. Drays of lumber are being unloaded in front of every ruin as far as CAMERA can see. Carpenters and masons are noisily busy on every hand. SCARLETT and MAMMY enter the foreground. They pause to look about them.

MAMMY: Ah's skeered of disyere town lak it is now, Miss Scarlett!

SCARLETT looks at her and smiles strangely.

MAIN STREET–CLOSE SHOT

SCARLETT [SMILES]: I'm not scared of it. They burned it and laid it flat but they didn't lick it. It'll grow back again as big and sassy as it used to be!

They step off the curb to cross the street.

MAIN STREET–TRUCK SHOT

The bustle is far greater than during the war. A group of Yankees [men] stand on the curb with their backs to the street. SCARLETT and MAMMY crossing, step up on the curb, try to get through. Though one or two of the men notice them, they pay no attention. Then one of them ogles SCARLETT and speaks to her. MAMMY flashes at him.

MAMMY: Look hyah, you!

SCARLETT [a low warning]: Mammy!

They go along the sidewalk, CAMERA FOLLOWING.

MAMMY: Ah nebber 'spec' Ah'd hear mah chile spoke to by no Yankee!

SCARLETT: Please, Mammy, please! Let's get out of this crowd!

But MAMMY's way is obstructed by a trio of Free Issue Negroes as they come laughing noisily toward them.

MAMMY: Soon's Ah kick dis black trash outer mah way!

She routs the enemy with a swing of her carpetbag, denouncing them as they cringe away from her.

MAMMY: Free Issue niggers! An' *impident*, too!

*She rejoins* SCARLETT. *A group of Yankee women, four or five in number, come chattering along the sidewalk. One of them in front, talking back to her companions behind, collides with* SCARLETT *and* MAMMY *so that* MAMMY *drops the bundles she is carrying. The Yankee woman does not apologize but only brushes off the arm which came in contact with* MAMMY. SCARLETT *helps* MAMMY *pick up the bundles.*

MAMMY: Whut's dem, Miss Scarlett?

SCARLETT: Yankees, Mammy. Never mind. [*They are standing in front of the National Hotel.*] I'm stopping here.

MAMMY: Ain't you goin' ter yo' Aunt Pitty's?

SCARLETT: Later I am. I'm going in here first.

MAMMY [*She is horrified.*]: Whut you fixin' ter do in disyere hotel, Miss Scarlett?

SCARLETT: That's my business. You go on to Aunt Pitty's without me.

*She is turning into the hotel, but* MAMMY *follows.*

MAMMY: Mah baby don' go into no hotel without me taggin' right along affer her. [*She follows* SCARLETT *into the hotel.*]

INTERIOR–HOTEL LOBBY–DAY

THE CLERK *at the desk.* SCARLETT *enters to him,* MAMMY *following.*

SCARLETT: I've come to see Captain Butler, please.

THE CLERK: You won't see Captain Butler in this hotel.

SCARLETT: Why won't I?

THE CLERK: Because, Ma'am, they've put the Captain in jail.

SCARLETT *shrinks back, horrified.*

SCARLETT: In jail!

THE CLERK: That's right.

HOTEL LOBBY

BELLE WATLING, *coming down the stair, recognizes* SCARLETT *and lounges over to her.*

SCARLETT [*to* THE CLERK]: But what did they put the Captain in jail for?

BELLE: That's hard to say. [SCARLETT *turns, startled.* MAMMY *inspects* BELLE *with eyes that go very wide.*] They claim he shot a Yankee infantryman for getting fresh with one of you prewar belles. [*She laughs.*] Maybe he did. All Southerners are fools about their women.

MAMMY *gasps.* SCARLETT *draws herself up and turns to* THE CLERK.

SCARLETT: Do you think they'll let me see the Captain in jail?

BELLE: The question is, will the Captain see you, dear. And if he doesn't want to get into trouble, he won't.

*She turns and sweeps out of the lobby into the street.*

MAMMY: Who dat? Ah ain' never seed hair dat color in mah life. It looked dyed ter me.

SCARLETT: It is.

MAMMY: Does you know a dyed-hair woman? Ah ast you who she is!

SCARLETT: She's the town bad woman. But I give you my word I don't know her, so shut up.

MAMMY: Ah don't know whut de Lawd thinkin' 'bout lettin' de bad women flourish lak dat w'en us good folks is hungry an' 'most barefoot!

SCARLETT: The Lord stopped thinking about us some years ago. You must go on to Aunt Pitty's alone, Mammy, like I told you.

MAMMY [shakes her head]: Ah's gwine stay right wid you an' keep you outer trouble.

EXTERIOR–PEACHTREE STREET–DAY

In front of the hotel as before. BELLE has just seated herself in her carriage and is driving off. Some street URCHINS acclaim her.

FIRST URCHIN: That's her!

SECOND URCHIN: That's old Belle!

THIRD URCHIN: I seen her red hair!

FADE IN:

INTERIOR–MAIN ROOM OF THE OLD FIRE HOUSE–CLOSE SHOT–FIRE ENGINE–DAY

A Yankee CORPORAL of the Guard enters. PAN WITH HIM as he passes the first engine upon which are hanging a couple of U.S.A. tunics and RHETT's hat. Voices off scene:

MAJOR [showing his cards and almost arrogantly]: Kings and treys.

RHETT's VOICE [over shot]: Oh, too good for me! [He throws in his cards, face down on the table; buttering the MAJOR.] You know it's a pity we couldn't have fought the war out in a poker game. You'd have done better than General Grant, with far less effort.

The MAJOR laughingly rakes in the chips, very pleased with himself. The CORPORAL of the Guard enters during this action.

MAJOR [looks up sharply]: What is it, Corporal?

CORPORAL: Sir, there's a lady to see Captain Butler. Says she's his sister.

MAJOR: Another sister? [good naturedly] This is a jail, not a harem, Captain Butler!

The two captains laugh. One winks to the other.

CORPORAL: No, Major. She ain't one of those. This one's got her mammy with her.

RHETT: She has? I'd like to see this one, Major, without her mammy.

MGM, © 1939, 1967. Collection of Richard Harwell.

Let's see, my losses for the afternoon come to what? Three hundred and forty? [*bends over to scribble his I.O.U.*] My debts do mount up, don't they, Major?

MAJOR: All right, Corporal! Show Captain Butler's—sister to his cell.

RHETT: Thank you, Major. [*He rises.*] Excuse me, gentlemen!

*He walks out of scene in direction taken by the* CORPORAL *of the Guard.*

MAJOR [*to the two captains*]: It's hard to be strict with a man who loses money so pleasantly. [*He looks at the I.O.U.*]

*They all laugh.*

OUTSIDE THE DOOR TO RHETT'S CELL

RHETT *enters scene, greets* SCARLETT *who is being ushered in from the other direction by the* CORPORAL *of the Guard.*

SCARLETT: Rhett!

RHETT: Scarlett! [*He takes her in his arms.*] My dear little sister! [*He kisses her delicately on the brow—turns to the* CORPORAL *who is looking on enviously.*] It's all right, Corporal. My sister has brought me no files or saws.

*The* CORPORAL *gives him a look, annoyed at his dismissal and because he can't be a witness to this scene. He exits.* RHETT *ushers* SCARLETT *into his cell.*

RHETT'S CELL

*The cell is a converted horse stall, the adjoining stall being occupied by a horse.* RHETT *and* SCARLETT *are just entering. He closes the door behind them.* SCARLETT *gives a suspicious little look at the door being closed.*

RHETT: Can I really kiss you now?

SCARLETT [*a sidelong glance from her. Then, too demurely*]: On the forehead, like a good brother.

RHETT [*drops his hands*]: No, thanks. I'll wait and hope for better things.

SCARLETT: Oh, Rhett! I was so distressed when I heard you were in jail! I simply couldn't *sleep* for thinking . . . it's not true they're going to hang you?

RHETT: Would you be sorry?

SCARLETT [*as though she couldn't stand the thought*]: Oh, Rhett!

RHETT [*laughing*]: Well, don't worry—yet. The Yankees have trumped up some charges against me but what they're really after is my money. They seem to think I made off with the Confederate treasury.

SCARLETT [*almost betraying herself*]: Well—well, did you?

RHETT: What a leading question! But let's not talk about sordid things like money! . . . How good of you to come and see me! And how pretty you look.

SCARLETT: Oh, Rhett, how you do run on—teasing a country girl like me!

RHETT: Thank Heaven you're not in rags. I'm tired of seeing women in rags. Turn around. [*She turns around slyly and flirtatiously. His eyes take her in greedily.*]: You look good enough to eat. Prosperous, too.

SCARLETT [*Her manner in answer is falsely too light.*]: Thank you, I've been doing very well. Everybody's doing well at Tara. . . . Only I got so bored, I just thought I'd treat myself to a visit to town.

RHETT: You're a heartless creature, but that's part of your charm. You know you've got more charm than the law allows. [*He has seated her on the couch and has drawn up a stool beside her.*]

SCARLETT: Now, I didn't come here to talk silliness about me, Rhett. I came because I was so *miserable* at the thought of you in trouble. Oh, I know I was mad at you the night you left me on the road to Tara, and I still haven't forgiven you . . .

RHETT [*with mock concern*]: Oh, Scarlett, don't say that!

SCARLETT: Well, I must admit I might not be alive now, only for you. [*She gently squeezes his arm.*] But when I think of myself with everything I could possibly hope for, and not a care in the world, and you here in this horrid jail . . . [*She tries lightening matters with a little joke, indicating* RHETT's *next door neighbor.*] And not even a human jail, Rhett, a horse jail! [*Then the tears come quite convincingly.*] Listen to me trying to make jokes, when I really want to cry. In a minute I *shall* cry!

*He stares at her incredulously.*

RHETT: Scarlett, can it be possible! . . .

SCARLETT [*sniffing*]: Can what be possible, Rhett?

RHETT: That you've grown a woman's heart? A real woman's heart?

SCARLETT [*eagerly, leaning provocatively toward him*]: I have, RHETT. I know I have.

RHETT: Well, it's worth being in jail just to hear you say that. It's well worth it. . . .

*Impulsively, really moved, he has seized her hands, leans over, and kisses them. He feels her hands, then turns the palms upwards, looks down at them. Unaware of what he is thinking, she closes her eyes and lifts her face to his, obviously waiting for him to kiss her. But his tone changes.*

RHETT [*with quiet sarcasm*]: You can drop the moonlight and magnolia, Scarlett. [*Her eyes open in surprise.*] So things have been going
well at Tara, have they?

*She nods, mutters a frightened* "Ye–es."

RHETT [*with violence*]: What have you been doing with your hands?

*Then she tries to wrench them away, but he holds them hard, run-
ning his thumbs across the callouses.*

SCARLETT [*hastily, panicky*]: Just because I went riding last week,
without my gloves . . .

RHETT [*angrily*]: These don't belong to a lady! You've been working
with them like a field hand! Why did you lie to me, and what are you
*really* up to?

SCARLETT: Now, Rhett . . .

RHETT [*disgusted with himself*]: Another minute and I'd almost
have believed that you cared for me—[*He drops her hands as though
they were two hot potatoes, and steps back from her.*]

SCARLETT: But I do care . . .

RHETT [*savagely*]: Suppose we get down to the truth. You want
something from me! And you want it badly enough to put on quite a
show in your velvets! What is it? Money?

*Then the mask comes off. She faces him, hesitates a second, then
blurts it out:*

SCARLETT: I want three hundred dollars to pay the taxes on Tara.
Oh, Rhett, I did lie to you when I said everything was all right. Things
are just as bad as they possibly could be! And you've got millions,
Rhett. [*Her emotion is genuine now and needs no play-acting.*]

RHETT [*with cryptic dryness*]: What collateral are you offering?

SCARLETT [*thinks, then, touching her earbobs*]: My earbobs.

RHETT [*quickly*]: Not interested.

SCARLETT [*fast*]: A mortgage on Tara.

RHETT [*equally fast*]: What would I do with a farm?

SCARLETT [*pleading; rapidly*]: You wouldn't lose. I'd pay you back
out of next year's cotton.

RHETT: Not good enough. Have you nothing better?

SCARLETT [*a deep breath; then*]: You once said you loved me . . .
if you still love me, Rhett—

RHETT: You haven't forgotten I'm not a marrying man?

SCARLETT: No. I haven't forgotten.

RHETT [*contemptuously*]: You're not worth three hundred dollars,
Scarlett [*bitterly*]. You'll never mean anything but misery to any man.

SCARLETT [*She breaks out.*]: Go on! Insult me! I don't care what you say! Only give me the money! I won't let Tara go! I can't let it go while there's a breath left in my body! Oh, Rhett, won't you please give me the money!

RHETT [*stopping her, his poise and humor gradually returning*]: I couldn't give you the money if I wanted to. My funds are in Liverpool, not Atlanta. If I tried drawing a draft, the Yankees'd be on me like a duck on a June bug. . . . [*Looks at her and smiles.*] So you see, my dear, you've abased yourself to no purpose.

*Her face goes ugly, and she swings at him with an incoherent cry.* RHETT *is beside her quick as a flash. He controls her body with one arm around both of hers, and claps his hand tightly over her mouth. She struggles against him, tries to scratch his face and bite his hand.*

RHETT [*as to a bad child*]: Here! Here! Stop it! Do you want the Yankees to see you like this?

*He takes his hand from her mouth, and her struggling ends as quickly as it began. She is out of breath, his arm is still around her.*

SCARLETT [*very cold*]: Take your hands off me, you skunk!

RHETT *releases her.* SCARLETT *arranges her clothing and starts out, talking as she goes.*

SCARLETT: You knew what I was going to say before I started. You knew you wouldn't lend me the money and yet—and yet you let me go on.

RHETT [*talking to her as she goes*]: I enjoyed hearing what you had to say . . . cheer up. You can come to my hanging. And I'll remember you in my will.

EXTERIOR–STREET–*TRUCK SHOT*–DAY

*It has come on to rain.* SCARLETT *emerges from headquarters. She walks up the street almost drunkenly. A passing Yankee officer is concerned for her. She is weeping. A wagon going by splashes her with mud. She does not notice. Passing Negroes laugh at her. She goes on, dabbing her eyes with her handkerchief. Then, from off-screen,* FRANK KENNEDY *calls out to her.*

FRANK'S VOICE: Surely it can't be Miss Scarlett!

SCARLETT *turns, astonished.*

STREET IN FRONT OF FRANK KENNEDY'S STORE

*A modest affair in a reconstructed wooden building, flanked on one side by a plot still occupied in part by ruins and, in the part adjacent the store, by various, not extensive, piles of lumber. The building has two show windows, one filled with furniture, the other with hardware. The sign above the doorway reads:*

FRANK KENNEDY COMPANY

## Hardware.   Furniture.   Lumber.

FRANK KENNEDY *stands in the doorway, beaming upon the passersby, bowing first to one, then to another. Suddenly his face goes blank with amazement and he steps forward as* SCARLETT *enters to him.*

SCARLETT: Why, Frank Kennedy! I never was so glad to see anyone in my life!

FRANK: It's a pleasure to see you, Miss Scarlett! I didn't know you were in town. [*He coughs.*] Did anyone else come up from Tara with you?

SCARLETT: No. I came alone. [*She shakes his hand, not warmly, but with relief at finding someone, anyone, whom she knows.*] I didn't know you were in Atlanta.

FRANK: Didn't Miss Suellen tell you about my store?

SCARLETT: Did she? I don't remember. Have you a store? [*His gesture points it out. It is a proud gesture. But her interest is not yet engaged.*] This?

FRANK: Won't you come in and look around a bit?

*They go in.* MAMMY *stays outside looking eagerly in at the window.*
INTERIOR–FRANK KENNEDY'S STORE
*A general merchandise store, stacked and untidy. A lady customer is doing business with a clerk.* SCARLETT *and* FRANK *enter.* SCARLETT *stops on the threshold. Looks about her bewildered.*

FRANK: I don't suppose it looks like much to a lady. But I can't help being proud of it.

SCARLETT *looks at him with a new respect.*

SCARLETT: You're not making money?

FRANK: I can't complain. In fact, I'm mighty encouraged. Folks tell me I'm just a born merchant. It won't be long now before Miss Suellen and I can marry.

*A new idea begins forming in her mind.*

SCARLETT: Are you doing as well as all that?

FRANK: Yes, I am, Miss Scarlett. I'm no millionaire yet, but I've cleared a thousand dollars already.

*But* SCARLETT's *interest is now very much alive. Her eyes are snapping up every detail of the store. She discovers the lumberyard outside the window.*

SCARLETT: Lumber, too!

FRANK: Well, that's only a side line.

SCARLETT: A side line, Frank? With all the good Georgia pine around Atlanta, and all this building going on?

FRANK: Well, if I had my own lumber mill, Scarlett . . . but I haven't.

SCARLETT: Why don't you get your own lumber mill? [*She seems to be making plans, definite plans, characteristic* SCARLETT *plans.*] Or did the Yankees burn all the lumber mills?

FRANK: No. As a matter of fact, I've got my eye on one. Buying a lumber mill takes capital, though. [*He laughs coyly.*] I've got to be thinking about buying a home!

SCARLETT: What do you want a home for?

FRANK: For Miss Suellen and me to set up housekeeping.

SCARLETT: Here in Atlanta? [*This is a setback.*] You'd want to bring her to Atlanta, wouldn't you? There wouldn't be much help in that for Tara!

FRANK: I don't rightly know what you mean, Miss Scarlett.

SCARLETT: I don't mean a thing. [*But she becomes more than usually feminine.*] Frank, how would you like to drive me out to my Aunt Pitty's?

FRANK: Nothing would give me more pleasure, Miss Scarlett.

*They go out together.*

DISSOLVE TO

EXTERIOR–THE STORE

SCARLETT *and* FRANK *emerge from the store.* FRANK *goes at once to the hitching post to remove the nose bag from his horse's head.* MAMMY *climbs up in the back seat.*

SCARLETT [*to* FRANK]: I think you'd better stay for supper tonight, too. I'm sure Aunt Pitty would be agreeable, and I know I'd like a good long visit with you!

FRANK: You act on me just like a tonic, Miss Scarlett! And will you tell me all the news? All the news of Miss Suellen? [*He is helping her into the buggy.* SCARLETT *looks down at him, then turns guiltily away. Is evidently upset.* FRANK *is frightened.*] What's the matter, Miss Scarlett? Miss Suellen's not ill, is she?

MAMMY *turns in surprise.*

SCARLETT: Oh, no! No! I thought surely she'd written you! Oh, I guess she was too ashamed to write you! She should be ashamed! Oh, to have such a mean sister!

FRANK *is now beside himself with terror. He hurries around the buggy, climbs up beside her, picks up the reins, but before he starts the horse:*

FRANK: You must tell me, Miss Scarlett! Don't leave me on tenter-hooks!

SCARLETT: Well, she's going to marry one of the county boys, next month! She just got tired of waiting, was afraid she'd be an old maid. Oh, I'm sorry to be the one to tell you! [*with an intimate gesture*] Oh, it's cold and I left my muff at home. Would you—would you mind if I put my hand in your pocket?

FRANK *is stunned.* MAMMY's *eyes are very large, indeed, as the buggy drives out of the scene.*

*DISSOLVE TO*

INTERIOR–MISS PITTY'S HOUSE–SCARLETT'S BEDROOM–DAY

SCARLETT *sits at her mirror, a wrapper around her.* MAMMY *is cleansing the mud from her velvet dress.*

MAMMY: Lamb, huccome you din' tell yo' own Mammy whut you wuz upter? You kain fool me. Ah seed Mist' Frank's face w'en he druv you up an' Ah kin read yo' mine lak a pahson kin read a Bible.

*A sharp look from* SCARLETT, *which* MAMMY *returns with calm omniscience.*

SCARLETT: Well, what are you going to do about it? Tell Suellen?

MAMMY: Ah is gwine ter he'p you pleasure Mist' Frank eve'y way Ah knows how.

SCARLETT: Well, then, you've got to go downtown for me and buy me a pot of rouge.

MAMMY [*She starts.*]: Whut dat?

SCARLETT: Never you mind. Just ask for it.

MAMMY: Ah ain' buyin' nuthin' dat Ah doan know whut 'tis.

SCARLETT: Well, it's paint, if you're so curious. Face paint.

MAMMY: You ain' so big dat Ah kain whup you! Miss Ellen be tuhnin' in her grabe dis minute! Paintin' yo' face lak a . . .

SCARLETT [*losing her temper*]: You can go straight back to Tara!

MAMMY: You kain sen' me ter Tara 'less Ah wants ter go. Ah is free. Lawsy, but you sho look lak yo' pa! Ah kain go buyin' no paint! Ah die of shame, eve'ybody knowin' it wuz fo' mah chile! Honey, doan nobody but bad womens use dat stuff!

SCARLETT [*looks up at her*]: Well, they get results, don't they?

MAMMY [*gasps*]: Lamb, doan say bad things lak dat! Ah'll go. Maybe Ah fine me a sto' whar dey doan know us.

*She is going out.*

INTERIOR–FRANK KENNEDY'S STORE–DAY

SCARLETT *sits at a desk, working over a ledger.* RHETT's voice is heard off-screen.

RHETT: My dear Mrs. Kennedy! [*He enters, dashingly dressed and quite his old self.*] My very dear Mrs. Kennedy!

SCARLETT *looks at him, far from pleased to see him.*

SCARLETT: What are you doing here?

RHETT: I called to congratulate you. So you couldn't wait even two weeks for me!

SCARLETT's *eyes blaze, but she has no answer.*

RHETT: Or are the charms of wedlock with old Frank Kennedy more alluring than? . . .

SCARLETT: What a pity they didn't hang you!

RHETT [*He grins and leans closer.*]: Would you mind satisfying my curiosity on one point? Have you no womanly shrinking from marrying men you don't love? This is the second time you've done it, you know.

SCARLETT *looks about her to make sure that she is not overheard.*

SCARLETT: Listen to me, Rhett Butler. I get what I want. If I can't get it one way I get it another. And I've got it now . . . or very soon will have. [*And she nods emphatically.*]

*DISSOLVE TO*

INSERT: BANK DRAFT–for $300.00 made to the order of the Tax Collector of Clayton County. SCARLETT's hand is just finishing writing her signature: Scarlett O'Hara Kennedy.

*DISSOLVE TO*

INTERIOR–HALL–TARA–DAY (WINTER 1865–1866)

SUELLEN *and* MELANIE *have just come out of* ELLEN's *study and are crossing the hall.* SUELLEN *is sobbing and* MELANIE *is trying to comfort her.*

SUELLEN [*sobbing*]: She's gone and married my Mr. Kennedy! He was my beau and she's gone and married him!

MELANIE [*her arm around* SUELLEN, *comforting*]: She did it to save Tara. You must understand that, Suellen.

SUELLEN: I hate Tara! And I hate Scarlett! She's the only thing I hate worse than Tara.

*During the last speech CAMERA HAS STARTED TO MOVE PAST THEM into ELLEN'S STUDY where we find* ASHLEY *and* SCARLETT *facing each other.*

ASHLEY: I should have committed highway robbery to get that tax money for you!

SCARLETT: I couldn't let you do anything like that! And anyway, it's done now.

ASHLEY [*bitterly*]: Yes, it's done now. [*He strolls to window, talking as he goes, his back to* SCARLETT.] You wouldn't have let *me* do anything dishonorable. But you would sell yourself in marriage to a man you didn't love. . . . Well, at least you won't have to worry about my helplessness any more.

SCARLETT [*suddenly*]: What do you mean?

ASHLEY: I'm going to New York. I've arranged to get a position in a bank there.

SCARLETT [*panicky*]: But you *can't* do that! . . . [*She desperately reaches for an idea.*] I counted on you to help me start a lumber business . . . I *counted* on you!

ASHLEY [*still looking out the window; his shoulders present a picture of defeat*]: I'd be no good to you, Scarlett. I know nothing about the lumber business.

SCARLETT [*frantic*]: You know as much as you do about banking. [*Gets sudden idea.*] I'll give you half the business.

ASHLEY [*embarrassed at being unable to say "yes," and pleadingly in the hope he can make her somehow understand*]: That's generous of you, Scarlett. But it isn't that—If I go to Atlanta and take help from you again, I bury forever any hope of standing alone.

SCARLETT [*suddenly angry*]: How can you be so hateful and bullheaded!

MELANIE *enters, now with little* BEAU *clinging to her skirts.* SCARLETT *quickly throws herself down on the sofa and bursts into wild crying.*

MELANIE [*sitting next to her*]: Scarlett! What is it?

SCARLETT [*blubbering*]: He won't lift a finger to help me! He doesn't care if I starve! [*She burrows her head into* MELANIE'S *shoulder.*]

ASHLEY *closes his eyes in pain.*

MELANIE: How can you refuse her, Ashley, after all she's done for us? How *unchivalrous* of you!

SCARLETT *peeps out slyly to see the effect on* ASHLEY *of her performance and of* MELANIE'S *arguments.*

ASHLEY: Melanie . . . [*He throws out his hands helplessly.*]

MELANIE [*vigorously*]: Think, Ashley, think! [*then, pleadingly*] If it hadn't been for Scarlett I'd have died in Atlanta—and maybe we wouldn't have little Beau. [*She strokes the child's head.*] And she—yes, she killed a Yankee defending us! Did you know that? She *killed* a man for us! And when I think of her picking cotton and plowing just to keep food in our mouths, I could just . . . [*She looks at* SCARLETT, *kisses her hair in fierce loyalty.*] Oh, my darling!

ASHLEY, *who has been taking this attack with his back to us, turns slowly. He looks, then speaks with resignation.*

ASHLEY [*quietly*]: All right, Melanie . . . I will go to Atlanta . . . I cannot fight you both.

*He turns, walks out of room. In his eyes [and also in his posture] we see the same look we have seen when he spoke about being lost forever if he went to Atlanta. This is* ASHLEY's *final defeat. All hope of his ever being a man able to face the new world is gone.*

*FADE OUT*

# Ninth

# Sequence

# EXTERIOR–A LUMBER YARD–DAY

*A sign, painted on framed canvas, both high and large, reads:*

WILKES & KENNEDY
### Fine Lumber

*Then CAMERA takes in the lumber yard which adjoins* FRANK KEN-
NEDY'S *store, as expanded and amplified by* SCARLETT'S *enterprise. Miss*
PITTY'S *carriage stands at the gate under the sign,* UNCLE PETER *on the*
*box,* SCARLETT *seated behind him.* ASHLEY *stands by. Both of them are*
*watching two Negroes who carry a 2 x 4 scantling between them to*
*a wagon which they are loading.*

SCARLETT: Look at 'em, Ashley! Two of 'em carrying one little stick
between 'em! If you can't get more work than that out of your men
. . . and don't be forever telling me you aren't fitted! I wasn't fitted
once! But didn't I learn?

ASHLEY *looks up at her eloquently.*

SCARLETT [*she flinches*]: I know I'm not as kind and gentle as I
was brought up to be. When I can afford it, I'll be as nice as you
please.

ASHLEY *comes to her appealingly.*

ASHLEY: Look at our old friends, though, Scarlett. They haven't
changed. They're going down, but with colors flying!

SCARLETT [*stiffens*]: They're all starving. They're a passel of fools!
[*then*] Get that lumber loaded and get back to the mill. Drive on,
Uncle Peter.

UNCLE PETER *drives her out.* ASHLEY *looking after her.*

STREET

UNCLE PETER *is driving the carriage along. He speaks to* SCARLETT
*over his shoulder.*

UNCLE PETER: Mist' Ashley wuz right, whut he said, Miss Scarlett,
an' it's jes' whut everybody hyah's sayin' 'bout you!

STREET

*The carriage passes* MISS INDIA WILKES *on her way to call on her*
*brother. She stops to blaze hatred in* SCARLETT'S *direction.*

UNCLE PETER'S VOICE: Dar's Mist' Ashley's sister, Miss India.

STREET

UNCLE PETER *and* SCARLETT *as before.*

UNCLE PETER [*continuing*]: She ain' goin' traipsin' 'roun' doin' men's bizness.

SCARLETT: She let's Ashley support her, though, on what he earns running my mill for me!
STREET
MRS. MERRIWETHER *and* MRS. ELSING, *walking along the street, see* SCARLETT, *bow very coldly, and eye each other.*

UNCLE PETER'S VOICE: Dar's Mis' Merriwether an' Mis' Elsing.
STREET
UNCLE PETER *and* SCARLETT *as before.*

UNCLE PETER [*continuing*]: Dey din' bow ter you lak dey used ter, Miss Scarlett.

SCARLETT: A lot I care about them!

UNCLE PETER: Dey needs money, too, but dey stays home w'ere ladies belongs. Mis' Merriwether bake pies an' Mis' Elsing she paint china.

SCARLETT [*furious*]: You mind your own business! And stop here. I'm going to speak to this gentleman.

UNCLE PETER *stops.* SCARLETT *is descending where a pile of lumber —decorated with the Wilkes-Kennedy sign—denotes building in progress.*

UNCLE PETER: He ain' no gempmum, Miss Scarlett. He's a Yankee.

*Three* YANKEE WOMEN *advance to* SCARLETT. *The first* YANKEE WOMAN, *tall and thin, with a Down East accent, speaks:*

FIRST YANKEE WOMAN: You're just the person I want to see, Mrs. Kennedy. My nurse says she won't stay another day down here, and I can't say I blame her. Tell me how to go about getting another nurse.

SCARLETT [*She laughs.*]: If you can find a darky just in from the country who hasn't been spoiled by the Freedmen's Bureau . . .

*The three* WOMEN *break into indignant outcries.*

FIRST YANKEE WOMAN: Do you think I'd trust my babies to a darky?

SECOND YANKEE WOMAN: I wouldn't have one in my house!

THIRD YANKEE WOMAN: I don't trust 'em any further than I can see 'em!

UNCLE PETER *is breathing hard and sitting up very straight.*

FIRST YANKEE WOMAN: Look at that old one swell up like a toad. I'll bet he's an old pet of yours, isn't he?

SCARLETT: It's strange you should feel that way about the darkies when it was you who wanted to set them free. [*angrily*] Uncle Peter is one of our family! [*She steps back into the carriage.*] Good afternoon. Drive on, Peter.

*Victor Fleming directs Vivien Leigh in postwar street scenes in Atlanta.
Snapshots taken on Selznick's Forty Acres lot, June 19, 1939, by Wilbur
G. Kurtz.*

UNCLE PETER *lays the whip on the horse so suddenly that the startled animal jumps forward, and the carriage jounces off.*

FIRST YANKEE WOMAN: Her family? You don't suppose he's a relative?

SECOND YANKEE WOMAN: More than likely, my dear!

PEACHTREE STREET

UNCLE PETER *is driving the carriage along Peachtree Street. Tears are rolling down his cheeks.* SCARLETT *reaches up to touch his arm.*

SCARLETT: I'm ashamed of you for crying, Peter! What do you care? They're nothing but Yankees!

UNCLE PETER [*sniffling*]: Dey talk in front of me lak Ah wuz a mule an' couldn' unnerstan' dem—lak Ah wuz a Affikun an' din' know whut dey wuz talkin' 'bout! An' dey call me a nigger an' Ah ain' never been call a nigger by no w'ite folks. An' dey call me "ole pet" an' say niggers ain' ter be trus'ed! You wouldn' ketch Miss Pitty wipin' her lil shoes on sech trash! [*He pulls up in front of* MISS PITTY'S *house.*] Ah 'spec' she ain' gwine want me ter drive you roun' no mo' affer dat. No, ma'am!

SCARLETT: Aunt Pitty will want you to drive me as usual, so let's hear no more about it.

*She is descending.* MISS PITTY *and* FRANK KENNEDY *are just turning in through the gate.* UNCLE PETER *lifts his voice in real lamentation.*

UNCLE PETER: Ah'll git mizry in mah back. Mah back huttin' me so bad dis minute Ah kain' ha'dly set up. Mah Miss ain' gwine want me ter do no drivin' w'en Ah got a mizry an' Yankee folks 'sult me!

MISS PITTY: What's that, Peter?

SCARLETT: Don't listen to him, Aunt Pitty.

UNCLE PETER [*insistent*]: Dey 'sults me, Miss Scarlett, an' you don' tek up fo' me, needer!

SCARLETT [*exasperated almost to the breaking point*]: I did so take up for you! I told them you were one of the family!

FRANK: Dear me!

UNCLE PETER: Dat ain' tekkin' up fo' me! Dat's jes' a fac'! You got no bizness havin' no truck wid no Yankees!

FRANK: I entirely agree with that.

SCARLETT: Oh, you're all driving me crazy!

MISS PITTY: Well, it's only what all our friends are saying, Scarlett. You are a lady born, you know, and . . .

SCARLETT [*beside herself*]: Stop telling me that! Where would the Kennedy family be if I didn't take hold and at least try to make some real money! I won't be one of those big mouthed fools and break my heart over the old days! If I've got to make friends with Yankees I'll make friends with Yankees and beat 'em at their own game! You can keep your old carriage! I'll buy me a buggy and drive it myself!

MISS PITTY: Scarlett, you wouldn't do that!

SCARLETT: Yes, I would, too!

MISS PITTY: But you wouldn't go about alone, Scarlett!

FRANK: Think, Scarlett! Think of that drive alone out to the mill! And the roads full of riffraff and poor white trash! Not to speak of . . .

MISS PITTY: Needlessly, vulgarly exposing yourself!

FRANK: It's dangerous, Scarlett! It's madness! It's just flying in the face of . . .

SCARLETT: I can shoot straight if I don't have to shoot too far!

*A faint scream, and* MISS PITTY *swoons against the gatepost.*

SCARLETT: I'll get my buggy and go where and how I please—and nobody's going to stop me, and I'm not going to stop at anything much either!

*QUICK DISSOLVE TO*

EXTERIOR–LUMBER MILL–NIGHT–SUMMER

*Open on CLOSE SHOT idle buzzsaw lighted only by a couple of oil lanterns which have been set on the ground. PAN CAMERA OVER to BOARD FENCE on which we see the shadows of a file of convict laborers, as we hear their chains on the sound track.*

*CAMERA MOVES BACK to reveal the convicts—a line of miserable white men silently trudging through the yard, starved, bent and weary. They are of all ages, but one thing they have in common: all are emaciated. Many of the men glisten with perspiration; they are unkempt and to varying degrees, unshaven.*

*A man stands over them, a tough, evil-looking little Irishman—* JOHNNY GALLEGHER.

GALLEGHER: Halt!

*The men stop in front of* SCARLETT, *who is standing at the side of the building, in a doorway leading into the mill office. Her figure is silhouetted against the light behind her. She stands like a general, feet spread, her hands behind her, looking down at the line of men, hard and businesslike. Behind her stand a terrified* FRANK KENNEDY *and a horrified* ASHLEY. *In the course of the scene,* ASHLEY *dejectedly leaves and goes back into the office.* GALLEGHER *approaches* SCARLETT.

GALLEGHER: Here's your mill hands, Mrs. Kennedy. The pick of all the best jails in Georgia.

SCARLETT [*hard and cold*]: Humph! They look pretty thin and weak to me, Gallegher.

GALLEGHER: They're the best you can lease, ma'am. And if you'll just give Johnny Gallegher a free hand, you'll get what you want out of 'em.

SCARLETT: All right, you're the foreman. All I ask is that you keep the mill running and deliver my lumber when I want it.

GALLEGHER: Johnny Gallegher's your man, Miss—but remember, no questions and no interference.

SCARLETT: That's a bargain. Start in the morning, Gallegher. [*She turns back into the mill office.*]

INTERIOR–MILL OFFICE

*As* SCARLETT *walks into the office we see that* ASHLEY *has gone over to a corner, immersed in his thoughts and in horror at what he has just seen.*

GALLEGHER'S VOICE [*from outside*]: Hey, you there on the end! Get a move on!

*We hear the clank of chains as the men start away.* FRANK *timidly approaches* SCARLETT.

FRANK: But, Scarlett, this isn't right and you know it! It's bad enough for a woman to be in business at all, but—

SCARLETT [*interrupting sharply*]: What are you complaining about? You never would have owned a mill if I hadn't taken things over.

FRANK: But I didn't want a mill in the first place! And we couldn't have bought it if you hadn't pressed all our friends for the money they owed me. [*Looks over at* ASHLEY.] Isn't that right, Ashley?

ASHLEY *doesn't answer. Only lowers his head and covers his eyes with his hands.*

SCARLETT [*to* FRANK]: What are you running—a charitable institution? Now go back to the store, Frank—and then go home and take your medicine. You're not looking very well. [*She gives* FRANK *a little kiss on the ear or nose.*]

FRANK: But, Sugar, don't you think you'd better come home with me?

SCARLETT [*disgusted and in a temper*]: Great balls of fire! Don't bother me any more! And don't call me "Sugar!"

FRANK: All right, all right. [*He withdraws, picks up his hat, calls to* ASHLEY:] Good night, Ashley . . . [ASHLEY *doesn't reply.* FRANK *exits, shaking his head.*]

FRANK [*on his way out*]: My, my! She can get mad quicker than any woman I ever saw!

*TWO SHOT–*ASHLEY *and* SCARLETT

ASHLEY [*looks up as* SCARLETT *walks toward him*]: Scarlett, I don't like to interfere, but I do wish you'd let me hire free darkies instead of using convicts. I believe we could do better.

SCARLETT: Why, their pay would break us! Convicts are dirt cheap. If we just give Gallegher a free hand with them—

ASHLEY [*bitterly*]: A free hand! You know what that means? He'll starve them and whip them—Didn't you see them? Some of them are sick,—underfed—

SCARLETT [*impatiently*]: Oh, Ashley, how you do run on! If I let you alone you'd be giving them chicken three times a day and tucking them to sleep with eiderdown quilts.

ASHLEY: Scarlett, I will not make money from the enforced labor and misery of others.

SCARLETT: But you weren't so particular about owning slaves!

ASHLEY: That was different. We didn't treat them that way. Besides, I'd have freed them all when Father died if the war hadn't already freed them.

SCARLETT *goes to him with some gentleness and some patience. After all, it is* ASHLEY.

SCARLETT: I'm sorry, Ashley. But have you forgotten so soon what it was like without money? . . . I found out that money is the most important thing in the world and I don't intend ever to be without it again! I'm going to have money enough so the Yankees can *never* take Tara away from me! And I'm going to make it the only way I know how!

ASHLEY: But we're not the only Southerners who've suffered, Scarlett. Look at all our friends. They're keeping their honor, and their kindness, too.

SCARLETT: Yes, and they're starving. I've got no use for fools who won't help themselves. Oh, I know what they're saying about me, and I don't care! I'm going to make friends with the Yankee Carpetbaggers, and I'm going to beat them at their own game—and you're going to beat them with me!

CLOSE TWO SHOT—MRS. MEADE *and* MRS. MERRIWETHER

MRS. MEADE: And did you know, Dolly Merriwether, that Dr. Meade actually saw her peddling lumber to those Yankees *herself!*

MRS. MERRIWETHER: And that isn't all!

DISSOLVE TO

CLOSE TWO SHOT—AUNT PITTYPAT *and* INDIA

INDIA [*with ill-concealed rage*]: I think it's shocking what she's doing to my brother Ashley!

AUNT PITTYPAT [*tearfully*]: And she's even taken to driving her own buggy! Oh!

*DISSOLVE TO*

EXTERIOR–KENNEDY STORE–DAY–SUMMER

*CAMERA IS SHOOTING UP at two workmen hanging a large, new sign over the storefront, which has been enlarged to twice its original size. The sign reads:*

WILKES & KENNEDY

Contractors, High Grade Lumber, Builders' Supplies

See us for furniture.

SCARLETT'S VOICE: That's it! Move it a little to one side.

*CAMERA MOVES BACK AND DOWN to reveal* SCARLETT *standing on the street directing the hanging of the sign. We note that the store has been enlarged and is very prosperous: customers are seen going in and coming out of the store.*

*A flashily dressed* YANKEE *approaches* SCARLETT.

YANKEE: 'Afternoon, Mrs. Kennedy. Business is certainly growing, ain't it?

SCARLETT [*turning on her sweetest smile*]: It certainly is. . . . I'm expecting to see you about that new saloon you're going to put up.

YANKEE: You will, Mrs. Kennedy. Wouldn't think of doing business with anyone else.

*He leaves with a wink to go into the store,* SCARLETT *sending him on his way with a coy smile. She turns to go toward the curb and stops dead in her tracks in amazement.*

*CLOSE SHOT–*RHETT*–[FROM* SCARLETT'S *ANGLE]*

*With his back to* FRANK KENNEDY's *old buggy, which now bears the sign "Wilkes and Kennedy,"* RHETT *stands at the curb smiling at* SCARLETT. *He is elegantly outfitted and is casually smoking a cigar.*

RHETT [*coolly*]: There's nothing much that money won't buy. [*Motions to the sign with his head.*] I observe it's even bought you the honorable Mr. Wilkes.

SCARLETT *closes her lips tightly and narrows her eyes, but controls herself and speaks coolly:*

SCARLETT: So you still hate Ashley Wilkes! . . . Do you know, I believe you're jealous of him!

RHETT [*throws back his head and laughs*]: You still think you're the belle of the county, don't you? You'll always think you're the cutest little trick in shoe leather and that every man you meet is dying of love for you.

SCARLETT [*brushing by him, advancing with contempt*]: Let me by.

*She climbs into her buggy.* RHETT *elaborately helps her in, talking as he does:*

RHETT: Don't get angry, Scarlett. . . . Tell me, where are you going?

SCARLETT: I'm going out to the mill, if it's any of your business.

RHETT: Through Shantytown? Alone? . . . Haven't you been told it's *dangerous* for you to drive alone through all that riffraff?

SCARLETT [*takes a pistol from under the cushion of the buggy, shows it to him*]: Don't worry about me.

*She cracks the whip on the horse and drives off, leaving* RHETT *standing looking after her admiringly, shaking his head.*

RHETT: What a woman!

*DISSOLVE TO*

*EXTREME LONG SHOT*–SHANTYTOWN–DUSK

EXTERIOR–SECTION OF SHANTYTOWN–*FULL SHOT*

*In background, amongst the trees are dirty tents and lean-tos, and around a number of open fires, degenerate looking whites and blacks are discovered, some lounging, others munching hungrily.*

*In the foreground is the silhouetted form of a powerfully built Negro lying with his back to CAMERA, his shoulder and head pillowed against a log, his slouch hat pulled over his eyes as he sleeps. This is* BIG SAM, *but his features are not recognizable at this time. Just beyond* BIG SAM *another big black is seen adding sticks to a fire, under a whisky still, while an evil-looking* WHITE MAN *tips an old five-gallon oil can and discovers that they are out of water. Picking up a stick close by, he passes it through the handle of the bucket and nudges the colored man by the fire. The black man takes one end of the stick while the* WHITE *grips the other. Both exit with the bucket. CAMERA PANS IN OPPOSITE DIRECTION, so that we see the road through the trees on the edge of the settlement, and see a buggy in the far distance as it comes along the road.*

WOODS ROAD–*CLOSE SHOT*

SCARLETT, *seen driving along in a buggy, is nearing the vicinity of Shantytown. She glances ahead and casually around as if in fear of passing through this section alone. She clucks to the horse and loosens the reins, urging the horse into a trot. A carriage robe is over her lap.*

SMALL STREAM–*MEDIUM SHOT*

MGM, © 1939, 1967. UGa Libraries, Marsh Papers.

*The two men, carrying the can on a stick, are just starting to fill the can with water. The black man is filling the bucket as the* WHITE MAN *stands, attracted by something off-screen. He taps the black man on the shoulder, calling his attention to the off-screen buggy approaching. They both start up the bank.*

BRIDGE

SCARLETT *slows the horse down slightly as she goes to cross a small, crudely built bridge. As the wheels of the buggy start over the bridge,* SCARLETT *is startled by the sudden appearance of the two men who are coming up the bank toward the opposite end of the bridge.* SCAR-LETT *clucks to her horse, and, at the same time, reaches for her whip. As the horse lunges, the* WHITE MAN *springs onto the road with a leap, grabbing the horse's reins and pulling him to a sudden stop. The rear end of the buggy has just cleared the bridge.*

SCARLETT [*thoroughly frightened*]: What do you want?

WHITE MAN [*leering at* SCARLETT]: Can you give me a quarter?

SCARLETT: Let go of my horse!

*She furiously lashes at her horse and at the man. The* WHITE MAN *grips the reins firmly in both hands, with jaw set, as he holds the horse, turning to the Negro.*

WHITE MAN: Hold this horse!

*As the Negro holds the horse, which lunges and rears, the* WHITE MAN *crosses and grapples with* SCARLETT, *who now turns the whip on him. He grabs her whip hand and is attempting to pull her from the buggy.* SCARLETT *fights like a wild cat, grabs gun and starts to level it, but the* WHITE MAN *grips her wrist.*

CLOSE ON GUN

*As the* WHITE MAN'S *hand twists the gun from* SCARLETT'S *hand, the gun falls to the floor of the buggy.*

CLOSE SHOT—BIG SAM

*Still in silhouette, his features unrecognizable,* BIG SAM *rouses lazily from his slumbering position, starts to stretch and yawn. His hat comes off. The faint off-screen noises of* SCARLETT'S *voice are heard:*

SCARLETT'S VOICE: Help! Help! Help!

*The huge black man is attracted by the faint off-screen calls. As he leaps to his feet, his hat falls to the ground and for the first time we see his face. He starts out of the scene toward the sound of the voice.*

LONG SHOT

*As* BIG SAM *runs toward the road.*

SCARLETT *and* WHITE MAN

ABOVE: *Yakima Canutt was listed in the cast only as the renegade in the Shantytown scene but was also Gable's double in the shots of the burning of Atlanta.* BELOW: *Scarlett's buggy is being wired to teeter on the bridge without quite falling off. Actor Everett Brown (Big Sam) stands to the rear of the buggy. The "Scarlett" is not Vivien Leigh but stunt-double Aileen Goodwin. Snapshots taken June 15, 1939, at Big Bear Lake.*

*Still in desperate struggle, in silhouette. The excited horse starts backing toward the bridge. One of the rear wheels drops off the side of the bridge and is on the verge of tipping over.* SCARLETT, *dropping to the floor of the buggy, is fighting like a wild cat. The buggy is now tipping at an angle.* SCARLETT *has fallen to the floor of the buggy and is hanging to it desperately and bracing herself against the* WHITE MAN'S *pull, who stands on the bridge and tries to drag her from the buggy.*

THE BRIDGE–MEDIUM *CLOSE SHOT*

*LOW SETUP WITH CAMERA ANGLING UP over the rear wheels while the rig tips at an angle with one wheel off the bridge and the other one moving back and forth; with each backward move it gets closer and closer to the edge. It is just on the verge of going off as the full figure of* BIG SAM *appears from thicket in background. He rushes toward bridge and buggy and braces himself as he grips bed of buggy with hands. He strains, and both wheels are lifted and swung onto the floor of the bridge.*

EXTERIOR OF BRIDGE–*CLOSE SHOT*

*Shooting over* SCARLETT'S *back and into the face of the* WHITE MAN. *The rig is now in a more level position. The* WHITE MAN *is about to drag* SCARLETT *from the rig as a big hand enters the scene and grips the* WHITE MAN'S *throat and a huge, black fist cracks against the* WHITE MAN'S *chin causing him to snap back and go out of scene. As the* WHITE MAN'S *face disappears,* BIG SAM *swings into the scene with his back to the* CAMERA. *He glances down at his fallen opponent, then turns, and goes toward* SCARLETT. *The sight of her face causes* BIG SAM *to stop and stare as if almost unable to believe his eyes.*

BIG SAM: Miss Scarlett!

*At this moment the other black crashes into the scene from behind, locks both arms around* BIG SAM'S *throat and taking him off balance, drags him back out of scene.*

CLOSE SHOT–SCARLETT

SCARLETT *comes slowly out of her daze, glances around, frightened and sees the two men off-screen fighting—but does not recognize* BIG SAM.

BIG SAM *and Negro–[As seen from* SCARLETT'S *angle]*

*They are in a desperate struggle close to the edge of the bridge. Finally,* BIG SAM *lands a terrific blow on his opponent's jaw, and the man goes down.* BIG SAM *bends to pick up his body.*

SCARLETT–*still not recognizing* BIG SAM, *grips one rein, and frantically starts the horse.*

MGM, © 1939, 1967. Collection of Richard Harwell.

BIG SAM *and Negro*

BIG SAM *throws his opponent's body over into the stream and turns hurriedly to go after* SCARLETT.

LONG SHOT

BIG SAM *chasing after* SCARLETT's *buggy.*

BIG SAM [*calling as he runs*]: Miss Scarlett! Miss Scarlett. . . . Wait! . . . It's Sam! Big Sam from Tara! Wait, Miss Scarlett!

MEDIUM CLOSE SHOT–SCARLETT *IN BUGGY*

*Riding furiously.*

BIG SAM's VOICE: Wait!

WOODS–LONG SHOT–BIG SAM *RUNNING*

*CAMERA PANS with him.*

BIG SAM: Miss Scarlett! Miss Scarlett!

CLOSE SHOT–SCARLETT

*She looks back over her shoulder and finally recognizes* SAM.

BIG SAM's VOICE: It's Sam!

SCARLETT [*incredulously*]: Sam! Big Sam!

*She pulls at the reins and the buggy stops.* BIG SAM *runs in, panting.*

SCARLETT [*hysterical*]: Sam, Sam!

BIG SAM: Is yo' hu't, Miss Scarlett? Did dey hu't yo'?

SCARLETT *starts to cry.*

BIG SAM: Don' yo' cry, Miss Scarlett. Big Sam'll git yo' out o' this in a jiffy.

*He gets into buggy, and takes the reins.*

BIG SAM: Hawse—Make tracks!

LONG SHOT–BUGGY

*Riding swiftly through woods.*

FADE OUT

FADE IN:

INTERIOR–AUNT PITTYPAT'S PARLOR–NIGHT

*Open on CLOSE SHOT* SCARLETT, *dressed as she was when we last saw her near Shantytown, her dress torn and her hair awry. She is frightened and is biting her nails nervously and watching* BIG SAM *and* KENNEDY *out of the corner of her eye. CAMERA PANS OVER TO-WARD* BIG SAM *and* KENNEDY, *on the way passing* MAMMY *and* PITTY-PAT, *who are also listening.* MAMMY *is sitting gloomily following the activity with wary eyes and occasionally stealing glances out of the corner of her eyes at* SCARLETT. PITTYPAT *sits tearfully sniffing at her smelling salts.*

FRANK's VOICE [*as CAMERA moves*]: You're a good boy, Sam, and I won't forget what you've done. . . .

*CAMERA HAS NOW REACHED* BIG SAM *and* FRANK, *who stand nearer the doorway.* BIG SAM *is frightened, but* FRANK *is curiously and unprecedentedly calm. He is wearing a light overcoat, ready to go out.*

FRANK [*handing him some money*]: You get to Tara just as quick as you can—and stay there!

BIG SAM: Ah sho' will. Ah's had ernuff o' dem Carpetbaggers. Thank you, Mistuh Frank . . . [*Turns to* SCARLETT.] Good-bye, Miss Scarlett. [*He exits as we hear* SCARLETT'S *voice.*]

SCARLETT'S VOICE: Good-bye, Sam, and thank you.

*We hear the front door close behind* SAM *as the CAMERA MOVES WITH* FRANK *OVER TO* SCARLETT. FRANK, *for the first time in their married life, is not the henpecked husband. He is kindly and sweet but speaks with authority:*

FRANK: Scarlett, change your dress and go over to Miss Melly's for the evening. I've to go to a political meeting.

SCARLETT [*in a rage*]: Political meeting! How can you go to a political meeting after what I've been through this afternoon? [*She bursts into tears of rage.*]

FRANK [*leans over and kisses her on the cheek*]: Now, Sugar, you're more scared than hurt.

*CAMERA MOVES in to a CLOSE-UP of* SCARLETT, *looking from right to left at* MAMMY *and* PITTYPAT, *complainingly, feeling very much the martyr at the lack of attention.*

SCARLETT: Nobody cares about me! You all act as though it was nothing at all!

*CAMERA MOVES BACK to* FRANK, *who calmly puts on his hat, and as he is deliberately putting his pistol in his pocket, we—*

DISSOLVE TO

INTERIOR–MELANIE'S HOUSE–THE PARLOR–NIGHT

*It is a poor little room, cheaply, even pathetically underfurnished.* MELANIE *sits by the stove, sewing. The other ladies—*SCARLETT, MISS PITTY, MRS. MEADE, INDIA WILKES—*are variously disposed in a circle.* SCARLETT *is also sewing. Silence. Great uneasiness.* MISS PITTY *leans over to examine* MELANIE'S WORK.

MISS PITTY: You're taking stitches an inch long. You'll have to rip every one of them out.

MELANIE *continues sewing without comment,* SCARLETT *looks about her at the others, then throws her mending down.*

SCARLETT: I'm too nervous to sew! I'm nervous enough to scream! I wanted to stay home and go to bed and Frank knew it and had no business going out! Talk, talk, talk about protecting our women! Then, after what happened to me this afternoon, he has to go to a political meeting! [*Her snapping eyes have come to rest on* INDIA's *face and she pauses.*] And if it won't pain you too much, India Wilkes, I wish you'd tell me why you're staring at me?

INDIA [*venomously*]: It won't pain me! I'll do it with pleasure! If you cared about being protected you'd never have exposed yourself as you've been doing all these months! What happened this afternoon is just what you deserved! If there was any justice you'd have gotten worse!

MELANIE [*impatiently*]: Oh, India! Hush!

SCARLETT: Let her talk, Melanie! She's always hated me! Ever since I took your brother, Charles, away from her! But she was too much of a hypocrite to admit it! If she thought anyone would take after her, she'd walk the streets naked!

INDIA *has hated too long to speak quickly. When she does speak, her words are filled with venom.*

INDIA: I do hate you! You've done all you could to lower the prestige of decent people! And you've put our men's lives in danger because they've got to . . .

MELANIE [*fortissimo*]: India!

*Now* INDIA *does stop.*

MRS. MEADE: I don't think we'd better say any more or one of us will be saying too much.

*Now* SCARLETT *rises and looks about her.*

SCARLETT: What's going on that I don't know about?

*But* UNCLE PETER *is on his feet.*

UNCLE PETER: Shh!

*The women all turn to him.*

UNCLE PETER: Somebody comin' up de walk. Somebody dat ain' Mist' Ashley!

MELANIE [*She rises calmly.*]: Will you hand me the pistol, please, Aunt Pitty? [*and, as* MISS PITTY *tremblingly obeys*] Now, whatever this is, remember we know nothing.

SCARLETT *is now completely bewildered. A knock on the door.*

UNCLE PETER: Who dar?

RHETT's VOICE: It's Captain Butler. Let me in.

MELANIE *goes to the door and opens it quickly.* RHETT *enters. He does not trouble to remove his hat, but speaks directly to* MELANIE, *closing the door behind him and standing with his back against it.*

RHETT: Where have they gone? Tell me. It's life or death.

SCARLETT *and* MISS PITTY, *startled, look at one another in bewilderment, but* INDIA *streaks across the room to* MELANIE's *side.*

INDIA: Don't tell him anything! He's a Yankee spy!

RHETT *does not even favor her with a glance.*

RHETT: Quickly, please, Mrs. Wilkes! There may still be time.

MELANIE: How did you know?

RHETT: Good heavens, Mrs. Wilkes! The Yankees knew there'd be trouble tonight, and they're ready for it! I've been playing poker with two Yankee captains! Your husband and his friends will walk into a trap if I can't stop them! They must have a meeting place!

INDIA: He's only trying to trap you!

MELANIE *stops her. Then, very steadily:*

MELANIE: They have. Out the Decatur Road. Just this side of those woods where the attack on Scarlett happened. The old Sullivan plantation. The house is burned. They're meeting in the cellar.

RHETT: I'll do what I can. When the Yankees come here be careful what you say. [*He goes.*]

MISS PITTY: The Yankees aren't coming here!

*She collapses on the sofa, too frightened for tears.*

SCARLETT: What's it all about? What did he mean? If you don't tell me, I'll go crazy! [*And she is shaking* MELANIE.]

INDIA: He means you've probably been the cause of Ashley's death and your husband's death! And stop shaking Melanie! She's going to faint!

MELANIE: No, I'm not. Pick up your sewing, Scarlett. I shall read aloud to you as though nothing had happened. The Yankees may be watching the house now. [*She has gone for a book.*] You should know, of course—though we thought it best not to tell you—that Ashley and Frank and Dr. Meade and others have gone to clean out those woods where you were attacked. It's what a great many of our Southern gentlemen have had to do lately for our protection. [*She sits in the big chair and opens the book.*]

INDIA: And if they're captured, they'll be hanged, Scarlett. And it will be your fault and their blood will be on your . . .

*So complete is* MELANIE's *control of herself now that she can cut* INDIA *off without raising her voice or looking up from her book.*

MELANIE: Another word and you go out of this house, India. Scarlett did what she thought she had to do. And our men are doing what they think they have to do.

*Music, the ominous strain again.* SCARLETT *sinks, dazed, into a chair.*

FADE OUT

FADE IN:

MELANIE'S HOUSE–THE PARLOR

*The reading is broken off. Those present all listen. A horse neighs off-screen.*

UNCLE PETER: Dar's a hawse, Miss Melly. Hyah dey come.

*A knock on the door.* MELANIE's *eye imposes discipline, then:*

MELANIE: Will you open the door, Uncle Peter?

*The door opened, a* CAPTAIN *and two other federal soldiers enter.*

CAPTAIN: Good evening, Mrs. Kennedy. And which of you ladies is Mrs. Wilkes?

MELANIE [*with great dignity*]: I am Mrs. Wilkes. And to what do I owe this intrusion?

CAPTAIN [*looks around the room quickly as though searching for male occupancy*]: I should like to speak to Mr. Wilkes, if you please.

MELANIE: He's not here.

CAPTAIN: Are you sure?

MAMMY: Don' you question Miz Wilkes' word!

CAPTAIN: I meant no disrespect, Mrs. Wilkes. Give me your word, and I won't search the house.

MELANIE: Search if you like. But Mr. Wilkes is at a political meeting at Mr. Kennedy's store.

CAPTAIN [*grimly*]: He's not at the store. There's no meeting tonight! No *political* meeting! We'll wait outside till he and his friends return.

*He bows stiffly and goes out. Then his voice is heard off-screen.*

CAPTAIN'S VOICE: Surround the house. Put a man at each door and window. Keep back out of sight among the bushes.

*Silence, then:*

MELANIE: Go on with your sewing, ladies, and I'll read aloud. [*She opens the book.*] "As the Cathedral clock struck two, Jean Valjean awoke . . ."

*A sound from* SCARLETT *startles her. She looks up.*

CLOSE SHOT–SCARLETT

*As she forces herself to resume her sewing.*

CLOSE SHOT–MELANIE

*Her finger on the page. She looks down at the page. The CAMERA goes close to the page. It is page 19 of* LES MISERABLES.

DISSOLVE TO

LES MISERABLES, page 27.

*The CAMERA BACKS AWAY while* MELANIE *is reading:*

MELANIE: "Ah, there you are," said he, looking towards Jean Valjean, "I am glad to see you. But! I gave you the candlesticks also, which are silver like the rest, and would bring two hundred francs. Why did you not take them along with your plates?"

*Over this sound track we have the following cuts:*

INDIA's FACE, *terrified.*

MRS. MEADE's FACE, *terrified.*

SCARLETT's FACE, *terrified.*

*Each Close-up is larger than the others—*SCARLETT's *Close-up being only her eyes.*

HANDS SEWING

FEET TAPPING NERVOUSLY

THE PENDULUM OF A CLOCK SWINGING

*BACK TO GROUP*

*From off-screen comes the sound of drunken singing, distant at first, then drawing nearer—the voices of* RHETT, DR. MEADE, *and* ASHLEY *—and the melody of "Marching Through Georgia."*

VOICE OF YANKEE CAPTAIN: Halt! You're under arrest!

*The women jump to their feet frantically—only* MELANIE *calm.* SCARLETT *starts running toward the door.*

MELANIE: Leave this to me, Scarlett. And please say nothing.

MELANIE'S HOUSE–THE HALL

MELANIE *enters and opens the front door.*

MELANIE [*like a very annoyed wife*]: So you've got my husband intoxicated again, Captain Butler! Well, bring him in.

*But it is the Yankee* CAPTAIN *who appears in the doorway instead of* RHETT.

CAPTAIN: I'm sorry, Mrs. Wilkes, but your husband's under arrest.

MELANIE [*quite steady*]: If you arrest all the men who get intoxicated in Atlanta, you must have a good many Yankees in jail, Captain. Bring him in, Captain Butler, if you can walk yourself.

*Now* RHETT, *weaving drunkenly himself, supports* ASHLEY *through the open door.*

MELANIE'S PARLOR

SCARLETT, MRS. MEADE, MAMMY, *and* INDIA WILKES *as before.*

ASHLEY *is still singing drunkenly as* RHETT *supports him into the room.* RHETT *is also acting like a wild drunk.* MELANIE *follows them.*

MELANIE: Put him there in that chair.

RHETT *obeys and* ASHLEY *forthwith collapses, most convincingly drunk.*

RHETT: *He's not himself.* [*He laughs drunkenly.*]

DR. MEADE [*plays up, with a drunken snicker*]: Who is he?

RHETT: Way he looks, I'd say no one in particular.

MELANIE: That's nothing unusual when he spends his evening with you. Will you leave the house, please? And try to remember not to come here again?

RHETT: That's fine thanks for bringing him home and keeping him out of jail!

MELANIE: As for you, Dr. Meade, I'm astonished at you! [*Then, to* ASHLEY.] Oh, Ashley, how can you do this to me?

RHETT *jogs* ASHLEY, *who makes a hazy effort to look up.*

ASHLEY: I ain't so very drunk, Melly.

MELANIE: Uncle Peter, will you take him to his room and put him to bed?

UNCLE PETER *steps forward. So does the Yankee* CAPTAIN.

CAPTAIN: Now, just a minute, lady! He's under arrest!

RHETT *turns to him.*

RHETT: What for Captain?

CAPTAIN: For leading a raid on that settlement out on the Decatur Road tonight where that woman got herself into trouble this afternoon.

SCARLETT *stiffens and is about to break out.* MELANIE *stops her.*

CAPTAIN: Lots of poor people's shanties got burned in that raid. A couple of men got killed. Don't you think it's about time you Rebels learnt you can't take the law into your own hands?

RHETT [*He is laughing.*]: Captain, this isn't your night to teach that lesson!—This pair have spent the whole evening with me!

*The* CAPTAIN *is not ready to believe this lie.*

CAPTAIN: So? Where was that?

RHETT: Well, I don't like to say—in the presence of ladies.

CAPTAIN: You'd better say.

RHETT: Do you mind stepping out on the porch?

MELANIE: Speak out, please, Captain Butler! I've a right to know where my husband's been!

*A pause for embarrassment before* RHETT *answers.*

RHETT: Much as I regret to say it, Ma'am, we've all been together at an establishment conducted by a friend of mine and the Captain's. A Mrs. Belle Watling . . . we played cards, drank champagne, there were ladies. . . . [*A gesture leaves the rest to the imagination.*]

DR. MEADE: Now you've done it! Now you've done it! Did you have to give me away! With my wife right here!

RHETT *snickers*.

RHETT: I hope you're satisfied, Tom! These ladies will not be on speaking terms with their husbands tomorrow!

*Now it is the Yankee's turn for embarrassment.*

CAPTAIN [*regretfully*]: Rhett! I had no idea! . . . Look here! Will you take an oath they've been with you at—er—[*with embarrassment*]—Belle's?

RHETT [*very steadily*]: Ask Belle if you don't believe me. She'll tell you, Captain.

CAPTAIN [*abashed*]: Do you give me *your* word as a gentleman?

RHETT: As a gentleman? [*He grins.*] Why certainly, Tom.

*He extends his hand; the Yankee* CAPTAIN *takes it.*

CAPTAIN: W-well . . . If I've made a mistake, I'm sorry . . . [*sheepishly, his eyes avoiding* MELANIE's] I—I hope you'll forgive me, Mrs. Wilkes. I—

MELANIE [*stiffly but with dignity*]: If you'll go and leave us in peace, please.

CAPTAIN [*backing away*]: I regret exceedingly . . . Indeed I do . . .

*He backs out, his men accompanying him.*

SCARLETT, *her knees shaking, catches hold of a chair beside which she has been standing. The front door closed,* DR. MEADE *springs to* ASHLEY.

RHETT [*to* UNCLE PETER]: Lock that door!

*But* DR. MEADE *has already opened* ASHLEY's COAT *and the shirt is seen to be bloodstained.* SCARLETT *points.*

SCARLETT: Look! Ashley's hurt!

INDIA: You fool! Did you think he was really drunk?

DR. MEADE: It's nothing much. It's only through his shoulder. Get him to bed where I can dress the wound.

*But* ASHLEY *has revived.*

ASHLEY: I think I can walk.

*He is going,* UNCLE PETER *on one side and* DR. MEADE *on the other.* MRS. MEADE, MISS PITTY, *and* INDIA *follow toward the bedroom.*

MRS. MEADE: Were you really there?

DR. MEADE: Where?

MRS. MEADE: At the Watling woman's place. What did it look like? Are there cut glass chandeliers and plush curtains and dozens of gilt mirrors? And are the girls? . . .

DR. MEADE: Good heavens, Mrs. Meade! Remember yourself!

MRS. MEADE: But this is the only chance I've ever had to hear what a bad house looks like!

MELANIE'S BEDROOM–NIGHT

ASHLEY *is stretched out full length on the bed.* MELANIE *sits beside him washing his face with the napkin which she dabs in the water pitcher.* RHETT *stands beside her.* SCARLETT *looks on from the foot of the bed.*

MELANIE: Now please tell me what happened, Captain Butler. All that happened! Captain!

RHETT: I was too late. When I got to the old Sullivan place, there'd already been a skirmish with the Yankees. I found Mr. Wilkes wounded and Dr. Meade with him. I had to prove they'd been *somewhere.* Any place but where they were. So I took them to Belle's.

MELANIE: And she took them in?

RHETT: She's by way of being an old friend of mine.

MELANIE [*Her eyes fall.*]: I'm sorry.

RHETT: *I'm* sorry I couldn't think up a more dignified alibi.

MELANIE'S *candor is never more clear or lovely as she rises to take his hand.*

MELANIE: This isn't the first time you've come between me and disaster, Captain Butler. I'm not likely to question any device of yours. I'll go help the Doctor find what he needs. . . . [*She goes out.*]

SCARLETT: Oh, Ashley, Ashley!

RHETT *looks steadily at her across the unconscious* ASHLEY.

RHETT: Have you no interest in what's become of your own husband, Mrs. Kennedy?

SCARLETT *snickers nervously.*

SCARLETT: Was Frank at Belle Watling's with you?

RHETT: No.

*The least pause.*

SCARLETT: Where is he?

RHETT [*quietly and without melodrama*]: He's lying out there on Decatur Road, shot through the head. . . . He's dead.

SCARLETT *reacts in horror, as we—*

FADE OUT

FADE IN:

SERIES OF LARGE CLOSE-UPS

PROVOST MARSHAL–DAY–[AGAINST BACKGROUND OF AMERICAN FLAG]

PROVOST MARSHAL: Are you ladies prepared to testify that the accused spent last evening at Mrs. Watling's?

WIPE TO

GIRL–*arranging her hair and rolling her eyes around in very un-courtroomlike attitude:*

GIRL: . . . the *whole evening* . . . I *never* had a better time!

WIPE TO

ANOTHER GIRL

GIRL: But of *course* we were drinking. What do you take me for, Your Honor?

WIPE TO

YOUNG NEGRESS

YOUNG NEGRESS: Yassir . . . Ah's Miss Belle's maid . . . and Ah can indemnify 'em, every one.

WIPE TO

PROVOST MARSHAL

PROVOST MARSHAL: But, Dr. Meade, aren't you a little *old* for such goings on?

WIPE TO

BELLE WATLING

BELLE [*a little too angry*]: What I want to know is—who's goin' to pay for the mirrors they broke . . .

WIPE TO

PROVOST MARSHAL

PROVOST MARSHAL [*disgustedly*]: There's always fifty witnesses to prove a Southerner was someplace he wasn't. . . . All right. . . . Dismissed!

WIPE TO

INDIA–NIGHT

INDIA: I'd rather they'd have *hanged* than be under obligation to that Butler man!

WIPE TO

MRS. MEADE

MRS. MEADE: . . . And that Watling woman! . . . It's intolerable!

WIPE TO

AUNT PITTY

AUNT PITTY: Well, what if they were drinking all night?

DISSOLVE TO

CLOSE-UP–MELANIE

MELANIE: Won't you come in the house, Mrs. Watling?

*CAMERA PULLS BACK to reveal that we are in* BELLE'S CARRIAGE. MELANIE *is peering in from outside through the open door; and* BELLE

*is within the carriage, sitting covertly back or in the corner of the carriage so as not to be seen by passersby.*

BELLE [*embarrassed*]: Oh, I couldn't do that, Miz Wilkes. You climb in here and set a minute with me.

MELANIE *enters the carriage, closing the door behind her, and sits down beside* BELLE, *reaching for her hand.*

MELANIE: How can I ever thank you enough, Mrs. Watling, for what you did today? How can any of us thank you enough!

BELLE [*embarrassed, changes the subject*]: I got your note this morning sayin' you was goin' to call on me to thank me. Miz Wilkes, you must of lost your mind! I come up here as soon as 'twas dark to tell you you mustn't think of any sech thing. Why, I—why, you—it wouldn't be fittin' at all.

MELANIE: It wouldn't be fitting for me to call and thank a kind woman who saved my husband's life!

BELLE: I'll bet the other ladies don't thank me none—and I'll bet they don't thank Captain Butler neither. [*with sudden venom*] I wouldn't of minded if all their husbands got hung. But I did mind about Mr. Wilkes. There ain't never been a lady in this town nice to me like you was—about the money for the hospital, you know—and I don't forget a kindness. And I thought about you bein' left a widder with a little boy if Mr. Wilkes got hung, and—[*wistfully*] I seen your little boy once. He's a nice little boy, Miz Wilkes. I got a boy myself, and so I—

MELANIE: Oh, you have? Does he live here in . . .

BELLE: Oh, no'm! He ain't here in Atlanta. He ain't never been here. He's off at school. I ain't seen him since he was little. [*Her mind and her eyes wander for a moment, then she remembers herself and quickly changes her tone.*] Well, anyway—I got to be goin'. I'm afraid somebody might recognize this carriage if I stayed here longer and that wouldn't do you no good. And, Miz Wilkes, if you ever see me on the street, you—you don't have to speak to me. I'll understand. . . .

MELANIE: I shall be proud to speak to you. Proud to be under obligation to you. I hope—I hope we meet again.

BELLE: No. That wouldn't be fittin' neither. . . . And, Miz Wilkes —[*looks at* MELANIE *tentatively*]

MELANIE [*kindly*]: Yes, Mrs. Watling?

BELLE: Meanin' no offense—I don't like Miz Kennedy much—but would you tell her I'm sorry about Mr. Kennedy?

MELANIE *presses her hand in thanks.*

BELLE: Goodnight, Miz Wilkes.

DISSOLVE TO

FADE IN:

EXTERIOR–MISS PITTY'S HOUSE–THE FRONT DOOR–
DAY–(SPRING, 1866)

CLOSE SHOT–A WREATH–of immortelles with a crepe bow on
the door. Through the center of the wreath:

DISSOLVE TO

CLOSE-UP–OF BRANDY BOTTLE

INTERIOR–SCARLETT'S BEDROOM AT AUNT PITTY'S

SCARLETT'S hand comes into shot, lifts up bottle. PULL BACK
CAMERA—to see SCARLETT, with a slight jag on, pouring drink into
a glass. She takes a big swig . . . hears carriage wheels from outside—
runs to the window and looks out.

EXTERIOR–HOUSE [FROM HER ANGLE]

RHETT stepping from his elegant carriage, and walking up the path
to the front door.

BACK TO SCARLETT

She runs back to the mirror—smooths her hair hurriedly—thinks
of her breath—holds her hand in front of her mouth—blows on it—
grimaces as she sniffs the odor on her hand from her breath—goes
hurriedly to the dresser from which she takes cologne bottle—tilts it
back and gargles cologne from the bottle.

A knock is heard on her door.

MAMMY's VOICE [disgustedly]: Miss Scarlett! Cap'n Butler here to
see you. I told him you were prostrate with grief.

SCARLETT affects a tragic voice which belies her appearance and her
hasty attempts to straighten herself up.

SCARLETT: I'll be right down, Mammy.

AUNT PITTY'S LIVING ROOM

RHETT has been pacing the living room floor. MAMMY comes in the
door—gives RHETT a dirty look.

MAMMY: She says she's comin'. I don' know why she's comin', but
she's comin'.

RHETT smiles, then looks at her reprovingly.

RHETT: You don't like me, Mammy. [MAMMY snorts.] Now don't
argue with me. You don't—you really don't.

MAMMY exits in a huff as SCARLETT enters. RHETT goes forward to
meet her.

SCARLETT enters to RHETT, slightly tipsy, putting on a great act of
the grieving widow. She extends her hand to RHETT. He bows over it
very low, kisses it, and sniffs.

MGM, © 1939, 1967. UGa Libraries, Marsh Papers.

RHETT [*as he rises from her hand*]: It's no good, Scarlett.

SCARLETT: What? [*She starts guiltily.*]

RHETT: The cologne.

SCARLETT: I'm sure I don't know what you mean!

RHETT: I mean you've been drinking. [*Goes toward her to look more closely.*] Brandy. Quite a lot.

SCARLETT [*bridles*]: What if I have? Is that any of your affair?

RHETT [*bows*]: Don't drink alone, Scarlett. People always find out and it ruins the reputation.

*He looks at her, amused, as she crosses into the room, still acting like mad.*

RHETT: May I close the doors?

SCARLETT *doesn't answer—just sniffs into her handkerchief, sobbing brokenly. He goes over and pulls the sliding doors together, turns back to her.*

RHETT: What is it, Scarlett? This is more than losing old Frank.

SCARLETT [*She looks up pathetically.*]: Oh, Rhett, I'm so afraid!

RHETT [*He smiles.*]: I don't believe it. You've never been afraid in your life.

SCARLETT [*She insists.*]: I'm afraid now. I'm afraid of dying and going to hell.

*He wants to laugh and rises and moves away to restrain himself. Then:*

RHETT: You look pretty healthy. And maybe there isn't any hell.

SCARLETT *looks up shocked and injured.*

SCARLETT [*very earnestly*]: Oh, but there is! I know there is! I was raised on it!

RHETT: Far be it from me to question the teachings of childhood. Tell me what you've done that hell yawns before you.

SCARLETT: I ought never to have married Frank to begin with. He was Suellen's beau, and he loved her, not me. And I made him miserable and I killed him! Yes, I did! I killed him! Oh, Rhett, for the first time I'm finding out what it is to be sorry for something I've done! For the first time I'm glad that Mother died! [*She dissolves into tears again.*]

RHETT: Here. [*He offers his handkerchief.*] Dry your eyes. If you had it all to do over again, you'd do no differently. You're like the thief who isn't the least bit sorry he stole, but is terribly, terribly sorry he's going to jail. [SCARLETT *looks up enraged.*] What's more, you're on the verge of a crying jag. [*She rises, furious, but still he continues.*] So I'll change the subject and say what I came to say.

SCARLETT: Say it, then, and get out! [*Then, in spite of herself*] What is it?

RHETT: That I can't go on any longer without you.

SCARLETT [*slowly; the great lady*]: You really *are* the most ill-bred man to come here at a time like this with your filthy . . .

RHETT [*interrupting and completely disregarding her performance*]: I made up my mind that you were the woman for me, Scarlett, the first time I saw you at Twelve Oaks. . . . Now you've got your lumber mill and Frank's money, you won't come to me as you did to the jail. . . . So I see that I shall have to marry you.

SCARLETT: Why, I never heard of such bad taste! I . . .

RHETT [*interrupting*]: Would you be more convinced if I fell on my knees? [*He kneels and takes her hand. She tries to draw it back, but he holds it fast.*]

SCARLETT: Turn me loose, you varmint, and get out of here!

RHETT [*play-acting*]: Forgive me for startling you with my sentiments, my dear Scarlett—I mean, my dear Mrs. Kennedy. But it cannot have escaped your notice that for some time past the friendship I have felt for you has ripened into a deeper feeling. A feeling more beautiful, more pure, more sacred . . . dare I name it? Can it be love?

SCARLETT [*furious*]: Get up off your knees. I don't like your common jokes!

RHETT: Scarlett, this is an honorable proposal of marriage, made at what I consider a most opportune moment. [*He rises.*] I can't go all my life waiting to catch you between husbands.

SCARLETT: You're coarse and conceited, and I think this conversation has gone far enough! . . . [*afterthought*] Besides, I shall never marry again.

RHETT: Oh yes you will, Scarlett. And you'll marry me.

SCARLETT: You! You! I don't love you. . . . And I don't like being married.

RHETT: Did you ever think of marrying just for fun?

SCARLETT: Marriage *fun?* Fiddle-dee-dee! Fun for men, you mean! [*This time he does laugh heartily and she is frightened.*] Hush up! Do you want them to hear outside?

RHETT: You've been married to a boy and an old man. Why not try a husband of the right age, with a way with women?

SCARLETT: You're a fool, Rhett Butler, when you know I shall always love another man. . . .

RHETT: Stop it! [*then, in a low voice, shaken, though, by the violence of his feeling*] Do you hear me, Scarlett? Stop it! No more of that talk!

*He takes her in his arms, bends her head back across his arm and kisses her hard on the mouth again and again, till she struggles for breath.*

SCARLETT: Rhett, don't! I'll faint!

RHETT: I want you to faint. This is what you were meant for, Scarlett! None of the fools you've known have kissed you like this, have they? [*continues kissing her*] Well, have they? Your Charles or your Frank or your stupid Ashley?

SCARLETT: Rhett!

RHETT: Yes, I said Ashley! What does he know about you? But I know you, Scarlett! I know you! And you're going to marry me—and we'll put everything else behind us and out of our minds! You hear me, Scarlett?

*He kisses her again and slowly* SCARLETT's *arms go around him. At long last* SCARLETT O'HARA *has surrendered. Through the embrace we hear her mumble.*

SCARLETT: Rhett . . . Rhett . . .

*We hold on this for a—*

SLOW FADE OUT

ADDED SCENE–INTERIOR–AUNT PITTY'S PARLOR–*CLOSE TWO SHOT*–RHETT *and* SCARLETT

RHETT *draws back from the embrace.*

RHETT [*hoarsely*]: Say you're going to marry me! . . . Say 'Yes'! Say 'Yes'!

SCARLETT [*whispers*]: Yes.

*She closes her eyes preparing for another kiss. He starts to kiss her again, then draws back and looks at her.* SCARLETT *opens her eyes.*

RHETT: You're sure you meant it? You don't want to take it back?

SCARLETT: No.

*He puts his hand under her chin and lifts her face to his.*

RHETT: Look at me. And try to tell me the truth! Did you say 'yes' because of my money?

SCARLETT [*taken aback*]: Well—yes, partly.

RHETT [*looks at her sourly*]: Partly!

*He drops his arms and walks away from her a few steps.*

SCARLETT [*floundering*]: Well, money does help, you know, Rhett—and then, of course—well, I am fond of you—

RHETT: Fond of me!

SCARLETT: Well, if I said I was madly in love with you, you'd know I was lying. But you've always said we had a lot in common.

*As she talks,* RHETT *bites his lip and shakes his head in despair, with*

MGM, © 1939, 1967. Collection of Richard Harwell.

which is mixed a degree of humor at what he's putting up with to get this woman. In the face of what she says he has no alternative but to control his emotions and assume as casual an attitude as hers.

RHETT: That's right, my dear. And I'm not in love with you any more than you are with me. God help the man who ever really loves you! . . . Well, what kind of a ring would you like, my darling?

SCARLETT: Ooo—a diamond ring! And Rhett, do buy a great big one!

RHETT: You shall have the biggest and most vulgar ring in Atlanta . . . and I'll take you to New Orleans for the most expensive honeymoon my ill-gotten gains can buy.

SCARLETT: Oh, Rhett, that would be just *heavenly!*

RHETT: And I think I'll buy your trousseau for you, too.

SCARLETT: Oh, that would be *wonderful!* [*on second thought*] But you won't tell anybody, will you, Rhett?

RHETT [*looking at her with slightly sour amusement*]: Still the little hypocrite! . . . [*He laughs, starts out of room.*]

HALL

SCARLETT *running in, after* RHETT *who is at the door.*

SCARLETT: Rhett! Aren't you going to kiss me goodbye?

RHETT: Don't you think you've had enough kissing for one afternoon?

SCARLETT: Oh, you're impossible! You can go and I don't care if you never come back!

*She turns and flounces toward the stairs, peering over her shoulder expecting* RHETT *to come after her. But he simply opens the door and calls:*

RHETT: But I will come back.

*He closes the door after him and we—*

DISSOLVE TO

INTERIOR–MISS PITTY'S HOUSE–THE PARLOR–NIGHT

*Music. CAMERA is close to a telegram, which reads:*

I MARRIED RHETT BUTLER TODAY AND WE ARE OFF TO SPEND OUR HONEYMOON IN NEW ORLEANS MUCH LOVE

SCARLETT

*CAMERA draws back to take in the group in the room.* MISS PITTY *lies back in her chair, just coming out of a faint.* MAMMY *waves the swoon bottle vaguely under her nose.* MELANIE *looks up from the telegram, both bewildered and shocked.* ASHLEY, *deeply disturbed, turns away to sit in a chair.*

MAMMY: Ah ain' never thought ter say it 'bout none of Miss Ellen's blood, but Miss Scarlett ain' nuthin' but a mule in hawse harness. She give herseff airs lak a fine hawse, but she a mule jes' de same! An' dat Butler man, he come of good stock an' he all slicked up lak a race hawse, but he a mule in hawse harness jes' lak her!

*DISSOLVE TO*

LONG SHOT–RIVERBOAT ON THE MISSISSIPPI

*Negroes are singing off-screen and the singing continues through next scene.*

CLOSE UP–WEDDING RING AND ENORMOUS DIAMOND AND EMERALD RING ON SCARLETT'S FINGER

*CAMERA PULLS BACK, and we see that* SCARLETT *is lying in bed in a cabin of an elegant riverboat of the period, dimly lighted.* RHETT *enters, or is found already sitting on the edge of her bed, in dressing gown.* SCARLETT *looks up at him, smiling and coy.*

SCARLETT: Oh, Rhett, I'm so happy!

RHETT: I'm glad, darling—

*She throws her head back luxuriously and thoughtfully on the pillow. She makes a very provocative picture.*

RHETT [*softly and romantically*]: What are you thinking about, Scarlett?

SCARLETT [*She closes her eyes romantically, and after a second, speaks.*]: I'm thinking about how rich we are.

*Taken aback,* RHETT *cannot help laughing nevertheless.*

SCARLETT [*suddenly nervous*]: And, Rhett—I can keep the lumber business, too, can't I?

RHETT [*tolerantly, as to an adored and spoiled child*]: Yes, of course you can . . . if it amuses you. And now that you're so rich, you can tell everybody to go to the devil as you always said you wanted to.

SCARLETT: But you were the main one I wanted to tell to go to the devil.

RHETT [*laughs*]: Well, do it whenever you like, if it makes you happy.

SCARLETT [*confused*]: But it doesn't make me specially happy.

RHETT, *laughing adoringly, takes her in his arms, as we*

*DISSOLVE TO*

INTERIOR–NEW ORLEANS CAFE

*CLOSE SHOT—A LINE OF CREOLE DANCING GIRLS, about seven-eighths covered by the smoke. The Cafe is gas-lighted and there are many shadows.*

MGM, © 1939, 1967. UGa Libraries, Marsh Papers.

*PULL BACK to reveal* SCARLETT *and* RHETT *in profile across from each other at a table.* RHETT *is smoking a long cigar.*

*On the table is the most elaborate possible food—an elegantly prepared dove, etc., etc. . . . wine glasses . . . two or three kinds— and buckets of wine.*

SCARLETT's *plate is almost empty.* RHETT's *is half-eaten but he has finished. She is stuffing herself and scraping her plate, and in between times gobbling champagne as though it were water. She is as tight as a tick.*

RHETT: Don't scrape the plate, Scarlett. I'm sure there's more in the kitchen.

*At this moment* SCARLETT *sees a waiter go by with an elaborate tray of pastries.*

SCARLETT: Oooh, Rhett! Can I have some of those chocolate ones stuffed with meringue?

RHETT: If you don't stop being such a glutton you'll get as fat as a Cuban lady. And then I'll divorce you.

*A waiter enters and lifts the tureen, revealing something particularly succulent and amazingly beautiful. Through the tureen and behind the food, we see* SCARLETT, *her wide eyes devouring already this next course. Her eyes turn questioningly to* RHETT, *turn back to the new dish. She wets her lips in anticipation and swallows more wine, as we—*

DISSOLVE TO

INTERIOR–A HOTEL BEDROOM–NEW ORLEANS–DAY

*CAMERA looks into a mirror, in which* SCARLETT *is examining a sumptuous frock.* RHETT *looks over her shoulder.*

SCARLETT: We're really a handsome couple.

RHETT: Handsome is as handsome does, my dear Scarlett.

*But the CAMERA draws back as she turns to him and shows the romantic sumptuousness of the room and every piece of furniture literally buried in other new frocks.*

SCARLETT: Just you wait, Rhett Butler! Now I've got money—well, now we've got money—I'm going to be the greatest lady you ever saw.

RHETT: Oh, I shall wait with interest!

SCARLETT: Look at these, too! [*She lifts her skirt to show her silk stockings.*] No cotton tops on these! And I bought fifty pairs! Perhaps that is a little more than I need at the moment. You don't mind my being a trifle extravagant, though?

RHETT: I want you to be.

MGM, © 1939, 1967. UGa Libraries, Marsh Papers.

SCARLETT: You're really very nice, Rhett. [*She goes into his arms.*]

RHETT: Buy whatever you want, darling, and more than you need.
. . . But don't you think it would be nice if you bought something for Mammy, too?

SCARLETT: Why should I buy her a present? When she called us both mules?

RHETT [*laughing*]: Mules? Why mules?

SCARLETT: Yes—She said we could give ourselves airs and get all slicked up like race horses, but we were only mules in horse harness, and we didn't fool anybody.

RHETT: I never heard anything more true. Mammy's a smart old soul and one of the few people I know whose respect I'd like to have.

SCARLETT: Well, I won't take her a thing! She doesn't deserve it!

RHETT: Then I'll take her a petticoat. . . . I remember my mammy always said that when she went to Heaven she wanted a red taffeta petticoat so stiff that it would stand by itself and so rustly that the Lord would think it was made of angels' wings.

SCARLETT: She won't take it from you! She'd rather die than wear it!

RHETT: That may be, but I'm making the gesture just the same.

SCARLETT: Oh, Rhett, would you do something for me if I asked you?

RHETT: You *know* I will.

SCARLETT: Take me away from here.

RHETT: Don't you like New Orleans?

SCARLETT: I love New Orleans, but I want to go home and visit Tara—Will you take me to Tara?

RHETT: Yes, Scarlett. Of course I will. We'll go tomorrow.

*As* SCARLETT *holds herself close to him, we*

DISSOLVE TO

INTERIOR–THE HOTEL BEDROOM–NIGHT

SCARLETT *lies sleeping in the bed at* RHETT's *side. The moonlight streams over them. He is shaking her.*

RHETT: Wake up, Scarlett! Wake up! [*She opens her eyes.*] You were having another nightmare.

*She looks about her, then turns to him in a little girl's terror.*

SCARLETT: Oh, Rhett, I was so cold and hungry and so tired! And I couldn't find it! I ran and ran but I couldn't find it!

RHETT: Find what, honey?

SCARLETT: I don't know! I've always dreamed that dream, and I never know! I just run and run and hunt and can't ever find what I'm hunting for! I know I'd be safe forever if I could find it! I know it's near, too!

RHETT: Darling!

*He kisses her.*

SCARLETT: Do you think I'll ever dream that I get to safety?

*He shakes his head, smiling tenderly at her.*

RHETT: Dreams don't work that way. When you've got used to being safe and warm, though, you'll stop dreaming. And I'm going to see that you are safe and warm.

*She looks at him a moment, then suddenly her face is troubled.*

SCARLETT: You . . .

*She turns away from him and sighs. He draws back, grimly, looking down at her.*

RHETT: I see you wish I were someone else.

*She looks back guiltily.*

SCARLETT: Oh, no! Oh, no, Rhett!

RHETT: You do! Confound your cheating little soul, you do!

*DISSOLVE TO*

EXTERIOR–FRONT OF TARA–*LONG SHOT*–DAY

*CAMERA PULLS BACK until* RHETT *and* SCARLETT *are revealed standing in the foreground.*

RHETT [*moodily*]: You get your strength from this red earth of Tara, Scarlett. You're part of it, and it's part of you.

SCARLETT [*nostalgically, almost with a cry of pain and hope*]: Oh, Rhett, I'd give anything to have Tara the way it was before the war!

RHETT [*kindly*]: Would you? . . . Then go ahead and make it that way. Spend whatever you want to make it as fine a plantation as it ever was.

SCARLETT *looks at him unbelieving.*

SCARLETT: Oh, Rhett, Rhett, you *are* good to me! [*She throws her arms around his neck.*] And can we still have our big new house in Atlanta?

RHETT: Yes. [*laughing*] And it can be as ornate as you want it. . . . Marble terraces, stained glass windows and all.

SCARLETT: Oh, Rhett, won't everybody be jealous! I want everybody who's been mean to me to be *pea-green* with envy!

*He laughs.*

*DISSOLVE TO*

INTERIOR–BEDROOM–TARA–SUELLEN *and* CARREEN–NIGHT

SUELLEN [*sobbing in rage*]: I don't care! Scarlett's hateful—building that new house just to show off! And even taking our servants!

CARREEN: Darling, you mustn't think unkindly of her. She's made it possible for us to keep Tara—always—

SUELLEN [*turns*]: Yes, and what good is Tara? She's had three husbands—[*screaming through her tears*]—and I'll be an old maid!

*DISSOLVE TO*

EXTERIOR–BUTLER HOUSE

*In the background through the trees we see the elegant new house. In the foreground,* PORK, MAMMY, *and* PRISSY *are standing agape, looking up at the house, bags in hand. Their luggage consists of old-fashioned, worn leather suitcases, which had probably belonged to the O'Hara family.* PORK *totes a small, square, leather hat trunk of the period, which he holds by its handle.*

PORK: Great Jehosophat! Great Jehosophat!

PRISSY: *Lawzee!* We sho' is rich now.

MAMMY: Huh! Dat fancy buildin' ain' no quality house lak Miss Ellen's wuz. *Naw suh!* Not lak Tara—*naw suh!*

*DISSOLVE TO*

EXTERIOR–THE NEW HOUSE–DAY

UNCLE PETER *is waiting with Miss Pitty's carriage.* WADE HAMPTON *stands on the verandah. The door opens.* MISS PITTY *appears, followed by* MAMMY.

MAMMY: Ah kinder 'pologized ter Mist' Rhett 'bout it not bein' a boy. Lawsy, Miss Pitty, he ack lak a gempmum 'bout it. Maybe Ah done been a mite wrong 'bout Mist' Rhett.

MISS PITTY: Perhaps we all were, Mammy. I hope we were.

MAMMY *is helping* MISS PITTY *into her carriage.*

MAMMY: Dis sho is a happy day ter me, Miss Pitty.

*FADE IN:*

INTERIOR–RHETT'S ROOM–NIGHT–(SPRING, 1867)

*CLOSE-UP–RHETT'S FEET pacing the floor—surrounded by cigar butts on the fine carpet. As another is thrown down on the carpet:*

RHETT'S VOICE: But it's ridiculous! Why can't I go in?

*CAMERA HAS PANNED UP and we are now on a CLOSE SHOT of* RHETT.

RHETT [*continuing*]: I'm entitled to at least see what my own child looks like.

*CAMERA PULLS BACK to show us that* RHETT *is in his room talking to* MAMMY. *The door to the hall is open.*

MAMMY: You control yo'seff, Mist' Rhett—you'll be seein' it fer a long time.

MGM, © 1939, 1967. UGa Libraries, Marsh Papers.

RHETT *continues mumbling, goes over and pours himself a drink and drinks it during* MAMMY's *following speech.*

MAMMY: Ah'd lak to 'pologize, Mist' Rhett, 'bout it's not being a boy.

RHETT: Hush your mouth, Mammy. Who wants a boy. Boys aren't any use to anybody. Don't you think I'm proof of that?

MAMMY *laughs uproariously at* RHETT's *joke. He pours a drink into another glass and hands it to* MAMMY.

RHETT [*suddenly worried*]: She is beautiful, isn't she, Mammy?

MAMMY *takes the drink, peering around and looking through the open door to see no one is looking.*

MAMMY [*gulps it down*]: She sho' is.

RHETT [*still worried*]: Did you ever see a prettier one?

MAMMY: Well, suh, Miss Scarlett wuz mos' near as pretty when she come, but not quite.

RHETT [*his worries assuaged*]: Have another glass, Mammy.

*He takes the glass from her, starts pouring another drink.* MAMMY *takes a step or two forward toward him, her skirts rustling.*

RHETT [*sternly, but with twinkling eyes*]: And Mammy . . . what's that rustling noise I hear?

MAMMY: Lawsy, Mist' Rhett, dat ain' nothin' but mah red silk petticoat you gave me. [*She giggles and swishes till her huge bulk shakes. She drinks.*]

RHETT: Nothing but your petticoat! I don't believe it. Let me see. Pull up your skirt.

MAMMY: Mist' Rhett, you is bad! Yeah-O-Lawd!

*She gives a little shriek and retreats about a yard, modestly lifting her dress a few inches to show the ruffle of her red taffeta petticoat.*

RHETT [*grumbling*]: You took long enough about wearing it.

MAMMY: Yassuh, too long.

RHETT: No more mule in horse harness?

MAMMY: Mist' Rhett, Miss Scarlett wuz bad to tell you dat. You ain' holdin' dat 'gainst ol' Mammy?

RHETT: No, I'm not holding it—I just wanted to know. Have another drink, Mammy—have the whole bottle.

MELANIE *appears at the door.*

MELANIE: Dr. Meade says you may go in now, Captain Butler.

RHETT *exits as though he'd been shot.*

MAMMY [*to* MELANIE]: Dis sho' is a happy day ter me. I done diapered three ginrations of dis fambly's girls, and it sho' is a happy day.

MELANIE: Oh, yes, Mammy. The happiest days are when babies come. I wish . . .

MAMMY *looks at her keenly.* MELANIE *is suddenly aware of her look.*

MELANIE: Oh, Mammy, she's beautiful! What do you suppose they'll name her?

*As* MAMMY *starts to answer, CAMERA STARTS TO MOVE UP CLOSER TO HER:*

MAMMY: Miss Scarlett done tol' me effen it wuz a girl she wuz goin' to name it *Eugenia Victoria!*

*For the last words we are on a LARGE CLOSE-UP OF MAMMY'S FACE, and from her big black face, we—*

*DISSOLVE TO*

*CLOSE-UP–THE BABY'S TINY WHITE FACE [AS IT LIES IN ITS CRIB]–DAY*

*Over it we hear* RHETT's *voice talking baby talk.*

RHETT'S VOICE: Yes, she's a beautiful baby, the most beautiful baby ever. Yes. [*clucks*] Do you know that this is your birthday? [*Leans farther into crib—CAMERA PANS with him.*] That you're a week old today? Yes. [*Starts to pick her up.*] I'm gonna buy her a pony the likes of which this . . . [*bent over crib;* MAMMY *left background*] . . . town has never seen. Yes, I'm gonna send her to the best . . . schools in Charleston. Yes.

INTERIOR–SCARLETT'S BEDROOM–*REVERSE SHOT*–RHETT

RHETT *turns, still talking baby talk, moves to background.* MAMMY *moves to crib in foreground as CAMERA PANS with* RHETT.

RHETT: And her'll be received by the best families in the South. [*He is crossing the room.*] And when it comes time for her to marry— Well—[*CAMERA REVEALS* SCARLETT *in bed.*] She'll be a little princess.

*CAMERA PANS OVER TO* SCARLETT, *who lies in the nearby bed.*

SCARLETT [*irritably*]: You certainly are making a fool of yourself.

RHETT: Why shouldn't I? She's the first person who's ever completely belonged to me.

SCARLETT: Great balls of fire! I had the baby, didn't I?

*A knock is heard.*

MELANIE'S VOICE [*off-screen*]: It's Melanie. May I come in?

SCARLETT: Come in, Melly.

RHETT: Yes. Come in and look at my daughter's beautiful blue eyes.

MELANIE [*crossing and laughing*]: But, Captain Butler, most babies have blue eyes when they're born.

SCARLETT: Don't try to tell him anything, Melly. He knows *everything* about babies.

RHETT: Nevertheless, her eyes are blue and they're going to stay blue.

MELANIE [*laughingly*]: As blue as the Bonnie Blue Flag.

RHETT: That's it! That's what we'll call her! Bonnie Blue Butler!

*CLOSE-UP*–SCARLETT–*looking at* RHETT *in disgust.*

*CLOSE-UP*–INFANT–in RHETT's arms.

*FADE OUT*

# Tenth
# Sequence

ADE IN:

INTERIOR–SCARLETT'S BEDROOM–NIGHT [ABOUT SIX WEEKS LATER]

*Just as in her girlhood days at Tara,* SCARLETT's *stays have just been laced by* MAMMY. *The lacing completed,* MAMMY *is pulling a tape measure tight around* SCARLETT's *waist.* MAMMY *looks up at her mistress.*

MAMMY: Twenty inches.

SCARLETT's *jaw drops.*

SCARLETT: I've grown as big as Aunt Pitty! You've simply got to make it eighteen and a half again!

MAMMY [*shakes her head*]: You done had a baby, Miss Scarlett, an' you ain' never goin' to be no eighteen an' a half inches again— never. An' dar ain' nothin' to do 'bout it.

*This statement provides* SCARLETT *with the most unpleasant possible food for thought. A pause while she digests it, then:*

SCARLETT: There *is* something to do about it! I'm not going to get fat and old before my time! I just won't have any more babies!

MAMMY: I heerd Mist' Rhett say he'll be wantin' a son next year.

SCARLETT: Tell Captain Butler I've decided not to go out after all. [*She picks up a wrapper from a nearby chair and slips it on.*] I'll have my supper in my room. [*Meditatively,* SCARLETT *crosses the room. She sits at dressing table and stares at herself in mirror.*]

*CLOSE SHOT*–MAMMY

*As she goes out, sighing, and shaking her head disgustedly.*

*BACK TO SCENE:* SCARLETT *at her dressing table.*

*Music a distant reminiscence of the old moonlight and magnolia days.* SCARLETT's *eyes drop to a little drawer in her dressing table. She opens the drawer. Takes out a daguerreotype in its case and opens it. It is a picture of* ASHLEY WILKES *in his major's uniform.*

*So absorbed is she that she does not hear* RHETT's *entrance. He comes toward her. Puts his hands on her shoulders tenderly. She starts and conceals the daguerreotype quickly in her lap.*

RHETT: I got your message. I'll have them bring my supper up here, too.

*He bends to kiss her neck. She gives a sudden quick shudder. She is on her feet. The daguerreotype slips from her lap to the rug.*

RHETT [*looks at her curiously*]: No objection to that, I hope?

MGM, © 1939, 1967. UGa Libraries, Marsh Papers.

SCARLETT: No. Yes. I mean, I don't care where you have your supper. [*She moves to the window, speaking over her shoulder.*] Rhett . . .

RHETT: Yes?

SCARLETT: You see—well—I've decided—well—[*She blurts it out.*] I hope I don't have any more children.

*Startled,* RHETT *takes a step toward her. His foot comes into contact with the daguerreotype. He looks down.*

*CAMERA WITH HIM.* It is open. RHETT's *jaw sets. He controls himself. His tone is cold.*

RHETT: My pet, as I told you before Bonnie was born, it is immaterial to me whether you have one child or twenty!

SCARLETT [*faces him*]: You know very well—[*She is embarrassed, lowers her eyes. Then looks at him again, belligerently.*] Do you know what I mean?

RHETT: I do . . . And do *you* know that I can divorce you for this?

SCARLETT: You're just low enough to think of something like that! If you had any chivalry you would be nice like—well, look at Ashley Wilkes! Melanie can't have any more children and he—

SCARLETT *stops, unable to explain further.* RHETT *looks at her silently for a moment, sees through her. His face takes on a bitter little smile.*

RHETT: Has Ashley Wilkes been over talking to you this afternoon?

SCARLETT [*guiltily*]: What has that to do with it?

RHETT: Quite the little gentleman, Ashley. . . . Pray go on, Mrs. Butler.

SCARLETT [*She chokes with rage, realizing the futility of any future hopes.*]: Oh, what's the use! You wouldn't understand!

RHETT *goes over and pinches her chin playfully, attempting to cover his hurt.*

RHETT: You know, I'm sorry for you, Scarlett.

SCARLETT [*with a sneer*]: Sorry—for me?

RHETT: Yes, sorry for you—because you're throwing away happiness with both hands—and reaching out for something that would never make you happy.

SCARLETT [*pushing his hand down from her chin*]: I don't know what you're talking about.

RHETT: You're a child crying for the moon, Scarlett—and what would a child do with the moon if he got it? What would you do with Ashley if you had him? If you were free, and if Miss Melly were dead and you had your precious, honorable Ashley, do you think you'd be happy with him? [*a bitter little laugh*] You'd never know him, never

even understand his mind—any more than you understand anything except money. [RHETT *gives her one last look and strolls away, talking as he goes.*] And the tragic part of it is that Ashley doesn't understand or even *want* your mind, the fool! And I don't want anything but your mind—and your heart.

SCARLETT [*laughs derisively*]: Are you trying to tell me that's all you care about?

RHETT: Exactly. You may keep your sanctity, Scarlett. It'll work no hardship on me.

SCARLETT: Oh, you're vile!

RHETT: The world is full of many things and many people . . . and I shan't be lonely.

SCARLETT: That's fine! But I warn you, just in case you change your mind, that I intend to lock my door!

RHETT: Why trouble? [*He is on his way to the door.*] If I wanted to come in, no lock could keep me out!

*He opens the door with one savage kick which tears the hardware out of the splintered jamb.*

SCARLETT *gasps, staring after him.*

DISSOLVE OUT

FADE IN:

INTERIOR–BELLE WATLING'S PLACE

*Which is a little too richly appointed.* RHETT *is pacing like a caged, enraged lion.*

CAMERA PULLS BACK TO REVEAL BELLE, *sitting at a table with her back to* RHETT, *moodily playing with a glass and listening to him.*

RHETT [*pacing*]: I always knew that most women were cheats . . . hard and hypocritical . . . but *this* one!

BELLE [*without looking at him*]: It ain't no use, Rhett.

RHETT [*stopping short and looking at her angrily*]: What do you mean?

BELLE: I mean that you're poisoned with her . . . I don't care *what* she's done to you . . . [*moodily*] . . . you're still in love with her . . . and don't think it pleasures me any to say it.

RHETT [*savagely*]: Maybe so! But I'm through with her, I tell you! I'm through!

BELLE: You got to think of the child, Rhett. The child's worth ten of the mother.

RHETT *takes this, and after a moment speaks:*

RHETT: Yes, Belle, yes. [*He goes to her, pats her hand, looking at her warmly and speaking kindly.*] You're a very shrewd woman, Belle, and a very nice one, and . . . [*He stops.*]

BELLE [*looking up at him*]: Yes, Rhett?

RHETT [*quietly but with a little bitterness*]: Oh, I was just thinking of the difference between you and . . . You're both hardheaded business women and you're both successful . . . but—[*sincerely*] you've got a heart . . . and a soul. [*He picks up his hat and coat, and turns.*] Goodbye, Belle. [*He is on his way out.*]

BELLE *doesn't look at him. There are tears in her eyes.*

BELLE [*without looking up*]: Goodbye, Rhett.

*He leaves.*

FADE OUT

FADE IN:

INTERIOR–THE NEW HOUSE–THE DRAWING ROOM–DAY

SCARLETT *sits at her desk, checking over a ledger. On the floor* WADE HAMPTON *is building a house of bricks for* BONNIE. RHETT *sits above them, watching them lovingly. The house collapses and* SCARLETT *turns from her desk.*

SCARLETT: Wade, you're driving me frantic! Go tell them to hitch up the carriage and drive you to play with Beau.

WADE HAMPTON: Beau isn't home. He's at Raoul Picard's birthday party.

RHETT: Why aren't you at the party, son?

WADE HAMPTON: I wasn't invited.

RHETT *rises and moves across to* SCARLETT, *saying as he does so:*

RHETT: Drop that figuring, Scarlett. Why wasn't Wade invited to this party?

SCARLETT: Oh, for heaven's sake, Rhett, don't bother me now! Ashley's got these accounts in a terrible snarl. Raoul Picard's old Mrs. Merriwether's grandson. She'd as soon have a rattlesnake in her house as a child of mine.

WADE HAMPTON *flinches.* RHETT *looks down at him darkly.*

RHETT: Would you like to be at that party, Wade?

WADE HAMPTON [*proudly*]: No, sir.

RHETT: Don't you like parties?

WADE HAMPTON: I don't get invited to many.

RHETT: Here. [*He pulls a bill out of his pocket and offers it to Wade Hampton.*] Go tell them to hitch up the carriage and drive you downtown where you can buy enough candy to give you a stomach ache.

WADE HAMPTON *thanks him and goes, not happily.*

SCARLETT: I'll thank you to let me manage my own children's lives!

RHETT: You're not much of a manager. You should have looked out for your children's social futures. You haven't even troubled to keep what position you had. So you've wrecked Wade's chance to get any fun out of childhood. I'm not going to let you do that to Bonnie. Bonnie's going to grow up a little princess and all the world's going to want her at their parties.

SCARLETT: I'd like to hear how you're going to bring that about?

RHETT: I'm doing it now. I'm cultivating every female dragon of the old guard in town. Especially Mrs. Merriwether. I crawl on my belly to 'em. I'm meek under their coldness. I make contributions to their charities and go to their churches.

SCARLETT [*laughing harshly*]: So the speculator and scallawag's turned respectable!

RHETT: You'll be good enough to refrain from undoing my work, my dear. [*He turns to* BONNIE.] Bonnie, want to go for a ride?

BONNIE *does. He picks her up and goes out.* SCARLETT *looks after him. Suddenly, quite unaccountably, she bursts into tears.*

> DISSOLVE TO

EXTERIOR–THE STREET–DAY

RHETT *is riding along on his big black hunter, holding* BONNIE *astride the saddle in front of him. Bystanders remark on the pair with friendly smiles. He comes up to a carriage in which* MRS. MERRIWETHER *and* MRS. MEADE *are seated. He reins in and doffs his hat.*

RHETT: Mrs. Merriwether, I've always had a great regard for your knowledge. I wonder if you could tell me something. [*The plumes on* MRS. MERRIWETHER's *bonnet barely move as she nods.*] What did you do when your Maybelle was little and she sucked her thumb?

MRS. MERRIWETHER [*looking her surprise*]: What?

RHETT: My Bonnie sucks her thumb and I can't make her stop it.

MRS. MEADE: You should make her stop it! It'll ruin the shape of her mouth.

RHETT: I know that. I know. And she has such a pretty mouth! But I don't know what to do.

MRS. MERRIWETHER: Scarlett should know. She's the child's mother, isn't she?

RHETT [*looking down and sighing*]: I've tried putting soap on her fingernails.

MRS. MEADE: Bah! Soap's no good at all!

MRS. MERRIWETHER: I put quinine on Maybelle's thumb and let me tell you, Captain Butler, she stopped sucking that thumb mighty quick.

RHETT: Quinine. I would never have thought of it! I can't thank you enough, Mrs. Merriwether.

*He bows and rides on. The ladies turn to each other.*

MRS. MERRIWETHER: Somehow, I don't think he's so bad. There must be some good in any man who loves a child so much.

MRS. MEADE: Well, what did I tell you? It's Scarlett's the bad one and he's ashamed of her. But he's much too much of a gentleman to let on.

*DISSOLVE TO*

EXTERIOR–BUTLER GARDEN AND LAWNS

*In the foreground* RHETT *has had erected a very low bar.*

BONNIE, *now four, stands watching as* RHETT *teaches her pony to jump.* RHETT *is on his large horse and holds a guiding rope in his hand attached to* BONNIE's *pony.*

RHETT: Now watch Daddy put your pony over, Bonnie. [*guiding the pony alongside a fence in the garden, toward the jump*] Now watch—if he's all right, you can *ride* him over next time.

*The pony, guided by* RHETT, *takes a successful jump over the low hurdle.* BONNIE *screams in delight.*

BONNIE: Daddy, let me—let me!

RHETT: All right, Bonnie—you get on him.

BONNIE *mounts . . .* RHETT *riding back alongside her, still holding the guiding rope as* BONNIE *goes back to run for the jump.*

RHETT: Now hold your reins properly, and a firm hand—and go with your pony. You take him right down the side of this fence— Take him down to the jump and lean forward.

BONNIE *starts down the run for the jump—*RHETT *riding a little off, still holding rope. . . . As* BONNIE *nears the hurdle:*

RHETT: Lift his head, Bonnie!

*LONG SHOT*

*As* BONNIE, *on her pony, comes up to the jump and makes it unsuccessfully, knocking over the bar.*

*CLOSE ANGLE* BONNIE *ON PONY*

*She wheels around, disappointed, as* RHETT *gallops up to her.*

RHETT: Not afraid, are you, Bonnie?

BONNIE: Who's afraid? I'm not afraid of anything.

RHETT [*proudly*]: That's my Bonnie. Now go on . . . try it again . . . [*as they ride back to the starting mark*] That was all right, Bonnie —but you didn't pick up your pony's head enough . . . and you should have kicked him with your heels—that's what sends him over the jump.

*CLOSE SHOT*–BONNIE

*As she turns her pony to try again.*

RHETT's VOICE: Grip tightly with your legs—and sit close . . . lean forward and be sure you go with him . . . Take him a little faster to the jump this time . . . that's it! . . .

*LONG SHOT*

*As* BONNIE *tries again, this time clearing the jump beautifully. She lets out a terrific scream of delight, and* RHETT *does the same, "just like Apaches after successful scalpings."*

RHETT: That was fine! I knew you'd do it! When you get a little older, I'll take you to Kentucky and Virginia. You'll be the greatest horsewoman in the South. Give your Daddy a kiss. [*He leans down from his horse and kisses her as she sits on her small pony.*]

MAMMY's VOICE: Mist' Rhett! Mist' Rhett!

TERRACE–*MEDIUM SHOT*–MAMMY

MAMMY *comes out on the terrace. She has been picking flowers, and has a basket of flowers on one arm and some blossoms in her other hand.*

*TWO SHOT*–MAMMY *and* RHETT

MAMMY *comes running across the lawn to them.*

MAMMY: Mist' Rhett!

RHETT: Did you see her, Mammy? Wasn't she wonderful?

MAMMY [*impatiently*]: Mist' Rhett, I done tol' you and tol' you it jus' ain' fittin' fer a girl chile to ride a-straddle wid her dress flyin' up!

RHETT [*propitiating*]: All right, Mammy. I'll teach her to ride side-saddle . . . and I'll buy her a blue velvet riding habit. She'll love that.

MAMMY [*grumbling*]: A nice black broadcloth is whut li'l girls wear.

RHETT [*arguing plaintively*]: Oh, now, Mammy, be reasonable.

MAMMY [*grumbling*]: Well . . . I don't think it's fittin', but . . . [RHETT *laughs, leans over and pats* MAMMY *on the back. He turns his horse to ride off and* MAMMY, *still grumbling, looks after him.*] It ain' fittin'. It jus' ain' fittin'. [*She turns to go back to the house, then looks back as if in afterthought.*] It ain' fittin'.

*DISSOLVE TO*

*CLOSE TWO SHOT*–BONNIE *and* RHETT

BONNIE: I wish Mother could see me jump.

RHETT: We'll get her to watch you, Bonnie—but not until we've learned to take some higher jumps . . .

BONNIE: I know, I know . . . but why did she have to go to that dirty old mill today when I want her here?

RHETT: Now, Bonnie, Mother enjoys going to the mill once in a while, just the way you enjoy riding. You want *her* to have fun, too, don't you?

BONNIE [*pouting*]: Well—doesn't she have enough fun with me?

DISSOLVE TO

INTERIOR–LUMBER MILL OFFICE–DAY–(SUMMER, 1872)

ASHLEY, *very tired, is closing the ledger as we come in on the scene. He gets up and is slipping into his coat when he is suddenly aware of the presence of* SCARLETT, *who has entered unknown to him. Though she looks no older, her face is perceptibly hardened and her whole bearing more mature.*

[*There has been a time lapse of several years since we have seen* SCARLETT.]

ASHLEY: Scarlett! What are you doing downtown at this time of day? Why aren't you helping Melly get ready for my surprise birthday party?

SCARLETT [*indignantly*]: Why, Ashley Wilkes, you weren't supposed to know a thing about it! Melly will be so disappointed if you're not surprised.

ASHLEY: Oh, I won't let on. I promise to be the most surprised man in Atlanta . . . but as long as you're here, let me show you the books so you can see just how bad a businessman I really am. [*He starts for the books.*]

SCARLETT: Let's not fool with any books today! When I'm wearing a new bonnet all the figures I know go right slap out of my head.

ASHLEY: Figures are well lost when the bonnet's as pretty as that one. [*Goes to her, takes her hands and spreads them wide, looking at her dress.*] Scarlett, you get prettier all the time. You haven't changed at all since the day of our last barbecue at Twelve Oaks when you sat under a tree with a dozen beaux around you.

SCARLETT [*shakes her head, saddened by the memory of her girlhood*]: That girl doesn't exist any more. . . . Oh, Ashley, nothing's turned out like I expected! Nothing!

ASHLEY: We've traveled a long road since the old days, haven't we, Scarlett? I've come slowly, reluctantly, and you swiftly—dragging me after your chariot. Because you've always known what you wanted and I've never wanted anything but the old days back again.

SCARLETT: I've wanted them, too. But they're gone, Ashley . . . [*pleadingly*] And you must make yourself believe these days are better.

ASHLEY [*shaking his head sadly*]: No . . . I'll always be haunted by the memory of a charm and a beauty that are gone forever . . . oh, the lazy days and warm still country twilights! . . . The high soft Negro laughter from the quarters! . . . The golden warmth and security of those days!

SCARLETT [*tears in her eyes*]: Don't look back, Ashley! Don't look back! It drags at your heart till you can't do anything but look back!

*He goes to her and puts his arms around her.*

ASHLEY: I didn't mean to make you sad, my dear. [*Puts his hand under her chin and turns her face up to his.*] I'd never want you to be anything but completely happy.

*He kisses the tear off her cheek. Suddenly his face changes as he looks off in dismay.* SCARLETT, *noticing the change in his expression, turns her face in the same direction in which he is looking.*

*WE CUT or SWING THE CAMERA to reveal the malevolent face of* INDIA *staring at them triumphantly.* INDIA *raises her head with a sneer and a smile, turns, and is gone.*

*TWO SHOT—*SCARLETT *and* ASHLEY

SCARLETT [*terrified*]: Oh, Ashley!

ASHLEY *drops his arms from around her, and as his eyes fall in dismay and fright as he realizes the import of the situation and the interpretation that will inevitably be placed on it, he draws the back of his hand across his head or makes some other gesture of dismay.*

ASHLEY: You'd better go home, Scarlett, and leave this to me.

*The full import of the situation comes home to* SCARLETT *as she scurries out past* INDIA, *tottering into the lens of the CAMERA.*

*DISSOLVE TO*

INTERIOR—SCARLETT'S BEDROOM—NIGHT

*Only the lamps are lit.* SCARLETT *is in a wrapper, stretched out full length on the bed. A knock on the door and she sits up frightened.*

SCARLETT: Who is it?

RHETT [*off-screen*]: Only your husband.

SCARLETT *gasps.*

SCARLETT [*calls out in terrified voice*]: Come in.

RHETT *enters. He is dressed for the evening. His mood is cold and murderous.*

RHETT: Am I actually being invited into the sanctuary?

*He comes to the bed where* SCARLETT *has shrunk back into the pillows, and jerks her upright.*

RHETT: You're not ready for Melanie's party!

SCARLETT [*terrified*]: I've a headache. You go without me, Rhett, and make my excuses to Melanie.

MGM, © 1939, 1967. UGa Libraries, Marsh Papers.

RHETT *looks at her disgustedly for a moment, then speaks.*

RHETT [*drawlingly and bitingly*]: What a white-livered little coward you are! [*then*]: Get up! You're going to the party and you'll have to hurry!

SCARLETT: Oh, Rhett, has India dared to . . .

RHETT: Yes, my dear, she has! Every woman in the town knows the story. And every man, too. . . .

SCARLETT: You should have killed them for spreading lies!

RHETT: I have a strange way of not killing people who tell the truth. . . . There's no time to argue now. Get up.

SCARLETT *gets up, clutches her wrapper close, her eyes searching* RHETT's *face, but it is dark and impassive.*

SCARLETT: I won't go, Rhett! I can't—until this—this misunderstanding is cleared up.

RHETT: You're not going to cheat Miss Melly out of the satisfaction of publicly ordering you out of her house!

SCARLETT: Rhett, there was nothing wrong! India hates me so! I can't go. I couldn't face it!

RHETT: If you don't show your face tonight you'll never be able to show it in this town as long as you live. . . . And while that wouldn't bother me, you're not going to ruin Bonnie's chances! . . . You're going to that party if only for her sake.

RHETT *takes a step toward the clothes closet.*

*CLOSE SHOT*–SCARLETT

*Reluctantly she gets up and trembling, starts to take off her wrapper.*

*CLOSE SHOT*–RHETT AT CLOSET

*—searching through the dresses.* RHETT *takes one of the gowns from the closet.*

RHETT: Wear that! [*throws it at her*] Nothing modest or matronly will do for this occasion.

*CLOSE SHOT*–SCARLETT

*—in her chemise—trembling—frightened, picks up the dress from where he has thrown it.*

*BACK TO SCENE*

RHETT: And put on plenty of rouge! I want you to look your part tonight!

*DISSOLVE TO*

*DISSOLVE IN:*

EXTERIOR–DOOR TO MELANIE'S HOUSE–[*SHOOTING*

FROM INTERIOR THROUGH OPEN DOOR]–TWO SHOT–SCAR-
LETT *and* RHETT

RHETT: Now you go alone into the arena, Scarlett. The lions are hungry for you!

SCARLETT: Oh, don't leave me! Don't—

RHETT *bows and goes, leaving* SCARLETT *standing in the doorway alone, looking inside.*

INTERIOR–MELANIE'S PARLOR

*Come in on birthday cake. The company, including* ASHLEY, MELANIE, DR. AND MRS. MEADE, *and* AUNT PITTY *are packed around the table. Evidently* ASHLEY *has just been led up to the cake by* MELANIE. *His manner is nervous; he is clearly under strain and clearly making all possible effort to do what is expected of him.*

*Ad libs:*

MRS. MEADE: Now, Ashley, blow them all out but one, and leave one to grow on.

DR. MEADE: And when you cut the cake be sure Miss Pitty gets the ring.

AUNT PITTY: Oh no! The thimble for me! The thimble for me!

ASHLEY: And you baked this, Melly? You baked this?

MELANIE: Well, I did have a little help from Aunt Pitty's Cookie.

AD LIBS [*almost simultaneously*]: A birthday cake's always so exciting, isn't it? . . . Count the candles, count the candles! . . . How do you know Ashley wants them counted? . . . He's a man. Men don't care. . . . It's the most beautiful cake I ever saw! . . . What's it going to be like inside? . . . Cakes again! Even yet I can't get used to having cakes again! . . . It's just like the old times! . . . I'll never forget my cousin Sue's birthday in Milledgeville. . . . I haven't had a birthday cake since before the war. That's years ago. . . . We always made so much of birthdays at home. . . . Many happy returns, Ashley! Many happy returns! . . . There's got to be a toast. . . . We'll lift all our glasses . . . Now, what is the toast? . . . Speech! Speech! . . .

*Someone begins to sing "For He's a Jolly Good Fellow." The company joins in. Of the three musicians, the harpist leads off.* DR. MEADE *chimes in with his violin and* RENÉ PICARD *with his flute.*

*The chorus is no sooner under way that* ASHLEY *takes a deep breath to blow, but he does not blow because he sees* SCARLETT *standing in the doorway. The startled look on his face attracts* MRS. MEADE'S *attention. Her singing stops. Then, as each one of the rest of the company* turns, the song dies out. Only the harpist continuing uncertainly until she also stops.

In the meanwhile MELANIE is the last to see SCARLETT. She brushes quickly through the tense silence of her guests, goes to SCARLETT. She slips an arm about her waist.

MELANIE [very clear]: What a lovely dress, Scarlett, darling! India wasn't able to come tonight. Will you be an angel? I do need you to help me receive my guests.

SENSATION!

FADE OUT

EXTERIOR–MELANIE'S HOUSE AT DOOR–CLOSE SHOT– RHETT–NIGHT

We see that the door is still a little ajar after SCARLETT's entrance into the house.

RHETT has stood there to see how SCARLETT would be received. He hears MELANIE's greeting to her, shrugs, shakes his head in disgust, and exits.

DISSOLVE TO

INTERIOR–SCARLETT'S BEDROOM–SAME NIGHT

CLOSE SHOT the gown SCARLETT has worn to Melly's party. It is on the floor where SCARLETT has stepped out of it. MAMMY is picking it up, also a few other articles of clothing which SCARLETT has dropped —and is talking sleepily as she does:

MAMMY: Did you have a good time tonight at Miss Melly's party, chile?

During above line CAMERA HAS PULLED BACK and now reveals SCARLETT sitting in her red dressing gown at her dressing table.

SCARLETT [impatiently]: Yes, yes! . . . Now you be sure and leave word. . . . [nervously] If Captain Butler asks for me when he gets home, I'm asleep.

MAMMY: Yas'm. [She gives SCARLETT a suspicious look as she exits, and we—]

DISSOLVE TO

FADE IN:

INTERIOR–BUTLER HALL–NIGHT

It is lit with simply one, or at the most two, of the elaborate lighting fixtures. We see long shadows of SCARLETT as she comes tremblingly down the stairs. Near the bottom of the flight she stops short as she sees light coming from the dining room. She is dressed in negligee and her hair is down.

DINING ROOM [FROM SCARLETT's ANGLE]

MGM, © 1939, 1967. UGa Libraries, Marsh Papers.

*A candle is burning on the dining table in the otherwise dark room.*
*CLOSE SHOT*–SCARLETT

*She descends a few more steps, stealthily and nervously.*

RHETT's VOICE [*thickly*]: Come in, Mrs. Butler.

SCARLETT *reacts in fright, pauses irresolutely, saying nothing.*

DINING ROOM [*FROM* SCARLETT's *ANGLE*]

RHETT's *face moves into the light of the candle. He is without a coat and his cravat hangs down on either side of his open collar. His shirt is open and his hair rumpled. He is drunk. On the table is a silver tray bearing a decanter with cut glass stopper out, surrounded by glasses. The glass from which* RHETT *has been drinking is on the table.*

RHETT [*motions roughly*]: Come here!

*TRUCKING SHOT with* SCARLETT

SCARLETT *has never seen him drunk before, does not know quite what to do—but she draws a deep breath, clutches her wrapper closer to her and goes down the remaining steps and into the dining room, her head up, her heels clacking.*

RHETT *stands up and approaches the door with mock gallantry. He bows to her as she passes him and enters the dining room.*

DINING ROOM

—*as* SCARLETT *enters. Monstrous shadows are thrown by the candle on the high ceilinged room, making the massive furniture look like huge crouching beasts.*

RHETT *follows her into the room.*

RHETT [*curtly*]: Sit down. [SCARLETT *is frightened.*] There's no reason why you shouldn't have your nightcap, even if I *am* here.

SCARLETT: I didn't want a drink. I heard a noise and—

RHETT: You heard nothing of the kind. You wouldn't have come down if you'd thought I was here. You must need a drink badly. . . . [*He picks up the decanter and sloppily pours her a drink.*]

SCARLETT [*protesting*]: I do not . . .

RHETT: Take it! [*Shoves the drink into her hand.*] Oh, don't give yourself airs. I know you drink on the quiet and I know how much you drink. . . . Do you think I care if you like your brandy?

SCARLETT *looks at him a moment doubtfully, then bolts down the drink, making an unbecoming grimace. She notices as she does, that* RHETT *has seen the grimace and that he is smiling sneeringly.*

SCARLETT [*coldly*]: You're drunk. And I'm going to bed.

RHETT: I'm very drunk, and I intend to get still drunker before the evening's over. But you aren't going to bed—not yet. Sit down!

SCARLETT *sits.*

"*His voice still held a remnant of its wonted cool drawl but beneath the words she could feel violence fighting its way to the surface, violence as cruel as the crack of a whip. She wavered irresolutely and he was at her side, his hand on her arm in a grip that hurt. He gave it a slight wrench and she hastily sat down with a little cry of pain. Now, she was afraid, more afraid than she had ever been in her life. As he leaned over her, she saw that his face was dark and flushed and his eyes still held their frightening glitter. There was something in their depths she did not recognize, could not understand, something deeper than anger, stronger than pain, something driving him until his eyes glowed redly like twin coals. He looked down at her for a long time, so long that her defiant gaze wavered and fell, and then he slumped into a chair opposite her and poured himself another drink. She thought rapidly, trying to lay a line of defenses. But until he spoke, she would not know what to say for she did not know exactly what accusation he intended to make.*"

RHETT [*finally*]: How does it feel to have the woman you've wronged stand by you and cloak your sins for you? [*She makes no comment.*] You're wondering if she knows all about you and Ashley— wondering if she did this just to save her face. And you're thinking she's a fool for doing it, even if it did save your hide, but—

SCARLETT: I will not listen!

RHETT: Yes, you'll listen. Miss Melly's a fool, but not the kind you think. It's just that there's too much honor in her to conceive of dishonor in anyone she loves. And she loves you—though just why she does, I'm sure I don't know.

SCARLETT: If you were not so drunk and insulting I would explain everything. [*She rises, recovering some of her dignity.*] As it is, though—

RHETT [*threateningly*]: If you get up out of that chair once more . . . [SCARLETT *sits.*] Of course the comic figure in all this is the long-suffering Mr. Wilkes! Mr. Wilkes—who can't be mentally faithful to his wife—and *won't* be unfaithful to her technically. [*Takes a drink.*] Why doesn't he make up his mind?

SCARLETT *springs to her feet with a cry.* RHETT *lunges from his seat, laughing softly. He is in back of her and presses her down into the chair.*

TWO SHOT–SCARLETT *and* RHETT–LARGE HEADS, ONE ABOVE THE OTHER–

SCARLETT *sits tensely as* RHETT *stands behind her. He puts his hands in front of her face, flexing them.*

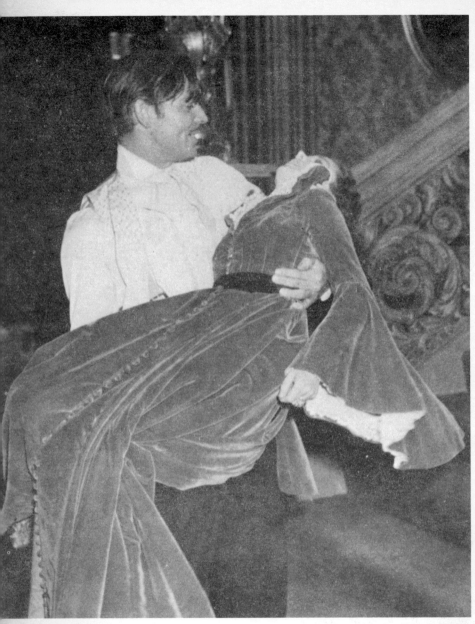

Atlanta Historical Society, Kurtz Collection.

*A previously unpublished snapshot taken at the Selznick studios by Fred Parrish*

RHETT: Observe my hands, my dear. I could tear you to pieces with them—and I'd do it, if it would take Ashley out of your mind. But it wouldn't. So I think I'll remove him from your mind forever, this way . . . I'll put my hands so, on each side of your head . . . [*He fits the deed to the word.*] And I'll smash your skull between them like a walnut . . . and that will block him out.

*His hands are under her flowing hair, caressing and hard. There is a moment of silence.* SCARLETT *is frightened, but she has never been without animal courage, which supports her now.*

*TWO SHOT*—SCARLETT *and* RHETT

SCARLETT *narrows her eyes and speaks coldly and slowly:*

SCARLETT: You drunken fool! Take your hands off me!

*To her surprise he does so, slowly removing them, and seating himself on the edge of the table, he pours himself another drink.*

RHETT: I've always admired your spirit, my dear. Never more than now when you're cornered.

*She draws her wrapper close about her body. She rises, but without haste so as not to reveal her fear—tightens the wrapper across her hips and throws her hair back from her face.*

SCARLETT [*cuttingly*]: I'm not cornered. You'll never corner me, Rhett Butler—or frighten me! You've lived in dirt so long you can't understand anything else. And you're jealous of something you can't understand. Goodnight.

*She starts casually toward the door.*

*There is a burst of laughter from* RHETT. *She stops and turns. He sways across the room toward her, still laughing. He puts his hands heavily upon her and pins her shoulders to the wall.*

RHETT: Jealous, am I? Yes, I suppose I am—even though I know you've been faithful to me all along. How do I know? Because I know Ashley Wilkes and his honorable breed. They're gentlemen—and that's more than I can say for you—or for me. We're not gentlemen and we have no honor—have we?

*He releases her, laughs and starts for the decanter.*

SCARLETT *stands a second then runs swiftly out into the dark hall.*

DARK HALL

*Out of the darkness comes* RHETT *after* SCARLETT. *He seizes her and roughly turns her around to him, holding her close.*

RHETT: It's not that easy, Scarlett. [*He kisses her violently.*] You turned me out while you chased Ashley Wilkes—while you dreamed of Ashley Wilkes.—Well, this is one time you're not turning me out!

*He swings her off her feet into his arms. He starts up the stairs*

*with her, her head crushed against his chest. She cries out frightened,
but the sounds are muffled against his chest.*

*He carries her up the stairs—up and up, into the increasing dark-
ness, their shadows on the stairs.*

*THE CAMERA DRAWS BACK as he goes further and further up
the stairs,* SCARLETT'S *cries diminishing. Then they are lost in the darkness at the top of the stairs and* SCARLETT'S *cries cease.*

*For a moment THE CAMERA HOLDS THE EMPTY STEPS, lit
only by the hall light, then we—*

SLOWLY FADE OUT

FADE IN:

INTERIOR–SCARLETT'S BEDROOM–NEXT MORNING

SCARLETT *in bed, just finishing her breakfast which is on a tray. She
is in a very happy mood. She wears her wedding ring. She stretches
luxuriously.*

*She hears someone approaching the door; quickly arranges herself
as becomingly as possible and looks anxiously at it.*

CLOSE SHOT–CLOSED BEDROOM DOOR [*FROM* SCARLETT'S
ANGLE]

*The doorknob turns.*

BACK TO SCENE

*Excited, embarrassed, nervous,* SCARLETT *gives a quick pat to her
hair, looking toward the door expectantly.*

*It opens and* BONNIE *runs in and over to her mother. A quick flash
of disappointment crosses* SCARLETT'S *face.*

BONNIE: Mummy, Mummy, will you come and play Confederates
with Beau Wilkes and me? Beau's promised to be the Yankees and let
us win!

SCARLETT [*distracted, absorbed in her thoughts*]: I'm sorry, baby—
I can't. Go ask your Daddy.

BONNIE: And can we have some cookies?

SCARLETT: Yes, yes. But run along—I'm busy.

BONNIE *wasn't expecting such an easy victory. She stops, looks at
her mother, surprised, lets out a whoop of delight and runs out, almost
colliding with* MAMMY *who is coming in.*

MAMMY [*to* BONNIE]: Whut you doin'? That ain' no way fer a lady
to ack . . .

BONNIE [*on her way out*]: Run along, Mammy—I'm busy.

*She disappears.* MAMMY *gives a takum and comes into the room.*

SCARLETT [*very gaily*]: How you feeling this morning, Mammy?

MAMMY: Well . . . my back ain' what it useter be with this ol' miz'ry.

SCARLETT, *paying no attention to* MAMMY's *complaints, starts to hum happily the first five bars of "Ben Bolt."*

MAMMY: You ack' mighty happy this mornin', Miss Scarlett.

SCARLETT: I am, Mammy! I am!

*She picks up the song, singing softly from "Ben Bolt."*

CLOSE SHOT–SCARLETT

SCARLETT [*singing*]:

"She wept with delight when you gave her a smile,
"And trembled with fear at your frown."

*As she sings, she adjusts her bedjacket more fetchingly over her shoulders, bites her lips and pinches her cheeks in a quick, almost forgotten gesture to bring color to them.*

*She stops singing and lies back on her pillow, thinking of the night before. Suddenly she is embarrassed—giggles like a girl and pulls the covers up tight around her neck.*

*She gets out of bed and wriggles into her wrapper as* MAMMY *opens the blinds.*

SCARLETT: Will you tell Captain Butler I'm awake and should like to see him?

*And she smiles to herself.*

MAMMY: Mist' Rhett he din' come home las' night.

SCARLETT: But he did! He was home when I came in and . . .

MAMMY's *eyes fall.*

MAMMY: Then he mus' hev gone out agin.

SCARLETT: Gone out? Before anyone was up? [*then*] Oh! . . .

*She stands looking at the bed.* MAMMY *gives no sign.*

DISSOLVE TO

SCARLETT'S BEDROOM–DAY

SCARLETT, *fully dressed, stands in exactly the same position. A sound, and she looks up. Through the open door she sees* RHETT *pass along the hall.*

SCARLETT: Where have you been?

RHETT *stops.*

RHETT: Don't tell me you didn't know! I thought surely the whole town knew by now. Well, the wife's always the last one to find out.

SCARLETT: You went from me to . . .

RHETT: Oh, that! [*He makes a careless gesture of apology.*] I will forget my manners. My apologies for my conduct last night. I was very

MGM, © 1939, 1967. UGa Libraries, Marsh Papers.

drunk, as you doubtless know, and quite swept off my feet by your charms. Need I enumerate . . .

SCARLETT: You went from me to that woman! [*Then, finally and forever outraged.*] Oh!

RHETT: Come, come, Scarlett! Don't play the injured wife. I've been living with that woman ever since the day when you and Ashley Wilkes decided we should separate.

SCARLETT: You have the impudence to stand there and boast to me, your wife . . .

RHETT: You haven't been much of a wife for the last few years. Belle's been a better one.

*TWO SHOT*

RHETT *approaches her.*

RHETT: Scarlett, I've been thinking things over and I really believe it'd be better for both of us if we admitted we'd made a mistake and got a divorce.

SCARLETT [*amazed and hurt*]: A divorce?

RHETT: Yes. There's no point in our holding on to each other, is there? I'll provide for you amply. You've plenty of grounds, and if you'll just give me Bonnie, you can say what you please and I won't contest it.

SCARLETT [*really angry now*]: Thank you very much, but I wouldn't think of disgracing the family with a divorce!

RHETT [*who has been quite simple and serious, now becomes angry at her hypocrisy*]: You'd disgrace it quick enough if Ashley were free! It makes my head spin to think of how quickly you'd divorce me!

SCARLETT *doesn't answer. She is hurt and furious.* RHETT *looks at her, "the old, puzzling, watchful glint in his eyes—keen, eager, as though he hangs on her next words hoping they would be—"*

RHETT: Wouldn't you, Scarlett? [*She doesn't answer.*] Well, answer me—Wouldn't you?

SCARLETT: Will you please go now and leave me alone?

RHETT: Yes, I'm going. That's what I came to tell you. I'm going to London—on a very extended trip. I'm leaving today.

SCARLETT [*stunned*]: Oh!

RHETT: And I'm taking Bonnie with me. So you'll please get her little duds packed.

SCARLETT: You'll never take my child out of this house!

RHETT: She's my child, too, Scarlett. And you're making a mistake if you think I'm going to leave her here with a mother who hasn't the decency to consider her own reputation!

SCARLETT: You're a fine one to talk! Do you think I'll let you take that baby out of here when you'll most likely have her around with people like that Belle—

RHETT *strides across the floor to her furiously.*

RHETT: If you were a man I'd break your neck for that! As it is, I'll thank you to shut your stupid mouth. Do you think I don't love Bonnie —that I'd take her any place where—and as for you giving yourself pious airs about your motherhood, why a cat's a better mother than you are! [SCARLETT *is terrified by his outburst.*] You have her packed up and ready for me in an hour or I warn you . . . I've always thought a good lashing with a buggy whip would benefit you immensely!

*He turns on his heel and storms out of the room.*

UPPER HALL

RHETT *striding out of Scarlett's room and crossing the hall in a rage. He passes* PORK *and almost knocks him over.*

CLOSE-UP–PORK–*looking after* RHETT—*startled and frightened.*

BONNIE'S NURSERY–[*SHOOTING FROM HALL*]

RHETT *throws open the door—revealing* BONNIE *and* BEAU *playing on the floor in the nursery.* BEAU *sees him first.*

BEAU: Hello, Uncle Rhett.

*As* BONNIE *looks up and runs to* RHETT:

RHETT: Hello, Beau.

BONNIE: Daddy! Daddy! I've been waiting for you all morning! Where have you been?

RHETT: I've been hunting for a rabbit skin to wrap my little Bonnie in. . . . Give your best sweetheart a kiss, Bonnie . . . I'm going to take you on a long trip to Fairyland.

CAMERA STARTS TO MOVE IN TO A CLOSE TWO SHOT *of* BONNIE *and* RHETT

BONNIE: Where? Where?

RHETT: I'm going to show you the Tower of London where the little Princes were . . . and London Bridge . . .

BONNIE: Oh, London Bridge! Will it be falling down?

FADE OUT

*FADE IN:*

THE THAMES, LONDON–(AUTUMN, 1872)

*Big Ben striking a late hour. As the chimes end, the CAMERA IS DRAWING BACK through a hotel window, and as the chimes end we hear a baby's voice, terrified, screaming over them.*

*As we get back in the* INTERIOR OF THE HOTEL ROOM *we*

*discover* BONNIE *in the completely dark room*—absolutely *dark except for the light from outside on the child's terrified face.*

*We hear* RHETT's *muffled voice from outside:*

RHETT's VOICE: Bonnie! Bonnie! It's all right, Bonnie.

CAMERA SWINGS TO THE DOORWAY, *through which* RHETT *enters. He wears evening clothes and a light overcoat. He crosses the dark room, the light hitting his face as he crosses.*

BONNIE [*screaming*]: Dark! Dark!

RHETT [*angrily, as he crosses*]: Who put out the light? Nurse! Nurse!

BONNIE *continues screaming until* RHETT *puts on a light.*

BONNIE: Dark! Dark!

RHETT *goes to her, tenderly lifts her from her bed and holds her in his arms.*

RHETT: There now, what's the matter with my Bonnie?

BONNIE: A bear!

RHETT: A bear? A big bear?

BONNIE: Dretfull big! With claws, too!

RHETT: Ah, claws, too.

BONNIE: And it sat on my chest.

RHETT: Well, I shall stay here and shoot him if he comes back! [BONNIE's *tears subside.*] That's better.

*He kisses the child and strokes her hair tenderly. She puts her arms around his neck. He looks at her adoringly, then puts her back into her bed.*

*Now the* NURSE *enters from the next room, rubbing her eyes. She has obviously been asleep and is startled at seeing* RHETT.

NURSE: Oh, good evening, Mr. Butler.

RHETT *advances toward her,* CAMERA PANNING WITH HIM.

RHETT [*angrily*]: Haven't I told you that you're never to leave this child alone in the dark?

NURSE: If you'll pardon me, sir, lots of children are afraid of the dark, but they get over it. If you just let her scream for a night or two—

RHETT [*interrupting*]: Let her scream! Either you're a fool or the most inhuman woman I've ever seen!

NURSE [*stiffly*]: Of course, sir, if you want her to grow up nervous and cowardly—

RHETT: Cowardly! There isn't a cowardly bone in her body! You're discharged. [*He leaves her and goes to sit on* BONNIE's *bed or on the chair near the bed.*]

NURSE [*coldly*]: As you say, sir. . . . But if I may offer one last observation, sir. Fathers are frequently given to spoiling their children. Her mother would most likely agree with me.

RHETT: I don't doubt it.

*The* NURSE *turns on her heels and exits.* BONNIE *opens her eyes.*

BONNIE: Where's Mother?

RHETT [*leaning over her tenderly*]: Now, Bonnie, aren't you happy in London with me?

BONNIE: I want to go home. I want my pony.

RHETT [*smiles tenderly*]: I could send for your pony, Bonnie.

BONNIE [*sleepily*]: I want to go home!

BONNIE'S *eyes close again, she drops off to sleep, her hand around* RHETT'S *finger.* RHETT *looks at her thoughtfully, leans over, kisses her on the forehead, makes a tentative attempt to release his finger, finds it caught tight. He smiles sadly, prepares for a long stay. AS CAMERA MOVES UP TO CLOSE-UP of the thoughtful, depressed* RHETT, *we—*

FADE OUT

INTERIOR–BUTLER HOUSE–HALL–DAY–(AUTUMN, 1872)

MAMMY *is running up the stairs, holding her back, which is giving her a bit of trouble with the years. [In the course of the scene the labor of running up the stairs also tells on her. The troubled years of the war and the Reconstruction, and the effort of them, have told on her. There is gray in her eyebrows and she hasn't her old spryness.]*

MAMMY [*calling*]: Miss Scarlett! Miss Scarlett! Dey's back, Miss Scarlett!

BONNIE'S *little figure is seen galloping up the stairs in back of* MAMMY, *as quick as its little legs will take it. She clutches a kitten to her breast.*

SCARLETT *appears, quite beside herself with joyous excitement. She runs down a few steps.*

CLOSE SHOT–SCARLETT

SCARLETT: Bonnie! Bonnie!

REVERSE SHOT–[SCARLETT *IN FOREGROUND, SHOOTING DOWN THE STAIRS*]

BONNIE *galloping up the stairs and* RHETT *below in the hall.*

RHETT *looks up at* SCARLETT, *sweeps off his hat in a wide gesture.*

CLOSE SHOT–SCARLETT

*She reacts to this—looks back at him in chagrin. But in a second* BONNIE *is in her arms and* SCARLETT *is embracing her frantically.*

SCARLETT: Are you glad you're home, Bonnie?

BONNIE [*showing her mother the kitten*]: Daddy gave me a kitten!

London's a horrid place. Where's my pony? I want to go out and see my pony!

[*During this speech* SCARLETT *hungrily clutches her child, speaking:* "You've been away so long—so long!"]

RHETT *has come up the stair to the scene.* SCARLETT *meets his steady, resentful look. Her eyes fall.*

SCARLETT: Mammy will take you, Bonnie. Go along with Mammy.

MAMMY *drops a curtsy and leads* BONNIE *out of the scene.*

BONNIE [*on her way out*]: Have you been riding my pony, Mammy?

*TWO SHOT*—RHETT *and* SCARLETT

RHETT *comes to the top of the stair.*

RHETT: Mrs. Butler, I believe.

SCARLETT [*smiling, glad to see him*]: Mammy said you'd come back.

RHETT: Only to bring Bonnie home. Apparently any mother, even a bad one, is better for a child than none.

SCARLETT [*dismayed*]: You mean you're going away again?

RHETT: What perception, Mrs. Butler. Right away. In fact, I left my bags at the station.

SCARLETT [*her face betraying her great disappointment*]: Oh . . .

RHETT *stands casually, his hand on his hip, and looks her over appraisingly from head to toe, and then back again to her face.*

RHETT: You're looking pale, Mrs. Butler. Is there a shortage of rouge? Or can this wanness mean that you've been missing me?

SCARLETT *flinches under the first word. Now she steps in, angry.*

SCARLETT: It's because—[*She can't go on.*]

RHETT: Pray continue, Mrs. Butler.

SCARLETT [*blurting it out*]: It's because I'm going to have a baby.

*In spite of himself,* RHETT *is startled and for a moment his supercilious expression drops. He takes a step forward as though to put his hand on her arm but she twists away from him and his former mood returns. Only for a moment has the shell disappeared.*

RHETT: Indeed! Well, who's the happy father?

SCARLETT *clutches the banister.*

SCARLETT [*her voice shaking with sick rage*]: You know it's yours! And I don't want it any more than you do! No woman would want the child of a cad like you! I wish—I wish it was anybody's baby but yours!

RHETT'S *expression changes suddenly into an expression of violent anger. He is silent for a moment, then the old impassive mask is back again.*

RHETT: Cheer up. Maybe you'll have an accident!

SCARLETT *stands appalled. Her fists clenching in rage as* RHETT *looks at her coolly. Then, after a moment, she lunges for him swift as a cat— but with a startled movement he side-steps her, throwing up his arm to ward her off. And as her arm with the whole weight of her body behind it strikes his out-thrust arm, she loses her balance, makes a wild clutch for the banister and misses it. She rolls down the stairs backward.*

LARGE CLOSE-UP–RHETT'S FACE

*He is aghast as he sees what has happened.*

LONG SHOT [*SHOOTING DOWN THE STAIRS PAST* RHETT]

*As* SCARLETT *rolls over and over to the bottom of the flight.*

CLOSE SHOT–SCARLETT'S FACE

*–distorted in torture as it rolls down the final steps.*

LONG SHOT

THE CAMERA ZOOMS *down to* SCARLETT'S *unconscious form.*

FADE OUT

*DISSOLVE IN:*

INTERIOR–SCARLETT'S BEDROOM–*CLOSE SHOT*–SCARLETT –NIGHT

*In bed, delirious, dimly lit by one lamp in the room. She can barely be heard in her delirium.*

SCARLETT [*very weakly whispering*]: Rhett! I want Rhett!

*The door opens and she turns slightly, eagerly, but in agony.* MAMMY *enters the room and approaches to her.*

MAMMY [*very gently*]: Did you call somebody, chile?

SCARLETT: It's no use . . . it's no use . . .

MAMMY *places a cold cloth on* SCARLETT'S *forehead, and as* SCARLETT *lapses back into semi-consciousness, we*

*DISSOLVE TO*

HALL–EXTERIOR SCARLETT'S DOOR–MORNING

RHETT *is waiting in the hallway outside the door as* AUNT PITTY *comes out from* SCARLETT'S *room.*

RHETT [*looking up anxiously*]: Is she better?

AUNT PITTY *doesn't answer, just lowers her head.* RHETT *reacts desperately to this.*

RHETT [*pitifully*]: Has she . . . has she asked for me?

AUNT PITTY [*avoiding his eyes*]: You must understand . . . she's delirious.

RHETT *controls his deep emotion and turns away.* AUNT PITTY *leans over and touches his arm gently.*

AUNT PITTY: You must try to get some sleep. You'll make yourself ill.

MGM, © 1939, 1967. UGa Libraries, Marsh Papers.

*DISSOLVE TO*
RHETT'S ROOM–BEDROOM WINDOW–RAINY NIGHT–
*CAMERA INSIDE*

*Against the window frame outside a loose shutter bangs methodically in the wind. The window is partially open and rain enters the room. CAMERA PANS to the bedroom wall showing the shadow of the gas chandelier swaying back and forth. CAMERA PANS FARTHER to the table where* RHETT *is seated with a whiskey bottle and a glass in front of him. He has been drinking and shows it. At the moment he is fondling a pistol, gazing at it in a dazed, morose way. From the hall door, now in background, comes the sound of someone knocking gently. He pays no attention. The knock is repeated. The sound at last penetrates his consciousness. He drops the pistol in one of his riding boots, standing by the table, or in any convenient place. Unsteadily he rises and opens the door.* MELANIE *stands there.*

MELANIE: Dr. Meade's left.

RHETT [*after a moment's silence, heavily, in a dead tone*]: Scarlett's dead.

*CLOSE SHOT–*MELANIE

MELANIE [*with a gentle, sympathetic smile*]: Oh no, she's much better—really she is.

*CAMERA MOVES WITH* MELANIE *as she goes to* RHETT. *As she moves to him she realizes that he is completely broken.*

MELANIE [*comforting him*]: There, there, Captain Butler, you're beside yourself. She'll very soon be well again. I promise you.

RHETT'S ROOM–LATE AFTERNOON

*Open on a table in Rhett's room, on which is a whiskey bottle and glass. The table is littered with cigar butts. Subsequently, as the room is revealed, we see that the entire room is untidy, with the bed tumbled and unmade; and we also see that* RHETT *is terribly unkempt. He has neither shaved nor washed since the night of the miscarriage—and his clothes are in a bad state; his shirt ripped open and his tie awry.*

*Over the close shot of the whiskey bottle on the table, we hear:*

RHETT'S VOICE: I killed her! I killed her!

*THE CAMERA MOVES OVER TO REVEAL* RHETT *who is seated clinging to* MELANIE'S *skirts, his head against her. He is sobbing and he speaks throughout the scene brokenly and chokingly.*

MELANIE [*comforting him*]: There, there, Captain Butler, you're beside yourself. She's much better—really she is. She'll very soon be well again.

"*At her words his grip tightened and he began speaking rapidly, hoarsely, babbling as though to a grave which would never give up its secrets, babbling the truth for the first time in his life, baring himself mercilessly to Melanie who was at first, utterly uncomprehending, utterly maternal. He talked brokenly, burrowing his head in her lap, tugging at the folds of her skirt. Sometimes his words were blurred, muffled, sometimes they came far too clearly to her ears, harsh, bitter words of confession and abasement, speaking of things she had never heard even a woman mention, secret things that brought the hot blood of modesty to her cheeks and made her grateful for his bowed head."*

RHETT: You don't understand. She didn't want this baby and—

MELANIE: Not want a baby? Why, every woman wants—

RHETT: *You* want children. But she doesn't. Not my children! She *told* me she didn't want any more children and I—I was drunk and insane! I wanted to hurt her because she had hurt me! I wanted to— and I did—

MELANIE: Hush, Captain Butler. You mustn't tell me these things. It's not fit—

RHETT [*continuing, heedless of her interruption*]: I didn't know about this baby until the other day—when she fell. I tell you—if I'd only known I'd have come straight home—whether she wanted me home or not.

MELANIE: Of course you would.

RHETT: And when she told me—there on the steps—what did I do?—What did I say? I laughed and I said—[*He breaks.*]

MELANIE: You didn't mean it. I know you didn't mean it.

RHETT: But I did mean it! I was crazy with jealousy! She's never cared for me! I thought I could make her care. But I couldn't!

MELANIE: You're so wrong. Scarlett loves you a great deal—much more than she knows.

RHETT: Oh, if that were only true! [*pitifully hopeful*] I could wait forever. If she'd only forgive me! Forget this ever happened . . .

MELANIE [*stroking his hair*]: She will. You must be patient . . .

RHETT [*His momentary hope vanishes as he suddenly recollects.*]: No, no! . . . It's not possible! You don't understand. . . . If you only knew who she really loved—but you wouldn't believe it, would you? [*Looks into her eyes.*]

MELANIE [*after a moment's silence, meeting his gaze squarely*]: Surely, you haven't listened to idle gossip? . . . No, Captain Butler . . . [*She shakes her head.*] . . . I wouldn't believe you. [*He lowers his eyes. She strokes his hair.*] There, there. Scarlett's going to get well. And there can be other children.

RHETT: No, no. She couldn't . . . even if she wanted to . . . after what she's been through . . .

MELANIE: But of course she could. Children are life renewing itself, Captain Butler.

*FADE OUT*

*FADE IN:*
EXTERIOR–BUTLER TERRACE AND GARDEN–*LONG SHOT* –DAY

SCARLETT, *dressed in a blue negligee, is stretched out in an easy chair with blankets around her and pillows at her back.* RHETT *enters from the house.*

MAMMY: Miss Scarlett's feelin' a heap bettah today, Mist' Rhett.

RHETT: Thank you, Mammy.

*CLOSE TWO SHOT*–RHETT *and* SCARLETT

SCARLETT *is pale and drawn from the agonies of the miscarriage from which she is recuperating. She gives* RHETT *one look as he approaches her, turns her face, and shrinks away from him. A moment of silence, then:*

RHETT: I've come to ask your forgiveness. In the hope that we can give our life together another chance.

*He is contrite, simple, serious—completely without any affectation of cynicism or any distrust of* SCARLETT. *He is the simplest and most sincere he has been in his whole life.*

SCARLETT [*without looking at him, sarcastically*]: Our life—together? When did we ever have a life together?

RHETT *lowers his eyes. He is determined to take full blame and not to let anything* SCARLETT *may say to him upset his final hopes.*

RHETT: Yes, you're right. But I'm sure if we could only try again— we could be happy.

SCARLETT: What is there to make us happy now?

RHETT [*simply*]: Well, there's—there's Bonnie . . . and . . . [*quietly and simply*] I love you, Scarlett.

SCARLETT [*jeeringly*]: When did you discover that?

RHETT: I've always loved you, but you've never given me a chance to show it. . . .

*During his speech* SCARLETT *has been moved just a shade, despite her will not to be moved.*

SCARLETT [*after a moment, not so bitterly*]: Well—just what do you want me to do?

RHETT: To begin with . . . give up the mill, Scarlett. We'll go away. We'll take Bonnie with us, and we'll have another honeymoon.

SCARLETT [*indignantly, her momentary softness exploded*]: Give up the mill! But why should I? It's making more money than it ever did!

RHETT [*patiently*]: Yes—I know. But we don't need it. Sell it. Or better still, give it to Ashley. Melanie's been such a friend to both of us—

SCARLETT: Melanie! Always Melanie! If you'd only think a little more about *me*—

RHETT: I am thinking of you. And I'm thinking that—well—maybe it's the mill that's taking you away from me—and from Bonnie.

SCARLETT [*blowing up*]: I know what you're thinking. And don't try to bring Bonnie into this. You're the one that's taking her away from me.

RHETT: But she loves you—

SCARLETT [*not listening*]: You've done everything possible to make her love you and not me. Why, she's so spoiled now that—

BONNIE'S VOICE: Mommy! Daddy! Watch me!

*They look off.*

GARDEN AND TERRACE

BONNIE *on her pony, calls to them from the garden. She is riding sidesaddle now, and wears a blue velvet riding habit with long, flowing skirt and a plumed hat.*

SCARLETT: We're watching, darling. [*She looks at* BONNIE *admiringly.*] You're mighty pretty, precious.

BONNIE [*generously*]: So are you. . . . I'm going to jump. Watch me, Daddy!

RHETT: I don't think you ought to do much jumping yet, Bonnie. Remember you've just learned to ride sidesaddle.

BONNIE: I will so jump! I can jump better than ever 'cause I've grown. And I've moved the bar higher—

SCARLETT [*alarmed*]: Don't let her do it, Rhett.

RHETT [*tolerantly*]: No, Bonnie, you can't.

*But* BONNIE, *unheeding, gallops away toward the jump.*

RHETT [*with a laugh, calling after her*]: Well—if you fall off, don't cry and blame me.

CLOSE SHOT–BONNIE

*Sticking her heels into the pony's ribs and starting across the grounds, emitting a terrific yell.*

CLOSE SHOT–SCARLETT *and* RHETT

SCARLETT [*rising and protesting as strongly as her condition permits*]: Rhett, stop her!

RHETT *looks at* SCARLETT, *realizes she is seriously concerned, turns, and shouts:*

RHETT: Bonnie! [*more insistently*] Bonnie!

CLOSE-UP–BONNIE

*Her eyes blazing delightedly in anticipation of the thrill she is about to get from the jump.*

BONNIE: Watch me!

CLOSE SHOT–SCARLETT

*She sinks back in her chair.*

SCARLETT [*with annoyance*]: Just like Pa!

*Suddenly terror comes into her face as she realizes the parallel. Instinctively she knows what is about to happen.*

SCARLETT [*terrified*]: Just like Pa!

*But it is too late. We hear* RHETT'*s terrified voice:*

RHETT'S VOICE: Bonnie! Bonnie! Bonnie!

SCARLETT *screams.*

ANGLE AT THE HURDLE

*As the pony runs up to the hurdle, he stops short and* BONNIE *is thrown over his head, her little body hitting the ground flat on its back. The pony turns and gallops off in panic, kicking up splinters from the shattered bar with his hooves.*

THE GARDEN

WADE HAMPTON *screams and covers his face.*

THE GARDEN

RHETT *yanks the pony to his feet and falls on his knees beside the prostrate child.*

RHETT: Bonnie! Bonnie!

SCARLETT *enters to him.*

DISSOLVE TO

FADE IN:

NIGHT–CLOSE SHOT–SMALL SPRAY OF WHITE ROSE-BUDS WITH WHITE CREPE STREAMERS ON DOOR OF THE BUTLER HOUSE

CAMERA PULLS BACK to reveal MELANIE standing waiting nervously OUTSIDE THE DOOR TO THE BUTLER HOUSE.

*The door opens and she is admitted by* MAMMY, *who is dressed entirely in black, her face puckered in sad bewilderment.*

MAMMY: Lawsy, Miss Melly, Ah's glad you'se come!

INTERIOR–HALL

*—as* MELANIE *enters and* MAMMY *closes the door behind her. She helps* MELANIE *shed her wrap and gloves,* MELANIE *talking the while:*

MGM, © 1939, 1967. UGa Libraries, Marsh Papers.

MELANIE [*sadly, looking around*]: This house won't seem the same without Bonnie. . . . How's Miss Scarlett bearing up?

MAMMY: Miss Melly, disyere done broke her heart. But Ah din' fetch you here on Miss Scarlett's account. Whut dat chile got ter stand, de good Lawd give her strength ter stand. It's Mist' Rhett Ah's worried 'bout. [*Tears flow down her face; she lifts the hem of her black skirt and dries her eyes.*] He done lost his mind dese last couple o' days.

MELANIE: No, Mammy! No!

MAMMY *starts toward the stairs and* MELANIE *accompanies her,* CAMERA FOLLOWING WITH THEM.

MAMMY: Ah ain' never seed no man, black or white, set sech a store by any chile. An' when Doctah Meade say her neck broke . . . [*She stops at the memory of the awful moment.*] . . . Mist' Rhett, he grab his gun and run right out an' shoot dat po' pony—an' fer a minit Ah think he gwine shoot hisseff.

*Tears fall again but this time* MAMMY *doesn't bother to wipe them away. Tears come to* MELANIE'*s eyes also.*

MELANIE: Poor Captain Butler!

MAMMY: Yas'm. An' Miss Scarlett, she call him a murderer fer teachin' dat chile to jump. She say, 'Give me mah baby whut you killt.' And he say Miss Scarlett hadn't neber keered nuthin' 'bout Miss Bonnie. . . . It lak ter turn mah blood cold, whut dey say ter one 'nother.

MELANIE: Stop, Mammy! Don't tell me any more!

MAMMY: An' dat night, Mist' Rhett lock hisseff in de nuss'ry wid Miss Bonnie an' he didn' open de do' even when Miss Scarlett beat on it an' hollered ter him. An' dat's de way it's been fer two days.

MELANIE [*horror-stricken*]: Oh, Mammy!

MAMMY [*nods ominously and shivers*]: An' den dis evenin' Miss Scarlett shouts through de do' dat de fune'l set fer termorrer mawnin' an' he say, "Try dat an' Ah kills you termorrer. Does you think Ah's gwine put mah chile away in de dahk when she's so 'fraid of it?"

MAMMY *and* MELANIE *have reached the head of the stairs, and the scene continues on the landing.*

MELANIE [*distracted and grief stricken herself*]: Mammy, Mammy, he *has* lost his mind!

MAMMY: Yes, it's de Gawd's truff . . . he ain' gwine let us bury dat chile. You gotter help us, Miss Melly.

MELANIE: But I can't intrude.

MAMMY: Ef you cain' help us, who kin? Mist' Rhett always set great store by yo' 'pinion.

MELANIE *steels herself, terrified at the prospect of what she has to do, but realizing that she must do it. She stands a moment while* MAMMY *looks at her pleadingly.*

MELANIE: I'll do what I can, Mammy. [*She goes to the door of* RHETT's *room and knocks softly.*]

RHETT'S VOICE: Get away from that door and leave us alone!

MELANIE [*she knocks again*]: It's Mrs. Wilkes, Captain Butler. Please let me in. I've come to see Bonnie.

*A pause, then the door is opened quickly from within and the drunken bulk of* RHETT's *figure, his face unshaven, haggard, looks huge and dark against the blazing forest of candles around* BONNIE's *bier. Grotesque shadows play on the gaily decorated walls of the nursery.*

MAMMY *shrinks back into the window recess of the landing as* RHETT *looks down on* MELANIE *for a moment; then grasps her arm and pulls her into the room, shutting the door.*

MAMMY *emerges, watches a second, and then slowly, ponderously, sinks down on her knees, raising her hands and her eyes in silent prayer.*

*DISSOLVE TO*

HALL–LATER THAT NIGHT
CLOSE SHOT–NURSERY DOOR

*It opens and* MELANIE *slips out. Before she closes the door quietly behind her, we see* RHETT's *figure in the background in the nursery, seated next to the bier, his head resting on his arm.*

MAMMY *steps forward to* MELANIE *from where she has been sitting in the recess.* MELANIE *stands swaying a little, supporting herself on the doorknob. She speaks steadily, but seemingly with a little difficulty.*

MELANIE: I want you to go make a great deal of strong coffee, Mammy. And bring it up here to Captain Butler. I'll go and see Miss Scarlett. . . .

MAMMY [*eager for news of what has happened*]: But—?

MELANIE: Captain Butler is quite willing for the funeral . . . to take place . . . tomorrow morning. . . .

*The steadiness of her voice has not wavered, but the volume has diminished.*

MAMMY [*raising her eyes*]: Hallelujah! Ah 'specks de angels fights on yo' side, Miss Melly.

# Eleventh
# Sequence

*ADE IN:*

INTERIOR–DR. MEADE'S OFFICE–DAY

DR. MEADE *sits at his desk.* SCARLETT *sits opposite him, handsome in her mourning, sobbing as she talks.*

SCARLETT: And when we do sit down to supper together he's always drunk now. Not like he used to be, I mean like a gentleman. Just drunk. Sodden drunk, too, before the evening's over. Sometimes I hear him come home long after midnight and the servants have to put him to bed! Put Rhett Butler to bed! I can't bear it! Dr. Meade, do you think he can have lost his mind?

DR. MEADE: I think this drinking will kill him if he doesn't stop it. My advice to you is to give him another baby just as fast as you can.

SCARLETT *looks at him in eloquent misery, then rises and turns away.*

SCARLETT: That's easier said than done.

*DISSOLVE TO*

INTERIOR–MELANIE'S HOUSE–DAY

MELANIE *sits on the sofa,* RHETT *beside her. She is holding his hand and looking up into his face. The face is changed. It is bloated now with drink and wants shaving, and the collar is rumpled and the linen soiled.*

MELANIE: It's breaking my heart to see you as you are now. Next to Ashley and Beau, I love Scarlett and you better than anyone. That's why I sent for you. If my heart weren't breaking I should never have had the courage to say what I want to say now. Bonnie's gone, Rhett. But Scarlett can give you other children.

*He recoils as from a sudden hurt.*

RHETT: No!

MELANIE: You need them. Think, Rhett. If you had a son, a son like you, with your dark handsomeness . . .

RHETT: No! No!

MELANIE: People like you . . . and me . . . are meant to have children.

*He looks at her wretchedly, then, his vision clearing, looks closer.*

RHETT: So you're going to have another child, Melanie.

MELANIE [*smiles*]: You see? You know that without my telling you. I've told no one. No one else has guessed; only you. You see? [*Now it is his turn to take her hand.*]

403

RHETT: But you shouldn't, Melanie. The doctors have said . . .

MELANIE [*smiling serenely*]: I have faith in life, Rhett. I want you to get your faith in life back again.

RHETT [*his head falling*]: May God bring you safely through. As for me, though . . . [*He shakes his head, rises and moves slowly away.*]

*DISSOLVE TO*

THE NEW HOUSE–SCARLETT'S BEDROOM–NIGHT

SCARLETT *stands listening, her wrapper held 'round her nightdress. The door into the hall is ajar. A sound from below and she goes to look out through the door. She recoils from what she sees.*

THE STAIR

*From* SCARLETT'S *angle* RHETT *comes drunkenly up the stair. He nearly falls once, catches himself on the banister and comes on.*

SCARLETT'S BEDROOM

SCARLETT *steels herself to face* RHETT *as he appears in the hall. She smiles.*

SCARLETT: Are you all right, Rhett?

*He looks at her soddenly for a moment, then:*

RHETT: You see how I am.

SCARLETT: I . . . I've been waiting up for you to come in.

*Their eyes meet for a long moment, then his fall hopelessly.*

RHETT: You can go to bed now.

*He moves on to the door of his room. She steps into the hall after him. The door of his room is heard to close and the key to turn in the lock. She turns back into her room, totters to the bed, sinks on the floor beside it, buries her head in the counterpane and sobs.*

*DISSOLVE TO*

EXTERIOR–THE NEW HOUSE–THE FRONT DOOR–DAY

*It is early morning, and* UNCLE PETER *drives Miss Pitty's carriage to the door. He is driving as* UNCLE PETER *has not often done. He springs down from his box in unaccountable agitation, runs up the steps and is ringing the doorbell.*

INTERIOR–THE HALL

*The doorbell is ringing frantically.* MAMMY, *startled by the sound, is on her way to answer, but* RHETT *enters from the dining room. He is shaved now and more presentable than in the last few scenes. He opens the door.*

RHETT: Why, Uncle Peter! What's the matter?

UNCLE PETER: Miss Melly, Mist' Rhett! She bad off! Seems lak she wuz gwine ter hev a baby an' de baby come too soon an' now de doctahs say she dyin'! [*He is crying. Exclamations from both* MAMMY *and* RHETT.] She ast fer Miss Scarlett! But Miss Scarlett better come quick!

MAMMY: She ain't awake yet.

RHETT [*to* UNCLE PETER]: Pull yourself together. I'll tell Miss Scarlett. [*He starts up the stair.*]

SCARLETT'S BEDROOM

RHETT *stands, looking somberly on, as* SCARLETT *dresses in desperate haste, tears coursing down her cheeks.*

SCARLETT: Oh, God, do please let her live! I'll make it up to her! I'll never even speak to Ashley again if You'll only let her get well!

DISSOLVE TO

INTERIOR–MELANIE'S PARLOR

AUNT PITTYPAT, SCARLETT, *and* INDIA *sit at the table.* AUNT PITTYPAT *dabs her eyes.* INDIA *is rigid.* RHETT *sits apart. There is a fire in the grate. A moment of silence then* ASHLEY *walks out from* MELANIE'S *room carrying his sobbing son.*

BEAU: Where is my mother going away to? And why can't I go along, please?

ASHLEY: We can't always go along, Beau, much as we may want to. You're going back to bed now.

*He starts across the room to take* BEAU *back to his bed.* SCARLETT *turns to* RHETT.

SCARLETT [*a whisper*]: Oh, Rhett, she can't be dying! She can't be!

RHETT [*low*]: She hasn't your strength. She's never had any strength. She's never had anything but heart.

ASHLEY [*looks back over his shoulder, to* RHETT]: You knew that, too.

BEAU: Why do I have to go back to bed? It's morning.

ASHLEY: It isn't really morning yet. [*He exits.*]

DR. MEADE *enters from the bedroom.*

DR. MEADE: You may come in now, Scarlett.

INDIA [*goes to the doctor and puts her hand on his sleeve*]: Doctor, please let me see her. I've been waiting for two whole days and I've got to tell her—that I was wrong about something.

DR. MEADE: She knows you were wrong. [*Turns to* SCARLETT.] She wants to see Scarlett. [*He leads* SCARLETT *into the hallway.*]

HALLWAY

*As* DR. MEADE *and* SCARLETT *enter.*

DR. MEADE: Miss Melly's going to die in peace. I won't have you easing your conscience telling her things that make no difference now! You understand?

SCARLETT *stops him with a gesture.* DR. MEADE *gives her a little push into the bedroom and closes the door after her.*

MELANIE'S BEDROOM

MELANIE *is lying very still on the bed. Her closed eyes are sunken in twin purple circles. Her face is a waxy yellow.* SCARLETT *tiptoes across the room to the quiet figure and stands over her.*

SCARLETT: It's me, Melly.

*The eyes open, then close again.*

MELANIE: Promise me?

SCARLETT: Anything!

MELANIE: Look after my little son! I gave him to you once before, remember? The day he was born?

SCARLETT: Oh, Melly, don't talk this way! I know you'll get well!

MELANIE: Promise me. . . . College? . . .

SCARLETT: Yes! Yes! And Europe. And a pony. Whatever he wants! But—Melly! Do try . . .

MELANIE: Ashley . . . [SCARLETT's *eyes go wide, but* MELANIE *continues.*] Ashley and you . . .

SCARLETT *bows her head in sudden prayer.* MELANIE's *fingers reach out to touch her.*

SCARLETT [*almost voiceless*]: What about—Ashley, Melly?

MELANIE: Look after him for me. Just as you looked—looked after me for him.

SCARLETT: I will, Melly.

MELANIE: Look after him. But never let him know.

SCARLETT *is almost on the point of breaking. She rises, abruptly sinking her teeth into her thumb to regain control. The door opens slightly.* DR. MEADE *stands in the threshold beckoning imperiously. She bends over the bed, takes* MELANIE's *hand and lays it against her cheek.*

SCARLETT: Good night.

MELANIE [*very faint*]: Promise . . .

SCARLETT: What else, Melly?

MELANIE: Captain Butler. Be kind to him . . .

SCARLETT [*surprised*]: Rhett?

MELANIE: He loves you so.

SCARLETT [*sobs*]: Yes, Melly.

MELANIE: Good-bye.

MGM, © 1939, 1967. UGa Libraries, Marsh Papers.

MGM, © 1939, 1967. UGa Libraries, Marsh Papers.

SCARLETT: Good-bye.

*She bends over and kisses* MELANIE's *forehead, then draws back. The eyes are closed again. A last look at* MELANIE *then* SCARLETT *goes.* DR. MEADE *follows her to the door.*

PARLOR

SCARLETT *and* DR. MEADE *enter.* INDIA *and* AUNT PITTYPAT *are standing now.* ASHLEY *sits at the table.* RHETT *looks on from the hall.*

DR. MEADE [*to the others*]: You ladies may come in now.

*They go in. The women hold their skirts close to their sides to keep them from rustling.*

SCARLETT [*calls to* ASHLEY]: Oh, Ashley! Ashley!

ASHLEY *displays a worn glove.*

ASHLEY: I don't know where the mate to this is. She must have put it away.

SCARLETT [*crying*]: Oh, stop it. [*Drops to her knees beside him.*] Hold me—I'm so frightened! I'm so frightened!

ASHLEY *clutches* SCARLETT, *pressing his head against her heart.*

CLOSE SHOT–RHETT

*He looks at* SCARLETT *in* ASHLEY's *arms. Then with an expression of mixed distaste and resignation, picks up his hat and coat and leaves.*

TWO SHOT–ASHLEY *and* SCARLETT

ASHLEY [*breaking their embrace*]: Oh, Scarlett! What can I do? I can't live without her! I can't! Everything I ever had is—is going with her.

*She looks at him, then the truth of things as they are comes clear to her.*

SCARLETT: Oh, Ashley! You really love her, don't you?

ASHLEY: She's the only dream I ever had that didn't die in the face of reality.

SCARLETT [*with a flash of her usual spirit*]: Dreams! Always dreams with you! Never common sense.

ASHLEY: Oh, Scarlett, if you knew what I've gone through—

SCARLETT: Oh, Ashley, you should have told me years ago that you loved her, not me, and not left me dangling with your talk of honor. But you had to wait 'til now—now when Melly's dying—to show me I could never mean anything more to you than . . . than this Watling woman does to Rhett!

"*Ashley winces at her words, but his eyes still meet hers, imploring silence, comfort. Every line of his face admitted the truth of her words. The very droop of his shoulders showed that his own self-castigation was more cruel than any she could give. He stood silent before her, clutching the glove as though it were an understanding hand and, in the stillness that followed her words, her indignation fell away and pity tinged with contempt, took its place."*

SCARLETT [*continuing*]: And I've loved something that—that doesn't really exist. Somehow I don't care. Somehow it doesn't matter. It doesn't matter one bit. [ASHLEY *bends his head, sobbing. She takes him in her arms and smoothes the back of his hair.*] Oh, Ashley, Ashley, forgive me! Don't cry. She mustn't see you've been crying!

DR. MEADE *enters.*

DR. MEADE: Ashley!

ASHLEY *starts up.* DR. MEADE *only snaps his fingers.* ASHLEY *goes in quickly. The door is left open.* SCARLETT *stands listening. A cry of real anguish:*

ASHLEY [*off-screen*]: Melly! Melly!

*Just the least sound from the motionless* SCARLETT. INDIA *comes out of the bedroom, sobbing in the most uncontrollable grief. She goes past* SCARLETT *to throw herself on the sofa.* AUNT PITTYPAT *follows and goes apart, crying. Then* DR. MEADE *comes and closes the door after him.* SCARLETT *looks at the three, then suddenly comes to life.*

SCARLETT: Rhett! Rhett! [*She looks for him and sees that the hall is empty. She goes to the hall.*] Rhett! Where are you? [*She goes out through the open door.*]

EXTERIOR–DOOR TO MELANIE'S HOUSE–MIST

SCARLETT [*as she throws open the door*]: Rhett! Wait for me!

*It is gray and there is a heavy mist.* SCARLETT *enters into the mist and is almost completely enveloped by it, so that we see only her face and part of her black dress in it. We hear her voice:*

SCARLETT'S VOICE: Rhett! Wait for me! Rhett! Rhett! Rhett! Rhett!

*TROLLEY SHOT–IN FRONT OF* SCARLETT *GOING UP THE HILL*

*The most we ever see of her through the mist is a bit of her dress and her face, and even these are lost occasionally as we trolley before her, up, up, up the hill.*

*INTERCUT with this is a REVERSE ON HER BACK.*

*In these angles she peers through the mist, attempting to see through it. She is frantic, eager to get home. Her tempo accelerates as she gets higher on the hill. Her hair becomes slightly awry, and she becomes increasingly breathless as she nears the top of the hill.*

*ALSO INTERCUT WITH THIS should be a LARGE CLOSE-UP of her, also trolleying in front of her.*

EXTERIOR–DOOR TO BUTLER HOUSE–CLOSE SHOT

*The mist is lifting. The door is slightly ajar.* SCARLETT *pushes it open eagerly and as the CAMERA goes behind her, she calls:*

SCARLETT: Rhett! Rhett!

*She looks from right to left and moving around the great hall. But there is no answer. She starts up the stairs calling:*

SCARLETT: Rhett! Rhett!

*SIDE ANGLE*

SCARLETT *half way up the stairs.*

SCARLETT: Rhett!

*ANGLE SHOOTING DOWN THE STAIRS*

SCARLETT *has reached the top of the stairs.*

SCARLETT: Rhett!

*She goes to the door to* RHETT's *room and throws it open without knocking. She stops short.*

RHETT'S ROOM

RHETT *is sitting morosely in a chair. Beside him is a decanter and a glass, but the glass is unused and the stopper is in place. He turns slowly and looks at her steadily. There is no mockery in his eyes. His emotion is that of a man who is saddened, first by the passing of* MELANIE *for whom he has had deep feeling, and second by the realization that an important phase of his life is ended.*

RHETT [*quietly*]: Come in.

SCARLETT: Rhett—Rhett!

RHETT: Melanie . . . she is? . . .

SCARLETT *nods. She enters slowly and uncertainly. Without rising,* RHETT *pushes back a chair with his foot. She sinks into it.*

RHETT [*heavily*]: Well . . . God rest her. She was the only completely kind person I ever knew . . . a great lady . . . a very great lady.

SCARLETT *shivers slightly. It is difficult for her to say what is in her heart.* RHETT's *eyes come back to her. He speaks again. This time his voice is changed and he is now light and cool, more like himself.*

RHETT: So she's dead? That makes it nice for you, doesn't it?

SCARLETT *is stunned and tears come to her eyes.*

SCARLETT: Oh, how can you say such a thing! You know how I loved her really!

RHETT: No, I don't know that I do. But at least it's to your credit that you could appreciate her at the end.

SCARLETT: Of course I appreciated her! She thought of everybody except herself—why, her last words were about you.

RHETT *turns to her. There is genuine feeling in his eyes.*

RHETT [*after a moment, quietly; he again drops his mockery*]: What did she say?

SCARLETT: She said, "Be kind to Captain Butler. He loves you so."

RHETT *drops his eyes. Suddenly he rises and goes to the window.*

RHETT: Did she say anything else?

SCARLETT: She said—she asked me to look after Ashley, too.

*He is silent for a moment, and then he laughs softly.*

RHETT: It's convenient to have the first wife's permission, isn't it? [*He walks out of the shot.*]

SCARLETT: What do you mean? [*Suddenly she sees something.*] What are you doing?

RHETT—IN ANOTHER PART OF THE ROOM

*He is standing over a partly packed bag in a part of the room which we have not yet photographed in this sequence, and which* SCARLETT *has not yet seen in this sequence. He is throwing into the bag toilet articles and a few other small things.* SCARLETT *rises to her feet, frantically.*

RHETT [*continuing with his packing*]: I'm leaving you, my dear . . . All you need now is a divorce—and your dreams of Ashley can come true.

SCARLETT: Oh, no! No! [*She runs to him.*] You're wrong! Terribly wrong! I don't want a divorce—[*following* RHETT's *steps as he packs*] Oh, Rhett, when I knew tonight that I—when I knew I loved you I ran home to tell you—Oh, darling—darling—

RHETT: Scarlett, please don't go on with this. Leave us some dignity to remember out of our marriage. Spare us this last. [*He continues packing.*]

SCARLETT: "This last?" . . . Rhett, do listen to me! I must have loved you for years only I was such a stupid fool I didn't know it. Please believe me! You *must* care! Melly said you did.

RHETT: I believe you. But what about Ashley Wilkes?

SCARLETT: I—I never really loved Ashley—

RHETT: You certainly gave a good imitation of it—up 'til this morning. [*He stops packing, laughs a bit, rather bitterly.*] No, Scarlett, I tried everything, and if you'd only met me half way, even when I came back from London . . .

SCARLETT: Oh, I was so glad to see you! I *was* Rhett! But—but you were so nasty!

RHETT [*He starts to put things in bag again.*]: And then when you were sick and it was all my fault, I hoped against hope that you'd call for me, but you didn't.

SCARLETT: I wanted you—I wanted you desperately! But I didn't think you wanted me.

RHETT: It seems we've been at cross purposes, doesn't it? But it's no use now. As long as there was Bonnie there was a chance we might be happy. I liked to think that Bonnie was you, a little girl again, before the war and poverty had done things to you. She was so like you—and I could pet her and spoil her, as I wanted to spoil you. . . . When she went, she took everything. [*Finished packing, he closes his bag.*]

SCARLETT [*crying frantically*]: Oh, Rhett! Rhett, please don't say that! I'm so sorry—I'm so sorry for everything—

RHETT: My darling, you're such a child. You think that by saying "I'm sorry," all the past can be corrected. . . . Here, take my handkerchief. Never, at any crisis of your life, have I known you to have a handkerchief.

*She takes the handkerchief, blows her nose, and sits down.* RHETT *picks up his bag, goes to the door, and exits.* SCARLETT *leaps up and runs after him.*

HALL

SCARLETT *runs out to* RHETT *on the landing, crying:*

SCARLETT: Rhett! Rhett! Where are you going?

RHETT: I'm going to Charleston, back where I belong.

SCARLETT: Please—*Please*—take me with you!

RHETT: No. I'm through with everything here. [*He sets down his bag, stops, looks at* SCARLETT. *With a faraway look; it is a new* RHETT— *new to us and new to him.*] I want peace . . . I want to see if somewhere there isn't something left in life of charm and grace . . . [*with just a trace of amusement*] Do you know what I'm talking about?

SCARLETT: No. I only know that I love you.

RHETT [*picking up his bag*]: That's your misfortune. [*Goes down the stairs.*]

SCARLETT [*going downstairs after him*]: Oh, Rhett! Rhett! Rhett! Rhett! Rhett! [*She reaches the front door.*] But, Rhett, if you go what shall I do? Where shall I go?

RHETT [*At the door, opens it.*]: Frankly, my dear, I don't give a damn!

*He goes out into the mist,* SCARLETT *looking after him.*

CLOSE SHOT—SCARLETT

*She is left stunned. She looks around, crushed by this blow, and speaks aloud:*

SCARLETT: I can't let him go! I can't! I won't think about losing him now! I'll go crazy if I do! . . . I'll think about that tomorrow.

*She closes the door and goes back into the hall, moving jerkily and without design. But the thought of it will not down. She throws herself on the stairs, defeated, and with nothing to look forward to. She lies face down with her head on her hands. CAMERA MOVES UP to a CLOSE-UP of* SCARLETT *sobbing and HOLDS for a moment.*

SCARLETT: But I must think about it! I must think about it! What is there to do? What is there that matters?

*Suddenly on the sound track we hear* GERALD'S VOICE:

GERALD'S VOICE: Do you mean to tell me, Katie Scarlett O'Hara, that Tara doesn't mean anything to you? [SCARLETT'S *sobbing quiets. She starts to lift her tear-stained face slowly.*] Why, land's the *only* thing that matters—it's the only thing that lasts.

ASHLEY'S VOICE: Something you love better than me, though you may not know it—Tara!

RHETT'S VOICE: It's this from which you get your strength—the red earth of Tara. [SCARLETT'S *face lifts a little higher as she listens.*]

GERALD'S VOICE: Why, land's the *only* thing that matters—it's the only thing that lasts.

ASHLEY'S VOICE: Something you love better than me, though you may not know it—Tara!

RHETT'S VOICE: It's this from which you get your strength—the red earth of Tara.

*Once again we hear the three* VOICES *repeating the same lines. The volume is still louder, the space between them still less, the speed of their repetition still faster:*

GERALD'S VOICE: Why, land's the *only* thing that matters—.

ASHLEY'S VOICE: Something you love better than me—.

RHETT'S VOICE: The red earth of Tara.

*CAMERA MOVES SLOWLY UP to a LARGE CLOSE-UP of* SCARLETT'S *face as we hear:*

GERALD'S VOICE: Tara!

ASHLEY'S VOICE [*louder than* GERALD'S]: Tara!

RHETT'S VOICE [*louder than either*]: Tara!

*A beautiful smile of hope crosses* SCARLETT'S *face as the realization comes to her that she still has Tara.*

SCARLETT [*lifting her face*]: Tara! Home! . . . I'll go home—and I'll think of some way to get him back.

*She lifts her chin higher. We see the stuff of which* SCARLETT O'HARA is made, and we thrill with the knowledge that she won't be defeated for long.

SCARLETT: After all, tomorrow is another day!

As the speech progresses we see and hear her strength return—her voice accelerates in power and volume and we must believe completely that what SCARLETT O'HARA wants to do, she can do.

SLOW DISSOLVE TO

FULL SHOT–TARA LANDSCAPE–SUNSET

With the huge tree where GERALD has spoken to SCARLETT. From behind the hill comes the silhouetted figure of SCARLETT until she stands outlined along the sky. She turns halfway and stands looking over the broad acres. Wind blows her skirts slightly.

CAMERA DRAWS BACK as we once did on SCARLETT and GERALD, until the tiny silhouetted figure of SCARLETT is outlined against GERALD'S Tara.

FADE OUT

## THE END

# SOURCES AND
# ACKNOWLEDGMENTS

The primary sources for this book are, obviously, the four versions of the screenplay of *Gone with the Wind*. I have used the copy of Sidney Howard's version which belonged to Susan Myrick and is now in the University of Georgia Libraries, her copies of the Howard-Garrett version, the shooting script, and the Moviola script, all now in the collection of the editor. The shooting script now in the Atlanta Historical Society's collections which belonged to Wilbur G. Kurtz includes some material not in Miss Myrick's copy and has also been used.

The Margaret Mitchell Marsh Papers at the University of Georgia, especially the sections devoted to the correspondence with Miss Myrick and with Selznick International Pictures, are the source of much of the information in the editor's introduction. Miss Mitchell's letters at Georgia are quoted with the permission of her brother, Stephens Mitchell, as are those to Mr. and Mrs. Kurtz now at the Atlanta Historical Society. Miss Myrick gave the editor permission to quote from her letters before her death in 1978. The letters from Katharine Brown are quoted with her permission. The letters from Sidney Howard have been used with the permission of Walter D. Howard. The quotations from David O. Selznick are from the souvenir program of *Gone with the Wind* prepared by Howard Dietz (New York: 1939) and from Roland Flamini's *Scarlett, Rhett, and a Cast of Thousands* (New York: 1975). The excerpts from Mr. Kurtz's journals are used with the permission of Mrs. Annie Pye Kurtz and the Atlanta Historical Society. His Hollywood journals have been published as "Technical Adviser: The Making of Gone with the Wind," *The Atlanta Historical Journal*, Vol. XXII, No. 2, 1978. Other quotations have been drawn from Sidney Howard's *Dodsworth Dramatized* (New York: c 1934), Andrew Turnbull's *Scott Fitzgerald* (New York: 1962), Fitzgerald's copy of a portion of the screenplay of *Gone with the Wind* which is now among the F. Scott Fitzgerald Papers in the Princeton University Library, and *Dear Scott/Dear Max: The Fitzgerald–Perkins Correspondence* (New York: 1971). *Memo from David O. Selznick* (New York: 1972) and William Pratt's *Scarlett Fever* (New York: 1977) have been particularly useful, but no quotations from them are included in this work. One brief quotation from Ben Hecht's *A Child of the Century* (New York: 1954) is included. Hecht's lines from the rolling title of *Gone with the Wind* have been copied from the cutting continuity in the collection of the Motion Picture Section of the Library of Congress.

Stills from *Gone with the Wind* are used with the permission of Metro-Goldwyn-Mayer, Inc. Copies from which the illustrations in this book have been made have been assembled from the collections of the Atlanta Historical Society, Mrs. Michael Curran of Rego Park, New York, the University of Georgia Libraries, and the editor. The snapshots made on the GWTW sets and locations were taken by Wilbur G. Kurtz. His original prints of them are in the collections of the Atlanta Historical Society. The reproductions used in this book are prints newly made from his negatives in the collections of the University of Georgia Libraries. The reproductions from out-takes from GWTW are from the collection of the editor, as are the reproductions of the call sheets and properties used in the filming.

It would be impossible to overemphasize my indebtedness in the making of this book to Katharine Brown, Karla Davidson, Walter D. Howard, Mrs. Annie Pye Kurtz, Stephens Mitchell, and the late Susan Myrick. I am deeply grateful to each of them. Among my colleagues at the University of Georgia Libraries I have special thanks for Mrs. Faye Dean, Larry Gulley, Judy Muse, Mrs. Geneva Rice, Marvin Sexton, Mrs. Dorothy Shackelford, Tracy Saveland, James A. Taylor, Jr., and Robert M. Willingham, Jr. Others whom I thank for a variety of reasons are William L. Pressly, Mrs. Grace Sherry, and Richard Eltzroth of the Atlanta Historical Society; Paul H. Anderson, Mrs. Margaret L. Branson, and Beverly M. DuBose of Atlanta; H. William Griffin, Mary Donchez, and Jed Mattes of New York; E.D.C. Campbell, Jr., of the Confederate Memorial Literary Society, Richmond; Clark Evans of the Library of Congress; Stephen Ferguson of the Princeton University Library; and Mrs. Marion B. Harwell of Greensboro, Georgia.

*Washington, Georgia*
*11 September 1979*